Men on a Mission

Men on a Mission

Valuing Youth Work in Our Communities

WILLIAM MARSIGLIO

The Johns Hopkins University Press
Baltimore

© 2008 The Johns Hopkins University Press
All rights reserved. Published 2008
Printed in the United States of America on acid-free paper
2 4 6 8 9 7 5 3 1

The Johns Hopkins University Press
2715 North Charles Street
Baltimore, Maryland 21218-4363
www.press.jhu.edu

Library of Congress Cataloging-in-Publication Data

Marsiglio, William.
Men on a mission : valuing youth work in our communities /
William Marsiglio.
p cm
Includes bibliographical references and index.
ISBN-13: 978-0-8018-8829-8 (hardcover : alk. paper)
ISBN-13: 978-0-8018-8830-4 (pbk. : alk. paper)
ISBN-10: 0-8018-8829-8 (hardcover : alk. paper)
ISBN-10: 0-8018-8830-1 (pbk. : alk. paper)
1. Men—United States—Attitudes.   2. Men—United States—
Psychology.   3. Mentoring—United States.   4. Children and
adults—United States.   5. Teenagers and adults—United States.
6. Youth development.   7. Youth—Services for.   I. Title.
HQ1090.3.M34 2008
362.7—dc22   2007038962

A catalog record for this book is available from the British Library.

*Special discounts are available for bulk purchases of this book. For more
information, please contact Special Sales at 410-516-6936 or
specialsales@press.jhu.edu.*

To my precious wife, Kendra,
and our treasured son, Phoenix,
for inspiring my life dreams

Contents

Preface

When I was a much younger adult, I freely approached unfamiliar children in parks, playgrounds, or on neighborhood streets—especially if they were playing with a ball. "Hey, can you guys make room for one more?" I don't recall ever hearing "No." I've always loved sports, so playing spontaneously with kids was natural and great fun. Few things match the contagious joy of being surrounded by children at play. Sadly, those days of unscripted recreation with young strangers are distant memories. Though I still love to play ball, the social rules governing adult-child interaction have changed. Furthermore, as an adult *male*, I'm now cast, in the eyes of many strangers young and old, as one of those "potential child abusers." Unfortunately, those projections affect me.

In recent decades, the news and entertainment media have ratcheted up their coverage of adults who have abducted, abused, or even killed unsuspecting youths. Who can forget the seemingly endless coverage John Mark Karr received in August 2006, and he was only a suspect in the JonBenet Ramsey murder case. This media frenzy—though providing a public service by raising concern for children—has created an unhealthy (though perhaps necessary) climate in which "good" parents must train their children in street survival skills. The lessons include the admonition "Never talk to a stranger!"

I still enjoy playing with kids, so I have a personal interest in how they see me. As a university professor and sociologist who studies how men live their lives as men, and as fathers in particular, I also have a scholarly curiosity about kids' reactions to men and men's reactions to kids.

My personal and scholarly worlds collide most often when I walk Jessie, my adorable 12-year-old Australian shepherd, still a puppy at heart. Once, when I was strolling with Jessie past a neighborhood swimming pool, six children flocked to Jessie's side. They showered her with playful petting and compliments. They greeted me with questions about her name, age, and "Does she do tricks?"

Mindful of the unwritten "adult-child protocol," I wondered how much I should talk to these gregarious kids. Jessie loved the attention, but I was self-conscious about being an adult male and a stranger. My decision: I was pleasant, I answered their questions but did not ask any, I allowed them to revel briefly in the excitement of being with Jessie, and then I left. The kids learned my dog's name, not mine.

Unfortunately, the discomfort I felt during this harmless episode is not an isolated occurrence for me and other men. I regularly avoid engaging young strangers in conversation, lest I inadvertently desensitize them to the potential dangers of being too friendly to that small cadre of men (and women) who prey on children. Ironically, the hard-line parenting advice sometimes given to children, "Don't speak unless you're spoken to," is turned on its head. I'm the one who adopts the silent demeanor in the company of unchaperoned children, unless spoken to first. I check my friendliness even when a child openly greets me.

A few years ago I discovered that even silence may not protect a man against false accusations. A friend of mine was misidentified in a police photo line-up by a middle-school girl as the stranger she thought had been too friendly on a few occasions. His photograph was placed in the line-up because he had been sitting in his car waiting to pick up his own daughter from the same school. He was charged with stalking the girl and his photo was prominently displayed in the local newspaper along with those of two other men arrested for taking advantage of children. Even though the state's attorney dropped the charges for lack of evidence, my friend's reputation and wallet took a significant hit. The girl probably filed her report in good faith, but her mistake was costly to this man, his children, and to men in general. Now he is even more cautious around children than am I; he intentionally diverts his eyes from children on the street.

Today, men in various occupations (e.g., school teachers, coaches, clergy, and daycare workers) are more self-aware than earlier male cohorts and more alert to the potential for being perceived as too child-friendly. Comparable sentiments reveal themselves in my recent research with stepfathers. Some ponder how they, as men not biologically related to their partners' children, can express wholesome physical affection without having the touching misconstrued as inappropriate or sexual.

Thus, men, as men, confront a unique challenge in donning a child-friendly personality in an era when fears generated by relatively few affect us all. Increasingly, we encourage dads to hug and kiss their children, but we caution them to avoid being too familiar with other children. Fortunately, many men can still be a positive force in children's lives without being demoralized by the prevailing cultural climate. This book captures a sampling of these men's experiences while noting how some have grown more cautious.

My journey in writing this book can be traced most directly to one early March afternoon in 2004 when my personal and professional insights about men and youth mingled. On that day I began to contemplate a project that reached beyond the borders of my roughly twenty years experience studying and writing about fathers and stepfathers, yet flowed from it. It seemed a logical next step to explore the lives of men who choose, through paid work or volunteering, to interact and develop bonds with kids in diverse public venues. Though I expanded my lens to focus primarily on men's involvement with youth outside a family context, I realized the value of showing how men's family life and public life overlap. I also reasoned that achieving a deep understanding of men's involvement with youth outside a family scenario required accounting for the larger cultural and social milieu in which that involvement occurs. Portions of that context had revealed themselves to me on walks with my dog and in my friend's unfortunate public humiliation.

My stepfather research followed a parallel course to my current one on men and youth because I studied how men's personal experiences were framed by the socially constructed world in which they lived. In particular, I examined how men without a blood tie to their partner's child negotiated their identities in a stepfamily, sometimes claiming the child as theirs, while living in a world shaped by institutionalized patterns and policies privileging biological fathers over stepfathers.

Immersed in a family context, men's lives as stepfathers unfold at times in public view, though more tends to occur in private. In or out of the public eye, stepfathers' experiences fuel contemporary debates about the value of genes versus love in defining family boundaries. Although many Americans still honor the sanctity of biological ties, others celebrate expressions of the heart as the defining symbol of family.

Public discourses about men as potentially dangerous and ones that focus on the merits of genetic versus social definitions of family, are tied tangentially to discourse relating women's work to mothering—a caregiving approach to relationships. A significant portion of the Western world still defines some public (and private) activities with infants, children, and adolescents as feminine—women's work. Indirectly, this social sentiment colors impressions about men's efforts to "care" for kids. In many people's eyes, men who are concerned about and care for kids in certain ways and in particular settings challenge conventional norms about manhood. When seen in this light, the men are often marginalized and viewed with suspicion.

After months of ruminating on these notions, I started the writing process in earnest in the winter of 2005. Several months later I began recruiting participants and conducting interviews. My initial interviews sold me on my project's merit, as I listened to the men's passionate descriptions of their jobs and their volunteering in service to youth. The full sample of personal stories and observations enhances the depth, breadth, and richness of the story I have crafted to capture men's experiences in what one man describes as "kid business." Though I repeatedly questioned whether it made sense to combine the diverse types of work and volunteer experiences represented in this book, in the end, I decided that painting a portrait of the forest along with the trees was worthwhile. Once I chose this route, I turned my attention to tailoring the book to a wide range of stakeholders interested in men and youth, most notably: social service professionals working directly with kids; scholars and students interested in gender, family, work, mentoring, volunteering, and community development issues; the general public; and policymakers interested in children's well-being. As I organized and developed the story of men's involvement with kids, foremost in my mind were the kinds of men I interviewed and their colleagues (male and female) who interact with youth in their paid and volunteer work. I was determined to prepare a book that they would "get" and find relevant. Three men with extensive youth work experience, Alejandro Romero, Andy Bachman, and Rashad Jones, graciously agreed to review the first draft of my manuscript. I greatly appreciate their insights regarding matters of organization, content, and style because they helped me refine the book to appeal to a broad audience. These men also provided a litmus test of the authenticity of the messages I share; they assured me that I have captured accurately the sentiments and experiences of men who work with kids.

From where I sit, one of the most compelling features of this book is that it is firmly grounded in a diverse sample of men's personal stories. Lots of books have been written about men, many on fatherhood in particular, but none to my knowledge has explored the vital ways in which men from a wide range of backgrounds can and do make a difference in kids' lives more generally. By emphasizing how many men experience their jobs and volunteering as part of a personal mission or a calling to reach out and help kids, this book broadens our understanding of how men try to shape our youngest generations.

A number of individuals helped me move from a vague idea to a coherent project. Several students played vital roles along the way as I turned my outline into an empirical study of men and youth. I had the good fortune of working with fourteen conscientious undergraduate students who assisted with library research, transcription, and editing. They are Chad Bernstein, Heather Christian, Angela Goddard, Judy Grimes, Andrew Jaeger, Tina Leger, Jessica Libbey, Jocita Manibusan, Michelle Phillips, Caitlin Samenfeld-Specht, Jenny Shimek, Frantz Williams, Ayme Winters, and Melissa Wolfe. Caitlin, Jessica, and Melissa in particular provided excellent editorial comments. Graduate students Louisa Chang and Jeanne Holcombe also provided useful help in several forms. On numerous occasions, my assistants' excitement for the project energized me to press ahead. Their constructive criticism repeatedly kept me on the right path as I sought to make the book accessible to a wide audience.

In addition to student assistants, several friends (Ed Blue, Betsy Dodd, Jim Faubel, Erin Oakley, Christina Paz, and Jon Visscher) and a Big Brothers Big Sisters staff member, Tambria Williams, provided me welcomed assistance identifying men to interview. Donna Balkcom, the department office manager, did a tremendous amount of valuable administrative work to facilitate timely payment of participants. Melisa Smith, a department secretary, offered her timely help with a few technical matters related to preparing manuscript materials. I also benefited greatly from my amazingly supportive wife Kendra's infectious enthusiasm for this project. Throughout my writing, I tested the flow and accessibility of my prose by reading aloud to Kendra. She was *always* eager to listen. Fortunately, Kendra is adept at flagging my academic jargon and she challenged me to find a more palatable way to express myself. Greer Litton Fox and Michael Kimmel, trusted colleagues who have offered me sage advice on numerous occasions throughout my career, also provided useful feedback on several important aspects of the book.

I was fortunate to have Anne Whitmore, a senior manuscript editor at Johns Hopkins University Press, provide wonderful stylistic recommendations for my manuscript. As a former social worker with a keen interest in seeing better social supports for youth, she is especially knowledgeable about and invested in my book, which benefited from her meticulous reading and substantive insights. Others at JHUP, notably editors Claire McCabe Tamberino and Henry Tom, were encouraging during my project's many phases, from manuscript review to marketing. I appreciate their willingness to let me personalize the book's cover by taking the photo for it myself. My hearty thanks go out to Keith Blanchard and Neal Gillespie of the Gainesville Boys & Girls Club for enthusiastically helping me recruit individuals for the photo, which symbolizes the web of supportive ties connecting male youth workers and kids. It was rewarding to watch the men and kids playfully manage two separate days of shooting, in ninety-five-degree heat, as we experimented with numerous arrangements while I took roughly one hundred shots. I am grateful for James Siler's generous and professional help organizing the first day of shooting. I am also thankful that the University of Florida's Research Foundation Professorship I received for 2005–2008 partially supported my research.

I wish to offer resounding applause to all fifty-five men I interviewed for this project. I was constantly amazed by their wonderful stories, accounts which illustrated their commitment, generosity, and concern for kids. An extra thanks goes to the eleven men who arranged for me to observe them in action with kids. More times than not, I walked away from my time with those men feeling that I had been watching a remarkable person. Often, their dedication made me feel that I had done very little by comparison to leave an imprint on the most impressionable and vulnerable members of our society. To ensure the men's anonymity, I have used pseudonyms when referring to them in the text.

Unfortunately, men (and women) like those in my study, the social stewards who care for and inspire ordinary and at-risk youth, too often go unrecognized. They regularly help kids learn new things, build character, grapple with troubling life circumstances, and find a life purpose. This book celebrates their passions, hard work, sacrifices, and contributions to making sure that the youngest generation has a chance to thrive.

Men on a Mission

CHAPTER 1

THE MISSION

My emotional reaction to this man's story was sudden and unexpected. As in other interviews, I began by asking Derek, a very tall, muscular African American police officer, to tell me about his life growing up. But this time, I was not greeted with the typical meandering, mundane storyline. Instead, pensive and direct, Derek launched immediately into his sad tale of vulnerability.

> *My first memory as a child—actually, I was 3 years old, because my brother was just born—is my dad leaving our family. . . . I can remember me and my sister propped up on the back of the couch looking out the window, watching my dad taking his bags to the car and get into the car with another woman and drive off. My momma had just had my brother and . . . she was really too weak to do anything for herself.*

My skin tingled as I listened to Derek candidly describe his life at age 3. In my mind's eye, I transposed this man of muscle into a small child helplessly gazing at a bizarre family scene. I reflected for a moment on my own life. My childhood offered only a stark contrast: my parents had been an exceptionally steady presence, but I snatched a taste of Derek's feelings when my mind landed on a vivid memory, twenty-five years old. I saw my son, almost 4 years old at the time, gazing at me with bewildered, teary eyes as he boarded a plane on the last morning we permanently lived together—an innocent victim of an impending divorce. That dark memory captured a piece of Derek's childhood pain for me, but what he shared later was beyond my personal experience.

He startled me once again with this account:

By the time I was like 13 years old, I had got shot, I had got stabbed, I watched my best friend die, and one of my other good friends had killed a guy—was robbing him and actually shot him, and they found his body in the bushes. That was his third strike, basically, cause he had already robbed somebody and already beat somebody with a bat or something before; and the judge said he was a menace to society and he would never see the streets again. So basically, to this day, he's in prison and he'll be in prison for the rest of his life.

Derek was stressing his friend's plight to accentuate his own good fortune. As Derek explained, he and his friend had hung out together all the time, but on the night of the murder, Derek was off doing something else. He knows that had he joined his friend instead, he might be in prison too.

Though relatively few of us are haunted by such unpleasant first memories or experience the multiple traumatic events that filled Derek's adolescent life, many youth struggle with the temptations of their age. Many kids experience persistent disadvantage as well as traumatic events that may or may not be of their own doing. As others have said, helping kids stay on a productive life path should not only be a family matter. It demands a "village" type of investment that extends beyond the home. My belief, shared by many, is that men are not as active as they could and should be in this collective effort to nurture, teach, and protect our children.

Unfortunately, little is known about how men's interactions and relationships with youth matter, for the kids, the men, or society more generally. Despite our spotty understanding of these involvements, their value should not be underestimated. A wide-angle view of how, why, and with what effect men are involved with youth needs to be explored.

Now 29, Derek overcame his youthful indiscretions to make a new life for himself by joining the ranks of men committed to helping kids. He became a youth intervention specialist nine months ago, with the goal of helping at-risk boys and young men stay out of trouble. The "at-risk" label implies a set of attributes such as low socioeconomic status, membership in a racial or ethnic minority group, and evidence of psychosocial stressors like parental divorce, family income loss, or the death of a loved one that place youth in danger of experiencing negative future events.[1]

Regrettably, many of Derek's teenage friends have not fared as well. Why Derek? Why was he one of the few among his circle of teenage friends who transformed his life from being a self-proclaimed "thug" to being a responsible family man and community member? Clearly, no single or simple answer exists. One factor is that during his teen years Derek began to see that he was at what he calls a crossroads. Adopting the vantage point and voice of his teenage self, Derek reflects: "Everybody and everything in my life is going negative right now. I can continue to go this way and I'm going to end up dead or in jail, or I have to go take this other fork in the road and see where it leads me." While mulling over these weighty concerns thirteen years ago, says Derek, it was a chance meeting with a middle-aged school teacher who had informally mentored a friend of his and the subsequent mentoring Derek received that helped him solidify his commitment to getting his life in order.

Though Derek's compelling story has the feel of a Hollywood script, it is real and ripe with lessons. It serves notice that some of the most disconcerting social problems are those involving children and adolescents. In recent times, the United States, despite its mixed record as a child-friendly place, has witnessed a surge in public awareness of the difficulties youth face and help perpetuate. The list is long, troubling, and complex. It includes drinking, smoking, drug use, eating disorders, abortion/pregnancy/childbearing, sexually transmitted diseases, prostitution, running away from home, poor school performance and dropping out, living as a "latch key kid," violence within and outside the home, pornography, and even suicide. In addition, the often hidden but precarious economic condition in which many youths live was brought squarely into public view as Hurricane Katrina's winds and floodwaters wreaked havoc on the Gulf Coast region in the late summer of 2005. The faces of hordes of poor youth, mostly black, were seen repeatedly in print and on television news broadcasts around the world. In short, far too many kids are at-risk and deserve more and better social support.

Equally impressive is the array of stakeholders at the local, state, and national level who are joining the ranks of those who care about kids and are attempting to make a difference. These stakeholders wear personal and group identities such as politicians, pundits, scholars, media personalities, religious leaders, teachers, healthcare workers, other professionals, and, of course, parents. Though they sometimes battle with one another over philosophy and pragmatics, collectively they draw attention to the status of youth.

For some time, the hands-on care of kids, whether in the home or in public spaces, whether paid or unpaid, has been viewed as women's work. For over a century, since the onset of industrialization, women have spent more time than men raising children in the home and, in recent decades, teaching them in the classroom. The pattern, termed by academics "the feminization of care-work," has been a main rallying point for the modern feminist movement. Achieving gender equity at home and in the workplace is intimately wedded to overcoming patriarchal ideologies and transforming the "culture of care."[2]

Not surprisingly, then, the voices and hands tackling contemporary youth-oriented social problems more often belong to women. The female army of youth workers and child advocates, like the depictions of the current American military, is talented and motivated, but it is decidedly understaffed. So where are the men? What will it take to transform the culture of care and youth work so as to entice more men to join and expand the army that supports and protects kids? How can we motivate more men to step forward to guide youth down a productive path when they arrive at a proverbial fork in the road, or, ideally, before they ever reach the crossroads? More broadly, what can be done to inspire men to participate more fully in creating a generative society—that is, one concerned about and committed to nurturing future generations.[3]

Public discourse has, for some time, highlighted adult men's value as mentors and role models for disadvantaged and at-risk youth, especially for kids who do not have an involved father. The social service and volunteering mantra resounds with the assertion: responsible adult men can help protect youth, particularly boys, from dropping out of school, becoming drug and alcohol abusers, acting violently, becoming chronically unemployed, and acting irresponsibly in their sexual relationships (contracting or spreading STDs or causing an unplanned pregnancy). However, actually getting men involved in caring for and working with kids, particularly in teaching, childcare, and one-on-one mentoring, has been challenging, to say the least.

Derek, a man intent on laboring in the trenches to make a difference in kids' lives says, "Everything that I do or that I have done in my life is basically because I wanted to somehow right a wrong in my life, and not have it be repeated." Derek's sentiment resonates with one definition of *mission*: "an inner calling to pursue an activity or perform a service; a vocation." Of course, not all men working with kids see their efforts as a full-fledged personal mission, nor do they have Derek's passion to change kids' life chances. However, numerous men are determined to reach kids through their efforts in public settings outside the family. This book is about such men.

I use the term "mission" because it captures the varied sentiments men personally express as well as the more general cultural messages or narratives. I show how various motives propel men into a life of working with kids. The individual motives are linked to broader cultural messages encouraging men to get more productively involved with their own children and with others as youth workers. Some messages are tied to feminist objectives, some are connected to more distinctly conservative masculine ideologies, and others represent a web of motives. Throughout, I highlight how accomplishing the mission in any of various ways can refine a man's commitment to youth, enhance kids' well-being, enable a man to experience personal growth, and advance gender equity in society.

As coaches, teachers, Big Brothers, Boy Scout leaders, 4-H Club agents, camp counselors, youth pastors, juvenile corrections officers, childcare workers, and other authority figures, men have the potential to alter how young persons think, feel, and act. Their influence can be felt through one-on-one mentoring arrangements or in social settings involving other kids and adults. Some settings are formal, others informal. Sometimes men are paid for what they do, other times not. Some men make their mark by working directly with kids, while others train youth workers and run the organizations serving young people. The common vision running through the diverse scenarios is of men trying to enhance kids' lives.

Michael, a 49-year-old, white high school science teacher, has spent his adult life getting paid to educate students in a relatively formal setting. He loves his work. Outside the classroom, Michael has pursued a more informal route for interacting with kids. He has been a Big Brother on two occasions, for three and eight years, respectively. Whereas Derek's mission is fueled by a desire to right a wrong and keep other kids from repeating his mistakes, Michael became a Big Brother to fill a void in his life and to give a few boys a small piece of the attention he received from his father and favorite uncle. Michael's father nurtured his curiosity by exposing him to new cultures through travel, books, and food. His uncle offered him an unwavering, deep friendship and taught him the leisurely pastime of fishing at his riverfront cabin. Similarly, Michael has tried to expose his students and Little Brothers to situations and things foreign to them while trying to lay the groundwork for a sincere friendship. Speaking as a teacher, Michael expounds:

I want kids to be diversified . . . to have a worldview. I want kids that I teach in my classroom to, like, want to eat sushi, instead of "ewww ughh ewwwww." . . . So, in my marine biology class, when we were studying algae . . . we made, like, our own sushi in class, made rolls, and I brought the sushi rice. We learned about the algae, but we made the sushi. When you have some black kid, say from the projects, that's probably never going to eat something like that . . . willing to try a piece of sushi, . . . or some redneck, deer-huntin', truck-drivin', mud-boggin' guy wanting to eat a piece of sushi, you feel like maybe you'll di-

versify their palate. And [in] my own way of thinking, having a taste for a wide variety of foods and stuff that are produced from the planet makes life more worthwhile.

Switching to his experiences as a Big Brother, Michael says it makes him feel "like I've contributed, in some way, to society. . . . I guess it's kind of satisfying to watch somebody grow up." Reflecting on his motives, Michael explains further:

Helping a kid makes you feel better about yourself, you know? When you look at your whole being, and you can think of . . . all the crappy stuff you did, you can say, yeah, but I did that; . . . nobody can take that away from you. . . . It was a time in my life when I pursued a lot of hobbies and I thought, I need that [positive connection to a kid]. And [now] when I'm sitting around I can say, "Hey, Alan [his Little Brother], what are you doing? Let's go play some pool or something, man." And you go do something, and I guess there's maybe a little bit of a selfish aspect in it cause it makes me feel good. It's not like I just give and I don't get anything, I get . . . it's rewarding. And it's rewarding after eight years, especially when you don't have kids of your own, when you have someone that sort of admires you. And looks up to you, and respects you, and thinks you're a nice guy, and thinks that you've been a good example for him.

We hear directly from Michael that helping a kid brings him joy, but this type of message is not widely circulated. Instead, the public and academic researchers tend to focus on how men's associations with youth influence kids' development, primarily in the context of fathering. What often goes unnoticed is that these involvements can shape the men's personal development as well. Men learn much about their own personality, interests, desires, and limitations by spending time with youth in assorted activities and situations. For example, Michael found that devoting his time, energy, and finances to help his Little Brothers forced him to become less self-centered. "It teaches you [to be] a little more giving. And I guess, from experiences I had being married, and stuff like that, I think maybe I need to learn to be more giving. . . . To actually practice it and improve my own self." It appears that being a Big Brother serves a dual-purpose mission for Michael. He seeks to help others while working to construct a new and improved self.

Men like Derek and Michael enable me to tell the big story of men's relations with kids in non-family relationships. My purpose is not to study in depth any particular category of adult men (e.g., coaches, teachers, youth ministers) and their relationships with youth, nor is it to evaluate systematically how much of an impact men make while participating in mentoring or volunteer programs. Rather, I paint a sweeping portrait of men's involvement with contemporary youth in all sorts of settings, at times placing this involvement in historical and crosscultural context. Although I suspect some of my observations may hold true for circumstances outside the United States, I largely restrict my commentary to an American context because my interviews were with American men and there is a paucity of rigorous research on men's youth work elsewhere. My book reveals how the shifting cultural climate in the United States breeds public scrutiny of men, and I suggest ways to get men more involved in youth work. I also show how men's experience with young people in one setting, including the home, affects how they interact with kids in another.

The story I weave is based on a combination of qualitative in-depth interviews, observations of men in action, news stories, published academic research, and personal insights. Readers interested in details about the study should consult Appendix A, where I elaborate on the methods used and outline suggestions for future research questions.[4]

Most of my main observations are either generated or illustrated by my interviews with a racially and economically diverse sample of men. At the time of the interviews, these men were doing youth work in paid and unpaid settings. During 2005 and 2006, I spoke to fifty-five men ranging in age from 19 to 65, including several gay men. Although I did not systematically assess the men's level of commitment to youth work, I suspect that the men I interviewed and observed tend to be more highly motivated than the average male youth worker because many were referred to me as men who are dedicated to kids. Thus, the story I develop focuses on the healthy dynamics of active and supportive male youth workers. I say little about men who avoid this type of involvement with kids or are involved with kids incidentally or in abusive ways.

My interviews, lasting over two hours in most cases, gave men the chance to share their life histories, to talk about their family, neighborhoods, school life, childhood mentors, and to chronicle their diverse experiences working or volunteering with kids over the years. Derek and Michael, one a black married father with a troubled past who survived and escaped public housing projects, the other a white single man without children who was blessed with a relatively privileged middle-class lifestyle growing up, demonstrate that men from all walks of life can enter kids' lives in meaningful ways.

In addition to my formal interviews, I spent time with eleven of the men I interviewed, listening to and watching them interact with kids in various settings, typically three to nine months after our initial meeting. Largely a silent observer,

I shadowed the men for hours, sometimes an entire day, at recreation centers, athletic fields, schools, camps, churches, or in transportation vehicles. My venture into the trenches where men's and youths' lives intersect confirmed many impressions I had formed from my interviews and identified new ways of thinking about men as youth workers. It also deepened my understanding of how organizational contexts and interpersonal dynamics shape men's relations with kids in diverse arenas.

The men you'll meet in subsequent pages share engaging stories rich in details and insights. They readily share sentimental accounts of wonderful experiences and bonds with children, though occasionally they express their frustrations in trying to connect with and help kids in today's fast-paced, increasingly materialistic culture. Many men can readily identify, in the youths with whom they work, personality traits and behaviors they find disheartening or offensive, such as, dishonesty, bullying, and lack of respect for adults. Most seem to agree, however, at least in principle, with the adage voiced by a few of the men: there are no bad kids, just bored kids or kids who do bad things.

Most of the men have worked with kids in at least several settings during their lives. Although I interviewed men primarily in the north central region of Florida and Miami, twenty-seven of the men grew up outside of Florida and have worked with kids in other states (and in several cases outside the United States). The men include coaches, teachers, Big Brothers, Boys & Girls Club staff, 4-H Club staff and adult agents, Boy Scout leaders, youth pastors, juvenile justice staff, camp counselors, daycare workers, youth employment directors, and volunteers at pediatric hospital wards.

This book is guided by questions about the status of contemporary youth in the United States and how men think, feel, and act in relation to them: How do men describe their motivation for and feelings about doing paid and volunteer youth work? How do men relate to youth and manage kids' behavior in diverse public and organizational settings? In what ways do their own experiences as youngsters inside and outside their families influence how they see and treat kids? What types of joys and struggles do men experience working with youth? How do men navigate the politics of touch and physical space that are intended to protect youth and adults alike but inevitably alter how they relate? How do men's involvements with youth make a difference for kids and affect men's personal growth and ties to their communities? How do men's perceptions of and experiences with their own families overlap with their involvement with youth outside a family context? What types of social policies and programs can improve men's relations with and commitments to youth?

Although I am interested in how men as youth workers are involved with both boys and girls, the men I interviewed and observed, on average, tend to have more experience with boys. For example, most of men's formal one-on-one mentoring in programs like Big Brothers Big Sisters is restricted to same-gender pairs; and the majority, but clearly not all, of men's formal and recreational coaching and criminal justice experience targets boys. These patterns are consistent with everyday reality. Thus, the larger story I weave out of men's individual accounts of their youth work is more heavily influenced by men's interactions with boys than with girls. Yet, I also discuss men's various encounters with girls and I compare men's perceptions and treatment of girls and of boys; men can leave profound, lasting, and healthy impressions in diverse settings on girls as well as on boys.

Clearly, to understand how and why men relate to children in public (and at home) in particular ways, we must explore how men develop preferences and make decisions about their involvements with youth in a multilayered, complex social world. Public ideologies and organizational policies, social movements, media imagery, changing household and family demographics, legal rulings, and the distinct properties of physical spaces and places all help determine what types of real and perceived opportunities men have to interact with other people's children. Cultural forces also come into play when gender, sexual orientation, race or ethnicity, and social class issues influence men's willingness, in their work and as volunteers, to be involved with children in specific ways. Finally, a full understanding of men's lives with kids must address a fundamental question: What is the connection between the cultural construction of parenting/fathering and men's public experiences with children?

Addressing these and related questions will clarify the conditions that either help or hinder men's involvement with youth in public and private settings. As I search for answers, I am mindful of the powerful historical and cultural forces shaping men's experiences with kids. Insights about the cultural, social, and personal forces affecting men's involvement with kids are pivotal if we are to develop initiatives that will inspire men to become more involved with youth in productive ways. Because the cultural landscape shaping men's youth work is complex and the climate sometimes not so friendly, I begin by exploring that context.

CHAPTER 2

THE LANDSCAPE

Among the many reasons why men should be encouraged to devote more of their time and energy to helping other people's children, one observation looms large. The United States is home to millions of at-risk youth with dubious long-term prospects for living healthy, productive lives. Most people who study or work with youth believe that having positively motivated men involved in children's lives can significantly improve young people's current circumstances, sense of well-being, and overall life chances.

Nick, an enthusiastic youth worker with seventeen years experience working with at-risk kids, shares a powerful first-hand account of how men can help kids turn their troubled lives around. One of twelve children, Nick barely survived his upbringing in a rat-infested home in the heart of a violent urban slum. In Nick's words:

> The boys would take turns at night . . . to sit and make sure that rats would not literally get in bed with my sisters . . . because they would crawl up in the bed. So we'd take turns, an hour and half a night a piece to make sure that didn't happen.

Sadly, having alcoholic, abusive parents worsened the effects of living in poverty. Nick was unable to think of a single positive life lesson he had taken from his parents. A hardened street kid, Nick had little interest in being a student. Often, he went to school for breakfast, then took his shoeshine box to the pier to earn honest cash or he stole to line his pockets.

At the age of 8, Nick saw his first murder. In subsequent years, he witnessed the deaths of six other people either by murder, suicide, or police action. These experiences scarred his psyche, shut down his heart for many years, and fueled nightmares that linger today. Imagine Nick, the boy, standing on a filthy, dark urban street watching two "winos" argue over a penny dropped by one man and aggressively claimed by the other. The man snatching the penny quickly takes the offensive and pulls a knife. "He stuck him in his throat and just ripped him right around," Nick remembers.

I had just got a brand new pair of tennis shoes and when the guy cut his throat, I had white tennis shoes on. The blood was all over me. I kicked my shoes off, kicked them in the street. And, I kinda went hysterical with it because that's the first time I ever seen that happen.

During his youth, Nick was always on the run from the horrors of his childhood. He roamed the streets as a thief and troublemaker, eventually spending four lonely, tough years in a juvenile prison for stealing cars and other crimes. He received no visits from family or friends, and he suffered physical abuse at the hands of guards and inmates. When his parents did not come to the bus station to pick him up after his release from the juvenile facility, he fled to the streets. He got involved with other street kids and hustled money. Then he ventured by bus to a relative's house in Florida.

Largely illiterate, Nick failed when he tried to pursue formal schooling in Florida in his mid-teens. With time, he recognized that his future would be bleak without a high school credential, so he looked for a tutor. George, a middle-aged man, diligently volunteered three times a week for eighteen months to help Nick earn his GED while providing the supportive guidance Nick so badly needed. Though Nick's determination to earn his GED was essential, George's mentorship made the difference. Nick, now a few months shy of 50, still holds George in high esteem for offering him hope and teaching him the skills to lead a better life.

He gave me an opportunity, and I took it. And, we still talk about it and I still laugh and tell him, I say, "I really did never think I would get a GED," but I felt that if he was willing to try to help me, I'd make that effort.

After securing his GED, Nick moved on to earn a respectable station in life. However, he has not forgotten his past. The memory of seeing his first murder and witnessing other senseless deaths during his childhood continue to shape his identity and commitment to kids.

If I can derail any kind of violence towards a kid, I'm gonna do that. . . . Anything I can do to keep that from happening to a child, I'm gonna do. That's just the way it is. . . . No child should have to see somebody get killed like that, at all. There's no reason for it. But, I seen my share of it. I don't want to see anymore. It still affects me. I still, 'til this day, have dreams, nightmares about that. It's real. It's something that you'll never get rid of. It's always in the back of your mind.

Nick's story is remarkable in the amount of misery he suffered as a child and adolescent. His situation is also noteworthy because he overcame incredible odds to become a well-respected professional who instills hope in kids. Unfortunately, many kids do not have the benefits of those who currently receive Nick's attention.

YOUTH WELL-BEING

Turning back to the big picture, it is reasonable to ask how youth, generally speaking, are doing today.[1] Assessments of young people's life circumstances and behaviors in the United States are typically cast in two basic ways. First, data can be assembled documenting how specific problems associated with certain subgroups of young people have changed over time. Second, indicators of youth's well-being in this society can be compared to indicators for youth living in other industrialized societies.

In the 1990s, numerous scholars and social commentators argued passionately that many American youth were awash in crisis. They were experiencing difficult times and the situation was worsening. Richard Lerner, a prominent developmental psychologist, captured this perspective:

Across the communities of our nation, children are dying—from violence, from drug and alcohol use and abuse, and unsafe sex, from poor nutrition, and from the sequelae of persistent and pervasive poverty. . . . And if our children are not dying, their life chances are being squandered—by school failure, underachievement, and dropout; by crime; by teenage pregnancy and parenting; by lack of job preparedness; by prolonged welfare dependency; by challenges to their health (e.g., lack of immunizations, inadequate screening for disabilities, insufficient prenatal care, and lack of sufficient infant and childhood medical services); and by the feelings of despair and hopelessness that pervade the lives of children whose parents have lived in poverty and who see themselves as having little opportunity to do better, that is, to have a life marked by societal respect, achievement, and opportunity.[2]

The general message of the mid-1990s was quite clear: the outlook for many youth in America was rather bleak. Drawing on the growing array of child well-being indicators produced by public and private sources, Lerner painted a detailed portrait of American youth's experience with numerous high-profile risk behaviors. He outlined disturbing patterns for the four major categories of risk behavior for older children and adolescents: school failure, including dropping out and underachievement; delinquency, crime, and violence; drug/alcohol use and abuse; and unsafe sex and teenage pregnancy/parenting. In all categories, the statistics revealed a troubling set of progressively worsening conditions for American youth.

In the first several years of the twenty-first century, indicators of youth's well-being show that many of Lerner's conclusions continue to hold true, though progress has been made on various fronts. Some of the mixed findings are illustrated in the 2007 *Foundation for Child Development Index of Child Well-Being (CWI)* report. Kenneth Land, the research director for the CWI, has constructed an overall national measure of well-being based on seven domains (family economic well-being, health, safety/behavioral concerns, educational attainment, community connectedness, social relationships, and emotional/spiritual well-being). The domains are assessed using twenty-eight annual indicators related primarily to children and teenagers in the United States between 1975 and 2005. Using 1975 as the baseline, the overall index indicates that youth's well-being has increased slightly, with the most significant improvements occurring in the safety/behavioral elements of teen childbearing, violent crime, cigarette smoking, alcohol drinking, and illicit drug use. The most significant declines in well-being related to youth's health, especially levels of obesity. Level of educational achievement as measured by the CWI has essentially remained the same for the thirty-one-year period.[3]

Selective data for key issues regarding youth's well-being provide a more detailed portrait of several recent national trends. Compared to the 20 percent poverty rates registered for youth under 18 years of age in the late 1980s, poverty levels declined slightly, to 17.1 percent in March of 2005.[4] The percentage of persons aged 16–24 categorized as high school dropouts (no diploma or GED) declined from 12.6 in 1985 to 10.5 in 2002.[5] However, trend data from the National Assessment of Educational Progress (NAEP) for students at ages 9, 13, and 17 show that math scores have improved only slightly between 1978 and 2004.[6] Reading scores increased slightly for 9-year-olds between 1999 and 2004, changed very little for 13-year-olds, and since 1992 have declined for 17-year-olds. Reports on sexual activity, pregnancy, and childbearing suggest more meaningful improvements. The proportion of high school students who have had sexual intercourse decreased almost 14 percent between 1991 and 2003; the pregnancy rate for women age 15–19 decreased 28 percent, from a high of 117 pregnancies per 1,000 women in 1990 to 84 per 1,000 ten years later; and the teen birth rate declined 32.5 percent, from 61.8 births per 1,000 women in 1991 to 41.2 per 1,000 in 2004.[7] National data on drug use among high school students indicates that in 2004 eighth, tenth, and twelfth grade students were less likely, on average, to have used illicit drugs and alcohol during the previous twelve months compared to their counterparts in 1996.[8] Finally, between 1993 and 2001, rates for criminal offenses by juveniles declined for all violent offenses and for most nonviolent offenses other than drug violations.[9]

Despite the good news that recent cohorts of youth are generally doing a bit better than their immediate predecessors, the significance of these statistics is often in the eye of the beholder. Little imagination is needed to conclude that many American youth, in both urban and rural areas, are still doing poorly. The number of children living in poverty should make everyone feel uneasy. The 17.1 percent poverty rate for children under 18 years of age translates into 12.4 million kids living in poverty—roughly the number of people living in Chicago, New York City, and Phoenix combined. Children living in a family with a female householder present but no husband present are most likely to be poor; roughly 43 percent of these children live below the poverty line.[10] That figure represents 7.2 million children, a number equal to the entire population of Delaware and Massachusetts combined. Circumstances are particularly bleak for female-headed families with children younger than 5 years of age; about 54 percent of these children live in poverty—2.3 million kids. Poverty rates deserve notice because living in poverty is associated with a wide range of disadvantages, including poorer health, lower levels of education, greater exposure to and personal experience with crime, and higher rates of risk-taking behavior. Thus, for kids, being poor typically means much more than not having enough money to buy the latest designer clothes or high-tech gadget. Poverty can pave a path to self-destructive behavior and limited life chances.

In recent years, public debate about youth's well-being—including initiatives to get men more involved with kids—is often linked to the hotly contested single-parent issue. Interested parties focus on whether, to what extent, and why youth in single-parent (especially mother-only) families might experience more negative outcomes compared to peers living in a two-parent family or household.[11] Unfortunately, getting clear answers from the research community is complicated for political and methodological reasons.[12] According to Andrew Cherlin, professor of sociology at Johns Hopkins University and past president of the Population Association of America,[13] much of the debate about single-parent families has focused on extreme positions: arguing either that children living in single-parent homes experience profound harm[14] or that parents and divorce are inconsequential for children's well-being.[15] Cherlin observes that once large-scale national data became readily available in the 1980s and 1990s, "substantial evidence" mounted indicating that "growing up in a single-parent family or a stepfamily is associated with a lower level of well-being and poorer life outcomes than living in a family with two biological parents."[16]

Obviously, many children living in single-parent families are able to thrive, but it appears that children in these families, especially when a nonresident biological father is not actively involved, must rely on their mother and her support network to put forth extraordinary effort to compensate for the resources (financial, emotional, psychological, time/monitoring) a father could contribute. Conditions limiting mothers' ability to provide an emotionally supportive environment with adequate supervision can lead to adverse outcomes for children, particularly boys. Sometimes, when a stepfather or cohabiting father figure enters a mother's family life, she finds herself better able to provide a supportive environment for her children. Yet, research suggests that even children in these circumstances do not fare as well as those who grow up with the involvement of two resident biological parents.[17]

Turning to a global view, youth in the United States, regrettably, are more likely to experience poverty than youth in other industrialized societies, according to a number of important indicators. For example, a recent UNICEF report comparing twenty-six rich countries, using as a relative measure of poverty half of the current median income for each designated country, found that 21.9 percent of children in the United States were living in poverty in 2000. Among the developed nations, only Mexico, at 27.7 percent, had a higher percentage of its children living in poverty. Japan, Canada, and the United Kingdom reported significantly lower percentages of child poverty, 14.3, 14.9, and 15.4, respectively. That said, the United States was one of only five countries to experience a reduction in child poverty during the 1990s. A report based on the child well-being index compares various child and youth well-being trends in the United States with those of four other English-speaking countries (Australia, Canada, New

Zealand, and the United Kingdom). The Foundation for Child Development study used nineteen key indicators measured around the year 2000 and grouped according to the seven domains of social life measured in the CWI mentioned earlier. The report concludes that,

> although no country outscores the United States on *all* domains of child and youth well-being, our comparison of five Anglophone countries shows deficiencies in U.S. child well-being, particularly in *Health*, and *Educational Attainment* domains. . . . The consequences of child poverty are far reaching, resulting in potential deprivation of basic necessities, poorer health outcomes, and behavioral and educational problems. This report highlights the need for continuing public and private sector efforts to support and enhance the well-being [of] children and youth living in households with limited economic resources in the United States.

Some societies, including the United States, have turned to adult mentoring of youth as a means to minimize the negative outcomes poor kids tend to face when government anti-poverty policies are too limited.[18]

This brief snapshot of how children and adolescents are doing in the United States suggests that, while many youth are doing just fine, a large proportion are struggling to varying degrees with one or more critical challenges.[19] Some belong to fragile families confronted by the ugly face of poverty; some grapple with troubled families and are besieged by neglect, discord, and abuse; and some have trouble handling the stress of navigating the turbulent tides of growing up, and in some cases of their own self-destructive tendencies. Whatever the origin and nature of their struggles, youth benefit if they have healthy relationships with their parents, but also with other adults in their communities. Youth who establish a meaningful relationship with one or more adults outside the family, through ingenuity or circumstance, typically fare best at managing their lives. Although many of these adults are men, more men can and should be involved with at-risk kids as well as with those kids who are thriving.

These interviews and ethnographic observations encourage interventionist caregiving by showing the actual and potential contributions men can make to kids in everyday life situations. Unfortunately, the myriad social problems affecting youth today will not be eradicated simply by having more men take a greater interest in working and volunteering with kids. Profoundly improving American youth's well-being will require significant structural changes in society, a shift in social policy and spending priorities to ensure that children's needs are taken more seriously, and the adoption of a new mainstream cultural narrative that more clearly equates masculinity with nurturance and caregiving—especially towards children.

CHILD AND ADOLESCENT DEVELOPMENT

Developmental psychologists say that children, in addition to basic physiological needs, also have emotional, cognitive, and social needs that must be met for healthy development. Researchers associated with the Minneapolis-based Search Institute have developed a strength-based approach to youth development relevant to the interpersonal bonds adults and youth form.[20] This approach delineates 40 specific developmental assets—critical factors or benchmarks—that identify healthy child and adolescent development. The assets refer to the "experiential outcomes of the youth's environment and socialization" and are divided into external and internal categories.[21] The framework uses insights from the literatures on child and adolescent development, resiliency, health promotion, prevention, and public health.

During the past two decades, Search Institute surveyed roughly two million sixth and twelfth graders throughout the United States to generate its age-specific assets. The assets have been extended to account for younger children's needs and abilities as well. Research shows that youth with more of these assets tend to experience positive outcomes, exhibiting, for instance, less risk-taking behavior (e.g., drugs, alcohol, violence, early sex), more thriving behavior (e.g., school achievement and leadership), and greater resiliency when faced with difficult situations and stress (e.g., parents' divorce). Unfortunately, recent surveys indicate that the typical American youth has only 19 of the 40 assets. Presumably, by enhancing men's motivation and ability to augment youth's developmental assets, strides can be made to improve youth's well-being.

The 20 external assets (those functioning outside the young person) are divided into four main areas: support factors, empowerment conditions, clear boundaries and expectations, and opportunities for constructive use of time. Not surprisingly, for kids to be supported they need to be loved and cared for by others. When they are empowered they feel valued by the community and are given options to contribute to others' lives. For this to happen, youth need to feel safe and secure at home, school, and in the neighborhood. As kids develop they need to learn what others expect of them and what is acceptable and unacceptable behavior. These lessons help them understand the behavioral boundaries associated with their activities. Finally, kids benefit from exposure to challenging activities in which they can develop their skills and competencies while growing in a productive way. Too much idle, unproductive time leads to boredom and stunted emotional, psychological, cognitive, and physical growth.

The internal categories reflect the processing of the external assets and refer to personal qualities that enable a young person to make wise choices and develop a focused, goal-oriented approach to life. They include commitment to learning, positive values, social competencies, and a positive identity. Learning to respect education and developing a life-long desire to learn are critical assets in life. People benefit from adopting a core set of values and living a principled life. Views differ on which values youth should select and apply, but the values identified by the Search Institute receive broad public support. For example, for kids ages 6–11, appropriate values are caring about other people, being interested in equality and social justice for the good of the community, integrity, honesty, age-appropriate responsibility, and striving for a healthy lifestyle and responsible sexual attitudes. Because social relations are essential for most people throughout the life course, youth need to develop the interpersonal skills necessary to build relationships and maintain them. The ability to achieve life goals is closely tied to self-concept; thus, helping youth to recognize their promise and enhancing their self-confidence can contribute to their success. People who possess these internal assets are better equipped to seek out, solidify, and make good use of interpersonal connections and to accomplish their goals and navigate their life circumstances productively.

In general, young people's needs fall into two areas critical to living in a contemporary society: relationships with other children and with adults, and how children spend their time.[22] Moreover, contemporary youth's ability to meet the challenges of the developmental phases associated with childhood and adolescence hinges on their exposure to resources and social support.[23] Because their needs cannot be met fully by family members, the community must share responsibility for providing the external assets and helping youth attain the internal assets.

From a sheer numbers perspective, if more men were involved with unrelated kids in productive ways they would augment the resources youth already have at their disposal to meet their developmental challenges. In addition, men are likely to be in a unique position to enhance some of the assets kids need. Some of the challenges boys and girls face involve learning various gender practices. One feminist scholar, Patricia Martin, refers to these practices as representing, "a class of activities that are available—culturally, socially, narratively, discursively, physically, and so forth—for people to enact in an encounter or situation in accord with (or violation of) the gender institution. Practices are per se conceptually distinct from people who practice them."[24] In other words, gender practices are ways of saying and doing things. They are the possible actions people know about and can perform in various situations. Gender practices, including the knowledge and preferences associated with them, change with the times and may be more or less appealing to particular people at any given time.

We learn lessons in gender behavior from others. Wise adults should prompt young people to assess critically how they practice gendered behavior—what they actually say and do when relating to others (e.g., "I love you" versus "I love you, *man*" and a shoulder hug versus a hand shake or a full intimate hug versus a half shoulder-to-shoulder hug). A teenage boy may become more mindful of how he practices gender after someone he admires alters the young man's view of physical intimacy among men. Derek, the muscular African American police officer, talks about his efforts to make a difference in how at-risk black male teenagers view physical and emotional intimacy.

> I hug the guys all the time. Actually, I have this thing. . . . Whenever I go to shake a guy's hand, I'll pull him in; I'll say, "Give me some love." . . . I don't know what it is about black men, black males, they're afraid to express emotion or they don't say anything like that. So I'll be . . . I don't go overboard or anything, . . . all huggy. But I'll bring them in, give them a little hug on the back. . . . I'll tell them to give me some love and I'll hug them around the shoulder. And just to show that you don't have to be hard all the time . . . it's not all about being tough. You can be tough without being distant from everybody. It's all right to share your feelings or it's all right to hug, take another guy and hug him around the shoulders, something like that. And I notice they've been doing it a lot more around the [facility], they'll even go up and they'll hug each other. . . . But before, when I got there, it was like, don't touch me . . . don't touch me.

By affording young guys the chance to confront their fear of male intimacy, Derek provides the young men a valuable interpersonal asset that may change how they relate to others and how they see themselves. Though the gesture may seem trivial to some, teenage boys are more likely to challenge unhealthy masculinity expectations if they are gently nudged to rethink their routine behaviors.

I got a glimpse of Derek in action when I spent a day with him at a community center for at-risk boys and while he visited several boys at their schools. At the center, I saw how effortlessly Derek connected with kids by shaking hands, giving hugs, or playfully wrestling with them. One kid, decidedly big for his age, approached Derek with a smirk and challenged Derek to an arm wrestling contest. As I sat next to Derek, watching him feign distress as he allowed the boy to get ever so close to pinning him, I got the distinct sense that this was a ritual between them; the boy seemed comfortable initiating the game. Meanwhile, several kids joked around with Derek, saying they were going to "take him" or one of their friends was going to do so. Some of the kids may feel more at ease than usual with Derek's being affectionate toward them because they revere him for his massive physical size and playful personality. They likely reason that if this big guy can express a soft side it must be okay.

Because we live in a socially constructed world organized around gender expectations, some youth will pay more attention to male adults who are sharing their "wisdom" and guidance on gender behavior, because they are perceived as more relevant and credible than women on certain topics. This pattern is probably most true for the social competencies in managing interpersonal relations between boys, or boys and girls. Men's contributions to asset building can be recognized without knowing what if any portion of their treatment of youth is connected to male genetic makeup. What is known is that being around responsible adult men can provide youths with distinct occasions for witnessing the process of healthy relations between people, in particular, men's treatment of adult females, and males, as well as children, in diverse situations. Directly and indirectly, the men's presence affords kids a chance to learn about their ability to effect outcomes in their lives, to feel good about themselves, and to develop a sense of investment in promoting their own growth and others' well-being.[25]

Obviously, being with irresponsible men exposes youths to negative experiences and examples. Some experiences may damage, perhaps crush, a youth's self-esteem while discouraging the young person from developing a healthy goal-oriented approach to life, but I emphasize men's potential to do good.

TODAY'S CULTURAL CLIMATE

Casual viewing of everyday life reveals that men interact and form diverse bonds with kids outside their homes. As I show later, my interviews with men illustrate an incredible array of situations in which men relate to youth and, in many instances, feel they have made a difference in kids' lives. Because our daily worlds are still touched by gender norms and stereotypes, the social forces of gender often affect the context in which men think, feel, and act around kids. Men are enveloped in an intricate web of cultural messages about what it means for them to be involved with youth in specific ways and settings. Cultural images and public discourse about men and kids make a difference in how men and

kids relate to one another. The images and language used in this public discourse affect how individuals define situations, perceive themselves, act, and
talk about issues.

Messages about men's relationships with youths are often filtered through
decades of feminist debate about egalitarian marriages, paternal responsibility,
and male violence. In the 1960s, feminists grew more vocal in prodding fathers
to increase their domestic labor, particularly childcare, and in the process they altered the cultural conversation about family life. The modern image of the involved father was born. Men embracing progressive ideas about masculinity and
gender relations became sensitive and attentive New Age fathers, some of them
choosing to become stay-at-home dads. A little later, more conservative voices,
some affiliated with the religious right, climbed on the bandwagon, challenging
fathers to take a more active role in caring for their children. Organizations like
the National Fatherhood Initiative emerged and created advertisements and
training resources promoting a certain brand of involved fathering in primarily
heterosexual, two-parent homes.

Pleas for men to increase their level of involvement in domestic labor were
accentuated because women, including mothers, were spending more time working outside the home. The debates were refined in the late 1980s and early 1990s
when scholars described employed mothers as coming home to a "second-shift"
of demanding work involving children and household chores, a shift fathers
largely ignored.[26] Although some scholars challenged the size of the gap between
mothers' and fathers' second-shift work,[27] most acknowledged that employed
fathers spent less time than employed mothers caring for their children.

Recent evidence does suggest, however, that, compared to previous generations of fathers, contemporary fathers do more domestic labor, including childcare.[28] Although the overall increase is not dramatic, fathers today have and take
more opportunities to hone their parenting skills, learning to address children's
basic needs, personalities, and activity schedules. Developing these parenting
skills transcends family or household boundaries; sometimes men learn important lessons while interacting with kids outside the home, in their paid work or
in community activities. Some men gain experience as adolescents relating to
younger kids; others venture down this road only after becoming adults. Phillip,
a 26-year-old graduate student in counseling with ambitions to do research and
work with kids in school settings, feels that his extensive experience as a camp
counselor, daycare volunteer, coach, and counseling intern in elementary and
middle schools taught him valuable interpersonal skills that will make him a
better father, such as

knowing how to take on . . . an authoritative role rather than dictator or au-
thoritarian role versus giving into every whim—taking on that authoritative
role, where you can kind of take on this hierarchical role and you can do the
discipline but you're also flexible and open minded and willing to engage in
conversation.

Phillip began working with kids in day camps as a teenager. Later, he accumulated practical hands-on experience relating to kids in a variety of settings while
gaining textbook knowledge about child development as he pursued his undergraduate and graduate psychology degrees. Together, his classroom instruction
in child psychology and practical experience working with kids should enable
him eventually to become a father with an informed perspective.

Research focusing on fathers' relationships with their children offers some
clues about men's basic ability to make a difference in children's lives. Although
the study designs and data are not ideal, it appears that when resident fathers
provide emotional support, give everyday assistance, monitor behavior, and engage in noncoercive discipline, their children experience a wide range of positive
outcomes.[29] The outcomes include greater academic success, fewer conduct
problems, less depression, higher self-esteem, and more competence in managing social relationships. Presumably, even though the process may differ somewhat, involved men who are not their fathers can also positively contribute to
children's development.

Let us extend the feminist lens beyond gender equity issues in the home to
look at men's orientation toward youth in the public sphere. If men and women
are ever to become equal players in managing the home and the larger social
world, and if we are to create a more generative society—one dedicated to helping the youngest generation thrive—the culture of caregiving must be transformed. Broadly speaking, providing paid or voluntary care for others—adults as
well as children—must be viewed as a human endeavor, not something for
which women are uniquely suited.[30]

In the world of youth, men and women must not only be more equally committed to and involved with their own children but with other people's children
as well, both at work and in leisure. Women still carry the bulk of the load when
it comes to teaching and caring for youth in elementary schools, daycare centers,
youth camps, and hospital settings. At the same time, men's greater fondness
for sports means that they are more likely than women to coach youth
recreational teams.[31] The predominance of male coaches is likely to diminish
with time as the proportion of girls involved in competitive sports increases,

providing a pool of adult females eager to coach soccer, basketball, softball, swimming, gymnastics, and other sports.

Overall, the gender gap in adult-child involvement in the public arena may have closed a bit in recent decades, but it persists, particularly in paid positions, because the public continues to view child-oriented occupations as primarily "women's work."[32] Even though the feminist movement has had some success in fostering appreciation of child-oriented occupations, they are still devalued. Staffed primarily by women, these occupations reap lower social prestige and fewer financial rewards. For example, at the national level only 9 percent of elementary school teachers are male, and the average salary of all elementary teachers in the United States was $48,091 for 2006.[33] In contrast, in a male dominated occupation like electrical engineering, in which 92.1 percent of workers are male,[34] the average salary was $78,633 in 2006.[35] Thus, when men choose a job or career devoted to children, they may face being marginalized as less masculine and can count on earning less money.

Fortunately, some men who choose jobs working with kids confront head-on the negative stereotypes of men as children's caregivers. I spoke with a number of men who were elementary and middle school teachers, childcare workers, and healthcare specialists working with kids. Listening to their passion for their work provides a powerful reminder that many men can and do love working with youngsters. Mariano, a 31-year-old school teacher of Cuban decent, spent more than two hours enthusiastically describing his teaching philosophy and efforts to inspire and support his students, initially in high schools and most recently at the middle school level. Asked if he had a preference for high school or middle school teaching, Mariano explains:

I love the interaction with the high school kids because they're at a different level socially, emotionally, creatively. . . . The other day I had a conversation with my eighth grade kids about U.S. immigration policy. Wow, I hadn't had a conversation like that in three years. And I came out of that second period—it was with my eighth grade Spanish kids—and I was like, "Man I miss that." But if you were to ask anyone that knows me right now, they'll tell you that I'm a better middle school teacher, that I was made to be a middle school teacher. And I'm seeing that. I miss my AP [advanced placement] kids, I miss my discussions on theology and politics and those things, but I think I'm making better high school students. I think that I'm where I'm suppose to be right now. And, I'm enjoying it a lot. I'm making a positive impact here.

Like Mariano, Richard, a 47-year-old black man who immigrated to the United States more than twenty years ago from Africa, is committed to his youth work. He shares his unusual and moving story about why he launched a childcare business. As children's playful voices and bustling energy seep through thin office walls, Richard describes the particulars of an event that occurred seven years earlier while he was working as a retail store manager. After viewing TV news coverage about a kidnapped 10-year-old girl who had been missing for about a week, Richard, "by a miracle," recognized the child when she was dropped off without warning in the store's parking lot. Working with the police, he was instrumental in reuniting the girl with her family. The child was about his own daughter's age at the time. He was initially content to have played a useful role, but his state of mind changed quickly.

> Three days later I start having an emotional problem. I started thinking if that was my child. I started thinking that, okay, I'm here trying to make money, everything like that, my child was in school too, and she has to go home by herself, just like [the kidnapped girl] did. So . . . I start[ed] dreaming. What can I do to make a difference? That was my point; that was my turning back from, I would say, the will of trying to make money, better myself, then to turn back and . . . to help some other people that might be in this kind of predicament, regardless of race, color, creed, or whatsoever. So I told my wife, I said, "how would you like us to open up a daycare?"

Richard's wife, who at the time was regularly providing daycare for a few kids at their home, was not immediately sold on the idea. However, she helped Richard process his feelings and soon thereafter gave Richard the green light to act upon his dream and open the childcare center. Now, Richard, his wife, and their teenage daughter work side by side in their family-owned childcare center. Though Richard is well aware that his career decision placed him in a female-dominated field, he has no regrets about his decision. He only wishes more men would pursue this important line of work.

Richard's story is but one of many examples of men making a positive contribution to kids' lives in a community context. Another such person is Peter Westbrook, the 1984 U.S. Olympic bronze medalist in fencing, who launched a different type of youth-oriented initiative. As a kid growing up in the dangerous public housing projects of Newark, New Jersey, Westbrook found refuge in fencing, a sport that he says transformed his life. "If not for fencing, I would have been another city kid on drugs, taking my hurt out on somebody else."[36] It was his desire to provide productive options and discipline for other disadvantaged youth that led Westbrook to use his own money to build the Peter Westbrook Foundation in 1991. In addition to providing top-notch fencing training, the foundation encourages children to develop a more structured lifestyle and to be more attentive to their schoolwork. Unlike Richard, Peter has gained national prominence, including an appearance on the *Oprah Winfrey Show* and a write-up in *Sports Illustrated* magazine. Other men across the country make similar commitments by devoting enormous amounts of time, money, and energy to helping youth.

The value of men's involvement in the community, particularly helping disadvantaged children, is captured aptly by the National Football League's partnership with the United Way Campaign and the "NBA Cares" social responsibility initiative targeting youth-serving programs. Television commercials sponsored by the NFL regularly show football stars promoting the benefits of reading as they recite children's stories to enthusiastic kids huddled around them. These ads display the rugged football players' caring side. When an icon of physical prowess reaches out to children, the viewing public's attention is captured by the contrast of power and vulnerability. The ads illustrate that even a traditionally masculine man can and should play an active role in nurturing youth outside the home.

Similarly, heroic scenes of police officers and fire fighters rescuing children from life-threatening situations are consistent with cultural images mentioned above and are part of the public mind. For many, especially in more affluent neighborhoods, masculine public servants receive the community's respect. Many children and young adolescents view these men as their public protectors and representatives of goodwill. Admittedly, some well-to-do older adolescents resent police authority, and many poor inner-city youth have jaded views of police officers, in part, because of racial profiling. But, on balance, many youth recognize male police officers and fire fighters as serving a useful purpose in the community, one that may directly or indirectly enhance their welfare.

Extraordinary circumstances often yield examples of men helping children. The devastating Indian Ocean tsunami of December 2004 created conditions for many images of heroic behavior. Countless strangers, doctors, and aid workers helped frightened, injured, and orphaned children. In the aftermath of Hurricane Katrina in the late summer of 2005, the public saw images of local strangers giving aid and professional rescuers dangling from helicopters plucking survivors from floodwaters and rooftops. Though the message was probably dulled because of public frustration over the delayed official rescue and relief response, people often saw men helping kids and others. The poignant images conveyed the notion that men can be protectors and nurturing forces in children's lives without having a family connection.

Closer to everyday life, male coaches are positively involved with youth in recreational leagues. Granted, some male coaches are overbearing, obnoxious, too aggressive, or dangerously competitive. However, onlookers typically appreciate men's willingness to volunteer their time and energy to work with kids. Outside of the sporting venue, parents may have similar appreciation for the conscientious male teacher, minister, or Boy Scout leader who takes a productive interest in their child.

Unfortunately, wholesome images of men displaying heart-felt concern for children in public are offset by gripping, sad tales of men acting badly toward children, inside and outside a family context. It was a man, for instance, who abducted the girl Richard found in the parking lot. Just as feminists played a critical role in highlighting men's limited involvement in the day-to-day care of their own children, they have been instrumental, along with other groups, in drawing attention to the emotional and physical abuse of children.

Only a few years ago, disturbing news flooded media outlets detailing how a significant minority of Catholic priests had for many years sexually molested young parishioners.[37] The priests, along with complicit superiors who essentially turned a blind eye to these troubling events, had violated their parishioners' trust. These men who had once possessed a privileged community status increasingly were compared to a stereotype—the despicable child molester. Their maleness grew more central to their public persona and social identity. Labeled as male predators or potential predators, the accused and suspected were stigmatized, their virtuous public image as men of God tarnished.

Other news reports, before and since the Catholic priest scandal have documented the expanding domestic and international sex industry's penchant for exploiting youth. The public learns about male sex offenders causing public havoc by snatching young children from homes, playgrounds, supermarkets, or shopping malls. News stories and documentary writings offer sordid details of how adults, mostly men, kidnap and coerce children into a life of prostitution worldwide. Abductions usually result in devastating abuse and ultimately the child's murder. Not surprisingly, the clients fueling this industry are largely male as well. Men also increasingly use the Internet to meet and lure unsuspecting children or precocious teens for inappropriate sexual rendezvous or worse. This infamous pattern has received extensive national visibility from the popular *Dateline NBC* series, "To Catch a Predator," which documents an undercover sting operation for identifying potential child sexual abusers. A 2005 national online victimization survey found that at least 73 percent of the perpetrators of sexual solicitation of youths ages 10–17 were male, though perhaps roughly half of solicitors were other youths.[38] Advances in computer technology have helped such men produce and consume child pornography at unprecedented rates. According to a congressionally funded project, reports of child pornography made to the National Center for Missing and Exploited Children CyberTipline™, launched in March 1998, had by April of 2007 reached a total of roughly 422,800.[39] Though most people are not well versed in the particulars of how men operate and support this industry, the public seems to recognize that men, not women, are primarily responsible for exploiting children in this way. If only they were as well attuned to the large percentage of male police officers and FBI agents who work tirelessly to disrupt this industry and bring those other men to justice.

Law enforcement, the courts, and legislatures are struggling to combat this societal problem. Horrific thoughts about sex offenders' lethal potential stunned the nation in the early months of 2005 when two Floridian girls, 9-year-old Jessica Lunsford and 13-year-old Sarah Lunde, were brutally killed in separate crimes. The men implicated in these murders were described as only two of the roughly 34,000 registered sex offenders living in Florida.[40] The well-publicized events inspired tougher legislation in Florida, the Jessica Lunsford Act, enhancing punishments for persons convicted of a sex crime.

Several years ago the public was also engrossed by news reports of the destructive mentor-disciple relationship between John Muhammad and Lee Malvo. The serial snipers thrust themselves into the media limelight for three weeks in 2002 by killing ten people and wounding three others in the Washington, D.C., area. The teenage Malvo reportedly had told his mother that he had chosen the much older Muhammad as his new parent figure. Over time, Muhammad was able to direct Malvo on what to eat, when to speak, and how to shoot a rifle. Prior to their capture, the prevailing suspicion, which proved to be accurate, was that the sniper was a man. Even though it did not appear that the sniper was targeting children, thoughts of a male sniper killing innocent children shocked the public at large, leaving a sour taste of masculinity's potentially destructive impact.

Of course, women sometimes are at the center of well-publicized child abuse stories, occasionally involving children not their own. But the relative rarity of these events limits the public's exposure to them. The press occasionally vilifies a female school teacher who seduces an adolescent boy into a romantic fling or a woman who has helped a man abduct children to secure a ransom. Yet, when the media showcases a woman for mistreating a child, she is most often a mentally unstable mother who has done horrific things to her own children. We think of Giberta Estrada's murder-suicide hanging involving her young daughters in Hudson Oaks, Texas, in May of 2007, or Andrea Yates, the mother living in Houston who suffered from postpartum depression and drowned her five children in the bathtub in 2001. Similar stories of abusive women make the national news, but the public's shock remains isolated and focused, not generalized to other women. The public continues to see women treating children so poorly as an aberration.

In contrast, negative stories about men appear to reinforce a common public sentiment that men, compared to women, are more likely to treat children badly. Thus, men's public interactions with youth are at times constrained by a gendered climate of distrust. Adult men in the United States today face conflicting images of their relationships with children, and a distinct negative stereotype prevails in certain contexts. Sometimes the unflattering image is thrust vividly upon us; other times it slips unnoticed into our intuitive understandings of daily life. What once was a seemingly uncomplicated public view—that men, compared to women, are by nature less attentive to and compassionate toward children in the community—has morphed into a more nuanced and sometimes much more ominous public sentiment, one fed by a media machine in search of tragedy. The media frenzy surrounding incidents of men's maltreatment of children has gradually generated a public consciousness beset with fear and distrust. Unfamiliar men are no longer simply strangers; they are potential child abusers. They are the flesh and blood incarnations of the imaginary monsters children fear lurk inside their bedroom closets. The fear-laden outlook implies that men are not simply less kid-oriented and caring than are women but also more likely to harm children—emotionally, psychologically, and physically. Though elusive and diffuse, this image affects people of all ages, creating a general distrust and suspicion of men who take an interest in children.[41]

This climate is perpetuated by parental fear and what social demographer Gill Valentine labels, "terror talk." "Stranger-danger discourses"—fearful ways of thinking and talking about the risks children face in public space—have altered how parents manage their children's lives. It appears that parents are imposing more rigid guidelines on where kids can go and to whom they are permitted to speak. Soon, individuals' quality of parenting may be judged by whether they strap a bracelet with a global positioning system (GPS) device on their child's wrist.[42] In fact, the local risks children face in public are exaggerated due to the global reach of modern media and the culture of control it breeds. The male body, says Valentine, is described as "saturated with threat and so contributes to shaping the way that adults and children relate to each other and (re)produce public space."[43] Meanwhile, "safe environment educators" advise children outside the protective care of parents to seek help by locating a mother—a woman with child in tow.

How does this depiction of the cultural landscape affect our understanding of how men treat children? Most importantly, it signals the need to appreciate the larger cultural context in which men's relations with children are framed. Men's attempts to be good guys committed to helping kids are often complicated by the destructive force of negative stereotypes, like those of the pedophile, child pornographer, and child abuser, all of which conjure up *male* images. Unlike discussions of the "good dad" and "bad dad" dichotomy[44] in which the attentive, loving father is glorified, partly because his behavior differs sharply from that of the dead-beat father, the negative stereotype of the "bad guy" casts an unfriendly shadow over the man with good intentions. Consequently, the man set on serving youth and parents often pursues his mission while wading through an undercurrent of stranger-danger fear.

Generally speaking, the public, or at least a sizeable portion of it, tends to view men in relation to youth in one of several stereotypical ways. Those men perceived most positively, like Peter Westbrook, the former Olympian turned community activist, and the many men I interviewed who have worked with kids for years, have earned others' respect and trust. They are recognized as exceptional individuals by those who know them personally or know of them because their actions suggest they are truly devoted to helping kids flourish.

A genre of Hollywood movies aptly captures the good guy stereotype by depicting the teacher or coach who exceeds public expectations in his commitment to youth. In the movie *Radio*, which recounts a true story, Ed Harris plays Coach Jones, a former high school football coach from South Carolina who in 1964 befriended a mentally challenged young man, James Robert Kennedy, played by Cuba Gooding Jr. Coach Jones, a white man, reached out to the young black man despite the objections of many in the community, coaxing successive generations of his players and others to accept him as a vital part of the team staff, school, and community. Another real life high school coach, portrayed by Samuel Jackson in the movie *Coach Carter*, embodies the essence of the good guy stereotype through his undying belief in, and commitment to, the at-risk boys playing on his basketball team. Parents, kids, and the general public recognize many other such good guys, though few achieve the same level of visibility as these, acknowledging them as decent men willing to devote their time, energy, and even money to youth. Those belonging to this subset of men are, in effect, your average run-of-the-mill good guys.

A cautious and less favorable image of a man often stems from having limited experience with and information about the man. Without specific information about a stranger, many people unknowingly rely on some combination of stereo-typical cues pertaining to social class, race or ethnicity, age, sexual orientation, and appearance to form their impression of him. A lone male stranger walking innocently by a city playground on his way to his destination who stops to watch a spirited group of kids playing kickball may be projected, to varying degrees, as a dubious guy by others in the area. The kids may think: Why is this man watching us? What does he want? Is he someone's dad? I wonder if he's like that bad man on the TV show I saw last week? Adults may think: Who is this man and what is he doing here? Has he been here before? Should I ask him what he's doing? Should I tell the security guard? Unknown in this setting, the man, like many others in comparable situations, is cast as a dubious guy, a potential threat. Chances are, had he been accompanied by a woman, others would have perceived him as part of a romantic couple enjoying the sights of children at play.

Of course, a man once deemed dubious may earn others' trust through deed or familiarity and become a good guy in the viewer's eyes, however, earning that trust is not always easy, and the trust may even be partial and fleeting. Some parents may label the male school teacher a good guy; others may see him as suspicious. Those who once viewed the school teacher as a good guy may change their minds quickly after hearing gossip about how he supposedly made a romantic pass at a student. In their mind he may slip from good guy, to dubious guy, to bad guy based on one rumored incident. Meanwhile, the school teacher is left to manage his self-image while contemplating what he believes others think of him. Among the numerous men implicated by these processes, guilty ones may realize that their inappropriate treatment of youth has been discovered. They may face disci-plinary action or legal proceedings, or make arrangements to pursue another path away from the kids in question. Others are left pondering how to challenge false accusations and regain their favorable reputation, sometimes amidst a formal or informal investigation into their behavior. As I discuss later, most men are aware of the politics of touch and physical space if they work with youth. Although some men sidestep the issue, many men's style of interacting with youths is affected by their vigilance in fear of false accusations for inappropriate behavior.

Men are often cautious about working with kids because the bad guy label can be debilitating, whether it is applied justly or not. The bad guy label serves a useful purpose when it informs youth and parents about men who have mis-

treated a young person or have acted in ways (e.g., murdering an adult, drug traf-
ficking) that signal they might endanger youth in some way. However, the bad
guy label can damage those who are wrongfully accused. In recent years, rising
public concern over sex offenders has made life difficult for some men who pose
no threat to children. For example, consider a man who was barely 19 when he
had consensual sex with his 16-year-old girlfriend one month shy of her seven-
teeth birthday. The girl's parents pressed criminal charges against the young
man for having sex with their daughter, who was considered a minor by state law
until she was 17. Once convicted, the man was labeled a sex offender by authorities and forced to comply with a monitoring protocol enabling his neighbors to
learn that a sex offender was living nearby. In some instances, neighbors will
warn their children not to talk to the bad guy living down the street. Though
some people obviously would deplore this young man's choice to have sex with
his girlfriend at that age and outside of marriage, it seems a stretch, perhaps
ridiculous, to argue that his having done so makes him a danger to children.

ACROSS THE DECADES

Men in the United States have always been involved with youth in public settings, but the picture has changed considerably over the years. To gain perspective on the meaning and consequences of the contemporary landscape, it is
worth mentioning how several major transitional periods affected the social organization of American society and, in turn, men's relationships with youth. In
addition to having direct consequences, these and other changes have been important indirectly because they shaped ideas about families and fathers' roles.
Views of men inside the home are tied to men's involvements with kids outside
it. (I take up these issues in Chapter 9.)

The companion processes of industrialization and urbanization set in motion
notable changes in men's public experiences with youth. The large-scale aspect of
industrialization and urbanization was accompanied by ideological shifts in how
individuals perceived and experienced childhood, family life, gender relations,
neighborhood, education, work, and leisure. Public ideologies were altered, too,
by technological developments like the car and telephone that expanded youth's
physical mobility and social opportunities. Most recently, the evolution and diffu-
sion of modern communications media have affected views of public space and,
more specifically, of men's involvement with youth in public.

With the movement of economic production outside the household and the
neighborhood beginning in the middle to late 1800s, children began to be raised

increasingly in a different type of social environment than ever before.[45] The growth of public schools, in addition to the parents' declining availability in the home due to their employment elsewhere, has meant that children have been spending more time in the public domain, a setting in which they encounter unrelated men and women through design or chance. It also means that the mix of human qualities and social resources available to children inside and outside the home has been changing. Hence, issues about how unrelated adults enter and affect children's lives, for better or worse, have become more significant with time's passing.

Together, industrialization and urbanization altered the physical and social spaces that brought men and children into each other's orbits. With the decline of the family farm, the immigration of men with and without families to more urban areas, and the tight housing arrangements of emerging inner cities, men were much more likely to come into contact with children other than their own sons and daughters. Typically, men who farmed were more physically isolated from other families and children. Although their own children often worked alongside them, their opportunities to cross paths with other young people outside the family were often limited to church or jaunts into the local town or village for supplies.

In the industrial North and Midwest in the 1880s and later, immigrants increasingly found themselves living in close quarters in burgeoning city slums. Here, men ran into neighborhood youth during their daily rounds. The presence of children and men traversing the same public space was normalized. In addition, prior to the child labor laws introduced in the early 1900s, men who did manual labor for a living rubbed elbows with child workers and apprentices on a regular basis. Given the view of childhood and adolescence of the day, men were less apt to coddle their young coworkers, whom they monitored and instructed in the workplace. Today, remnants of this adult-child work system are still found among transient migrants working the fields in various regions of the United States. Male migrant workers instruct youth on how to manage this Spartan, nomadic, labor-intensive way of life.

During the late 1800s and early 1900s, concerns about the feminization of American culture ran rampant as urban growth altered fundamental social and cultural patterns.[46] Fears of a culture perceived to be increasingly soft were pervasive; urban life was deemed by many to be gentler and less invigorating than farm life. In addition, adult males' involvement in public and many private schools was declining as the proportion of female school teachers grew. Boys were spending more time during their impressionable years being taught and, according to some, softened by adult females. These concerns prompted men to create youth-oriented organizations to remasculinize boyhood. The guiding logic was that boys needed to be around rugged, adult male role models so they could learn how to become masculine men capable of leading families and assuming their station in the workplace.

A remedy championed by some was to create organized settings for "boys to be boys." The Rev. William Forbush, author of *The Boy Problem*, published in 1901, stressed the value of creating summer camps for boys so they could "develop those savage virtues which are the admiration of boyhood."[47] Forbush established two organizations, the Men of Tomorrow and the Knights of King Arthur, in order to increase adult men's influence over boys. The Men of Tomorrow promoted a fellowship of men committed to learning and sharing information about male adolescent development and the Knights focused on instilling a brand of Christian virtues into young boys through rituals.[48] Because these and most other male-segregated organizations were open only to whites, black boys' gender socialization occurred largely outside organizational borders.

The Boy Scouts of America is the most prominent of the organizations launched during this era in order to counteract the cultural trends precipitated by urbanization. It offered men new and structured settings in which to interact with children other than their own offspring. However, because this organization excluded girls, men's options for recreating with unrelated youth were restricted to boys—white boys in particular. Adult males' involvement with youth was occurring in an increasingly gender-segregated environment.

Lord Baden-Powell founded the Boy Scouts in England. For him, adult male intervention in boys' lives was essential. "We badly need some training for our lads if we are to keep up manliness in our race instead of lapsing into a nation of soft, sloppy, cigarette suckers."[49] Across the Atlantic, Ernest Thompson Seton launched the Boys Scouts of America in 1910. The initial philosophy of the American rendition reflected Seton's influence, accentuating aspects of the frontier spirit while honoring Native American Indian culture and lore. But his standing in the organization was quickly challenged, and other voices began to shape the Boy Scouts within five years. The new leaders disputed portraying Indians as "manly heroes" for boys; instead, they emphasized the Boy Scouts as a "patriotic youth brigade."[50] Scout leaders agreed with Seton, however, that the main threat to male youth's vitality was the urban, industrialized way of life. It had supposedly given us soft men.

According to Seton, men were also becoming softer because they were being exposed to spectator sports. For him, "spectatoritis" was changing "robust, manly, self-reliant boyhood into a lot of flat chested smokers with shaky nerves and doubtful vitality."[51] For boys actually engaged in athletics, sports was seen as an ideal setting for exploring and demonstrating their emerging manliness. Boys could learn discipline, test their physical prowess, and compete with one another as they navigated their adolescent years in pursuit of becoming men. During their developmental journey they received instructions from men, who had once experienced the same transition.

Fortunately, the gendered philosophy of the modern Boy Scouts of America, especially as expressed in the folk culture at the local troop level, has evolved *a bit* since the early days—despite the current national office's intolerance of gays, represented by their essentially "don't ask, don't tell" policy.[52] In his detailed ethnographic study, *On My Honor: Boy Scouts and the Making of American Youth*, Jay Mechling, a professor of American studies, offers a compelling account of how the production of masculinities in Boy Scout culture changed throughout the twentieth century. As a longtime Eagle Scout (highest honor for a Boy Scout), scholar of folk culture, and interdisciplinary student of masculinity, Mechling is an astute observer of both rigid official Boy Scout positions and the messier immediate experiences of kids and adults at the troop level. Mechling crafts his story of Boy Scout culture largely out of his twenty-five years of field experience (1974–1999), including camping excursions in Sierra Nevada, where he joined the boys and their leaders during numerous summers, and other troop activities during the school years.

Mechling's rendering of the Boy Scout experience at the troop level reveals that, irrespective of the scout master's personality, plenty of traditional, aggressive, and antifeminine masculinity is on display. But Mechling also notes that a troop's own folk culture can be influenced by the kinds of men who lead the troop. For example, Pete, the man who served as troop leader throughout Mechling's study period, "would not tolerate homophobic or misogynist utterances at troop campfires, assemblies, or dining tables."[53] Pete also worked diligently to eliminate boys' use of shame as a control mechanism. More generally, a shift of sorts in gender performance can be seen in the experiences and traits once viewed as traditionally feminine, like cooking, nurturance, and attentive listening, all of which now appear to be incorporated more readily into the scouting experience throughout the country.

Part of the shift in how gender is practiced may be due to mothers' greater involvement in the organization. Jeff, a 50-year-old veteran scout troop leader I interviewed and observed, offers a mixed reaction to moms' involvement.

The scouting culture: very very dominated by females now, which was very hard for me to get used to. I got to honestly say it is a good thing. And a bad thing. Moms are much more resourceful; there is many many families where there is single moms running the show. They are mostly the ones who pick scouting because they are looking for some father figure or mentor to help with their kids and they get as active as they can. The ones that get trained and actually camp with us are typically very very good, but there is that little problem. Little Johnny is not the same in the woods when mom is around. You know, it is different. . . . You can't pee on a tree, you can't do this, can't be bad with your buddies. I don't know really how to explain it but . . . it is not the best. But women have a place now, a big place. They do well.

Jeff goes on to allude to how his wife sometimes alters the gender dynamics of the scouting environment when she participates. "My wife has learned the kids love her. She sneaks in, and the little things that she teaches them about cooking, and you don't have to go exactly about recipes, and she makes it fun." Having a woman teach boys how to cook while in a scout setting suggests that scouts may be incorporating a broader image of masculinity. In addition, Jeff's comments remind us that, whereas the Boy Scouts' appeal for many in the early 1900s was its role in compensating for the effects of the expanding urban, industrial culture, today the Boy Scouts help redress perceived deficiencies resulting from the larger numbers of boys being raised in single-female-headed households.

Another important youth organization that took root in the United States, 4-H, can trace its formal beginnings to the rural Midwest in the early 1900s. Although they didn't use the official 4-H label, a club for farm boys and girls was first established in 1902 in Springfield, Ohio, by A. B. Graham, a school principal.[54] Between 1905 and 1914, clubs were initiated in almost all states. In the early days, boys and girls participated in gender-segregated clubs organized around stereotypical themes: boys focused on exhibits of garden products and livestock contests whereas girls' exhibits included sewing and cooking. In 1927, at the first National 4-H Camp, or conference, the 4-H pledge was adopted: "I pledge my head to clearer thinking, my heart to greater loyalty, my hand to larger service, and my health to better living, for my club, my community, my country, and my world."[55] In 1958, males represented 43 percent of the total membership and today about 49 percent of members are boys.[56]

From its early beginnings as a gender-segregated organization centered in the rural Midwest, 4-H has evolved into an organization in which boys and girls are more likely to be involved in shared activities and competitions, and it has a presence in both rural and urban areas throughout the country. It offers a wide range of programs enabling youth to develop life competencies, including citizenship and leadership skills. Overnight 4-H youth camps are typically co-ed, providing boys and girls opportunities to enjoy the outdoors while learning to interact with and respect their gender counterparts. In recent decades, adult men increasingly have interacted with girls as well as boys, although little has been written about the interpersonal dynamics of these encounters.

Little League Baseball is a popular organization firmly rooted in the twentieth century. With currently over four million players and volunteers worldwide, Little League is purported to be the largest organized sports program for youth.[57] But, unlike 4-H, it has predominately been an organization run by men for boys.[58] Carl Stotz, along with his nephews Jimmy and Major, is credited with organizing the first Little League game, in Williamsport, Pennsylvania, in June of 1939. Stotz quickly realized his dream of encouraging men around the country to start leagues of their own so that more boys could play—307 leagues were formed by 1949. Notably, African Americans were participating in the league in its second year. Although some franchises left the organization during the 1950s in opposition to racial integration, Little League continued to promote itself as providing boys opportunities to play regardless of background or race. In the 1980s, an urban initiative was launched in South Central Los Angeles and in New York's Harlem to bring baseball to poor, largely minority kids. The Harlem program, founded in 1989, now has fifty teams. As for gender equality, it was not until 1972 that a girl, Marie Pepe, successfully challenged the "boys only" policy, in Hoboken, New Jersey. Interestingly, Kathryn "Tubby" Johnson has been credited with being the first girl—disguised as a boy—to play Little League, in 1950 in Corning, New York. And while a few girls do play in Little League, the vast majority of players continue to be boys with male volunteers serving as their coaches. In 1996, responding to public concerns about child safety, Little League created programs to educate volunteers and kids about pedophiles. The national office also encourages local leagues to run background checks on volunteers.

In these youth organizations, aside from 4-H, interactions between men and youth that were once tied to workplace and school settings, took on new meaning as they shifted to recreational sites. The once serious purposes of work and school where men and youngsters interacted were supplanted largely by arrangements promoting fun and competition. Men were now expected to teach life lessons, including those pertaining to adult manhood, by connecting them to the ethos of competitive team sports and the earthy self-sufficiency championed by the Boy Scouts. While each of these organizations helped boys to learn how to cooperate in ways useful for the growing industrial economy, they also stressed the value of men interacting with boys in an all-male setting.

In recent decades, girls have increased their participation in recreational sports significantly. Although exact figures are not available, men often coach girls' school and recreational softball, soccer, basketball, volleyball, and other teams, and many in the recreational leagues coach their own daughters. Thus, men today are much more likely than their earlier counterparts to have an opportunity to interact with girls other than their own daughters. Although the consequences for this new arrangement are largely undocumented, the men who participate in these activities presumably develop a more nuanced understanding of how young girls express themselves, relate to one another, and interact with an older unrelated male authority figure.

Darnell, a 37-year-old African American man currently coaching a high school girls basketball team, has coached boys as well. He frames his thoughts about interacting with his female players by comparing it to his involvement with boys.

> Well, girls are a lot more sensitive. They take things to heart what you say, so you really have to watch what you say and how you say it. Boys these days are getting to be . . . very . . . what have you done for me lately, or you owe me this, you owe me that. . . . But the girls you have to be careful how you say stuff to them or what you say. You can't get mad at them, cuz they really, they take it personal.

Darnell continues his commentary on girls by observing how he feels they relate to one another.

> Phew!! . . . You have to keep an eye out, because there will be some drama. Two girls getting along you have to keep an eye on them, because this girl don't like this girl because she likes her boyfriend, or this type of thing. Guys are pretty laid back, girls are more, you know, "she's talking about me" or "I heard she said," you know, more he say–she say stuff for girls than boys.

Darnell clearly is not alone in believing that men must orient themselves a bit differently toward boys and girls if they want to relate effectively to them. Yet, some men working with kids in varied settings discern few, if any, significant differences in how they relate to boys and girls. Increasingly, though, men's perceptions about kids have evolved because of shifting social expectations of what girls can and should do with their lives.

DEMOGRAPHICS OF MEN'S INVOLVEMENT

One way to gauge the level of men's public involvement with youth today is to look at how many men we know are involved with kids as paid workers or volunteers. Estimating the total number accurately is impossible, because much of this activity is informal and not clearly documented. There is "formal" volunteer work and then there is casual time men spend with kids. For instance, like many other men, I have taken friends' or neighbors' kids from time to time on outings to movies, arcades, dinners, or simply played sports or other games with them. Though clearly incomplete, available data and anecdotal observations provide a rough portrait of some general patterns.

School settings are the most obvious employment site providing men opportunities to interact with children. Unfortunately, relatively few men pursue careers in elementary school teaching, so young children's degree of exposure to men in schools is rather limited. This pattern has prompted various news commentators[59] and the National Education Association (NEA)[60] to label the shortage of male teachers a serious problem. According to the NEA's 2000–2001 survey, only 21 percent of public school teachers are male, a 40-year low. The picture is bleakest in elementary schools, where males represent only 9 percent of teachers; 35 percent of secondary school teachers are male. Men are particularly scarce in kindergarten and the lowest primary grades.[61] In comparison, the proportion of male elementary school teachers in 1981 was at an all-time high of 18 percent; about 50 percent of secondary teachers were male in 1986. Minority male teachers are the least represented, a pattern some commentators see as uniquely problematic because of the high percentage of single-female-headed African American families.[62]

Males' relative absence in the expanding childcare industry is even more striking. Childcare workers fulfill a wide range of basic care and instructional duties for children. This involvement can influence children's early development and reinforce childcare workers' sensitivity to children's needs more generally. In 2004, according to government statistics, childcare workers occupied about 1.3 million jobs, with about 33 percent being self-employed and 21 percent working for private households.[63] When paid home-based providers (including paid relatives) are included, there are roughly 2.3 million childcare workers serving children ages 0–5 at a single point in time and nearly 2.5 million over the course of a year, which reflects high job turnover.[64] Based on reports from the mid-1990s, males represent only 3 percent of those working in childcare centers (including prekindergarten and Head Start programs) and 1 percent of nonrelative family childcare providers offering care in their own home.[65]

Men represent a large proportion of youth workers in the juvenile justice system. The magnitude of men's exposure to these youth is underscored by the fact that courts with juvenile jurisdiction handled over 1.63 million delinquency cases in 2000.[66] In 2004 there were an estimated 93,000 probation officers and correctional treatment specialists in the United States, with a significant majority of those being male.[67]

Men's involvement in youth ministry is another area that has grown over the years. Since the first recorded youth minister was hired by a local congregation in 1937, thousands of men (and some women) have worked with kids in this role. Unfortunately, there are no sound national estimates of the number of men who serve as Christian youth ministers or youth leaders in other religions, but we do know that 7,500 youth ministers representing various denominations attended a conference in Atlanta's Georgia Dome in 1996.[68]

Although teaching, the juvenile corrections system, and youth ministry are three of the more obvious employment sites that provide willing men the chance to interact with children, much of men's involvement with kids occurs through their volunteering. National data indicate that roughly 23 percent of men and 30 percent of women age 16 or older reported volunteering during the one-year period ending in September 2006.[69] Among volunteers, 5.4 percent of men and 5.5 percent of women indicated that their main organizational involvement included mentoring youth. Men were more than three times as likely as women (10.2 versus 2.7) to be involved in coaching, refereeing, or supervising team sports. Among parents with children under 18 years of age, roughly 36.5 and 45.1 percent of fathers and mothers, respectively, volunteered primarily for an "education/youth-service" related organization, for example, a school or sports team. These rates were more than twice as high as the 17 percent volunteer rate among persons without children under age 18.

Among men, whites are more likely to report volunteering than African Americans or Hispanics: 24.5, 16.0, and 10.9 percent, respectively. This pattern is significant because it suggests that only a relatively small percentage of African American and Hispanic males are spending time with kids through institutional forms of volunteering. These figures may be most alarming to those who emphasize the value of male role models and are concerned with the roughly 51 percent of African American children living in mother-only households.[70] Some men in lower socioeconomic groups may be interested in volunteering with kids but may have limited spare time because they are juggling multiple jobs. Reliable estimates are not available to document how many men from various racial backgrounds and community settings spend time informally hanging out with kids in the neighborhood or with young kin other than their own children.

A more focused report, by the Corporation for National and Community Service, documents volunteering from 2002 to 2005 by college students ages 16 to 24 and indicates roughly a 20 percent rise in volunteers during those three years.[71] Much of this increase is attributed to the compassionate response of students who were attending high school or were first-year college students at the time of the terrorist attacks of September 11, 2001. Overall, college students volunteer at twice the rate as age peers not enrolled in college (30.2% vs. 15.1%). As is true of volunteer rates for the general population, college males volunteer at lower rates than their female counterparts (26.8% vs. 33%). Male college students are most likely to volunteer for an educational or youth services organization (33.6%), compared to serving at a religious (22%), social or community service (14.8%), or some other site. Among male volunteers, 21 percent tutor or teach youth and 20.5 percent mentor youth.

In 2005, over 1.7 million youth were members of 4-H Clubs and 440,000 adults volunteered.[72] Other organizations, like Little League Baseball with its 2.5 million kids playing in fifty states,[73] Pop Warner Football with over 130 leagues and 380,000 participants,[74] and numerous other sporting leagues and camps, provide men many opportunities to instruct, mentor, and supervise youth. The Boy Scouts of America is one of the largest youth programs in the country. In 2005, almost 3 million youth were involved in some level of scouting (Tiger Cubs, Cub Scouts, Webelos Scouts, Boy Scouts, Varsity Scouts, and Ventures) and 1.1 million adults served as scout leaders.[75] The Boys & Girls Clubs of America, with 4,000 club locations and 49,000 trained staff, serve roughly 4.8 million boys and girls.[76] Among the adult leaders of these groups, roughly 70 percent are male.[77]

CHAPTER 3

SOCIAL PLACES

Camping excursions are perhaps the signature activity of scouting for men and boys. Countless other kids, including girls, not participating in the Boy Scouts of America also enjoy organized camping trips or visits to one of the diverse wilderness youth camps. Being involved with kids in a camping environment offers men unique opportunities to observe and interact with them. Ben, a youth pastor and director of a family-run summer camp for boys in the Midwest, describes with considerable excitement how the natural elements of a camp setting help define the context for working with boys.

> The nice thing about camp is the context is so pure. There is no television, there's no electricity, there's no running water in the cabins. We literally live in four wooden walls underneath mosquito nets. They're not walking around with their iPods on all day. . . . When you literally live in the elements of nature—like when it's cold out, when it's forty-five degrees out and you have to wear a hat, when you're literally at . . . the ebb and flow of the natural cycle of the outside world, it allows you to look at life in a different way.

Seeing life differently enables the men and kids to relate to one another in unique ways, and, in the process, to experience personal growth not easily replicated in other settings. The wilderness, of course, is but one of many settings in which men as paid workers or volunteers interact with youth. That physical and social settings often set the tone for how men and kids relate to one another should come as no surprise, but the effects of place are too often ignored by researchers and those who work with kids.

Adults encounter kids in diverse physical and social places.[1] The places include athletics venues, schools and classrooms, indoor and outdoor camps, the wilderness itself, churches, playgrounds, buildings and fields used by youth clubs, daycare centers, juvenile detention facilities, the neighborhood street, and others. It is in these settings that men must manage their identities as youth workers of one sort or another. Sometimes, they need to navigate across the borders between these public places and their home and family domains or similar private settings where they might interact with a young person—a topic I explore more fully in Chapter 9. In short, aspects of social places influence how men and kids perceive one another and interact.

What takes place in these various settings is also affected by the public discourse about kids and adults in public places. The "terror talk" noted earlier sets for parents and public officials a framework for thinking about adults, kids, and places.[2] Whether discouraging men from closing doors to classrooms and offices when only one or a few children are present, or dissuading men from spending time with kids out of sight of others when camping, the current ideology promoting greater scrutiny of adult male behavior takes into account features of physical and social settings.

Varied in form, the settings that bring men and kids together have distinct and often interrelated physical, social, and symbolic attributes. Although the attributes of individual spatial and social contexts can overlap, making it difficult to view them independently, discussing the attributes separately brings them into sharper focus. Insights can emerge by dissecting the practical realities, social aspects, and symbolic meanings of the diverse physical sites where men and youth spend time together. For instance, how do particular settings influence the way men and kids perceive each other and behave? To what extent do settings provide men and kids distinct opportunities to shape their environments and interact? Although some men are aware of the subtle ways spatial properties of settings affect social life, many are largely oblivious to them. Being ignorant of the conditions defining social places does not, of course, mean that the conditions do not matter.

At times, men act deliberately to orchestrate their identities and the interaction while accounting for aspects of social places. They may escort, invite, or force youth into specific places. They may take kids on camping and hiking trips in the wilderness, on mission trips to poor areas in or outside the country, or into restricted rooms in a detention center in order to create and share certain types of social experiences, and to teach specific life lessons. Changing the look and feel of a physical site, perhaps by integrating certain objects into it, can alter individuals' emotions and behavior. For example, one Big Brother took his 6-year-old Little Brother shopping for toys so that the boy could keep them at the Big Brother's house to play with when he was there. Another Big Brother bought an aquarium and fish for his Little Brother and allowed the boy to keep them at his Big Brother's house. In each instance, the men were searching for ways to help their brothers feel more at home by letting them claim some space and possessions in their houses.

Brandon, a 41-year-old American Indian who is a seventh grade science teacher, presents a more elaborate example of space management. He is keenly aware of how physical aspects of place affect students' energy, curiosity, and behavior. Entering Brandon's uniquely decorated classroom, where I interviewed him, both of us sitting at student desks at the end of a school day, I quickly realized I was in a natural wonderland. His room was littered with artifacts which I imagined embodied personal stories of intriguing places and adventures. Later, Brandon confirmed my suspicion about the objects while describing how and why he organizes his classroom as he does:

> My classroom is a lot different than a "teacher's" classroom. . . . I have bones and skeletons and furs and rocks from every place I have been around the Earth. And kids, when they come in, they're like, "Wow," and I'm like, "Touch it," and they're like, "We can touch things?" And they can take things home, if they want to . . . like that chunk of rock or something; all they have to do is sign it out. . . . I can look around and I can put a name and a face to just about everything that's in here. Where it came from, when I collected it, why I picked it up, why it's significant to me. . . . Why do I keep doing and decorating the room the way I do? Because I think that it makes a difference. When I look at kids, I want them to feel, you know, kids are gonna spend a major portion of their life, this year, in this classroom. . . . I want them to look around and be curious and learn about things. If the kid wants to go around this room and go, "What's this? What's this? What's this?" I try to make the time to say to that kid what each one of those are.

A number of the objects Brandon displays symbolize his Native American heritage. School policy prevents Brandon from speaking openly about some of the spiritual meanings and rituals associated with the items, but he conveys in broad terms to students how the physical artifacts symbolize the longstanding ties between his cultural heritage and nature. By letting students take objects home on loan, he offers students a tangible means to merge their school and home learning environments. Thus, Brandon accentuates the significance of physical and cultural artifacts while extending his learning message beyond school property.

My own curiosity about how the physical and social aspects of places make a difference in people's lives stems from an earlier book in which my colleagues and I explored how spatial aspects affect fathers' involvement with their children and how men express their identities as fathers in diverse settings.[3] To name but several, we explored sites related to dwellings and adjacent yards, vehicles and highways, family farms, prisons, inner-city streets and neighborhoods, military venues, and community buildings used for public gatherings. We identified a set of interrelated properties that define sites where fathering tends to take place, several of which I modify and mention below to illustrate how physical and social spaces matter for men and youth.

Like fathering activities, nonrelated men's experiences with youth as paid workers and volunteers occur in social places packed with practical and symbolic attributes. Granted, fathers' involvement with their minor children can be influenced considerably by the circumstance of living together and their sense of being part of a family. Although these circumstances seldom matter for men's paid and volunteer involvement with unrelated kids because the men do not live with or have biological family ties with the kids, unique situations sometimes bring family-type sentiments and rituals to the fore. That said, the spatial issues shaping fathers' experiences with their own children parallel how male youth workers interact with kids in various ways.

Two basic considerations capture how physical and social aspects of places matter to men's involvement with youth. The first, *interaction form,* focuses on how men in broad terms behave in their youth-oriented positions. In their interactions with youth, men instruct, give advice, provide comfort and care, monitor, discipline, play, act as a spiritual guide, build social capital, and more. Much of what men do as youth workers involves talking to and interacting with kids directly—behaviors I explore at greater length in subsequent chapters. In addition, meaningful indirect interaction can take place even when youth are absent from the setting. Men sometimes talk about kids to parents, teachers, coaches, neighbors, ministers, counselors, and others involved in the child's life. Though technically not a form of interaction with that young person, the purely mental labor the youth worker undertakes on behalf of the kid is relevant. While grocery shopping, eating a meal at home, shopping, exercising, or whatever, a man can ponder how he might address kids' needs and make a difference. Thinking time away from youth may be invaluable if it helps the adult to respond effectively to kids' needs. At the same time, these thoughts can be stressful, as 22-year-old Ray expresses, reflecting on the consequences of listening to at-risk kids throughout a long day. "You take it in and you live it; you take it home with you sometimes. In your car it will be on your mind; you won't get sleep [because of] some stuff that you hear."

The interaction form between men and youth can incorporate a wide range of youth-related activities either directly or indirectly involving kids. In this chapter, I focus on direct forms of contact.

A second consideration, *identity work*, refers to how men manage their identities as people relating to kids in particular ways and settings. This activity is a mixture of both meanings tied to why the men are involved with youth and the cultural materials and personal narratives out of which the men construct their personal identity. Identity work includes men's conscious and unconscious efforts to create, present, and sustain their personal identities as certain types of youth-oriented workers or mentors—the fun-loving Big Brother, the disciplined but fair coach, the morally consistent religious teacher, or the fatherlike Boys & Girls Club director. Men may feel compelled to convince the youths, themselves, and others that they are a particular type of youth worker or mentor.

Sometimes the men are fully conscious of how they perceive themselves and want to be perceived; other times they may have only a vague conception. Generally speaking, men express their desire to have kids trust them. They want children to see that they have the kids' best interests in mind and that the kids can feel safe around them. Individual men may accentuate different aspects of who they are in different settings. Brandon, for instance, is aware that he wants to present himself to his seventh grade students as the cool science teacher with a rich American Indian heritage and an affinity for nature. On the other hand, when Brandon works nights in a residential facility for emotionally troubled youth, he stresses his image as the fair and calm arbitrator of disputes and the informal leisure director, nicknamed "Coach," who monitors groups of kids on public outings, including regular trips to the gym where he is a member.

PHYSICAL CONDITIONS

Interactions between men and kids are influenced by the physical conditions of the places where they meet. Conditions matter when they affect individuals' moods, posturing, and willingness to participate in certain types of activities.

The quality and neatness of structures and the material objects in them are obvious aspects that help define physical sites. Are men relating to youth in a dilapidated, messy, excessively hot or cold youth center or one reasonably well furnished, tidy, and equipped with an adequate heating and cooling system? If they look on the bright side, youth workers may sometimes focus on their rundown surroundings or the threat that their facility might deteriorate and use that as a way to generate a valuable learning experience for youth. Frank, a 36-year-old unit director for a modest Boys & Girls Club, continually encourages the kids at his center to respect their physical surroundings. He describes how he helps youth orient themselves to their physical surroundings:

> [The kids] take pride in what they do because they see me taking pride in what I do. And, and if I ask someone to do something, I get right beside them and do it too. . . . I don't believe in, "make sure you get that spot, make sure you get that spot." . . . When you working beside young kids they work all day, and they don't ask for anything. I don't have to bribe 'em with pizza and all that kinda stuff, they just do it. . . . I think that they have a sense of knowing that, yeah this is our club, and I tell them it's their club, but also you have to maintain the place. I say because you never know when visitors are gonna come by . . . if you keep nasty bathrooms and windows all smeared, "what kinda place y'all runnin'?" . . . They can be eatin' some chips and drop something on the ground or whatever, they'll just, automatically, they'll just pick it up and put it in the trash. Other places, they'll probably just leave it down there. But it just something that I constantly tell them. Now, when I first started it was hard, and they thought I was crazy, but over a period of time, they bought into it. And it works. And the other kids, new kids'll come in and they'll drop something on the ground, and "hey, you droppin' that on the ground now we got to clean this up now."

By encouraging the kids to claim the center as *their* club, Frank inspires them to assume responsibility for their physical environment. Now, seeing the place as theirs, they are more apt to keep it clean. Frank offers a valuable lesson in managing kids when describing the partnership he forges with them through shared manual work. He teaches kids the value of being neat, working hard, and taking pride in personal or shared property by focusing attention on the center's physical conditions. The kids' eagerness to stake a claim in the center shapes how they relate to Frank and to each other. Men working with kids in other recreational facilities describe similar scenarios; kids are encouraged to take ownership of their facility and behave accordingly.

Settings can be thought of as being closed, like the sheltered domain of a detention center or classroom, or open and spacious, such as a neighborhood park or forest. Sites like some recreation centers and many schools may include a combination of places—buildings and adjacent fields. Brandon's seventh grade classroom represents a physically closed environment. Though Brandon prompts his students to think creatively about places beyond the classroom through his collection of artifacts, seeing and touching objects in the closed room differs from exploring in person the places where the objects were found. The physical conditions associated with the wilderness, the advantages of which Ben praises in describing the summer camp experience, can provide men and kids unique challenges and learning opportunities.

Joseph, a 34-year-old man with vast experience working with at-risk and troubled youth in diverse settings, expands on this point by sharing an impressive story about his early youth work managing delinquent kids assigned to an outdoor residential camp. He describes the camp as "there's no bars, there's no fences. They're just deep in the woods." Joseph was in his element at the camp, because his Native American great-grandfather, who lived off the land, had taught him much about the ways of the woods during Jospeh's visits to his rustic cabin. One lesson Joseph learned from his great-grandfather was the value of being prepared for a task, especially those involved with wilderness adventures. His boyhood training came in handy when Joseph simulated the youth campers' experience during a three-week training program to prepare him to work on site with the kids. He paints a vivid picture of the labor-intensive rituals at the isolated, alternative juvenile detention camp.

> They've got a very primitive camp site where they have to cut down pine trees, take a big blade, skin the bark off, bleach them out, sink them in holes. They don't get to use any real tools. The only saws they get to use are the two-person shove back and forth saws. They use the bit and brace, the big drill that you go like this [motioning]. . . . And, they would have to design and build their own shelters for their sleeping tents . . . these wooden structures. The only thing the camp provided was a wooden platform as a floor on blocks and a piece of the big tarp that went on as the roof. But, they put on the rafters and all the side poles and the tent poles, uprights. They had to do that all together and they had to figure out what design, how many poles they'd have to cut, what

*size. . . . That's where a lot of their math came in and a lot of their schoolwork
came from actually having to do things.*

In the primitive wilderness setting, Joseph got his first taste of managing
kids using the camp philosophy grounded in "group consequences." The philosophy encouraged kids to think about the consequences of their decisions and
behaviors while learning to work more cooperatively with others. However, in
practical terms, applying the philosophy often produced unpleasant consequences for the youth workers. Joseph explains that if a kid caused any sort of
trouble,

> *then, no matter where we're at, what we're doing, the whole group stops,
> moves away from where the problem started, a hundred yards away or more,
> sits in a circle on the ground and discusses it. . . . the person that's having the
> actual problem is the last one that really has any input. He's sitting there lis-
> tening to everyone else go around talking about how it's affecting them, how
> it's affecting the group, what they have done in these situations before. Every-
> body puts their two cents in. The counselor, really puts in very little. And, then
> it comes to the person that's having the problem or the people that are having
> the problem. And nobody moves until the entire group's satisfied that this per-
> son has recognized what they're doing wrong, set a good plan to avoid this
> problem again, and gave some type of commitment to the group. And if
> everybody's satisfied, we move. And if one person is not satisfied, then we stay
> there and the process starts over. I have sat sometimes in freezing cold, in rain
> at three o'clock in the morning and mosquitoes that were unbelievable for
> some six and seven hours. And, during that time each group was scheduled to
> the one shower house we had on property to take showers. They're only sched-
> uled once a day and if that's the time you're sitting having a problem, then
> you go to bed as dirty and smelly as you are until that time comes up the next
> day. If you're having a problem through a meal, you'll catch the next when it
> comes.*

Although Joseph admits to being frustrated at times when he had to endure
unpleasant circumstances due to kids' inconsiderate behavior, he recognized
that it was useful for the youth to see him suffering alongside them. Just as
Frank's kids learn by working next to him, the kids at the juvenile camp could
learn a lesson by seeing Joseph and other counselors suffering with them.
They recognized that the counselors must be committed to helping youth succeed. From Joseph's description, it's clear that the hardships associated with

the physical conditions of this site accentuated how the kids were likely to interpret the consequences. It would have been difficult to achieve the same effect if the program were run in a protected, air-conditioned building. The take-home message Joseph and the other counselors wanted the kids to embrace was that they have responsibilities in real life, and that their actions—whether in the camp or in their roles at home, school, and work—affect other people.

The openness and tranquility of the outdoors, and perhaps the reality of being away from familiar surroundings, can offer kids, especially boys, a unique opportunity to reveal their vulnerable, feminine side. Carlos, a 33-year-old pastor, captures this image when he describes his experience with taking boys on camping excursions:

> There's something about just being out in the outdoors around an open fire
> that gets people talking. It's really weird, it . . . I still don't understand it to this
> day. You get [a] bunch of guys sitting around a fire, just staring at a fire . . . it's
> like everybody's an open book. Somebody mentions something about their
> childhood or what they've been through, and this person over here will chime
> in and go, "yeah, I know what that's like" and blah blah blah. There really is a
> dynamic to that. That's the kind of stuff that goes on when they're just pulled
> out of their environment, I guess.

Perhaps the natural and pulling-together dimensions of living outdoors offer boys a safe place to set aside their emotional armor and open up in ways that they otherwise might not.

Carlos's comments remind me of an ABC television documentary shot in the mid-1990s and narrated by Hugh Downs that followed his involvement in a "Wildman" therapeutic weekend retreat set in a wooded area in a rural section of Texas. There, grown men shared intimate, emotional life stories either huddled next to a small campfire or around a fire in a darkened sweat lodge. The wilderness setting of such "talking rituals" can provide boys as well as men a meaningful place to reflect, share, and bond. The boys' response to the campfire ritual is consistent with Brandon's philosophy when working with kids in camp settings: "let's go out and be part of the environment instead of trying to be master and commander of it." So, whether it is intimate talk around a fire or a respectful and curious appreciation for nature's mysteries, the wilderness can foster openness in boys. The wilderness can also provide youth and their adult guides with natural challenges to conquer as they attempt to hike through it and live off it. In outdoor settings, campers have opportunities to demonstrate self-reliance and leadership skills. In these situations, nature provides boys the means to be tested and to express themselves in traditionally masculine ways.

Unfortunately, the divide between kids and the outdoors in the United States is growing wider by the day. Journalist and child advocate Richard Louv sounds the alarm in his provocative book, *Last Child in the Woods,* in which he reports that youth's disconnect from nature appears to be tied to troubling trends in declining youth mental and physical health.[4] Worried by the rising rates of depression and obesity among kids as well as our society's declining appreciation for nature, Louv waxes poetic about the transformative energy of the outdoors for youth.

> Nature—the sublime, the harsh, and the beautiful—offers something that the street or gated community or computer game cannot. Nature presents the young with something so much greater than they are; it offers an environment where they can easily contemplate infinity and eternity. . . . Immersion in the natural environment cuts to the chase, exposes the young directly and immediately to the very elements from which humans evolved: earth, water, air, and other living kin, large and small.[5]

I agree wholeheartedly with Louv that youth have much to gain by experiencing the outdoors on their own or with their peers, but I also believe that natural sites offer men and kids unique opportunities to relate to each other and to grow as they explore nature's wonders together.

Outdoor places need not be exceptional places for men and kids to enjoy themselves and bond. My afternoon on an expansive athletic field with Derek, the police youth worker introduced in Chapter 1, one of his male coworkers, and about twenty middle-school-age boys reaffirmed what is common knowledge to many: it's fun to throw, run after, and catch a football or a Frisbee. On a seemingly endless field and under warm and sunny skies, I saw wide-eyed boys test their athletic prowess as they sought the men's affirmation. Derek whipped a Frisbee for kids to chase, he taught throwing and catching tricks, and he orchestrated competitions for the kids. When he took charge of a football drill, he threw himself into the moment and demonstrated the specific plays he wanted the kids to execute. The size and openness of the space made it easier for the boys to revel in their energy, to let loose, to cooperate, and to compete. By constructing the boys' free time in this manner, Derek challenged them to step away from the sedentary lifestyle of high-tech electronic games. Because few of the boys live with their fathers and most do not have fathers who spend much time with them, their physical play with adult men like Derek appears to take on special meaning.

It may seem a bit odd to think that how men and kids react to each other is affected by weather (warm/cold, rain/sunshine, light/darkness), but these conditions sometimes do matter. Both the hardships of excessive weather that Joseph describes having to endure at the detention camp, and the pleasant weather conditions during my time with Derek and the boys can make a difference. Had Derek's kids been greeted by a cold, rainy afternoon, I suspect they would have been far less enthusiastic about spending the day outdoors running around.

With one exception, my participants were currently living and working in sunny Florida, and a number of the men capitalized on their freedom to engage in outside activities with kids year round. Those who spent time with kids in after-school programs typically spent a lot of that time supervising and playing with kids on the playground. The men had a chance to horse around with the kids on jungle gym equipment and play sports on the nearby fields and courts. Having a spacious field immediately outside a school or recreational building offers convenient options to organize games and play spontaneously with youth in specific ways, some of which are cooperative and instructional (e.g., kicking a soccer ball, playing catch).

However, having an appropriate physical place does not mean that people will know what to do with it. Brandon was once hired to reorganize a preschool facility. When he began this job, he discovered that the teachers were complacent about their work, in part because the nice weather fostered a laid-back attitude and an effortless passing of time. Brandon remembers with dismay what things were like when he arrived:

> The kids would be dropped off; there would be absolutely no interaction between the teacher and the kids all day long. Basically, what the teachers did was they would take the kids out on the playground and then the kids would run around, and the teachers would all sit together talking.

Even though good weather and accessible outdoor facilities provide wonderful opportunities for youth to develop physical and interpersonal skills through play, some initiative and organization are usually needed to take advantage of the opportunities. Staff should devise creative ways to balance kids' free play with instructional activities supervised by adults that encourage youth to think and acquire new insights.

Most people assume that more space is better, but sometimes smaller, more confined spaces, especially those offering a degree of privacy (e.g., car, bus, small room) can produce novel opportunities for men to relate to kids. In an earlier study, I found that stepfathers sometimes talked about how they had revealing conversations with their stepchildren when they were alone on a walk or riding in a car.[6] Compared to fathers and stepfathers, male youth workers have fewer opportunities to converse with kids in private settings such as cars, rooms, or in the wilderness. Big Brothers were the subset of unrelated men who spent the most one-on-one time with kids, and it was fairly common for Big Brothers to pick up their Little Brother in their car and take him to various places and activities. Unlike most organizations that offer men opportunities to interact with youth, the Big Brother Big Sister program encourages men and kids to have one-on-one time, to solidify their relationship. Twenty-two-year-old Gerald's most memorable experience with his Little Brother, 11 years old at the time, occurred on an enjoyable two-hour car ride returning from a weekend road trip they took to visit Gerald's family. Gerald was stunned by how talkative his Little Brother was on the return leg of the trip. He would like to go on a similar trip with his Little Brother, he says, because the boy truly carried on a sustained conversation. "So, it was definitely something that was rewarding, definitely memorable. . . . That was the first and the last time . . . he actually carried on a conversation, and actually held it and it was good." Although Gerald's Little Brother did not talk about anything exceptionally revealing on the ride, his willingness to talk about a variety of topics—football, a science project, and other casual topics—was remarkable. The few private hours spent in a confined car, without the usual distractions, channeled the Little Brother's energy into a meaningful conversation.

If we push the envelope a bit, we see how space can be used creatively in unusual ways and how a large site can be a safe and intimate place. Jeff, a scout master, says, "When a young man needs a Scout Masters conference or something, they come to my place. I got ten acres and we walk around, but mom is there or dad is parked." Scout masters are not supposed to be alone with members of their troop, but Jeff's extensive acreage enables him to have a semiprivate one-on-one conference with a scout. He and the boy are in sight of a parent but out of hearing range. A scout master who lives in a small apartment or even a house with little land would have more difficulty creating a spatial arrangement that would be equally successful in balancing the need for supervision with the desire for privacy.

TIME, PLACE, AND COMMUNICATION

Because time always unfolds in a setting or context, time and setting are closely related. How men construct their identities, as teachers, coaches, camp counselors, probation officers, and the like depends not just on where they act in these roles but when men get "into character." Elements of time shape people's orientation to a particular situation by defining the "pace, duration, value, and cadence" of an event.[7] Thus, temporal issues affect men's involvements with youth. Focusing on how time is experienced in relation to settings highlights how men's relationships with youth are affected by perceptions and limitations of both time and place (and space).

When men go about their daily routines, their movements and activities are bound or defined by time. For instance, a married Big Brother living in the suburbs may invite his inner-city Little Brother to join him at a Saturday afternoon Major League baseball game. To make good on the invitation, the Big Brother chooses to leave his home and wife to escort the child to and from the stadium. If the man lives relatively far away, he will incur high costs in time as he treks into, across, and then out of the city. Or, imagine the male teacher who may not be too alarmed by spending a few seconds alone with a child in a classroom as students arrive in the morning but may grow increasingly anxious of sharing this private space with a student as the minutes pass before other students arrive or if classes have ended for the day. Hence, spatial concerns defining men's efforts to be involved with kids are also temporal concerns.

Men and kids often define time and place in terms of their preferred level of accessibility. Modern communication technologies add a unique twist to understanding how individuals perceive, manage, and negotiate time and place/space. Technology can alter social institutions, and in the process change social expectations about how men should and can be involved with youth. Cell phones and e-mail displace face-to-face talks, but they provide men and youth more opportunities to touch base and access one another's lives. They make available times outside the typical one when two people would come into contact, such as, the Wednesday evening Boy Scout meeting or the after school basketball practice. Armed with this new technology, youngsters may be more willing to seek advice and open up to teachers, coaches, ministers, Boy Scout leaders, and mentors. Several men I interviewed believe that the kids are likely to say things in e-mails that they would not otherwise share.

Monitoring how men and youth manage their time and physical access to one another reveals the shifting relations between generations of men interacting with youth. Technology allows today's male youth worker to be more accessible than his counterpart who worked with kids prior to the cell phone and e-mail. Older men tend to see a clear increase in how often youth contact them in the e-mail and cell phone era, and even many of the younger youth workers have noticed an increase in recent years.

The men differ in their preferred level of accessibility to youth. Some freely provide contact information and welcome contact from kids outside of the immediate context in which they typically meet. Others guard their privacy by monitoring the real and symbolic borders separating their youth work activities from their personal life. Some manage the borders by not revealing cell phone and e-mail information or by selectively answering the phone. Even men highly devoted to their work with kids admit to sometimes being reluctant to give kids unfettered access to them. For example, Michael, the enthusiastic school teacher with eleven years of highly active Big Brother experience, sheepishly admits to not answering his Little Brother's phone calls occasionally when he is at home relaxing on a weekend.

Communication is two-way. The men can also initiate contact with youths, either informally or formally. Doing so in some ways involves making the decision to "enter" the places where kids reside, work, or play. In Joseph's case, this means that he can keep track of kids who are either under court order or have volunteered to attend his diversion program for at-risk youth. Joseph is authorized to unexpectedly visit a kid at home to make sure that he or she is following the curfew rules, or he may make telephone curfew checks. Mark, a white 58-year-old educator, mentored several African American young men as part of a high school program and is still closely involved in their lives, even though they have graduated. Cell phones provide Mark a convenient tool for fielding and initiating regular "check-in" and information calls with the kids. Some of the calls may even lead to getting together at the young men's favorite local restaurant, a site that has afforded Mark and the guys a comfortable place to hang out.

PERCEPTIONS AND SYMBOLS

Both men and youth often come to a place with ready-made definitions to the setting; they also form new perceptions once there. Perceptions of a setting have various dimensions: being safe/dangerous, work/leisure oriented, child-centered/adult-centered, poor/affluent, informal/formal, emotionally warm/-cold, own space/others' space, and so on. Obviously, how people perceive places and situations can influence how they view and treat each other. For example, when men are with youths in neighborhoods they perceive as unsafe, they may assert their protective role more forcefully and intensify their supervision of the youngsters. For their part, young people in a similar setting may scrutinize adults warily, hoping to avoid dangerous men while finding trustworthy older allies who can protect them from rampant street violence. Thus, the perception of danger has the potential to both bond and separate people. Consider Frank, at the Boys & Girls Club, where he encourages youth to claim the physical site as their center—their home away from home. He expects youth to respect the property in a special way, investing time and energy into shaping its appearance. Frank is also trying to build a collective spirit, sense of community and club identity, in which the youth monitor each other when they use "their" place and their equipment.

Certainly, segregation of the occupants of a place, whether by age, race, or gender, is likely to be consequential to the interactions that happen there. A Boys & Girls Club unit director, eager to build a sense of community, may challenge a tendency to age segregate by creating play activities in which the older youth are given responsibility for helping the younger kids.

People's perceptions of a setting are based in part on their first-hand experience and in part on reports from others, like coworkers, family, friends, and the media. A man who has lived his entire life outside an urban center comes to an urban youth program with different experience than one raised in an inner city. Although a suburban man volunteering to help kids with their reading at an inner-city school will develop first-hand experience of what the physical and social space is like once he's in the school, his initial perspective will be shaped by other sources. Familiarity with a setting can influence how men treat youth while in it. For example, a man who regularly takes care of kids in an outdoor adventure setting is likely to feel more comfortable than someone who enters this place for the first time to assume the responsibilities associated with being a supervisor there.

Some projects engaged in by men and youth profoundly affect the kids' perceptions of their relationship to others and to their community. Sometimes this takes place when kids contribute their labor to a neighborhood project, such as painting an elderly person's porch, or building benches for a residential transitional facility for women who have recently been released from prison. It may involve traveling on a mission trip to another state or country to help disadvantaged families refurbish their homes or community buildings. A number of the men spoke enthusiastically about taking groups of kids away from their homes and neighborhoods to see and help poor families in far away places.

Here again, when men create opportunities for kids to live and work side by side with them on volunteer projects, for a weekend, a week, or longer, kids get to see the male youth workers devoting themselves to helping others. Not only do the kids get to work with the men and other adults; they also work with each other in unfamiliar physical and cultural surroundings. For many kids who are relatively well off financially, spending time in an impoverished area can inspire personal growth and lead them to appreciate their own life and home more fully. For anyone, providing such volunteer assistance gives them a chance to feel a sense of pride that they are helping others in concrete ways and in specific locations. Ministers spoke highly of their excursions with youth to other areas, stressing the profound changes in how kids thought about their own experiences and themselves.

But, getting kids to join what essentially is a traveling work team sometimes requires youth workers to frame the venture as involving more than work, to manipulate the young people's perceptions of an activity with which they do not yet have experience. The men leading these trips face the challenge of helping kids see the activity as a form of leisure or civic volunteerism, rather than hard, boring, manual work. If the leaders are successful, the beneficiary houses and community are symbolically transformed into special spaces and places, to the youth and men alike. Ben, the camp owner and minister, speaks fondly of one church-sponsored mission trip he led to a community in the southern United States. The kids who went on the trip had been "asked" by their parents to devote their spring vacation to helping others a long way from home. Most of the kids, as Ben recalls, were quite reluctant and apathetic about the venture when it began, but all quickly grew to enjoy their time together helping poor families. The following year, a hurricane hit the southern community they had worked in, and it became clear that the homes and their occupants still held considerable meaning for those young people. The kids expressed genuine concern for the people they had helped and the houses they had restored. Fortunately, they learned that the specific structures they had worked on were spared significant damage.

Men's concerns about their own physical safety and health affect and reveal their perceptions about working with kids in different settings. Most men's contact with kids is in places where they do not have to worry about their personal safety, but in some cases there is risk. A few of the men vividly recall what it is like to work in unsafe places dealing with unruly and unpredictable kids who can—and sometimes do—physically harm the adults working with them. Joseph explains his feelings about his previous job as a behavioral technician at a school for emotionally handicapped and severely emotionally disabled kids from area schools. "I was putting in all this time and going home bloodied and bruised and bitten and everything and spit on each day and coming back early the next morning to do it all over again." Joseph eventually decided to pursue a different job. In a similar tone, Thomas, a thirty-year-old

African American first grade teacher, describes his earlier experience as a direct care professional at a children's psychiatric facility where he had to use the full range of crisis prevention intervention techniques, including forced takedowns:

> It was a pretty extreme environment. . . . every day was like starting from square one, every day was a clean slate. . . . You never know what factors will cause them to behave the way they do, whether it's positive or negative, so, that was a difficult job, working with kids. . . . I can remember plenty days coming home frustrated. . . . I never knew what my day was going to be like. . . . I can remember being sent to the hospital on two occasions [from attacks].

Like Joseph, Thomas's experiences led him to find a different, less stressful job. Work-related stress also eventually forced Frank to quit his job after nearly seven years as a corrections officer in a juvenile detention center. As he explains,

> It really took a toll on me because when you go into work you locked up too. . . . Can't leave, you're dealing with these young kids who have a lotta attitude, liftin' all these weights, and you got to kinda stay fit because you might have to lock one down or whatever. So, it's almost like a police officer, and I got to the point where I got very aggressive, you know, because that was the nature of my job, and you know, when I get home I'm still wired up or whatever, and it wasn't healthy. And my doctor told me that I probably need to find another profession, because high blood pressure runs in my family.

Frank's comments are telling because he alludes to his negative feeling of being out of control. In his work experience, he was literally "locked up." Even in less confining circumstances, the physical space parameters associated with some kinds of youth work can lead some men to feel confined in particular physical settings, especially those populated by certain types of kids. Together, the three men's stories about being bitten, kicked, punched, cursed, spit on, and attacked with weapons, in schools for at-risk kids, adolescent psychiatric wards, and juvenile detention centers, illustrate that not all men are comfortable with their youth work and that even some who may accept the circumstances initially can be worn down over time. But, despite their frustrations, Joseph, Thomas, and Frank have all taken a series of new jobs that keep them working with kids. The good news for each is that they now spend time with kids in more appealing and less dangerous places.

Finally, some men try to turn settings that some kids view as threatening into safer environments by informing the kids' perceptions and teaching them new ways to deal with unsafe situations. Phillip, the school counselor doing his graduate training, recently worked with another counselor to develop a group counseling program targeting victims and bystanders of bullying. The school-based, three-month program is in a middle school in a small city. Phillip talks to the kids about preventative strategies while drawing attention to the "triangle" of victim, bully, and bystanders who come together in various school-related settings. Helping kids feel safer in the places they encounter is an important contribution men can make to youth.

Although concerns about helping kids feel safer typically involve helping them feel less physically or verbally threatened by others, men can also foster feelings of safety by altering the kids' approach to emotional vulnerability. This is what Derek, the youth intervention specialist, does in the informal social support group he runs for at-risk teenage boys. He calls the group the "circle of trust," and it is held at a daytime resource facility monitoring at-risk boys. It includes a group of roughly fifteen young men who sit in a circle in a specific room sharing personal stories about their life struggles and dreams. Derek initiated this part of the program to encourage the young men he interacts with to become more introspective, reduce their posturing, and seek emotional support from friends. One broad goal is to provide them an opportunity to learn about and experience the process of trusting others in a safe environment.

Trust issues are visible in another story shared by Nick, about how he once creatively and effectively managed his workspace in a residential facility for emotionally troubled youth to regain kids' trust when his role changed. Early in his career, Nick worked in maintenance at a facility populated with troubled kids, and he was encouraged to work with them on the premises, teaching them basic carpentry and maintenance skills. The kids liked and trusted Nick when he held this job, but he noticed that the kids "backed off" once he took a supervisory position in the facility. He reconstructs the events that took place when he asked the kids about their new demeanor toward him. They responded, "Well now, you've got that title and you have an office."

> I said, "Well, if that's a problem for you we can get rid of the office. I don't need the office. I'll sit right out here and do my paperwork." . . . They looked at me as an authority figure. Now, I had the ability to help 'em or hurt 'em. I could write the letters to the Department of Juvenile Justice. I could call their probation officers. I could do things that as a maintenance person I wouldn't

do. So, there again, with the name came power, with the title now I receive power. Now I became a threat. I wasn't a threat then, but what I did was I took the office that I was given and I shut the door and I never worked at that office, never went in there to make a phone call, never went in there to do anything in that office. I moved all my books that was in that office out to the outside of the wall. And, the building that we was in, it was open. . . . We had benches for the kids to sit on. I would sit out there on a daily basis and do my paperwork, right there with them. When they were sitting there, I was sitting there. So, all of a sudden, I became again one of the group . . . non-threatening.

Although Nick's clever strategy for managing space and his presence around the kids earned him the trust he sought, his tactic did cause other problems. The kids started to ask other staff members why they weren't working out in the open area like Mr. Nick. By changing his own orientation to space, Nick made the kids aware that alternative definitions of space/place and staff-youth relations were possible.

INSTITUTIONS, NORMS, AND POLICY CONSTRAINTS

Each institutionalized setting in which men interact with kids has its own set of formal and informal norms and rules clarifying how participants are expected to act and treat each other. Many such norms touch on basic etiquette, like showing respect for others and for property. Some institutional administrators also must monitor child protection policies with specific written conduct guidelines designed to protect kids and adults alike from inappropriate behavior and false accusations. These policies may stipulate that adults not be alone with a child, interact with a child behind closed doors, or interact with a child in particular ways. In addition, each setting includes individuals with differing levels of power, privilege, knowledge, and access to valued resources. Status in a formal setting is often defined by the rights and responsibilities associated with the person's standing in the organization.

In a school classroom, for instance, a teacher has considerable say in how he or she interacts with students, although administrators intent on following formal or informal organizational policies are likely to set boundaries for what is permissible. Program directors can stipulate that male childcare workers not change children's diapers. This happened to Eric, a 22-year-old, with three years experience providing childcare at a formal center as well as a year and a half of paid experience taking care of his brother's infant. He describes how the director explicitly told him that he was not allowed to change children's diapers, whereas she said nothing to the four women who worked at the site. Supposedly there were concerns about the threat of child abuse. One explanation he received was that this was the way things had always been done and so the organization was just going to continue the practice. Because the director has since left, Eric admits to changing infants' diapers occasionally because he wants children to be presentable when their parents arrive to take them home. Eric stresses that "it was my duty, because I'm not gonna, send a child with a soiled diaper to their parents . . . because that was one of the specific rules of being a childcare worker at this location" (to change diapers 10–15 minutes prior to parents' picking up their child).

Administrators might also enforce rules about the topics adults can lecture on or chat about with kids. In Nick's work with emotionally troubled kids, the administration forbids him and his colleagues from divulging anything about their own troubled past. Consequently, Nick has never told the kids he has worked with over the years anything about his dysfunctional family and the incredible personal struggles he has overcome. Apparently, administrators are fearful that such stories might trigger anxiety and negative reactions among some of the kids who have been abused and neglected.

Institutional norms and administrative rules controlling the flow of information may reflect community sentiments about the use of physical and social settings in which adults and children interact. According to one pervasive norm in the United States, parents should have control of the types of religious and sexual messages their kids receive in places like schools, childcare facilities, and recreational organizations. This norm has been translated into policy in various organizations, including the Boys & Girls Club and schools. Staff members at Boys & Girls Clubs are not permitted to offer religious-based guidance to youth under their supervision, unless parents have signed an approval form for each specific event. Of course, religious organizations are free to use their own buildings to provide Sunday school classes and other faith-based recreational and instructional programs to youth. Youth ministers and adult volunteers are permitted to offer religious instruction and spiritual guidance when the program is operated and paid for by the church.

In addition to formal policies, public stereotypes that many people assign to types of individuals (e.g., gay, unmarried, feminine) may be of consequence to men who wish to stay on good terms with administrators and kids. Alan, a 43-year-old volunteer with a church youth group, describes himself as being mindful of how he presents himself around youth. But Alan has the additional burden of managing society's concerns about gay men. Consequently, he is self-conscious about how other boys might perceive him and respond to his innocent gestures when he's interacting with them in youth group meetings or on mission trips. He tries to avoid any action that might make the boys in the group feel he is making advances toward them. Over time he has become more comfortable with how he manages his identity, and he feels more accepted now—in part because some younger boys who joined the program seem okay with gays. Alan meticulously details how he tries to be attentive to boys' feelings and monitor his actions when he's around them, whether on or away from church property, including on church mission trips.

I tend not to do solo flights with guys, whether it's luncheons or things like that . . . unless I know they're real comfortable with me, and I know that it won't be a problem with them. . . . When we do the overnights and stuff . . . it's just Kristin [female adult] and me, so you know, I have to be roomed off separate with the guys. . . . When you're getting close to [a] sleeping situation or showering, worrying about that kind of thing, . . . scared that someone, if I walked in the shower, someone was gonna say I was trying to peek at 'em or something like that. That was a hard thing for me . . . and still is, 'cause you still have to worry about it. But I just try to make sure that I'm the last one in bed. I wait until everybody's gotten in bed, everybody's had their showers, . . . then I'll go in and shower . . . especially if you're in a rustic situation. . . . You have to worry more about it as a gay man, about being around a guy, 'cause the guys are a little more funny about that than girls are. . . . [When sleeping] I make sure that I'm fully dressed in either pajama or jogging pants or something. . . . At home I just might wear a T-shirt and underwear, that's it. I won't do that when I'm out with them, 'cause I got to consciously think about it. You know, just every little thing . . . anything I can think of . . . I don't want them to . . . give them the wrong idea. . . . I still constantly try to keep myself aware of . . . not being around when they're undressing or whatever. If we're in a, a dorm area and I see some of the kids are startin' to undress, I just find myself a reason to get out for a while and let 'em change. And it's really more me than them, because obviously if they're gonna just start yanking their clothes off they don't care, but I just . . . don't wanna be in there when they do that, just to keep problems from happening.

Clearly, Alan is alert to how his gay identity may disrupt his attempts to develop productive relations with the kids in this church youth group. Compared to heterosexual men, Alan is probably more sensitive about infringing on the boys' comfort zone, especially when he is sleeping and showering in the same place. Alan's self-conscious orientation towards boys in certain places is not surprising in a homophobic society, where genuine acceptance of gays is still withheld in many settings, further compounded by his working with kids.

Although the awkwardness Alan describes is shaped in part by his being gay, straight men can also feel awkward about the intimacy borders of particular social places. Brandon, for example, once took exception to a summer camp practice of staff and campers sharing the same shower facilities. When Brandon approached the camp director about this policy, the director simply indicated that it had always been done that way and that it would remain the practice; so Brandon, who is extraordinarily sensitive to potential problems in such situations, quit.

The men interacting with kids in organizational settings express a range of perspectives on the policies and the more general philosophies of how adults should or can relate to youth. In general, they are fully aware of negative public sentiment and stereotypes regarding "bad men" who take advantage of children in various situations. Not surprisingly, then, most men typically monitor their conduct with kids so as not to jeopardize their own reputation and lose their opportunity to work with kids. A few men go to the extreme of not even shaking a kid's hand, when a boy or girl extends it. One of the ways Brandon deals with kids extending a hand is to joke, "I don't know where your hands have been." He explains his behavior by saying, "You never know what's going to be misconstrued nowadays, whereas in the past. . . . You know, I remember teachers and everybody putting their arm around me, hugging me, and things like that. But now, you just can't do [that] because everybody is litigious."

Others do whatever they can to avoid kids' innocent efforts to hug them or hold their hand. Sidney, 28 and new to being a second grade school teacher, says, "If I have kids that are coming up trying to grab my hand, or do different things, I'll be like, 'Hey you need to be in line, hands by your side, that's not the way we walk in line.'" He also mentions that he holds a notebook or places his hands in his pockets when walking through the halls and playground, to avoid children's hand-holding requests. These gestures were initially done intentionally to avoid contact; now they are second nature.

Some men speak passionately about how they sometimes struggle to respect organizational policies while trying to honor how they feel they should interact with the kids in their care. And others, like Mariano, who is so enthusiastic about the importance of teaching in middle school, acknowledge that bad things do happen to children but express a more nonchalant attitude about their personal circumstances, because they are convinced of their own good intentions and feel that most kids need and want genuine, uncomplicated emotional support.

On a practical level, men discuss how policies discouraging adults from being alone with kids sometimes inconvenience them and require creative remedies. One 34-year-old man, Donny, participated as a youngster in a religious youth group, then returned in his early twenties to be the youth minister for the same group. He has witnessed first-hand the evolution of child protection policy in his church from nothing to a formal, written document. Other men have seen similar transitions in camps, schools, and other facilities where they were present as the cultural climate shifted and a child protection policy emerged; some even were the ones who drafted the document for their organization. Speaking about the effects of his church's current policy, Donny says:

> It's a part of our everyday life here. Liability is something that we have to think about all the time. We can't drive a kid home by ourselves. We can't be put in a situation where it's one adult and one youth, unless we're in the plain view of other people. . . . At the end of any of our program time, we always have to be aware of never being caught in a situation where everyone's been picked up and you're waiting for that last kid to be picked up and you're the only adult with the one kid.

In addition to the practical inconvenience, Donny describes how the policy sometimes makes it more awkward to practice his youth ministry because he is apprehensive about physical contact with kids.

> Our group tends to be kind of a huggy group at times when we go away on trips or whatever. [The counselors and] the kids get really close. And I for one don't actively go out hugging kids. I let them hug me. I mean if a young lady approaches me to hug me I let her hug me but I don't actively go out hugging kids. And I think that's mainly because of some of this stuff. I don't ever want someone to take something the wrong way. But I think that the flipside of that is maybe they think that I'm not as approachable. . . . Maybe they think I am standoffish. But again it's 'cause this is at the forefront of my thinking, unfortunately. So yeah, I would say that has affected me. . . . I put the arm around them kind of deal. I feel like that's different than a full high embrace.

Donny is one man among many who pointedly distinguish between side and full hugs. A number of men suggest that they intentionally position their body when around kids so that only side hugs are possible. Donny also struggles when he is in settings in which a youngster is emotionally distraught, perhaps crying. Reflecting on these "crisis" situations, Donny offers,

> That's actually tough for me 'cause again its like, unfortunately, my thought process is, "Okay, how should I react to this?" So generally I put an arm around them and try to talk to them rather than a full body embrace, hug kind of thing. "It's going to be okay." It's more of a pat on the back, it's more of an arm around the shoulder kind of deal. Doing it in public or at least in clear [view], not taking 'em off and "Oh, let's go talk about this over here," or whatever. Maybe I'm erring on the side of, I don't know, of this whole liability stuff. I don't know. So, yeah, it's not good.

Although Donny recognizes his struggles, he takes some solace in knowing he has a team of younger male and female youth leaders who are able to connect through touch with the boys and girls in his church. So, even though he feels *he* is unable to connect with the kids as well as he would like, others can pick up the slack.

Fifty-two-year-old Paul has several decades of experience working with kids in religious settings and is currently the director of religious education for a Catholic church. Compared to Donny, Paul appears much more frustrated with how the cultural climate and related child protection policies impinge upon his ability to work with kids. Paul acknowledges that the safe-environment movement targeting kids has made his "life miserably difficult from a bureaucratic point of view" because of his new responsibilities, which include doing extensive background checks and maintaining databases on volunteers and employees. But he believes that the recent scandal in the Catholic Church probably has not affected him, as a lay professional, as much as it has the priests, whom he describes as "burdened in a way that's unique, because of that status." Paul shares his mixed sentiments:

> I feel a considerable burden in the rules of touch and, not touch, and the door being closed and not being closed. I know the rules, and sometimes [it] feels to me like it prohibits some of those basics that I was saying I went into church work for. There are certain times when—how to put it—people need a hug, or people need a, at least a handshake, and I feel like I'm in a position now where

I cannot do that, because of the politics. . . . I don't want to say it's all bad; it's very good. So I feel some of that burden [when working with] . . . my Sunday school class, and I [teach] kindergarten through sixth grade. . . . Little kids have their natural tendency to run up to me and hug me. . . . When I first started teaching I hugged all my kids, that was what you did; now I feel my head going, "Should I do this? Can I do this? Is this improper? Am I doing something wrong or am I doing something right? How will that parent perceive this if I do it?"

Paul's reflections reveal that as his career has evolved he has become much more mindful of the public's scrutiny of male youth workers. The need for heightened self-consciousness appears to have taken some of the spontaneity, affection, and joy out of his youth work. Responding to my request that he clarify how this "burden" has affected him on an everyday level in terms of his willingness to hug kids and to be friendly with them, Paul again asserts his frustration:

I think it's directly affected the way I act, especially [with] high school kids of the opposite sex. . . . How would you say it? I feel incapacitated sometimes, that when I'm with . . . my high school confirmation class, tenth, eleventh, and twelfth graders, one of the tasks of that class is to foster in them a sense of connectedness to the church, you know, community. It's hard to build community among teenagers without gathering together and putting your arms around one another and feeling some sense of looseness and camaraderie . . . and, with the guys as well as the girls. But I feel like I can't do that. I don't know whether I'm interpreting rules or if I'm off the mark from other teachers who are in similar situations, but I feel incapacitated.

Although Paul continues to wrestle with making sense of what the rules mean and how to apply them, he has witnessed significant changes in how adults and kids interact in those religious settings with which he's most familiar. Paul asserts, too, that he is not alone in his frustration. His colleagues around the country have shared similar sentiments with him.

Trying to confront the issue head-on, Paul discusses these matters with his students. From these conversations Paul extracts a deeper appreciation for how youth interpret and react to the heightened public scrutiny of adults. Taking a cue from his confirmation class, he senses that a "group consciousness" exists among youth who feel entitled to admire religious figures and hold them in awe; unfortunately, many kids seem "lost" because they do not know whom to trust. They may also feel cheated out of feeling safe. According to Paul, the kids' distrust extends well beyond the walls and rituals of the Catholic Church. The sentiment is captured by the question Paul feels underlies his students' perspective: "How the hell do I navigate the world? It seems like a tough place." Unfortunately, Paul's struggles to reach out to kids in productive, compassionate ways are exacerbated by developments inside and outside the Catholic Church.

Kevin, a 37-year-old minister, offers a slightly different view, appearing thankful that his church has policies in place that predate his arrival. With time, he has grown more at ease with them.

> I see their significance. Whether you're a high school teacher, male or
> female, . . . unless you're just ugly as I don't know what, somebody's gonna
> have a crush on you, or somebody's gonna have feelings towards you that
> might be inappropriate. And I think these guidelines keep those things from
> turning into anything beyond just a crush. They don't ever give them the op-
> portunity to turn into anything greater.

Concerns about how the recent public discourse and child protection policies affect male youth workers' effectiveness are not, of course, restricted to religious organizations. Similar worries surface in all youth organizations, including schools, camps, 4-H Clubs, and residential facilities for troubled youth. Like religious settings, these physical sites are marked by their own rules of conduct for adults and youth. Generally speaking, the men who spend time with kids in these settings are either very reserved in how they treat kids or they provide what they believe to be safe physical contact in the form of high-fives, handshakes, or an occasional pat on the back.

A long-time 4-H leader, Sandy, comments on men's limitations in offering kids emotional support.

> It is tough to take a child one on one and counsel them through a situation.
> Most of the time you have to have some other kids with you or a teen with you
> or an adult. There are certain things that you cannot go into, can't talk about,
> when you have another adult present. The kids are going to relate to you differ-
> ently. It makes the job a lot harder.

Sandy acknowledges the reality that an adult having a private conservation with a kid is likely to cast a distinct meaning on the site they occupy. Ironically, kids facing personal difficulty may perceive a place occupied by multiple adults and kids as safer in a physical sense but less inviting and safe emotionally.

Tony, a director of an alterative school for at-risk kids who have been dismissed from their regular schools, is "extremely" conscious of the "the stigma of being an adult working with kids, because these days, it's—this is a bad pun—but it's a touchy-feely situation." Tony is particularly aware of the politics of touch in his office because several years ago in a previous job a disgruntled girl and her boyfriend submitted a false report claiming that Tony had behaved inappropriately toward the girl. Although he was quickly cleared of the charges, the incident has made him more sensitive to avoiding the perception of wrongdoing. Now, when counseling a student about a private matter, if he feels inclined to close the door to his interior office, even though it has windows between it and adjacent offices, he gets another staff member to sit in the room. Asked about this monitoring policy, Tony candidly replies, "Oh, I hate it. I hate it. I understand it, and I don't argue with it, and I've come to understand the need for it, . . . you would be a fool to not acknowledge it." But while Tony understands the need for these measures on a practical level, he struggles to make sense of how gender stereotypes have distorted perceptions about his or other men's well-intentioned, supportive gestures involving physical touch:

> The thing I have always had trouble with is, what's the difference if after a soccer game, you know, a huge game, a guy's coming over, one of my players is coming over to give me a hug for the victory, but this girl's bawling her eyes out because her dad—whatever—and she needs a hug. So, is it the stigma because I am a male and it's a female student? Not that it can't happen the other way. It's just so delicate.

Listening to the men who work in institutional settings talk about the limitations they face and their efforts to connect with kids, I was struck by the contrast between the standard organizational policies governing adult-child contact and the Big Brother Big Sister organization, whose entire focus is one-on-one relationships. Youth workers in most other organizations are discouraged from orchestrating private one-on-one encounters with kids, either on site or away from the organization's property. This is unfortunate, because many youth in need of emotional support and guidance can sometimes benefit from spontaneous and private exchanges with caring adults in varied settings.

Of course, some youth workers and kids may have only a vague understanding of the regulations, and some will modify or loosely interpret whatever rules they do know. Thus, some settings are relatively rigid while others are much more flexible in how men and youth are expected to manage their conduct. Mariano, the energetic middle school teacher, provides a glimpse of how a man can sidestep policies to relate to students at school. A key principle underlying Mariano's approach is that he wants to avoid treating students like many of their parents do, so he emphasizes emotional support and hugs. He clearly sees kids as the products of their parents and environments but also notes that kids are free to make life-altering choices. Mariano describes his approach while referring to some kids who display their anger and hostility.

> I try to react with open arms. It's like, "Did you get a hug this morning? It doesn't seem to me like you got a hug this morning. Come here let me give you a hug. You'll feel better; you're not going to be angry anymore. And please, tomorrow morning before you leave your house, get a hug from your mom that way you can be a better kid tomorrow." And they respond to that, ya know.

Mariano feels that his approach works because he knows his kids and is aware of who is open to hugging and who is not. As he explains:

> I've never had a kid fight me off or tell his mom or tell the principal or be angry at me and shove me off. Because they know that I'm treating them with respect. In no way, shape, or form have I ever put my hands on a kid where the kid is offended by it. And the whole hugging thing, well I'm Hispanic, ya know. I'm very . . . , I'm a touchy guy. But I know my boundaries. . . . And I've never crossed 'em. I've taught seniors and I'm teaching seventh graders and I know exactly what is appropriate and what's inappropriate.

In addition, Mariano believes he has a firm grasp of the psychological reasons underlying kids' needs for attention and affection as well as the school policies that discourage certain types of interactions. "I've understood where my kids are coming from and I understood where I'm coming from, what my role is in their lives." For example, he asserts that if a teenage girl were seeming to develop a crush on him, he believes it would most likely be because she was looking for a strong male figure to substitute for her uninvolved father. Understanding her needs enables him to help her in appropriate ways.

Child protection policies clearly inspired most of the men to be more careful about how they develop relationships with youth, a pattern most likely found throughout the United States. But some cultural developments promote men's greater involvement with kids. Male teachers' chances of relating to students have been enhanced in the current cultural climate regarding girls' and women's roles. Title IX of the Federal Educational Amendments in 1972 ushered in one notable set of changes in school policies by making it illegal for schools to deny educational benefits on the basis of gender. This law requires equal gender treatment in the distribution of equipment and supplies as well as in the scheduling of athletic games and practices. Viewed from a coach's perspective—whether he is in charge of a boys' or a girls' team—the negotiation of access to gym and field space for practices and games presents the coach and players a real-world situation for interpreting and discussing gender rights. If a coach of a boys' team tells his players and others that they are going to practice early in the morning, in part because he doesn't want girls traveling in the dark for morning or late night practices, he is sending a gendered message about violence and chivalry in American culture. Moreover, he is saying that girls have a legitimate and vested interest in playing sports. Alternatively, if a coach presses to secure the best practice time immediately after school, on the grounds that the boys' team is superior and draws more fans, he is sending a message about the privileging of male sports. Meanwhile, if the girls team coach is a man, he has an opportunity to demonstrate to his players that he values girls as athletes and that they deserve to have the same opportunities as boys. Prior to the 1970s, these types of interactions between male coaches and youth were unheard of or rare, but now they are relatively commonplace.

PRIVATE VERSUS PUBLIC PLACES

Institutional policies and cultural norms influence how men and youth differentiate and manage private and public places. Unlike fathers, who usually spend lots of time with their children in private, men's experiences with nonrelated youth usually occur in a public context in the presence of other adults, multiple kids, or a combination of the two. In fact, as described above, in many organizations men must maneuver themselves to avoid being alone with a child. Sometimes chaperones are explicitly incorporated into settings to avoid the appearance or actual violation of behavioral conduct rules regarding adults and children being alone. Common rules are that men (or women) cannot transport a solitary child in a car or bus, or be in a room with a child without another adult present. However, even in organizations in which individuals attempt to follow the rules, practical reality may take over, placing a man in an awkward situation. Andre, a 49-year-old administrator for a Boys & Girls Club and former police officer, provides an insider's view of the real-life difficulties youth workers face in managing public and private spaces by recounting a weird situation.

I had one little boy who came in [my office] one day [because] he was being a
real pain. I said, "just come back here and hang out for a while," because the
instructor didn't wanna deal with him. And I let him stay back here, and he
was sitting in that chair, and he was playing that triangle football game, and
he shot it off of here [the desk] and it landed right there [next to Andre behind
his desk], and he got up and bent down to pick it up so he was on his knees
right here picking it up, and his dad walked in. And from there, you know,
what did he see, and I [thought], "Oh God, no." So for the most part we have
a rule that you can't be alone with a kid, you have to have at least two staff
members present, especially if [the kid is] the opposite sex. But the reality is it's
just not possible all the time. I mean, the kids . . . when you're sitting there typ-
ing, they're gonna walk in. What are you gonna do? There's nobody around.
You gonna stop every time that happens and get up and run, find another staff
member, bring 'em in? So I always keep the windows open, I always keep the
doors open, and I pretty much don't allow [kids] back here, but it happens. And
I have to always be aware of it because we've had two or three situations
where kids who had crushes on counselors and have accused them of some-
thing that was in their, you know, a fantasy, or they got mad because the coun-
selor wouldn't do anything, wouldn't act on their crush. And then we had to go
through this big long investigation, and all it takes is if that gets out, it's on the
news, you're done. . . . . That's why I have video cameras all over the place. I
have fake ones, real ones. I'm getting ready to install a video surveillance sys-
tem at all the clubs—that I can monitor; it's web based so I can sit here and
watch it, and that will cut down on—just knowing it's there really cuts down
on stuff.

As Andre's story reveals, it is not always easy to keep private space private and
when the conventional rules are broken, men may worry that their innocent actions will be misconstrued. Moreover, not all men react to the contemporary
public scrutiny of men in a measured way, like Andre. Some withdraw, sup-
pressing their inclination to be a nurturing caregiver or attentive listener in certain situations.

For those unconstrained by organizational policies, private times are often
filled with seemingly mundane experiences that occur while riding in a car,
spending time in a business office, hanging out in a home, or engaged in a
leisure activity away from others. But some private experiences can create powerful moments of important sharing, relationship building, and self-discovery.
Kenny, a Big Brother to a 6-year-old, describes a sequence of spatially oriented re-

lationship milestones: he initially went to his Little Brother's home, then took his Little Brother to the high-profile business Kenny owns, then they went to a retail toy store, and finally visited Kenny's home. By taking his Little Brother to his work and home, Kenny provided the boy an opportunity to see him in the places where he constructs his key identities as a business man and husband. Such gestures offer kids a chance to feel closer to a man as they see him in the spaces and with the people who matter most to him. Similarly, a couple of Big Brothers in their early twenties had made a point of taking their Little Brothers to the Big Brothers' parents' home for overnight visits, to introduce them to their families.

A different type of private sphere is accessed through e-mail, text messages, and phone talks. Though individuals are physically not present, the private exchanges fostered by these communication technologies require men and youth to negotiate interpersonal channels often viewed as private. Finally, semi-private exchanges may occur between men and youth in public places populated with people. In stadiums, malls, public squares, and the like, men and youth can experience a bit of privacy and anonymity, for they are among strangers—the passive public eye.

The private-public distinction seems to be a tangible, physical one, but places can be defined by their social and symbolic dimensions as well. A coach and his team may view a locker room or dugout as private physical space—a kind of back stage; the "private" team secrets and camaraderie they share transcend the physical borders of the site. The coach and players may experience their private bond while on a bus, plane, or walking together on school property. Similarly, a private place may become a public one; the public face of a coach may appear in the locker room or dugout when parents, reporters, or fans breach the borders of the team's back stage haven. This intersection between the physical and social dimensions of privacy breeds unique "situated" contexts for men to coach, teach, counsel, and supervise. Those settings in which parents help coordinate youth activities being directed by a coach, teacher, or supervisor of some sort can introduce a novel set of circumstances, blurring the line between private and public places.

GENDERED PLACES

Physical, social, and symbolic attributes of specific sites can lead people to see places as gendered. Certain athletic venues, the natural outdoors, and inner-city areas are commonly assigned masculine attributes; whereas church, daycare centers, and school (especially elementary schools) tend to conjure up less masculine, perhaps even feminine imagery. The result is that attributes of different types of places influence the gender practices men and youth are likely to see as appropriate or possible in a given setting.

Depending on the physical and social particulars of a situation, gendered images may shift as men, youth, and others change the way they label a site. A specific school that was once viewed largely as a feminine domain by those who worked and studied there may be transformed gradually into a battleground for gang warfare where male youths assert their vision of masculinity through intimidation and violence. When influential youths practice gender in this way, their daily activities can transform the gender practices of the school setting. The attempt to turn the school grounds into gang turf may inspire forceful reactions from male (and female) administrators, teachers, and law enforcement. Responses such as metal detectors, more visible and plentiful security, a stricter code of conduct and dress, and a less forgiving school suspension policy may curtail the violence in the short run, but these measures may simply alter the ambiance of the school from "pervasively unsafe" to "potentially unsafe." In the eyes of students and adults who spend time on school property, a masculine, potentially dangerous aura may have seeped into the physical and social qualities of the building and surrounding grounds. To get by, some students may be compelled to don a more defensive, "bad ass" personal front. Moreover, the pervasive fear of violence may alter how teachers perceive and treat their classes and individual students. Their affection and social support may take a back seat as they consciously display a more protective posture toward their students and themselves. The idea of mentoring youth or of youth accepting mentoring from adults may fade because of the growing climate of distrust and fear.

Irrespective of the good or bad images defining an interaction site, images can affect how men and youth treat each other. Even though more masculine environments probably predispose men to accentuate a masculine style of interaction, some men may make a concerted effort to balance this site-based masculinity with a more expressive, nurturing style.[8] Looked at differently, the masculine climate of, say, the athletic field, may enable some men to express a nurturing style selectively because they sense that the masculine climate offers a secure buffer, allowing expression of feelings of vulnerability and caring. However, a man coaching a girls softball or soccer team may use the energy and perceptions of the outdoor athletic field as a signal to take a more rugged stance with the girls than he would in physical contexts depicted as less masculine—a band room or language arts center. In general, sites exuding a softer image may prompt men to see and treat youth in a gentler way, though some men may compensate for a feminine site by resorting to more masculine displays around boys.

In addition to the gendered attributes of particular interaction sites, men's involvement with youth is influenced by a mix of gender, adolescent, and sexuality discourses, which in turn may be affected by attributes of a situation, including the gender composition of participants. In practical terms, people use threads of gender discourse to make sense of and talk about individuals and social life. Certain phrases from a type of masculinity discourse are frequently used in people's assessment and treatment of boys in particular. The traditional "boy code" discussed in Chapter 4 guides not only how boys often relate to other youth; it also affects how adults treat kids. A biologically based discourse of gender is quick to point out boys' "innate" aggressive tendencies, that "boys will be boys." Statements like "We're going to make a man out of you," "We'll whip you into shape," "Big boys don't cry," and "Stop acting like a girl" capture the real and implied social influence adults can have on kids. Even though the traditional masculinity discourse focuses on males, it indirectly addresses girls and how femininity is portrayed because it is tied to a larger gender discourse related to men's patriarchal privileges.

Though often pervasive across settings, a masculinity discourse is sometimes closely tied to specific settings. Settings associated with all-male sports, juvenile corrections, schools, and summer camps may reinforce a masculinity discourse and shape how men and boys relate to one another in those places. A parallel discourse about adolescence and the transition from boyhood to manhood may come into play in these and other settings as well. When men teach boys lessons of toughness, responsibility, independence, aggression, teamwork, and fierce competition, they often rely on a discourse designed to move boys beyond the bounds of boyhood into the world of adult manliness. This is what takes place in the school-based, Afrocentric rites of passage described in Chapter 5, in which boys are trained to appreciate the significance of making the transition to adulthood. The meanings boys assign to this rite of passage are closely connected to their exposure to male mentors in an all-male, African American environment.

A masculinity discourse can also be intertwined with discourses about sexualities, particularly as they apply to youth. As we saw in Chapter 1, part of the public's characterization of men with stereotypes of good guy, dubious guy, and bad guy is connected to images of some men as sexual predators. How this discourse is applied in specific settings is often contingent on the physical and social circumstances. For example, few parents would be comfortable with an adult male taking a group of girls from a Boys & Girls Club on a hiking trip in a state forest without an adult female chaperon, but most are willing to accept a male coach running his girls' basketball team through drills on a Saturday morning in the school gym without a chaperon.

To understand the consequences of different contexts for men's relations with kids, we must look at each setting's physical conditions, how time and place are connected, how participants perceive situations and assign meaning, how institutional policies and norms shape adult-youth relations, and how men and youth may sometimes struggle to manage the borders of private and public places. We must also take into account the cultural norms, legal constraints, and general perceptions and discourses that affect these relationships. Part of the larger context also involves the real or imagined public scrutiny of men's activities with kids in the course of their work, play, and community service, especially in the more female-oriented professions.

But what motivates men initially to devote time, energy, and resources to be with kids? And what keeps them active in kids' lives year after year? In some areas, like coaching, men's entry into working with kids may seem like a natural choice, but in settings like elementary education and childcare, men are pursuing an unconventional path. The stories men share about why they work and volunteer with kids expands the study of the social places where men are involved with youth. Thus, exploring men's motivations for doing youth work reveals another layer of the larger story of male youth workers. Those motivations, and related competencies, are often nurtured over the years while men accumulate valuable lessons from interacting with kids in various types of youth work environments.

CHAPTER 4

MEN'S MOTIVES

Andrew, the eldest of five children, grew up in a suburb of New York City in a two-parent household with a loving father who was a basketball coach, teacher, and pastor at a private high school. Though Andrew felt his mother was more nurturing in a traditional sense, he is quick to assert that his father was a caring person in his own way. In addition to his biological siblings, between two and nine surrogate siblings—kids experiencing some type of difficulty whom Andrew's parents took into their home—were part of his family at any point throughout most of his childhood. Reflecting on how he reacted to seeing his father manage a house overflowing with kids, Andrew says,

It's funny, because you would think I would have been jealous at the time, and I suppose there's a part of me that probably would have, would have liked some more attention. Although my dad, because he included us along with everybody else in family events and group events, you never felt left out. I don't ever recall having feelings of being neglected at all. I thought it was actually pretty fun to have all this activity, hustle and bustle, around the house. . . . I think I learned a tremendous amount. A lot of the values; and the reasons I've worked and tried to give back, in my own way, to younger men that I've tried to mentor in some respect, is the direct result of my dad. So I saw the tremendous impact, positive impact, he had on people's lives. Again, I had the fortune of being in proximity to . . . guys [former players and current coaches] who would tell how your dad was pretty remarkable: "He made a big impact on my life." And you hear this over 10 or 15, 20 years, you say, "That's pretty cool";

you're proud. But you also saw, as my dad got older, [that] relationships he had
established 30 to 40 years ago were maintained and how much joy it brought
to his life. And I'd said that's definitely something, in terms of relationships,
that I was taught, that relationships were very important. And you got to work
at it, but it can add a richness to life, which I am fortunate to be able to partic-
ipate in.

By all accounts, Andrew had a wonderful childhood and an excellent relationship with his father, whom he greatly admired. The life lessons Andrew learned
from his father were ones repeatedly taught by example in the context of family,
faith, and sports. As Andrew notes, he is honored to carry his father's legacy forward by mentoring youth in the same fashion in which he and others were mentored. Coaching is the primary avenue through which Andrew works with youth,
trying to instill the values he inherited from his father.

Most people would agree that, compared to genetics, cultural and social
forces play a much larger role in shaping how men view and treat babies, children, and adolescents. Cross-cultural research indicates that men in some societies are quite capable of being loving, nurturing caregivers for children,
whereas in other societies men are largely emotionally distant, economic
providers.[1] Research and everyday observations clearly show that boys and girls
in the United States tend to be socialized and engage in play activities in gendered ways. Boys are much less likely than girls to engage in doll play, sibling
care, or babysitting.[2] These activities are common ones through which kids acquire and practice skills relevant to parenting while developing empathy toward
other children in general.

The contemporary and heated debate over the relative power of "nature versus nurture" in boys' disposition, interpersonal style, and play preferences rages
on, with much of the discussion mired in political dogma. Advances in cognitive
and neurological sciences will continue to sharpen the lens for interpreting why
boys and girls see the world and act the way they do. I do not discount the real
possibility that physiological differences may in some complex way contribute to
boys' and girls' different experiences and treatment of others at a young age, but
such potential differences are likely to be relatively small and either accentuated
or lessened by social forces.[3] In other words, given the right conditions, most
boys can be taught to care for, respect, and feel committed to children.

Compared to women, men during their youth tend to have fewer preparatory
experiences for being parents and spend less time thinking of themselves as
prospective parents. American boys, relative to girls, are less likely to develop the

motivation and aptitude to care for or to respond to children in a nurturing way—though many men eventually learn to do so in spite of their boyhood experiences. In short, although research has not clearly revealed a relationship between early socialization experiences and later fatherly involvement with children,[4] boys' experiences may influence the perspective they adopt as men toward caring for kids, in and outside a family context.

THEORIES OF BOYS' EARLY YEARS

Numerous theories try to explain how boys' childhood experiences help shape their adult orientation toward family, childcare, and work.[5] Some focus on the psychodynamics of boys' relationships with their mothers as they struggle to distance themselves from their mothers and things feminine in order to establish their male identities.[6] Others deal with social learning experiences in which boys identify with their fathers or other adult males and strive to model their attitudes and behavior.[7] Kathleen Gerson, a family sociologist, argues that while these theories "isolate different mechanisms of transmission, they predict a common result: men who share a package of psychological traits that leads them to prefer *and* to choose work accomplishment over family involvement and individual achievement over interpersonal attachment."[8] In general, it seems reasonable to extend the results predicted by these theories to settings beyond the family household. Having experiences as youngsters with non-nurturing models of masculinity would seem to minimize men's chances for developing a strong desire to volunteer or work with children, even though some men do strive for individual achievement in professions focusing on children (e.g., teaching, pediatrics, child/adolescent psychology/psychiatry). Although these theories about boys' socialization are appealing in some respects, Gerson challenges them because they do not address the contradictions existing in boys' socialization environments.

Unfortunately, the academic theories typically applied to men's childhood experiences often fail to distinguish adequately between the socialization contexts and boys' reactions to them. The evidence indicates that boys who must deal with a deceased, physically unavailable, emotionally distant, or abusive father during childhood may grow up to treat children poorly or fairly well or may go to great lengths to compensate for how their father treated them. In the case of men who lived through a father's death, they may simply want to "be there" for kids—their own or others—to reassure the kids that they matter and are not alone.

I sought to place the men's orientation toward youth in a life course and developmental context by asking them at the outset of their interviews to share their childhood stories about their family, extended kin, neighborhood, friends, and mentors. My invitations elicited diverse and detailed accounts of how the men were raised, who was important to them, what life lessons they felt they learned from key adults, and, to a lesser extent, how they spent their time. Not surprisingly, the men's stories reflected a wide range of experiences. Some of the men, like Andrew, were exposed to nurturing fathers (and mothers) who spent a lot of time with them, their siblings, and other neighborhood kids. However, even in families in which the father was viewed as caring, the mother and grandmother were generally viewed as more sensitive caretakers. At least four-fifths of the men describe having reasonably enjoyable childhoods in which one or more parental figure, and in many instances grandparents, provided them with love, attention, and steady support.

Thirty-five of the fifty-five men I interviewed had parents who were either currently married or had remained so throughout the men's boyhood years. Most of the men raised in two-parent households report that, as kids, they were at least reasonably happy with their relationship with their father, but some men had been disappointed. For example, Jackson, a 37-year-old man born into a military family that moved frequently, continues to lament the limited time his workaholic father spent with him. While describing his desire to reach out to kids and provide them with opportunities he missed, Jackson repeatedly calls to mind how he longed for such attention from his father while he was growing up.

> It has a lot to do with my father not spending time with me. Had he, maybe I wouldn't be as out there, looking to get that time that he didn't give me. I'm sure there's some psychological stuff going on in my head about, he didn't spend time with me.

Unlike Jackson, whose father, though not attentive, was around, seven of the men were 13 years old or younger when their father died. One learned around age 9 that when he was 3 months old his uncle had killed his father. Another man at age 2 lost his father to an illness.

Two of the men we met earlier, Derek, and especially Nick, overcame difficult family circumstances to pursue a path helping kids. Derek longed to have his father in his life after he walked out of Derek's day-to-day existence when he was 3 years old; Nick tried to avoid his abusive, alcoholic father, who remained firmly implanted in the household. Barry, a devoted 27-year-old youth worker with no memory of his father, provides yet another glimpse of how some men move be-yond their tragic childhoods. Responding to my initial question that he talk about his childhood and the family context in which he was raised, Barry hesi-tates momentarily, then shocks me with his family tale:

Okay. Um, my, my father was murdered, when [I was] 3 months old. My uncle shot him and killed him. I never got to see my dad. My mom couldn't take care of me so, my grandmother decided to step in and pretty much take care of me. There were, like, no real male role models in my life. I had an uncle. He had a drug problem so I never really got a chance to see him—on occasions I would.

Now adults, each of these three men expresses his passion for passing on in-sights to make young people's early years more peaceful and productive.

Finally, scholarly theories say little about boys' opportunities to change dur-ing adulthood, that the experiences during childhood and adolescence need not represent lifelong destiny. Boys once disinterested in caring for or being around younger kids may grow up and develop a strong desire to be involved with youth. For instance, when they were boys, Derek and Nick never showed an interest in helping younger kids, even though Nick did take his turns at protecting his sis-ters from the rats in their house. My interviews suggest that most men who eventually work with youth showed signs of wanting to help kids during their teens. Many got involved as teens or young adults in formal activities like day and summer camps, Boy Scout and 4-H leadership roles, or supervisory roles in church youth groups. Others, like Barry, a talented football player as a kid and still, as a young adult, took advantage of informal street opportunities to be with even younger kids. Barry notes:

When I first started playing . . . Pop Warner football, the smaller kids would always come up and say, "Oh, you know, I saw you running. You scored a touchdown tonight." And it was some type of—I don't know what to say—gratification. It felt good that they looked up to me. And they asked me, "Okay. How do you do this? And what do you do when you do this?" And, that was a good feeling because I never had anyone look up to me before. So from, being what . . . 10, 11, 12, that's when I was like, "Alright, you know, well, that's a good feeling." And the other kids around the neighborhood, I would try to help, show them how to catch, show them how to throw, show them how to run. So from, from like 10 to 12, that's when I first realized . . . there was a positive something I could do.

For more than ten years, since he was 17, Barry has held jobs enabling him to work with kids in several contexts, including most recently after-school childcare settings. Barry's self-described nurturing and attentive style with children was fostered by his interactions with the neighborhood kids and also by his caretaking responsibilities for his younger brother and sister and his ill grandmother. Although describing himself as initially an "angry child" who "didn't want to do anything for anyone," Barry eventually realized that, even as a youngster, he had been called upon to be a caregiver.

> This is my place in life I guess you could call it. They [his siblings and grandmother] have been placed here for a reason and this is something that I need to deal with, so I just have to accept it. I think it helped me become more of a patient person and not think of myself all the time—only myself.

Like Barry, some men, especially those raised in large families, are enlisted during their childhood and adolescent years by their parents or guardians to provide childcare for siblings and cousins; they exhibited varying levels of responsibility and attentiveness in fulfilling these roles. This type of experience was pivotal for Travis, a 24-year-old graduate student studying to be a school psychologist. When he was 9, his parents, divorced since he was 6 months old, each remarried, and within the year Travis had two more brothers. A sister came five years later. Travis feels as though in many ways he raised his new siblings. He changed diapers, helped with schoolwork, went to his sister's school to visit her for lunch, babysat, and taught them sports and karate. Learning that he could affect them left him with a lasting, favorable impression about childcare.

Though relatively rare, some teenage boys take on more formal babysitting responsibilities. When boys become active with kids in this way, they place themselves in the position of learning by doing. They experientially encounter the joys and struggles of playing with and caring for younger kids. These experiences can produce enduring images upon which men draw when they meet kids in the public realm through volunteer or paid work and when they become fathers.

GENDER AND THE BOY CODE

Boys' upbringings, of course, vary considerably, in family circumstances (e.g., parenting style and sibling structure), social class and racial or ethnic background, exposure to religious teachings, community norms, and much more. Thus, a search for the common threads that define boys' lives in the United

States is fraught with difficulty. Just as individual boys should not be viewed as passive creatures marching in step to prevailing cultural norms, culture is not a tidy collection of clearly articulated, uniform guidelines. So too, whatever circumstances and norms prevail, boys can successfully challenge them. Nonetheless, people construct their self-images by reacting to what they perceive to be the surrounding social expectations defining acceptable male and female behavior. The dominant ideology of masculinity impinges on all boys, even those who choose to navigate a course at odds with prevailing assumptions about masculine behavior and children's place in men's lives. For many men, investing time and energy into caring for children requires them to challenge or reinterpret this ideology. The power of this ideology over boys as well as men is apparent when we consider how many people would react to the following story illustrating men's capacity to develop strong and lasting bonds with youth.

Jackson established an unusual nineteen-year friendship with a woman he met when she was 7 years old and he was a 19-year-old in charge of an amusement ride. Feeling guilty because the girl fell and broke her arm while he was on duty, Jackson quit his job. He also sent the girl a teddy bear. They began to exchange letters and Christmas presents, and they met again when the girl was 9. A fan of rituals, Jackson took pictures of the girl and her mother every Halloween while she was growing up. He still calls her every Christmas and they exchange ornaments. Although Jackson notes that they are very different people, he values her friendship, says that he loves her, and is saddened that she doesn't occasionally initiate phone calls with him. He admits that in some ways the girl is like his substitute child because he has developed unconditional love for her.

Given the current public scrutiny of men, some people—perhaps many—will find Jackson's story a bit odd, partly because they are unaccustomed to thinking of men developing wholesome, close friendships with young girls. Related concerns were drilled into Jackson's head during his Boy Scout leader training—adults were not supposed to be alone with kids—so he was quite surprised when the girl's mother allowed her daughter at age 9 to get in a car alone with him. Clearly, without the mother's trust and support Jackson would have been unable to nurture this long-term friendship with her daughter. It is illustrative of how restrictive cultural elements come into play if we imagine how many fewer people would have found this story odd had Jackson been a woman.

Much has been written about how boyhood culture is inundated with images and messages of a brand of masculinity that restricts a boy's self-expression. Roughly thirty years ago, psychologists Deborah David and Robert Brannon labeled four main expectations for stereotypical male behavior: "sturdy oak," "give 'em hell," "big wheel," and "no sissy stuff."[9] More recently, clinical psychologist William Pollack (1998) discussed how these "injunctions" collectively shape the "boy code," constraining boys' ability to develop emotionally while restricting their chances to bond with adults.[10]

The rule of the "sturdy oak," encourages boys to be stoic, avoiding any sign of weakness. They are expected not to cry or complain when they are troubled or injured. Reacting to their environment, they learn to manage the impression they display to others, so that others will not see any self-doubt, fear, or grief. Boys influenced by this rule become adept at wearing a masculine mask when they interact with others, especially those they assume will criticize them for showing weakness. Though some commentators suggest that boys following this rule are placed in an emotional straightjacket, it is actually only the softer emotions, signaling vulnerability, which they must suppress. Emotions displaying anger or competitive fire are far less likely to be constrained by the dictates of the boy code. Indeed, boys are applauded in some circles for outbursts of aggressive energy. Moreover, greater latitude to display nurturing behaviors is given when they are revealed inside the sanctuary of an all-male enclave or in the course of the masculine ritual of an aggressive sport.

When guided by the "give 'em hell" norm, boys act with bravado, taking risks to showcase their sense of adventure and invincibility. Ignoring danger—in fact, inviting opportunities to explore it—is part of this aspect of the boy code. At times, boys will respond to this masculine ideal by embracing violence as a way of life and an acceptable means to resolve conflicts. The colloquial phrase "boys will be boys" aptly captures the essence of this injunction. Consequently, boys' penchant for risk-taking behavior often translates into increasingly self-destructive behavior as they transition from childhood into and throughout the teen years. For some boys, carrying weapons, driving recklessly, and abusing substances are simply a reflection of their desire to be "respected" as a masculine male.

In a related vein, the "big wheel" imperative offers boys a relational context for expressing their masculine self by emphasizing the importance of achieving status, dominance, and power. Boys are expected to compete and to win. They are taught to strive for a position of dominance over others, boys and girls alike, while dodging shame if they are tempted to feel it, and ignoring doubt if they privately question their own abilities. Though the forum for competing will vary, attempts to express power typically occur in settings involving physical prowess, sports, girls, and sometimes education. Emblems of financial status take on more importance among some teens as they age, especially those who have interpersonal ties to young adults.

Finally, and perhaps most important for how boys view childcare, boys are repeatedly reminded that they must avoid being seen as a sissy, or girl-like. Boys are taught to fear the feminine by having their identity as a male questioned if others see them acting in ways they characterize as feminine. This pattern of assessment of behavior is often linked to homophobic concerns, because being gay is associated with having feminine traits.[11] To be sure, the fads and fashions of popular culture in recent decades have obscured the edges of feminine boundaries, making it less likely that aspersions will be cast on boys because of their style of dress, self-adornment, or social behavior. Although the range of what is acceptable has broadened, most young boys are still prepared to deride a boy who drifts too far from one of the relatively standard badges of masculinity. And, for certain age groups and certain cultural subgroups, the expectations can be very narrow and rigid. Though many experts are trying to enlighten us about the harmful consequences of this process, it remains a powerful force embedded in our everyday culture.

Throughout childhood and adolescence, boys face versions of these four basic norms to varying degrees and in diverse contexts. Irrespective of how they feel about the norms, boys quickly learn that they will be rewarded or chastised in particular settings depending on whether they present themselves as independent, aggressive, competitive, emotionally cool, or anti-feminine. They are confronted with the boy code while playing at home, in school, on playgrounds, and in their neighborhoods. Other boys, and to a lesser extent girls, assert themselves as gender police, holding boys accountable for deviations from the code. Although individual boys actively construct their masculine identities, they do so in relation to gender definitions perpetuated and enforced by peer groups.[12] Parents, other relatives, and unrelated adults also reinforce gendered messages, out of habit, sometimes knowingly, other times unwittingly. Adults convey their message by treating boys in specific ways or treating others in ways that enable boys to observe how the gender game can or "should" be played. Boys are also exposed to similar cultural messages through the video games they play and the TV shows and movies they watch. Together, these messages reinforce the commonly recognized image of maleness. It implicitly tells boys that they should not adopt a nurturing, caregiving disposition. It may be okay for some to feign a nurturing disposition to impress a girl while she is babysitting, but fully embracing this role is a different matter altogether.

In recent decades, alternative messages for male behavior have crept into the cultural tool kit, offering boys (and others) images of ways to experience life and express personal meaning that are less restricted by the boy code. Perhaps the best known is the widely popular British fictional character Harry Potter, who offers boys and girls a clever image of what a powerful yet emotionally sensitive boy might look like. Harry expresses respect and compassion for others while using his wizardry and social intelligence to confront injustice.[13] Meanwhile, the recent Hollywood depiction of the American superhero Spiderman conveys traditional notions of masculine power and valor while also presenting softer personality qualities in a positive light. In the 1990s, Hollywood brought us *Kindergarten Cop*, with Arnold Schwartzenegger playing an undercover cop who exposes this softer side as he grows more familiar with his temporary classroom of energetic kids. The depiction of Schwartzenegger's ineptitude at working with young children is juxtaposed against his huge physical frame and law enforcement responsibilities.

Other comic films also cover stereotypical gender terrain related to men's involvement with children. Formulaic films such as *Three Men and a Baby, The Emperors Club,* and *Daddy Day Care,* depict men's stereotypical bumbling but heartfelt efforts to understand, care for, and bond with children. In the 2003 film *Daddy Day Care,* Eddie Murphy and co-star Jeff Garlin portray two men, Charlie and Phil, who lose their high-profile advertising jobs. As fathers of two preschool children, the unemployed men are forced to remove their kids from an expensive daycare program and care for them by themselves. In response, the business-minded Charlie launches an innovative daycare operation with Phil. Overwhelmed initially due to their ineptitude as caretakers, Charlie and Phil taste success once they learn to appreciate the childhood spirit and incorporate a third male caretaker, who has a unique ability to communicate with kids. Their program provides kids fun and creative ways to read, play games, and interact. The new business also enables Charlie and Phil the chance to develop stronger bonds with their own children. The film, along with others like it, shows men challenging the gender borders initially reinforced by the boy code.

Most of the time, when young males confront the boy code they are doing things that have little, if anything, to do with caring for children directly. They are hanging out with friends, playing sports, flirting with girls, and so forth. But the boy code's insidious power and long reach are apparent, for it encourages boys to develop attitudes and feelings that dissuade them from pursuing formal or informal childcare. The attitudes and feelings males develop can be affected in ways extending beyond the immediate issues targeted by the boy code. As boys learn to control their emotions, especially those that might signal a weakness to others, they may also be slow to develop a compassionate disposition that would enable them to empathize more easily with others, including children. The result is that boys too often are left with an underdeveloped form of "emotional literacy."[14] They may have to step beyond the path of least resistance to develop the nurturing qualities critical to effective childcare.

Boys do not perceive childcare as one of the domains in which they can achieve a sense of masculine dominance and respect. Thoughts about their ability to procreate may be the only child-oriented area in which boys ever think they can garner a degree of respect. Even so, the vast majority of adolescent boys do *not* report that having a child as an adolescent would make them feel more like a man.[15] Similarly, when boys recognize that people often equate caregiving, childcare in particular, with the feminine world, they will be less apt to express curiosity about child-oriented issues. They will tend to see it as irrelevant to the immediate or long-term set of life skills they are compelled or wish to develop.

Although most young males have grappled with the boy code, some encounter alternative images of masculinity that are more compatible with a nurturing approach to kids. To date, researchers have done little to map the terrain of alternative masculine images, but one can speculate about the types of experiences that might inspire boys to develop an interest in working with kids, either as volunteers or as a job, especially in female-oriented settings.

Travis's memorable experiences as an older brother looking after his siblings helped inspire him to pursue a career working with youth. His mother, an elementary school teacher, also affected Travis's comfort with kids. She took him to her class for the day at least once a semester as a helper. She also created intensive tutoring opportunities for him in summer school. Being exposed to the world of elementary education and receiving encouragement from his mother, Travis took a special liking to helping kids learn.

Imagine another boy, who grows up in a family in which his parents own and operate a large childcare facility. As a child, the boy spends countless hours at the center immersed in the day-to-day lifestyle of playing with kids and being supervised by various childcare workers. Later, as an adolescent, his parents incorporate him into the business by hiring him to organize activities for the children. Raised in this environment, it is reasonable to assume the boy may develop more attentive caregiving skills than many of his male peers. His first-hand experiences with younger children could enhance his appreciation for child development issues and the excitement of being around kids.

Unconventional experiences such as these may make it easier for boys to challenge the boy code during their youth. The experiences may also prime them, once they become men, to spend time with kids in settings traditionally thought of as more feminine. However, men who have traditional upbringings are still sometimes inspired to work with kids, especially in settings viewed as more competitive and rugged, like sports and camping.

GETTING AND STAYING INVOLVED

Stories of men like Derek, Michael, and Nick represent a first step for exploring in greater detail why men get involved with youth and what such men hope to accomplish. Derek works with at-risk kids to right a wrong in his own life—he was a delinquent "thug" as a kid. He became a police officer and more recently began devoting his time to kids as a way to better the local neighborhoods that were a part of his life growing up. He compares his current work as a youth intervention specialist to his earlier working life as a regular patrol officer.

> I feel like I'm serving more of a purpose now. . . . I'm trying to keep them . . . instead of arresting them after they've done something, I'm preventing them from even looking that way . . . going that route. So . . . it's more satisfying in that sense, thinking that, okay, this kid, instead of seeing him four or five years down the road and arresting him for something that he might do, just showing him, saying, there's a different route . . . let's not even look that way, let's go this way. Let's turn them into taxpayers instead of tax takers, basically.

Michael has been a Big Brother on two occasions, as a way to reduce his loneliness from a divorce, to do something productive with his life, and to address his unfulfilled desires to be a father. And Nick wants to protect at-risk youth from the ugliness of death, abuse, and neglect he survived as a kid. When he applied for his first job with his GED in hand, despite being a poorly qualified candidate, Nick prayed daily at a local church. "I said, 'Lord, I just want the opportunity to give something back.' You know, to give an opportunity for a child to have a better chance than I had." Nick believes his prayers were answered. He makes clear his enthusiasm for what he does for a living, noting that it is the only type of job he finds rewarding.

> The only thing I fear is a broken heart. Man, that broken heart will get ya; when your heart hurts everything hurts. And, if you look at these kids' faces, you can see broken hearts, I'm tellin' you. I have had opportunities to make a

lot of money doin' a lot of different things, but I don't make a lot of money here. But, this is where I'm happiest now. If I quit working with kids. . . . I tried it one time, and I was miserable. I was making over a hundred thousand dollars a year and I was miserable. I just had to come back. It just wasn't where my heart was. So, it's real if you're real.

Of course, because my study participants represent a wide range of experience working or volunteering with youth, not all of them share Nick's intensity and conviction. But, to varying degrees, his sentiments ring true for a considerable number of the men who are working with kids for a living, and all were motivated to continue their involvement in kids' lives.

The stories show that men emphasize different reasons for working with kids; some also have multiple reasons for staying involved. Men's reasons are sometimes rooted in their personal life histories and the specific settings in which they choose to spend time with youth. The activities in these settings involve monitoring and managing potentially disruptive behavior, play, skills and values training, education, religious instruction, friendship, and childcare. Men often work with disadvantaged youth, but sometimes only with advantaged youth, and sometimes with a mix. Some of their interactions with kids are tangential to whatever they are doing at the time. For example, thinking back to his teen years when he bagged groceries at a local store, Travis notes that his desire to be around kids began to crystallize at that time. "I would be having the worst day, and a little kid would come in and just come up and give me the biggest hug." It was often a highlight of Travis's day. "[I] started realizing that these kids have a direct effect on my mood." Meanwhile, 50-year-old Jacob's approach to being a Jewish Sunday school teacher for many years, and a rabbi for the past several years has been shaped by his camp counseling experiences as a young man. Jacob asserts that working with special needs children in a novel program at a Jewish summer camp for four consecutive years back in the early 1970s helped solidify in his mind that he wanted to "work with kids for the rest of my life." Now, compared to other rabbis, he sees himself as having a distinctively youth-oriented perspective and stronger commitment to spend time with youth.

Because a man over the course of his life typically relates to youth in a variety of settings, he may experience a mix of motives over time as he moves in and out of different situations. Michael, in addition to being a Big Brother, has been a high school science teacher for many years. He initially chose this profession in part because of his lifestyle preferences and the appeal of a flexible summer schedule. Helping kids was not the driving force that led Michael to become a teacher. Now that he has had the experience of being a teacher, he is committed to connecting with students and providing them a creative learning environment.

Many men are compelled to contribute to society, to kids in particular. Some feel a sense of obligation because others helped them when they were growing up. This perspective reflects a desire to pay back society for benefits received or to give to others in return for what someone gave to them. Many believe they can help fill a void in a youth's life while giving a youngster some healthy life opportunities. A subset of African American men are called to action because they perceive disadvantaged youth as having limited access to positive black male role models. Some of the men emphasize the prospect of nurturing younger people by teaching them life lessons and instilling key values. Finally, sometimes men are inspired to work with kids because they believe the experience will contribute to their own personal development and enable them to feel better about themselves.

GIVING BACK

When men get involved with kids, especially disadvantaged youth, as a way of giving back to their communities, the giving back sometimes occurs in the community where the men live and grew up themselves. But often they live somewhere other than where they were raised, so they perceive their contribution more generally. Charles, a gregarious 32-year-old unit director for a neighborhood Boys & Girls Club, captures this sentiment quite well. He identifies his experience as a freshman in a high school ROTC program as pivotal in shaping his commitment to helping kids.

> I had juniors and seniors starting to spend time with me. It was like a right of passage. Those older kids taught me and said, "Look, whatever you got to do, you got to learn to give back." And even on sporting teams, the leader of the team isn't always the star player, but it's the one who can talk to the kids that may be struggling, who's not picking up the offense or the defense. . . . Maybe there's a kid in your classroom who's just not comprehending that one math problem. Once I moved to Green Coast Springs, which was a smaller community, . . . the community expected you to do those sort of things. And, I started there. I started working for a lot of different youth groups and going to a lot of youth camps. . . . My great-grandmother told

me when I was growing up, she said that "a man's gifts will make a room for him [in heaven]." . . . A lot people talk about [that] they are for the kids, but it's about actions and deeds. You got to get out and do it. You got to be the one to role up your sleeves and get in the trenches. . . . It's not if my director thinks I care for kids, it's not if the staff care for the kids, but it's when the kids know that I care for them, because I'm not just Mr. Charles at the club, which they expect to see me here. But when I start showing up after school, showing up when they have a football game, when they have a play, after a graduation, showing up after church, that's when the kid really starts to say, "Wait a minute. He maybe really does care," because those are things that I don't get paid for.

Charles's commitment to the kids who frequent his club was palpable throughout our conversation. He thrives on being in the trenches, and Charles sees the frontline as extending beyond the club property. Not surprisingly, our morning interview was delayed twenty-five minutes because Charles unexpectedly needed to run an errand for one of the neighborhood boys. He went to purchase a white T-shirt, with his own money, and then swung by the boy's school to drop off the shirt so the boy could complete a school art project. This personalized gesture is consistent with his view of what giving back means. Charles clearly recognizes that his commitment to kids transcends the time he spends with them at the club. He sees the kids as being embedded in their families, schools, and the neighborhood. Consequently, giving back to the community— the kids in particular—means that Charles does a great deal of community outreach, all of which is above and beyond his specific job duties. It does not matter that he had nothing to do with this particular community during his youth. What matters is that his job situates him in a neighborhood club frequented by poor African American kids, and he is committed to doing all that he can to nurture them.

For Donny, his giving back as a minister is not directed at a geographical community but to a religious one, the youth group and church he participated in as a kid. Asked why he puts so much time and energy into youth ministry in particular, Donny says:

I think that inside I did feel a little bit of a calling to working with kids and, eventually I was able to get to the point in college where I said, "Well what I really want to do—I have no clue what occupation I want to do—but what I really feel called to do is to somehow make a difference in the life of kids." . . .

*whether it is because of what I received, I want to give that back, or whatever. I
just, . . . I recognize the importance of being involved with kids.*

As Charles does, Donny embraces the value of working with kids and is committed to staying involved in their lives.

FILLING GAPS, EXPANDING HORIZONS

Men committed to helping kids often see themselves as having insights and a
broad range of resources that particular youth lack. Ron, a 26-year-old white
graduate student, has had several types of mentoring relationships with kids in
South Carolina, and he currently is a Big Brother to an African American
teenager in Florida. Speaking of his mentoring relationships collectively, Ron
describes what motivates him.

*I had a stable home and I was given opportunities as a child and had nurturing
people in my life. . . . I know that there are a lot of kids out there that don't
have that . . . especially a lot of underprivileged boys don't have men, male role
models. A lot of times they live with their mom or grandmother, aunt, which
I've seen. And, they just need some, . . . they just need a guy there, even if it's
just hanging out.*

In Ron's eyes, being a man and having time to devote to developing mentoring relationships with boys are basic resources he can share. In addition, he
mentions wanting to provide kids the chance to experience new things. Prior to
his first solo meeting with his current Little Brother, Ron asked what the boy
liked to do and learned that he was thinking about being a veterinarian. So Ron
found a place where older horses were kept on a farm, then he and his Little
Brother bought carrots, went to the stable, and hung out feeding the horses. Ron
has also provided his Little Brother with a chance to experience what were for
him new activities: hitting golf balls, going to movies, going out to dinner, playing video games, attending athletic events, and playing the trumpet.

Others are also quick to point out how many kids do not have sufficient access to positive male role models, an observation teachers and Big Brothers often make. Asked what keeps him coming back to his second grade classroom,
Sidney, a 28-year-old, white teacher whose students are nineteen low-income
African Americans, offers this explanation:

*Just the chance to be a positive influence in these kids' lives, maybe, . . . be one
part of their life . . . that's safe, I guess, reassuring. I know the kids I have now,*

*a lot of them don't have much of a home life, so anything positive they can get
from me or from the school is definitely beneficial. And maybe down the road,
something I've done or something I've taught them this year will make them
make a good choice and keep them out of a bad situation.*

The home life of many kids like those in Sidney's class and Charles's club is disproportionately characterized by the correlates of poverty—poor nutrition, family violence, parental drug and alcohol use, limited parental involvement in monitoring school work, and a home environment not conducive to quiet study time.

Several African Americans among my participants are quick to point out that they feel compelled to get involved because African American children should receive the attention they deserve and witness positive men in their lives. Kenny, who is 58 years old, has contributed time and money to youth organizations throughout his adult life, but he got more directly involved several months ago as a Big Brother. He recounts how the director of the local Big Brothers Big Sisters organization moved him to act this year when she spoke at his company.

*She started tossing out some stats about Littles who were waiting, particularly
the shortage of African American males. My heart melted, I couldn't help but
say, "I'll do it." She didn't ask, she was just sharing how contributions and allo-
cations from United Way help in this effort. I was struck [by] the disproportion
and lack of African American males. I had no choice—"if it is to be, it is up to
me"—words that a lot of people use, but that is how I feel; I can't complain if
I don't do my part. My wife thought I was crazy. She says, "When do you have
time to do this?" I said, "I will make time."*

Kenny has made good on his commitment to take a more active mentoring role and speaks fondly of how his several-month-old relationship with his Little Brother has evolved.

Like Kenny, two African American elementary school teachers, Thomas and Reggie, profess that their rationale for becoming teachers was to make a valuable contribution to African American kids' lives. Thomas observes:

*from my experience I didn't see a black male in elementary ed. . . . With me
as a teacher . . . I don't want my students to lose hope at a young age. As
best as I can I'd like to provide a positive experience for them, and hopefully
they'll continue to stay motivated. I've noticed, again, just like in my own
experience, the further along I got in education, the more the crowd
thinned out.*

Thomas's comment on the crowd thinning is a reference to how relatively few African American males graduate from high school and continue their education. Reggie, a fourth grade teacher, is one man who challenged this trend by taking advantage of an unusual opportunity to earn his college degree. Several years ago, he received emotional and extensive financial support from several men who belonged to a country club where Reggie was working. The men, and others at the club, freely acknowledged Reggie's knack for interacting with kids at the club, so they offered to pay for his college education. Asked if it registered with him that he was a successful African American male teacher whose presence in the school the past six years might be noticed by the students, Reggie says:

> Oh yeah. I think about that a lot. I think that's why I wanted to be in a predominately African American school. To give them hope that they can be something other than what they experience on the streets. "You can't be successful; black man can't be a teacher." "Yes, you can." I'm a living example of that. Because they don't see it very often, you know, that you can be successful. . . . I purposely wear a shirt and tie, to tell the kids, "You can be a professional. You can do that. You don't always have to think that you are limited." . . . I'm involved in an African American group. . . . We're trying to evoke change in our community and let kids see lawyers and doctors and have them come out to the school to talk to the kids. I want kids to see that they can be whatever they want to be. Here are people, living, breathing, right here and now. I love the fact that I can come out here and they can see me. [Parents say] "Man, my daughter's so happy to be in your class. You're the first male teacher that she's had." Or "You're the first male teacher." . . . "They have a male teacher in fourth grade. He's a black man?" I'm like, "Yeah." . . . At the beginning of the year, the kid's [with his mother] and like, "What are you whispering about?" "Mommy, he's black. He's the first black teacher I've had . . . since I've been in school."

Although other African American men explicitly share the sentiments expressed by Thomas and Reggie, some do not. With all the men of color, I explored whether their racial identities affected how they related to kids. The men's responses vary widely. Some, like Reggie, say they are conscious of race and bring it to the fore intentionally to make a point, whereas others claim they never say anything about it, and some do not even think about it when working with kids. Reggie regularly has candid talks about race with his fourth grade students, particularly the boys, who are all African American. Being male, from his point of view, enables him to offer an informed perspective. He simulates his talks with the boys:

*"I see how people look at us [African American males]. . . . Look at the num-
bers. I guarantee somebody in here knows a boy or man that's in the jailhouse.
We don't need to be in the jailhouse. We need to be in the schoolhouse. That's
the house that I want my boys to be in." And I talk to them just like that. I say,
"Not all people are going to talk to you like I do, but that's because I think I
need to talk to you like that. And it's not to hurt anybody's feelings; I'm just
showing you the way we are, that people look at us." And I always put that
"us" there. The majority of the boys I deal with look like me, so I always talk to
them, I do talk to them differently. We of all people need to stay focused.*

Meanwhile, Dwight, a 36-year-old, African American teacher's aide, feels that the kids he works with at an alternative high school are indifferent to his being black. In his words:

*I don't see where it makes a whole lot of difference; I'm sure it makes some.
But in the situations that I've had to deal with here, I don't see where it played
a big role. . . . I feel like I'm a man about business and when they see this they
recognize this. I don't think my race has a whole lot to do with it.*

In addition, Dwight confirms that during his several years at the school, he has never had an explicit conversation about race with any of the students, many of whom are African American.

GENERATIVITY AND "PASSING IT ON"

More than fifty years ago, Erik Erikson, a renowned theorist of lifespan development, introduced the term "generativity" to capture forms of adult caring that contribute to the spirit of future generations. A generative person is one who seeks to pass on valued traditions, to teach key skills and viewpoints, to communicate wisdom, and to help younger generations reach their full potential.[16] Caring can foster more mature persons or new products, ideas, or works of art. John Snarey, a more recent theorist who focuses on fathers' expression of generativity adds that "generativity's psychosocial challenge to adults is to create, care for, and promote the development of others, from nurturing the growth of another person to shepherding the development of a broader community."[17]

Of the four types of generative care commonly practiced, I focus in this book primarily on men's expressions of cultural or societal generativity.[18] Those practicing this form of care direct their activities toward younger adults, or, as in my study, toward youth who are not biologically related to the men who work, teach, monitor, and play with them.[19] As I show, some men are clearly motivated to work with youth because they value the opportunity to express themselves in a generative way.

The other three forms of generativity—biological, parental, and technical—may also factor in to why and how men relate to kids outside as well as inside their families. Biological generativity refers to procreating and caring for infants, whereas the parental variation pertains to caring for children and incorporating them into the family system. The technical form involves passing on particular skills to others and the larger symbolic system in which they reside (e.g., how to shoot a basketball and the love of the game). Erikson tended to conceptualize biological and parenting generativity as providing the foundation for the subsequent expression of social generativity, and the comprehensive concern with generativity was a task associated with middle adulthood.[20] However, he recognized that different forms of generativity may occur simultaneously and aspects of generativity may be expressed at an earlier age. Thus, here and in later sections of the book, I explore how these forms may have a complex temporal ordering, may reinforce one another, or may serve as substitutes.

In the course of their youth work, men sometimes bring kids into their home and adopt them in spirit, or even legally, as family members. In addition, technical generativity with youth outside the family may help serve as a substitute when biological generativity is absent. As I show later, experiencing cultural generativity encourages some men to grow more excited about the prospects of becoming a father to their own children.

When Reggie talks about his motivation to become a teacher and about his teaching methods, the cultural generative spirit driving him to teach life lessons in the classroom is apparent.

I knew going in . . . that education . . . wasn't about the money, really; it was about change in the kid. . . . I knew that I wanted to work in a predominately African American setting and I was blessed that it did happen to me. . . . I'm teaching a lot of kids certain things about life . . . some subjects that may be more important in life [than academic subjects], you know—about responsibility, about anger, and about managing your life, staying out of trouble, and doing

*what authority people say. I think that right now [this] may be more important
to a certain extent, 'cause I think if you can get them under control, you can handle about everything else life throws at you. You can learn about authority, you
can learn about responsibility, you can learn about character. . . . They're learning that, okay, if I want to disrespect authority then I'm gonna have to deal with
the consequences.*

The generativity-related motives men describe are expressed in various ways.
A quick sampling of what men in different settings say about their motivation to
be involved with kids sheds light on men's desires to nurture and pass on life lessons to youth.

*It's worth a million dollars to see a kid that takes something that you instilled
in them and they display it later on in life, and that's joy for me. That's worth
a check to me, you know, because you get to see that result. (Frank, Boys &
Girls Club director)*

*They're still eager to learn, for the most part. I think the love of the game, the
love of kids, trying to help kids succeed in whatever it is they want to do I think
is a big motivator. (Steve, high school basketball coach)*

*I enjoy working with children because I see potential and possibility of poten-
tial, that's another way of looking at growth and development I guess. And I
enjoy seeing the potential of dreams awakening and hopes being realized.
(Paul, director of religious education)*

*Some of the things that keep us [his wife and himself] going: being part of their
developing and seeing what we planted, giving them the trust, giving them the
ability to move on in life. And it all started from here, and we're continually doing it. And they come back, and we've seen the outcome of it, with the parents
being satisfied with their children. (Richard, owner of daycare facility)*

*Right now, I'm focusing on young men. If we can't develop the men, leader-
ship, true leadership qualities, not being a boss, not being a bully, not being a
manager but a leader, then our society is lost. (Matthew, Boy Scout troop
leader)*

*I knew I'd be working with kids and I kinda looked forward to that 'cause I saw
it as a chance, and maybe I could instill some of the principles that I learned in
life in them. (Grady, probation officer)*

It just brings a joy on the inside that . . . it's just, it's hard to explain. To see them grow, to be able to teach them basic things and see them take heed and get a kick out of just simple, you know, everyday tasks that they haven't been taught. It just kinda lightens me up on the inside. (Dwight, teacher's aide)

Whether the implication is instilling values, planting seeds of trust, helping kids realize dreams, developing leaders, or teaching basic things, the common thread woven through the men's sentiments is their interest in extending themselves so that kids will grow and develop. The men taking this stance are moved by their convictions and thrilled to see the fruits of their labor.

Two men who became close friends because of their shared religious convictions and commitment to helping youth illustrate the power of the generative spirit. Their stories also show how the fruits of generativity can be passed on via a chain of interpersonal ties. Malik, a 27-year-old training specialist for a program of abstinence education and leader of a church youth group, was inspired nine years ago by Pastor Carlos to devote his life to working with kids. It was because of Malik's glowing portrait of Carlos's special ability to touch his soul that I arranged to interview Carlos a few weeks later. Referring to Pastor Carlos, Malik exclaims with resounding force:

Every time he preaches I love to hear what he's talking about. It inspires me, it motivates me, and I feel more connected to my destiny. I don't feel like I'm just walking around aimlessly through life. There's more clarity, every single week that I hear this man . . . I wanna be able to provide priceless insight for young people. I wanna be able to motivate somebody who's never tasted what motivation is. I wanna be able to say something to somebody that's gonna drive them towards their destiny, towards their goals, towards, you know, achievement and accomplishment.

The wisdom Malik tries to pass on to youth in schools and at his church accentuates sexual abstinence outside of marriage, living drug and alcohol free, and respecting others and oneself.

So what was Carlos like—the man who moved Malik to speak so passionately about finding his life purpose? Driving to my interview with Carlos, I was filled with anticipation. Fifteen minutes after meeting Carlos, I saw why Malik held him in such high esteem. Carlos's joy in working with kids is largely due to his excitement over knowing he has mentored individuals like Malik who have grown into exceptional mentors themselves. He enthusiastically talks about the value of "passing it on" and about his progress in accomplishing this goal.

To me, true mentoring takes place when the person that you've reproduced re-
produces. That to me is the goal of mentoring. You don't just want to have
someone's life turned around, or pointed in the right direction. To me, they
need to be pointed in the right direction, turned around, and passing on what
they've been given. And I remember when Malik came here, he was just 18
years old, I believe. He was homeless at the time. Got into it with his mom,
she kicked him out of the house, he was staying at the Salvation Army. . . .
Some girl he was trying to get with invites him to church, he comes to church,
makes that connection with the Lord, and then we hook up. And through the
relationship of me just encouraging him and seeing the potential in him and
then him beginning to work with me, he's found his whole direction in life. And
not only has he found his direction in life, he's passing on what I've taught him
and the things that he's learned, and that he's putting in now in some of these
young people. And to me that's what it's all about, man. Because in the long
run, I'm affecting more people because of what I did with Malik. His fruit, and
his impact, is a part of my impact.

Carlos's approach to youth work in school and church settings extends the generativity beyond one generation.

In various settings, other men voice similar perspectives on encouraging youth not only to embrace specific life lessons but also to make a concerted effort to share their message with others. Derek is one such man who takes this approach when mentoring at-risk boys and young men in his program. Making a wide encircling gesture with his hands and arms, he illustrates part of his thinking by using the well-known village metaphor.

It takes a village to raise a kid, . . . and I think that's what we need to get back
to, because no one wants to take the time now to raise anyone else's child. So,
just trying to teach these guys . . . if you feel wronged in any way in life, . . .
think life's treating you wrong, you've been dealt a bad hand, you know, you
don't have to keep that hand, for one. Like, I think I was dealt a bad hand, so I
didn't keep it, know what I'm sayin'? Hand me the deck, pass me the cards,
and then make sure that you don't repeat it, you don't repeat the cycle. 'Cause
I can tell these guys to straighten up their own lives, and if I was to get 100 per-
cent of these guys in this program to be productive citizens in the world, it
wouldn't be enough. Because I didn't teach them to pass that on, know what
I'm saying? That's just 85 guys . . . that comes to this program, go out and be
productive citizens. And all of them grow up and be productive citizens and do

something wonderful in life, but they don't pass it on, and they don't help out little kids coming up behind them, I've left them nothing. So, I'm telling them to make sure that they right the wrongs in their lives, and make sure they don't repeat the cycle. . . . Whatever knowledge you get, pass it on, because there's some kids . . . their little brothers, their little sisters, their little nephews, little next door neighbors that's coming up behind them that need that guidance also. And I'm not always going to be here. . . . I tell the guys, older guys in my program, I was like, once you get a certain age, people are less likely to help you. I mean you're going to find some people out there that was just willing to help you out, but they're more willing now that you're a child. But once you turn 18, they're less likely to help you, so take advantage of the program, take advantage of all the help that's given to you right now. And then once you get in a position to help people out or help the guys that's coming up behind you, by all means do it. So that's my thing I want them to take from this program, take from me.

Derek is well-positioned to share his message that boys need to straighten out their lives and become productive citizens, because he has personally made that transition, after spending his youth in poverty and tough neighborhoods and presenting himself as a tough kid. But he feels that unless he can also get kids to spread the message he will not have truly made a difference. Derek's story underscores one of the obvious risks associated with youth work: having the desire and making the effort to be generative does not necessarily mean that a man will be satisfied with the results. His story also illustrates the optimism most of the men display about inspiring kids to effect some positive change in the years ahead.

RECIPROCITY AND FEELING GOOD

Though most of the men say they want to contribute to the kids' leading better lives, some comment directly or allude to how spending time with kids makes *them* feel good and enhances their *own* personal growth and development. I take up these issues more fully in Chapter 10, but it is worth mentioning here how part of men's motivation to be involved with kids is tied to their personal benefits. A slightly unusual example of this comes from Blake, a 22-year-old volunteer for the 4-H Club.

I even see some kids in 4-H that, they can't stand their parents, and I want to be at least that positive role model; if they don't get it from their parents, at

least to get it from me. . . . And, too, . . . I feel it helps keep me younger. . . . I
can still, if only in my mind, be a kid. Because when I'm out doing stuff with
them, I'm putting myself on their level, and the only time I ever have to be an
adult is when they do something silly or do something stupid where I have to
reprimand them.

Blake was an active youth member in 4-H for a number of years, and he has good memories of being a part of this organization. Now he has an opportunity to share his insights with younger kids while expressing his youthfulness.

Another 22-year-old, Gerald, also cites personal enjoyment as a reason for pursuing his Big Brother relationship with his 14-year-old Little Brother, who was 11 when they were matched initially.

It [going to clubs and partying] really got old very soon for me. And, so it was
just like, there was nothing else to do and I thought that I needed to be more
productive. So, it was just like that was a way for me to actually be a positive
role model for him and it was actually a way for me to get out and do more
fun things. You know, take my mind off the other stresses. So, it was kinda tit
for tat, in a sense. He was providing me with different activities to do in my
leisure time and I was just being that positive role model in which I hoped to
be for him.

Both Blake and Gerald recognize that they are receiving something in return; mentoring is fun. Unlike Blake, who is involved with a number of youth, Gerald focuses his attention on developing a friendship and mentoring relationship with one boy. In both cases the young men appreciate doing fun and productive activities that they would not be doing otherwise.

The line between altruism and personal gain is often a fine one, and categorizing the perceived kindness of others is not always easy. Clearly, though some people feel that the joys of giving are themselves a personal reward. José, a 20-year-old who volunteers his time mentoring in schools, candidly admits, "I like to do the service and I feel like it makes me more of a charitable person. . . . I feel good about myself."

Another enjoyable reason for working with kids is that it can fill an emotional need for someone who does not have children of his own. For example, Alan's eagerness to work with the kids in his church youth group is flavored with a blend of motives by this gap in his life. Framing his comments from the perspective of a gay man without children of his own, he declares his youth work *my way of giving something to society, as you would with your, through your kids. I can do it through [other people's kids]. And a lot of the families here tell me [the kids are] like my surrogate kids, you know, 'cause they're that at-tached. But yeah, . . . this kind of makes up for that void, the not having kids. I would have loved to have been a parent.*

Alan's opportunities with the youth group allow him to experience the genera-tive spirit while appreciating indirectly the self-satisfaction and warm feelings parenting can produce.

SEEING THE IMPACT, BEING RECOGNIZED

Many men are inspired and energized to get involved and stay active with kids by the reality or hope of having a positive impact on the kids. Because cir-cumstances vary greatly, some men are more apt than others to see how their ef-forts affect youth. The ideal situation occurs when a man receives relatively quick feedback. He sees how he has had a positive effect and to what extent. However, in reality, the adult must frequently wait a long time to observe some sort of change in the youngster or to receive recognition for the involvement. In addition, men, especially those with limited youth work experience, are at times slow to realize that in some settings it can take much longer to notice change in kids. Thus, those possessing high expectations about effecting quick, positive change in kids are sometimes disappointed. But for those who see that they are making a difference, the child's joy is infectious and provides a powerful moti-vating force to persist. Ray is spurred on by the feeling he experiences when he notices his contribution.

It does my heart good to see people make something of themselves. I use the expression, "Don't be like me, man, be better than me." If I see a slight change, it just more motivation. "Hey, man, I'm gonna try this. I'm gonna keep going." It's like a scientist, man. Can you imagine how many times, man, that joker was tryin' to make peanut butter out of peanuts? . . . You know how many little changes they had to make and then keep going? They gave them drive, baby, 'til they finished. That's the kind of drive I got.

Unfortunately, some kids simply don't progress while the men are working with them, or the change or interpersonal bond goes undetected. This reality is particularly apparent to Tom, who has worked with kids in various settings in-volving youth ministry and teaching. Most recently, his work as a behavior analyst helping special needs children has revealed to him how much easier it is in this field than most to see his contribution to kids' lives using concrete evaluation measures. Many of his interventions with the special needs children are based on stimulus-response patterns that can be precisely assessed. However, when Tom thinks about his possible contributions to other types of kids he banks on reasoned hope.

> I guess it's like investing . . . you put your time and money to something and you hope that it pays dividends somewhere down the road, stock goes up. . . . It's one of those things that, I guess it's an altruistic thing, you do it because you know it's the right thing to do, and you hope—it's like throwing putty against the wall, some of it's gonna stick and some of it's not. I can always speak about people in my life who basically threw it against me and it stuck, and they never—to this day, they don't know what kind of impact, positive impact, they had. But I was watching, observing, paying attention, looking at them, analyzing, studying who they were, why they did what they did, . . . in terms of trying to search my own identity and who I wanted to be. So I felt like that was something that if it was true for me then it has to be true for a certain amount of people in this world, especially at this age too, in terms of youth culture, they are looking for examples, patterns, people to model their lives after. So, whether it made a difference? I am hoping it did.

A Boy Scout leader, Matthew, has also come to terms with the reality that there is no guarantee that the difference he makes in a kid's life will ever be recognized, either by the kid or others who have a vested interest. Drawing on his experience working with youth in various settings since his college days, Matthew has grown more relaxed and trusting that his efforts are likely to matter in some way, even if he never sees it.

> It's kinda funny, I don't know if you've experienced this, but as you get older, you become more patient . . . you got less time but you're more patient. . . . I've started to look at it more on the impact that I make. You might not actually see the effect that you have, it may happen after you're dead, after you're long gone. But you gotta understand that if you're able to invest yourself and your time, there is a payback. And that, to me, that's probably the most important life lesson.

Sandy, a 56-year-old 4-H Club "extension agent," who spent many years working with youth in Minnesota before moving to Florida, never understood the depth of the bonds he had developed with some kids in his program. He says:

Surprisingly I didn't notice how close some of the bonds were until I got here. Because when I arrived here, within that first year, I had one of my former counselors call and ask for help. . . . he was a kid that had two of his brothers also in the State Pen. And he was really going through something, so he actually moved in with me for a couple of months while we were living here, until he could get his head back together; then he went back to Minnesota.

Having a former counselor reach out across the country to ask for help signaled to Sandy that he must have left a significant impression on the young man as a supportive mentor.

Travis, the Ph.D. student mentioned earlier who is training to be a school psychologist, has witnessed his effect on some children, but he is comfortable framing his experience in a more abstract fashion. Talking about what drives him to work with kids, Travis offers that it is the daydream of having someone twenty years later get in touch with him to let him know that he made a difference in his or her life. He likens it to his own feelings for some of his school teachers who left an indelible impression on him.

If Travis eventually works in one school for a long period of time, his chances to receive student visits and retrospective "thanks" are likely to improve. Actually, given the pervasiveness of e-mail, it may become increasingly less important for a person to remain in the same place. Today, those committed to expressing their gratitude to someone from their past can track the person down relatively easily. Belonging to an organization like the Boy Scouts or 4-H Club probably improves options for finding former mentors. That seems to be the case for Sandy, who reports that kids are able to find him if they want. Given his longstanding association with 4-H, Sandy readily draws upon first-hand experience to claim that there is often a delayed recognition.

You really don't see the impact until several years down the road. I have been around long enough to see that impact. Example: yesterday I had a young girl [club member]—and this is from a different county—stop by to say hi. She was going to one of our camp counsels. . . . She ended up sitting here talking to me for about an hour. She is going to school [nearby] and just wanted to visit with me and see if there is any way she could be involved in our program here. She just graduated from high school but you could tell that I must have had some impact someplace, otherwise she wouldn't have made a point to come in, to initiate that contact. So I think those are some of the things [signs of positive impact] . . . to keep you motivated and keep

you moving. But it builds your own self-confidence. Now that . . . I am work-
ing with the young agents, the hardest part is helping them understand that
those first four or five years you are not going to see that. Because the teens
you have when you come in, you are not going to have a great deal of impact
on, it will be those other kids who go through the program with you. Ten
years from now, you can really see the impact that you have had. I think
that is why, the more experience you get as an agent the more self-confidence
you have.

Men mention diverse ways that others have helped them feel important and let them see that their youth work mattered. Several men note being pleased when little kids initiated contact with them through a wave or simple hello in settings away from their formal youth work. A former camp counselor recalls feeling important as a teenager when a kid he had worked with recognized him on his hometown street. A Little League coach reminisces about being approached by a player at the local mall. And, a youth worker who periodically gives talks in the schools glows when describing how he was greeted with big smiles and friendly chatter in the school hall a year after his presentation. Men in these situations can assume that the kids enjoyed their experience if they go out of their way to acknowledge the men at other times and places. Though simple acknowledgments, the gestures matter to the men.

Some youth reach out in a more invested way, by opening up to men, months or years later, about what they have been doing in their lives since they were relating to the men in that other setting. Youth sometimes share their success stories and in the process implicitly acknowledge that the men's efforts mattered in the past, and still do. Because of Joseph's years of experience working with troubled kids in the same city, he runs into youth around town all the time who interacted with him in one setting or another. He is moved when he describes what it means to him when kids he worked with previously approach him.

It's very humbling. To think that the time that I spent there after all these years,
that all that must have been going on in their life, they still are eager to share
their successes with me and that means that much to them. . . . I mean, the
kids that I used to come home bloody and bitten and scratched up from, having
to tango with all day, and getting called horrendous names and my mom
names and my wife names, that's not what they remember. They remember

*that I was there for them. I was there every day going through that with them
until . . . they straightened up.*

In many conversations the kids say nothing explicitly about what they feel
Joseph has contributed to their personal development. They simply speak in a
friendly way, implicitly acknowledging Joseph as a person worthy of hearing
their good news. Joseph is clearly touched by such casual conversation, an implied confirmation that his dedication and style work.

Sometimes, kids and others may explicitly show appreciation for the contributions men have made and the changes they helped bring about. Carlos fondly
recalls a conversation he had with a young man whom he and his mentoring
team had taken under their wing a number of years before.

*He just said, "You know, I just really want to thank you guys for everything
that you did back in those days." And it meant, it means a lot, to hear them
say that, and, years back they're still thinking about the impact that you
made. So we did get that a lot.*

Brandon, reflecting on his memorable experiences working at kids' summer
camps and in his teaching job, mentions:

*I've had people tell me that they're better people because they've met me. . . .
Camp jobs don't pay very much but I think those are probably the rewards
that I'm looking for, like "Wow, you made a difference."*

For some of the men, hearing a simple "thank you" is sufficient recognition
for them to register that they have done something worthwhile and appreciated.
Dwight mentions that after he bought a jacket for a boy at school who did not
have one, the kid said, "Mr. Dwight, I appreciate it. You didn't have to do this."
Feeling emotional recalling the memory, Dwight quickly says that that was all he
needed to hear.

Like Dwight, Brandon was noticeably teary-eyed while describing a teaching
ritual he performs with middle school students the last day of class each year. He
retells the "pebble story" his Native American grandfather told him: Two braves
were sent out to look for food and resources to help their people. On their journey, a goddess told them to pick up as many stones as possible and return to
their people, but the braves picked up only a few. The next morning, the stones
turned to gold and the goddess reappeared. She pointed out to the braves that
had they followed instructions, their people would have benefited much more.

After sharing this story with his students, Brandon asks each one to pick a stone out of a bucket that he passes around. Then, he reminds them that throughout the year he has been offering them pebbles of knowledge and that they have freely chosen to accept or reject them.

This ritual is a moving experience for Brandon and his students. Reliving it with me is deeply emotional for Brandon; it calls to mind the powerful mentoring role his grandfather has had on him. It also reminds Brandon of his own lasting effect on kids. During the past few years the story has taken on added significance because of an unusual phone conversation Brandon had with a former student, Lance, who had contemplated suicide the night before:

> He said, "You know, I don't even know why I looked your number up. But I found your number in the school directory and I wanted to tell you that last night I was gonna kill myself." I asked, "Why didn't you?" "Because I looked up on my shelf and I saw that stupid rock you gave me." "Well, good!" I said. "You have a piece of gold."

Most of us will never experience what Brandon felt that night and ever since—realizing that a relatively simple gesture might determine whether a person chooses life or death. Lance's phone call, although the most dramatic, is only one of many signs of his impact that inspire Brandon to value his involvement with kids so highly.

Some of the men I interviewed have stayed at the same setting or at least remained in the same community for years. These men often receive visits from kids whom they have worked with in the past or they simply run into the kids in public places. The men often beamed with excitement as they talked about this legacy aspect of their work. Some kids, once they have made a connection with a man, are inclined to return to seek advice about school, jobs, and other personal matters. Echoing Sandy's comments, Nick remarks that these return visits symbolize that kids feel comfortable with this adult advisor.

> If they're gonna come back now and ask me a question, I know there's something that I did right with 'em. I know there's a trust there. There's a bond that we have that was built over the time that we had together.

Trust is the sentiment Nick flags as being critical to kids' returning to visit him. These informal one-on-one visits are manifestations of unspoken bonds.

More formal ceremonies focusing attention on men for what they have accomplished through their work with kids are another means by which men can be made aware that they made a difference. Jeff describes the value of his experiences at Boy Scout award ceremonies, which make him conscious of an aspect of his service that he doesn't think about most of the time.

> I keep telling everybody it is for the kids, I am not interested in awards; but before you know it, the kids are interested in the awards you get. They are proud of you, so you got to go to these things and do it.

In several instances, the men were rewarded with public ceremonies at church or in schools in anticipation of their moving away from the locality. For example, members of Sandy's 4-H program in Minnesota arranged an elaborate surprise going-away party in his honor. After being escorted to a packed gym, he was treated to a program of teasing and toasting in which the kids reminded him of how much he had done for them over the years.

In short, all sorts of experiences help men develop and sustain a commitment to kids. Various circumstances enable them to feel that they are doing the right thing, despite the sacrifices they are making in their personal lives, especially in terms of time and money. When men are truly motivated and committed to working with kids, they are likely to see their paid youth work as more than a job and their volunteering as being an essential part of who they are and what they want to be.

Fortunately, some men develop a passion for working with kids. Those with the strongest passion for youth work often think of it as a mission or calling. In my interviews, some men used these terms on their own, while others acknowledged that they fit when I asked them if they see their efforts in this way. Although most of them appear to view "mission" and "calling" as interchangeable, Ray suggests that individuals choose a mission but a calling chooses them. When asked if he felt as though he were on a mission, the religiously inclined Ray explains:

> I don't feel like it's a mission, man. I feel like it's a calling. You know, everything happens for a reason, that's my belief. Everything is predestined, man, through the word of God, from the time I'm coming from my mother's womb, to me sitting right here, right now. . . . Everything's predestined right from the beginning. . . . And, right now, with me working with these kids, I supposed to be there, man. . . . That's what God meant to happen. He meant for that, he

meant for me to be there, no matter what's going on with the program, no matter who I'm working with. I'm supposed to be there.

Irrespective of whether men view their youth work as a choice they made or as having been chosen for them, when they reflect, they typically see their efforts as contributing to youths' development and to the larger society. Of course, in an ideal world more men would be motivated to devote time and energy to help other men's children. But there are plenty of foot soldiers already in the trenches, helping kids find their way through the troublesome times of youth.

CHAPTER 5

RELATING TO KIDS

On a whim, at the end of our interview, I asked Malik to free-style rap as he might when he uses rap with kids in schools to help them find purpose in their lives and avoid unhealthy choices. These are the opening lyrics of what he produced:

Yo, yo check it out
This is for real
I'm chilling at the desk with Bill
Yo, we gotta write this book
We got some stuff to build
My lyrics don't kill
They build up your spirit and your soul
I'm on a roll
Listen to all of these lyrics unfold
I got stories untold
About all of these youth and sex
When they start doing that
That's when their life get wrecked
They don't got nobody to put 'em in check
So they livin' reckless
And nobody that rolls around will respect this
But when I start spittin' these lyrics

It penetrates their heart and they minds
So you know they wanna hear it . . .

Malik then described his approach:

> When we first go into a lot of these classes, we do this thing, it's called the
> MC test. And, we'll tell the kids, "All right, we need y'all to give us three
> crazy, off the wall topics, but they have to be school appropriate. And I'll tie
> all three of those topics together in a free-style rap." They're thinking, "You
> can't do that, dawg, you trippin? How you gonna make up a rhyme right
> now about three crazy things?" So right there, we've got all their attention.
> And, it's working to our advantage, because they think we can't do it, they
> think I can't do it. So it gives me an opportunity to connect with them and
> prove myself. And they're wanting to think I'm going to mess up, so it's like
> we captivate their attention.

Six months after our initial interview, I went to see for myself how high
school students respond to his rapping. Having already presented to the same
kids earlier in the week, Malik and a coworker ran sessions of a sexual abstinence program for three separate classes as I quietly observed. I quickly realized
that Malik's assessment of his bond with students was perfect. In one session,
Malik gave the kids the option of coming up with four topics for the MC test. Because the kids had seen him do the test with three topics earlier in the week, they
appeared motivated to stump him. Their choices: "African Malaysian fairies,
hippopotomonstrosesquippedaliophobia, zella zippy zero zebra zippers, and
amniocentesis." After asking the students for a show of hands to see who
thought he would mess up versus do the rap cleanly, Malik effortlessly put together a high-energy two-minute rap incorporating all four expressions. As one
might expect, the kids were mesmerized throughout the rap, as was I, and they
enthusiastically participated in the program that followed.

Making use of his gift for free-style rapping, his affinity with hip-hop culture,
and his extroverted personality, the 27-year-old Malik has found his niche for
sharing his messages with school age youth. Carlos, Malik's minister, mentor,
and sidekick for some of the youth programs, is equally convinced of rap's
power. As Carlos explains, "hip-hop has seemed to transcend all the cultures
nowadays. I would say it's probably one of the only things in pop culture that
touches Blacks, Hispanics, Whites, I think all kids on every level." He asserts
that young people respond favorably to Malik's raps, as well as his own, because

in the kids' minds they imagine "you're trying to get on my level." As a result, Carlos believes, they open up. From what I saw at the high school where Malik conducted his program, I agree.

The men have been involved with kids of all ages, in various settings, doing all sorts of activities. Consequently, it is a challenging task to sort through their varied stories in hopes of identifying themes to capture how male youth workers relate to kids. With this caveat in mind, let's take a look at several key notions that are useful for dissecting how men often think about and describe their relations with kids: leveling; inviting comfort, contact, and trust; the power of touch; expressing bonds; and rituals.

LEVELING

Like Malik and Carlos, lots of men search for ways to put themselves on the same level as kids. Defining what this means and making it happen in practical terms takes diverse forms, depending on the circumstances. The youths' developmental stage and the types of activities that have brought the adults and kids together (e.g., sports, juvenile justice system, faith-based situations) are two obvious factors affecting the leveling process. Others include whether the men are actively participating in an activity with the kids versus instructing or supervising them; whether kids are participating voluntarily or not; whether kids are interacting with adults alone or in groups; and whether interactions are singular, short-lived episodes or are repeated over a considerable period of time.

For men working with very young kids, finding ways to get on their level appears to go more smoothly if men express themselves physically and emotionally in specific ways. David, 48, is currently working as a teacher's aide in an elementary school. He has plenty of experience working with small children in daycare (including Head Start) and with special needs children in healthcare settings. He perceives himself as having a knack for relating to young children, more so than most men. Reconstructing and blending images from two previous jobs, David conveys his personal style with kids:

> Little kids . . . they are running around, you are playing with them. . . . I try to play with them; the others, they sit and watch them. . . . When I was in pre-K, I had kneepads; I would crawl around with the kids, . . . at their eye-level. All of the time, because it is a comfort zone . . . I become the kid. I become them.

Unlike his coworkers in those classrooms, David took a more active role by throwing himself into the action; he played with the kids. Figuratively, David takes on a kid's mindset. Literally, David takes the initiative to get physically and emotionally closer to the children by entering their "comfort zone" on the floor.

Like David, Sidney, now a second grade teacher, made the effort, several years ago while working at a daycare center, to kneel or sit next to the youngest children in order to be "eye-to-eye" with them. Talking about why he did this, Sidney explains:

> I feel it's pretty important. I mean, when you get down on a kid's level, they relate to you a little bit better. With me being as tall as I am, I tower over the kids anyway, and if they're looking up it's a little more intimidating for them, so if I get down on their level they feel a little more reassured and calm, and they're easier to deal with and talk to.

As grown men working with decidedly smaller children, David and Sidney are conscious of how they can manage their bigger bodies in children's physical space. Imagine for a moment, in your own adult body, trying to relate to someone two or three times your height, just trying to look up at that giant's face. This is how the small children must have felt when David and Sidney stood next to them.

In addition to thinking of leveling in a spatial sense, men sometimes speak about how they get on kids' level by being playful, childlike, and spontaneous. Research shows that, among the many ways fathers relate to their own kids, they spend the most time playing with them.[1] It should come as no surprise, then, that men often enjoy using play to connect with kids. By interacting side by side with kids in activities like coloring, roughhousing, sports, and playing video games, men can share common ground with the kids, making it easier to appeal to them. For example, Phillip, now a graduate student in counseling, says, "I guess, because of my early experience with children, I always connect with children on just kind of being funny or being goofy and kind of building a rapport that way." Playfully wrestling with kids when he was a teenage counselor at a day camp is one of the experiences Phillip fondly remembers.

> There was this kind of big mat, and a lot of times, if there was some kind of physical activity that we were in, [the campers] would get really riled up; and then one guy would, one of the little kids, would jump on my back and then another one would kind of grab my leg; so I'd start to just kind of throw them

all on the mat and just have a good time. . . . That's something that I remem-
ber enjoying as a little kid and I enjoyed when I was 17, too.

Here we see another example of how physical space and objects provide men
with the chance to interact with kids in particular ways. Without the mat, Phillip
and the kids may never have experienced this type of physically oriented bonding with each other.

Reggie, the fourth grade school teacher, offers a more nuanced view of how
he casually reaches out to kids.

I can relate to them on their level. . . . Children feel like they can trust me.
I'm very fair to them. I think fair is a very important thing. You don't look at
them as children, you just look at them as people, which they are. And I al-
ways try to make them laugh, I'm always joking with them, and they like
that.

Though Reggie explicitly speaks of relating to kids on their level, he qualifies his
approach. He admits to seeing kids more holistically as people, emphasizing, it
would seem, their shared humanity. At the same time, he uses humor to take
them to the same emotional space.

Men's incentive to be playful is not restricted to elementary school kids.
Though the style and content of their playful interaction tends to differ when directed at teenagers, some men are willing, even eager, to be carefree in various
settings. For example, Alan laughs as he describes how his male partner's presence or absence in a setting influences his behavior around kids in his church
youth group.

When I'm with just the kids, sometimes I tend to get down to their level, I [act
like] . . . more of a kid. And then, when he's around I kind of keep myself more
at the adult level; I get, I don't know, it's just weird, you don't want to look
foolish, I guess, in front of other people. But the kids, I don't care about looking
foolish in front of them.

Alan's willingness to let his guard down and allow the kids to see him acting
foolishly appears to signal his comfort with entering teenagers' emotional
space.

In addition to hearing descriptions about their playful style, I saw some of the
men bonding with kids through lighthearted teasing, a joking demeanor, or silly
antics during my visits to different youth work sites. Of course, some adults are

more adept than others at being playful while retaining a latent aura of authority. Such adults are able more readily to build casual rapport yet ultimately keep kids' respect.

Charles seems especially capable of managing the delicate balance of being accessible to yet authoritative with the kids at his Boys & Girls Club. Asked to comment on what role spirituality plays in his interactions with kids, Charles, a man with strong faith convictions, begins by mentioning that through his work he meets kids from a range of religious backgrounds—Jewish, Catholic, Muslim, atheist.

> *You have to be able to relate to them, and like I say, a lot of the kids they have this saying that says "get on my level," . . . that's something from one of their songs they listen to. And sometimes, you know what, we really do. We have to get on their level to understand them, to connect with them. And through spirituality, that's, I think that's really what religion and spirituality is about. It's about meeting a person where they're at and helping them to grow and mature to be something else.*

By using the "level" metaphor in this instance, Charles captures the notion that adults should be aware of differences among youth while striving to find a spot where kids feel comfortable. So an adult's first task is to discover what a particular youth may be experiencing. Next, he or she must figure out how to relate to the kid in terms consistent with the youth's experience.

For some men, the discovery process is straightforward, because they need only look inward at their own experiences to realize what particular kids may be experiencing. Men like Barry, Derek, and Nick speak of how their childhoods of poverty and exposure to violence enable them to relate to poor kids in a deeper way than is the case for men who have lived a more privileged life. Thinking about the disadvantaged kids he currently cares for in an after-school program, Barry says:

> *There's so many of them I just feel like I can reach out to and give some type of knowledge about living life. And let them know, that things will get better. "Hang in there. If you need someone to talk to, I'm here." . . . I feel like I see a part of me inside most of those kids.*

Most of us can relate to Barry's powerful vision—of having the intuitive sense of seeing oneself in others. Those feelings tend to pull us closer to others. Thus, it stands to reason that Barry's strong affinity with the kids may be one reason he feels he's more effective than many of his coworkers in helping kids who appear to be struggling.

Like Barry, Nick believes he is better positioned than many of his colleagues to connect with troubled kids because of his difficult childhood. Alluding to meetings with his peers, Nick stresses the value of personal experiences in relating to at-risk kids.

> I've asked in meetings, "Have you ever been in trouble, you know, with DJJ [Department of Juvenile Justice]? Have you ever been? No. Have you ever been hungry and never had anything to eat? No. Then how you gonna understand how these kids feel? How can you basically understand and feel some real emotions to try [to] communicate with them? It's impossible. It's impossible for a person to walk in and be that effective for the child without having them experiences." It shows. . . . when I'm communicating with [the kids], I reflect on me, so it would be hard for me to be upset with them, because I had to look back at myself. So, to get upset with them, I'd had to be pretty pissed off with myself.

Nick continues by talking about how his African American coworkers in facilities for troubled youth have difficulty understanding why black teenagers often find him, a white man, to be more approachable.

> I lived the same life that a lot of young black men live. Came up similar even though my skin wasn't black. I still had the similar traits of trouble, alcoholism, drugs, feeling no worth, no self-esteem, and you know that most black men have those traits. They just don't have the abilities to try to push yourself any further. So, when people start seeing me building a bond with the black kids off the street, they're like, "How do you relate to them? You don't know nothing about their background." And, I just kinda look at them. I said, "Well, you only know what you learn. So if you learn something, then you can give it back to 'em." And, I would, even with the people I worked with. They didn't know my background. . . . I never relayed it to them, where I come from as a child, what happened to my family, how I was raised. To them, they thought I was educated and went to school and had a perfect life. Well, little do they know. Huh, there was no perfect life there. But . . . a lot of staff, especially black staff that work there, the black kids wouldn't talk to 'em. They be like, "No, we don't wanna talk to you. We want to talk to Mr. Nick." And, [the coworkers] asked me, "How they understand you and here I'm a black man and they won't talk

to me but they'll talk to you?" I said it's how you set yourself. You know, if you
[sit] down and just be a neutral space and just [sitting] there and you listen. Let
them lead the direction. Let them lead where they wanna go with it and have
no barriers; color, creed, religion. Let them just vent on what they feel like they
need to vent on. I give them—this is their floor. This is your option. I'm not
even here. I'm just air you're breathing. Talk just like you're talking to yourself
if you want to make yourself understand something. And, some of the conver-
sations I would hear, it would be unreal . . . it's a lot of hurt. I feel hurt. I feel
aggravation. I feel frustration. I feel no worth to the point where I reflect. When
they cringe, I would cringe, because I know what they're cringing about.

Though Nick does not reveal his childhood troubles to the kids because work rules prohibit his doing so, he believes his own personal pain enables him to be a more empathetic listener. In some respects, he feels that he has walked in their shoes, so he is able to be at their level as they describe their pain. I have no concrete way of verifying how accurately Nick describes his listening style, nor kids' willingness to open up to him, but my intuition tells me that he is good at what he does and that kids trust him.

Though memories of a hard life as a child are valuable tools for some men in relating effectively to a specific segment of youth, David offers a less common but potentially important window for peering into kids' emotional worlds. Because David spoke candidly, and often, about the practical difficulties and stigma of his own learning disability, I asked if his experiences shaped how he works with kids. "It gave me the empathy and the patience. . . . I learned how to control it," he says, referring to his frustration with his learning disability. David also indicates that his patience enables him to "just keep repeating something until someone understands it" and "to sit there and listen when some kid is yelling or screaming" instead of doing what he or she is being asked to do. In these seemingly tense situations, where David is trying to change a child's bad behavior, he is able to "keep calm and smile," because he taps into the awkward feelings he has had about the way others have reacted to him. Even though David did not want for money while growing up or see the violence that some of the men did, his life journey has been filled with other obstacles, providing him a reservoir of feelings for appreciating intimately the struggles facing young people with any kind of special need.

Although experiential knowledge helps the men in various settings, in many instances they must seek out information about particular kids or about youth in general if they are to figure out a way to get their message across to kids. Some men go out of their way to learn details about certain kids—their names, family circumstances, and the like—or they attend functions in which the kids are participating outside the context they usually share, functions such as sporting events, school plays, and graduation ceremonies. Although these efforts to be attentive away from their typical encounters with the kids do not always foster a kind of interpersonal leveling, sharing these experiences seems to increase men's chances of getting kids to accept them.

Male youth workers who work extensively with kids sometimes try to remain as current as possible with youth styles and fads. Kevin describes how he once spent a week watching videos of popular music artists like Usher, 50-Cent, Britney Spears, and Eminem on his office computer. He prepared a video as part of an exercise he did with his church youth group in which they broke down song lyrics and talked about them. Carlos is also attentive to the youth entertainment media and tries to use it to enhance his connections with kids in his youth ministry.

> I'll go to Barnes and Noble; I'll go through some of the magazines, and I'll know just enough to make me dangerous. . . . I'll look through a skateboarding magazine, and I'll find two names, so I'm talking to a kid, and I'll say, "So tell me a little bit about, you know, Tony Hawk. What's going on with him now?" And they look at me like, like I know. And I don't know, I saw the name in a magazine! But then he'll tell me something about him, and then I got that for the next kid. Flipping by MTV, and I'll see a music video by some rock group that I don't like, but I'll wait to see who it's by, and then next thing you know, I'll mention that in a conversation. I'll say, "What do you think about this band. I saw that video," and they're just intrigued that I knew who it is and I saw a video. . . . I'm not trying to be fake. I'm not trying to claim like I'm all in their world; I'm not gonna show up with a skateboard in my hand, but at least I'll have some kind of knowledge in it when I'm in a message, or when I'm talking to them, that I can refer to. And I believe that does a lot, and I know a lot of guys that don't do that. They don't know, they don't know anything about what the African American kids are into, or what, the Hispanic kids are doing, or what's cool there. . . . I'm not gonna change who I am to try to fit that, but I'm just gonna be a little educated, to try to know what's going on.

As Carlos sees it, studying pop culture is a vital part of his youth ministry because the lessons enable him to enter the emotional space where the kids live. He knows he doesn't have to pretend to be in their world completely, but he must acknowledge it and feel comfortable chatting with kids about it.

Though most male youth workers embrace some version of the idea of leveling, some shy away from it or resist it adamantly. Calvin, a 60-year-old former military officer working at a youth employment service helping teenagers develop job skills and find employment, prefers his own adult approach:

> I never try to talk down to the kids. Some folks here like to try to talk the kids'
> language, and they say, "Oh you can't communicate with them if you don't
> talk their language." I can't do that. I can't talk that street talk. It is not me. I
> try to talk to communicate with kids on an adult, mature level and in a clear
> direct way so that they understand where I am coming from, and there are not
> any, a lot of shades of gray in there. You made a mistake, let's talk about it,
> and here is what we can do.

Calvin prefers to deal with kids on terms more familiar to him. He confesses to finding it hard to understand kids at times because of the slang they use and their unclear speech. In addition, as someone who grew up in a two-parent, rural family, he candidly admits he struggles to understand many youth, especially African Americans raised in what he perceives to be such a different subculture.

> Learning to deal with their styles of dress, their music, their hairstyles, their lan-
> guage, the culture. . . . I am "white bread," I am white-bread culture. The mili-
> tary, what I was raised in was just so different that you really have to force
> yourself to be tolerant.

Calvin is committed to helping these kids get jobs, and part of his reluctance about their style may stem from his awareness of how employers view youth who fall too far outside the mainstream normative order. His decision not to embrace and utilize youth culture in his work is consistent with his belief that employers are more accepting of youth who closely fit the image of a conscientious, nonthreatening, and dependable person.

Calvin is not unique in his unwillingness to relate to youth on their level or support how some youth wish to present themselves. A number of the African American men speak vehemently against permitting the youth with whom they work to dress in gangster garb. Unwilling to embrace certain aspects of hip-hop culture, these men enforce a relatively strict dress code, prohibiting the baggy, beltless pants look in the facilities where the men supervise them. Some even frown upon boys wearing their hair in cornrows, a practice followed almost exclusively by African American kids.

INVITING COMFORT, CONTACT, AND TRUST

A common thread linking many men's orientation toward youth work is that they want kids to feel comfortable enough to come to them with their concerns and problems. They often speak of wanting kids to trust them, especially the kids old enough to carry on a conversation. Men express this sentiment in different ways depending on the parameters and purpose of their interactions with kids.

Trying to meet kids on their level is one way to produce the kind of comfort necessary for the kids to confide in a man. This is what Derek is attempting in his "circle of trust" sessions, sitting on the floor with the at-risk teenage boys. One strategy, if permitted by the organization for which they are working, is for the men to open up and talk about their past and current lives, discussing their own struggles with drugs, alcohol, crime, or poverty; life accomplishments; and sentimental experiences. Using this approach often casts the adult in the role of the experienced forecaster who has learned firsthand what can happen when a young person makes certain decisions. Such sharing is a deliberate act to establish trustworthiness.

Winning kids' trust is often closely linked to a man's ability to appear credible to kids and, sometimes, to the adults who determine whether their children spend time with that man. Speaking of why kids value his opinions or those of other mentors, Carlos explains:

> They see that I'm open, or that I understand, you know, what's going on out there. . . . The minute they see you're just, you're out of touch—I'm not saying you gotta be fake and, you know, be what you're not, but you should at least have an awareness of what's taking place out in the world, 'cause I think when a young person sees that, that gives you credibility. When you're out of touch, they're thinking, "Why do I need to listen to this person? They don't even know what's going on. They don't understand," you know, that's the worst thing you want to hear from somebody you're trying to mentor, is them thinking you don't understand. So when you enter into their world, and you, I mean you know what's going on with music, you know what's going on with style, you know what's going on, there's a sense of "Man, this guy really gets it, I wanna listen to what he has to say," type of thing.

In some youth work settings, particularly those in which men have one or only a few chances to make an impression, adults need to establish credibility quickly if they are to have any chance of getting youth to embrace their message.

This is what Malik's opening rap does for him when he shares abstinence programming with classrooms filled with strangers.

In settings where interacting with kids over an extended period of time is the norm, youth workers can establish their credibility at a more leisurely pace. In many situations, trust and credibility evolve as byproducts of shared activities. Mission trips are a fascinating example. The kids come to see their religious leaders in a different light when they have a more intimate vantage point from which to watch the leaders conduct themselves. Away from church buildings and scripted rituals, the adults navigate a different type of terrain with the youth they take on mission trips. Carlos has taken kids on numerous trips to distant places including El Salvador, Brazil, Croatia, Germany, Iceland, and Puerto Rico. Reflecting on how these trips create unique opportunities for him and the kids to relate to one another, Carlos says:

> They're with me for twelve days, every day, on a bus, on a plane. So there's a little bit more access, and there's a little bit more relatability, and there's a little bit more where we all kinda let our hair down to another level, and things like that. So yeah, there's a little different perspective. But I think also, . . . they get to see what I do when I travel, because I travel out a lot on my own. So they get to see what I'm doing with my life, with my career, with what God's called me to do. They get to see me in that perspective as I'm out there. They understand me a little bit more. I think it adds something to what I bring to them.

Under these circumstances, Carlos is able to solidify his connection with kids and improve his ability to communicate with them. While the kids' casual encounters with their minister bring Carlos into *their* world, Carlos highlights that the mission experience brings the kids into his world by helping them see more clearly what he does to honor *his* faith. The bottom line: the kids appear to feel more connected and open to him, and also to each other.

Jacob, the 50-year-old rabbi, offers a concrete example of why he feels teenagers from his youth group benefit when they see him away from the synagogue. He describes what happens when the kids travel to New York City with him and other chaperons for a "patrol trip":

> They see me in an informal role. And I try and show them the kind of consistency in my life, that the things that they see me doing here in the synagogue I do when I'm outside of the synagogue. . . . When they're in the synagogue and they see me eating, they know that I'm eating kosher. . . . When we're in

New York City and I take them to a kosher restaurant they see that I'm totally consistent. They're not gonna have a time when they see me, you know, eating a ham sandwich. . . . they're very keen into seeing . . . does the Rabbi behave in . . . you know, does he act differently here or there. And you know, if they see me in the grocery store they look into the grocery cart to see what's in there, and they look on the back of my head to see if I'm still wearing a yarmulke.

Thus, for these Jewish teenagers, hanging out with or seeing their rabbi informally can provide them unique opportunities to develop a deeper appreciation for the principles and symbols of a Jewish lifestyle.

On an even lighter note, Jacob tries to build rapport with kids by using puppets. During his rabbinical internship, he was impressed with how kids responded when his mentor took a stuffed bear adorned with a *yarmulke* and *tallith* (prayer shawl) into a preschool classroom. Jacob has since secured a few puppets and uses them from time to time to connect with kids and put them at ease. In one instance, he helped a small boy who had recently moved from out-of-state overcome his tears and fear of going into a Sunday school class. Jacob describes what he did when the teacher notified him that the boy would not enter the classroom or stop crying.

I brought him in here and [I] had no idea what I was gonna do, but I had the puppet [named Taz], and so I sat the puppet down and the puppet had a conversation with the little boy. And the little boy was completely scared of me, but he just looked at that puppet and he just talked to that puppet and the puppet told him everything was gonna be fine. The little boy laughed and laughed and laughed and thought that it was ridiculous. He's talking to this puppet and he was calmed down, and then after it was over I said, "Are you ready to go into class now?" And he said, "I'm ready," and he went back into class. And every time I've seen him since, he's come up to me and says, "Where's Taz?"

By using these creative props, Jacob grabs kids' attention while stimulating healthy talks.

My appreciation for Jacob's artful tactic was enhanced one Monday afternoon while attending a weekly faith program he coordinates for middle school kids at his synagogue. After his staff read a play, Jacob energetically moved about the inside of a circle of thirty seated kids playfully leading them in an up-tempo Jewish song. He made eye contact with individual kids while clapping his hands, smacking his knees, and making other scripted hand gestures in harmony with the class. As the song was winding down, he quickly retrieved a "special visitor" and brought his male puppet back to the group. At this point the puppet took charge and began to ask the kids questions about the play they had heard. Most of the kids seemed genuinely interested and comfortable with both Jacob and the puppet. Not surprisingly, Jacob's efforts to connect with the kids appear to have worked. The kids cast Jacob as the friendly and approachable rabbi, rather than a stuffy religious leader.

Building rapport is also critical for Ben, who practices his ministry and also directs an unrelated summer camp for boys. Talking about how he negotiates his relationships with kids, Ben says, "I want it to be a level playing field where the kids can confide in me with anything they need to and where even I can confer with them. I want that equality." The equality Ben tries to create underscores his desire to be accessible to the kids in a way that minimizes the hierarchal relationship that technically exists between a minister or camp director and the parish youth or campers.

The theme of openness permeates the main message many of the men shared about how they want school-age kids to see them. Contrary to stereotypical images of men as lazy, inattentive communicators in relationships, numerous men like Ben work at making kids feel comfortable confiding in them because they believe it is vitally important. My participants frequently asserted that kids want and need to express themselves to adults without being judged. For these men, being there for the kids means being willing to listen attentively, with an open mind and in a nonjudgmental way. Youth may ask them for guidance or simply the opportunity to vent without the fear of parental interrogation and judgment. Male youth workers often pride themselves on providing kids the space to share their problems and ask questions. Charles is one such man.

I think everyone's looking for somebody who they can confide in or they can talk to and not be judged. Someone who's trustworthy, someone that they know will always be there and willing to listen. And I think that . . . if you listen to kids talk, that's the first thing they say. . . . You hear them, if they argue with their parents—"You never listen to me." And sometimes that's all kids want to do, they just want to talk and be heard. And then they're finished with it, but if they never feel like what they're trying to convey gets across, then yeah, that builds up in them, and anger and disappointment and rage. So I mean, I think that's something that I provide for them.

Many men are mindful that appearance also often matters in kids' eyes. As a result, these men may sometimes go out of their way to convey an image of approachability to kids. Nick, for example, tall and an avid weightlifter, is aware that his large physical presence may illicit particular images from others.

> Whenever I walk into a room and especially . . . females, they're intimidated by a big person anyway, and I let 'em know, yeah I'm big, but I'm soft. I'm just easy; I'm just a big teddy bear. You ain't gotta worry . . . and within a couple of minutes they more or less know that I'm not that kind of intimidating factor. I'm not here to be a strong hand. I'm here to talk to 'em.

In Nick's situation, working with emotionally troubled youth, it is significant that he disarms these youths' defensive tendencies while encouraging them to handle their frustrations by talking rather than through violence.

THE POWER OF TOUCH

Even though youth workers do most of their relating to kids through talking and listening, touch enters the picture in subtle and occasionally dramatic ways. Recall the discussion in Chapter 3 about how the public scrutiny of adults' involvement with children affects how men think about and deal with the rules regulating their physical contact with youth in diverse settings. Dwight echoes a sentiment shared by many when he says that "everybody needs a hug sometimes." But hugging at what cost? Some men clearly struggle with the constraints they now face in a world highly suspicious of men's motives. Although most men seem to believe that, in principle, hugs may be helpful, some feel it is out of bounds for them to initiate hugs with kids; others regard it as inadvisable even to respond to youths' invitations for this type of touch. Thus, because the prospects of touch are significant and controversial, in either their presence or absence, I explore how some men use touch to define their relations with youth.

Generally speaking, men use touch as either a spontaneous and casual means to acknowledge a preexisting bond; a gesture to congratulate, reinforce, and encourage kids' efforts; or as a way to show emotional support. Some casual touching is incorporated into greetings and goodbyes, whereas other episodes occur in the natural flow of activities, such as, playing contact sports. Moments of creative touching sometimes convey unspoken respect as part of a playful ritual of masculine intimacy. Though men typically share this latter form of ritual touch with boys to convey male bonding, I saw men sharing similar moments with girls. For example, while sitting on a small stool with his fourth grade students next to him on the floor, Reggie was teaching the kids the value of looking at a person while offering a firm handshake. He engaged the girl immediately next to him in an extended and exaggerated handshake, moving their hands up and down. All the while, he looked her in the eye and asked her how her weekend was. The girl's smile and attentive response led me to believe she appreciated this playful bonding gesture and the spotlight.

Blake sheds subtle light on how touch can enhance men's relations with kids by describing how it adds special meaning to his interactions with teenage 4-H Club members. Referring to how he touches the shoulder of a kid who is having a bad day, Blake reveals the special meaning of touch.

> I try to do things like that, because it's the little things. Somebody can come up and say, "Oh, well I feel where you're coming from," but you don't necessarily, you know. You might say, "Okay, well they're just saying that to make me feel better," whereas if you put your arm around them or you touch them on the back, on the shoulder, and say, you know, "Okay, I feel where you're coming from. This is what I've had to deal with, which is similar to that." Then you kind of relate to that person more. And, not only that, but it makes the relationship a little bit more intimate.

As I begin to nudge Blake to clarify whether it's the hugging or the words that matter, he quickly and confidently continues.

> The touching, necessarily. The putting the arm around the shoulder or the neck, the touching of the shoulder, shaking hands. If we're having conversation and I leave the conversation, I try to shake your hand. Again, . . . even though they're young, you never know if that might be the last time you see them. You wanna leave that impression with them, that they do matter. To me someone that is an associate but doesn't necessarily matter in your life has no impact, you might nod, walk away. There's no physical contact. But when the person actually matters in your life, then there should be some kind of physical contact, whether it's a hug. I don't necessarily hug any of them, just because that would be fairly awkward at their age and at my age, but there are handshakes. Like I said, there's pats on the backs. If they're having a bad day I'll come behind them and, squeeze their shoulder up in this area just to show 'em, you know, "Hey, I'm behind you" or "If you ever, . . ." just "It's okay, relax a little bit."

In an era steeped in public scrutiny over sexual harassment and inappropri-ate touching of children, Blake offers a sober reminder that, under the right cir-cumstances, the high-fives, handshakes, pats on the back, hugging, and even incidental physical contact in the throes of an activity can inject healthy emo-tional energy into men's relationships with kids. Gentle, well-meaning touch can infuse interactions—including the verbal and facial gestures through which men convey meaning to kids—with a much-needed dose of humanity, a genuine sense of concern.

That the power of touch sometimes goes unnoticed may be due to its being mixed with verbal exchanges. Carlos reflects on how he has sharpened his awareness of the power of touch in recent years.

> Now that I'm older I really tend to use the power of touch to a degree, because I really believe in the power of human touch. I'm talking about appropriate touch, like you said, a handshake, a pat on the back, "How's it going?" In the church setting there's hugs, and even outside of church, a hug is a powerful thing. And so what my wife and I have seen, probably in just the last couple years of working with young people, that the power of touch is a really, a posi-tive influence in a young person's life. So now we see in the mentoring process, it really is important . . . of course, appropriate touch.

Over the course of a school day, I saw with my own eyes how Mariano ex-celled at using simple physical gestures to display his investment in kids' well-being while teaching middle school students and coaching the girls' vol-leyball team to a victory. In the hallways and classroom, as well as on the vol-leyball court, Mariano and students regularly swapped playful touches and smiles when they greeted one another or when Mariano congratulated them. Consistent with Blake's practice, Mariano would often place his hand on a student's shoulder as he moved about his classroom helping kids one-on-one or in small groups. The subtle validating power of touch also surfaced during an early morning conference where I observed seven teachers, including Mar-iano, and two parents and an eighth grade boy discuss the boy's recent indif-ferent attitude and declining grades. As the teachers took turns assessing the boy's waning commitment to his schoolwork, Mariano sat next to the essen-tially speechless boy, who hung his head throughout. When Mariano spoke, he casually placed his hand on the boy's forearm. My reading of this gesture was that it conveyed to the boy that, even though Mariano was frustrated with his lack of effort, he cared about the boy's well-being and wanted to help. Later that afternoon I noticed Mariano and the boy having several friendly and productive exchanges in class, one of which the boy initiated. I can only speculate that Mariano's touch had encouraged the boy to trust Mariano, but I sense that he had taken Mariano's gesture to heart, whatever meaning he derived from it. Seeing how comfortable other kids appear to be with Mariano's physical and joking style gives me good reason to believe that this boy also appreciated Mariano's demeanor.

Unlike Mariano, who is susceptible to a supervisor's judgment, Tony's leadership position at an alternative school for at-risk kids had enabled him to initiate an informal "hug day" about a month before we chatted. He directed his entire staff to give three hugs to kids during the day while making sure there was a reason behind each hug, such as a student doing something good. Tony took this novel step because he shares Mariano's belief that touch is a powerful tool by which adult professionals can express warmth, care, and love for kids. Despite his staff's initial skepticism of his plan, Tony sports a wide smile when reporting the feedback he received.

> Oh, it was great! . . . That was a great day, I mean, our [bad] behavior was down, we didn't have many negative situations to deal with, the kids were in good moods, the staff were in a good mood that day, so it definitely worked. . . . When the kids got off the bus, there were like two or three staff who went to a kid who wasn't in uniform yesterday; they acknowledged the uniform, and the kid smiled and got a hug for being in uniform. That kid wasn't going [to] have a problem the rest of the day; their first experience in stepping onto the campus that day was positive. It's going to be, it's going to be a good day.

Tom provides another insightful example of how touch can be used, in this instance with a group of kids for whom verbal logic is typically less appropriate. As a behavior analyst, Tom uses touch when working with autistic children. He mentions that

> deep pressure for a lot of kids with autism is stimulating to them, highly stimulating, and something they enjoy. So whether it's pressing on their back or their shoulders or wherever their specific, you know, particular location is—that can be very rewarding and reinforcing to them.

Tom also notes that autistic children sometimes respond well to being tickled or having their hair rubbed, so he pairs those responses with particular reactions and behaviors he's trying to reinforce.

Although my interviews and observations lead me to believe that various conditions affect the extent to which men can use touch effectively in their work with kids, there are plenty of situations in which it helps. I noticed, too, during the time I spent watching Mariano and Derek interact with kids that their skill at banter and joking around with kids seems to open doors to incorporating touch into their playful exchanges. If used wisely, joking and appropriate touch can encourage many kids to trust the men who work with them.

EXPRESSING BONDS

As we saw in Chapter 3, when men interact with kids outside the home, they frequently do so while participating in other institutional settings, such as school, the criminal justice system, religious organizations, community recreation programs, or mentoring programs. The meanings men and kids assign to their interactions are often significant enough to create some sort of interpersonal bond. Sometimes bonds develop out of the natural flow of people's everyday lives as neighbors, teachers, or coaches. Others emerge because people invest in a formal mentoring arrangement with organizational oversight. Either way, the bonds are part of an interpersonal process, often embedded in an ongoing relationship.

Myriad settings and circumstances surround men's interactions with kids, influencing what sort of bond develops. Some bonds resemble a form of friendship, brotherhood, or extended kin relation; others appear similar to a surrogate parent-child relationship; and some take on characteristics similar to an apprenticeship, mentorship, supervisory, or teaching relationship. Bonds vary in duration, intensity, breadth, and impact. Typically, bonds involve two or more overlapping types of expressions: behavorial, emotional, cognitive, and spiritual.

Behavioral Expressions

Behavioral expressions arise during activity. For example, the Big Brothers Big Sisters program emphasizes one-on-one time with a youth, ideally immersed in activities the young person enjoys. This strategy is stressed during the early phases of matches, when mentors and kids are learning about each other. For many boys and men in this program, becoming successful companions requires doing things together, whether it is playing basketball, watching a movie, going bowling, playing a video game, or doing homework together. Similarly, adults working with groups of kids in Boy Scouts, 4-H Clubs, Boys &

Girls Clubs, and other programs spend much time immersed in various activities.

Men and youth often develop feelings for one another as they make decisions and share time together doing these activities. An unspoken behavioral rhythm sometimes surfaces, guiding the activity and generating an emotional tie. For example, shooting baskets together can involve turn-taking, tossing a ball back and forth, counting makes and misses as part of a friendly competition, playing a game of one-on-one, or paying attention while one person displays a skill. In addition, power sharing can enter the process as persons in a relationship make suggestions then decide what to do next.

For men and kids, especially boys, the activity sometimes comes to resemble a silent dance of human spirits. With the passing of time, a shared comfort, perhaps even silent intimacy, colors the joint participation in the activity. This quiet, behavioral intimacy is often found in the game of catch, as individuals, without ever touching, toss a ball back and forth.[2] The 1989 movie *Field of Dreams*, staring Kevin Costner, poignantly captured the nostalgic force that sharing ritual play can bring to the human bond. In recent years, another dance may have emerged in how some men and youth play video games together. Even though logistics may limit the number of men who actually play video games with kids outside their own family, and these games tend to be a more competitive experience than tossing a ball back and forth, the silent rhythm and emphasis on sharing time and space can still help mentors and kids solidify bonds. Several Big Brothers among the participants talk about how they enjoy spending time hanging out in their apartments playing video games with their Little Brothers, though a few confess that they should probably spend more time exposing their Little Brothers to the world outside of Xbox.

The physical touching aspects of behavioral activities can also be significant for men and youth. By sharing his detailed story about playing with his Little Brother, a Big Brother interviewed for a different study paints a delightful image.

We would play football, and it was just the two of us, but he liked to make it a game, so that . . . when he caught the ball, then I would have to get him. . . . This one time I like threw him the ball about ten yards away, or maybe more. So he catches the ball and starts taking off. So I take off after him. And actually a year ago, it was much more easy for me to catch him—he's gotten a lot faster to the point where we play now, I really have to like struggle. But anyway, I threw it to him, he was way out front, he started running and I started to come up from behind him and I could just hear him giggling, just like really,

really giggling hard. And I got him from behind and we like went down in a heap and all our limbs are just like flying all over each way, tangled up in each other. And when we got down we were both just like lying on the ground just like really laughing hard for a while, just laying there on the ground.[3]

This story conveys the power that play and unspoken expressions of bonding have in sustaining interpersonal relationships between adult men and kids. Without words, with just laughter, the game of pass and chase coupled with the ensuing tumble in the field allowed this pair to reinforce their friendship. The emotional energy resulting from the physical activity clearly reinforced their bond.

Emotional Expressions

Men in the United States find themselves in an awkward position when it comes to establishing bonds with youngsters and expressing their genuine concern for them. Homophobic fears, though apparently less pernicious than in recent decades, continue to hinder how many males relate to one another.[4] This pattern plagues relations between similarly aged males, fathers and sons, and unrelated men and boys. In general, males' reluctance to bear the stigma often attached to those perceived as being gay or gaylike discourages them from being more physically affectionate with one another. Although sports are increasingly accepting of coaches' and players' embracing one another without sanction in times of jubilation or defeat, these expressions are conditional. They are legitimized most clearly in the heat of manly competition or shortly thereafter.[5] Settings that bring men and kids together but are devoid of athletic competition are typically defined as less masculine.

Furthermore, the negative stereotype of the unscrupulous male pedophile can force men to curb their emotional expressions with boys and girls alike. Concerns about being accused of inappropriate, perhaps sexually abusive touching, can dissuade men from hugging or even showing minimal signs of physical affection toward boys and girls in various settings. Seldom does our culture celebrate images like former United States Women's Olympic coach Bela Karolyi sweeping the diminutive Kerri Strug into his arms after her remarkable vault on a badly injured ankle, winning a team gold medal in 1996. Although Karolyi, a native Romanian, regularly gives his pupils bear hugs after they complete their routines, male coaches seldom treat their young female athletes in such a physically affectionate manner. For example, Darnell, who coaches girls' basketball as well as boys', describes being extremely careful to avoid such demonstrative displays. In one respect, Bela's gesture at the Olympics and his fondness for bear hugging his pupils represent unwittingly defiant reactions against the norms that discourage such physical displays between grown men and unrelated girls. These emphatic physical expressions may be well-remembered, in part, because they are an obvious departure from how our culture expects men to express their emotions with youth (or even adults in many circumstances).

After sober reflection, and realizing that their behavior is risky in the public eye, some men still defy the cultural restrictions on men's display of physical affection toward young girls. Herman, an African American stepfather I interviewed a few years ago for another study, confirms that some men are willing to challenge how their gestures are interpreted, because the cultural and institutional constraints, while justifiable for some reasons, can cause emotional pain for the youth. Recalling his time as a counselor for female juveniles in a detention home, he says:

> They could come to me and they could sit there. And I know they wanted me to hug them. I'm not talking physically, sexually hug. They wanted an adult-to-child hug, a male-to-female adult-to-child hug—they wanted to be loved. Man, I could feel that. They just—man I could just feel them longing for a positive adult in their lives, a positive male adult that would just hug them.

Despite his female coworkers' warnings, Herman from time to time stepped beyond the institutionally defined borders of his interpersonal encounters with the girls he was counseling. In his mind, he was called by duty to do so, because the girls had no other positive male role model in their lives and they needed to see that adult men can express love in a safe, healthy way. Herman accentuated the value of these gestures toward the girls while redefining the meaning others might associate with it. As we saw earlier with the middle school teacher, Mariano, a small number of teachers are compelled to disregard public scrutiny and hug students they feel are in need of a supportive embrace.

Andre, the former police officer currently working as an administrator for a Boys & Girls Club, spoke passionately about his commitment to responding to many kids' need for physical attention in the form of hugs.

> Well, I know these kids are starved for attention, so I hug 'em all. All that wanna hug, I'm gonna hug 'em, and if someone says something, oh well, I can

do something else; if I get in trouble or whatever, I'll move on. I'm not gonna worry about it, 'cause I know how important it is, just that physical contact is, you know. They might not get it anywhere else. So a lot of times, for me to walk from here [the office] . . . to the front door might take ten minutes (laughs), because I gotta, if one of them gets a hug then they all want hugs. So you gotta be careful of—there's not that many teenage girls; . . . I might be a little more careful with, you know, 14-, 15-, 16-year-old girls—but with the little kids especially, I don't even think about it, I just do it.

Even though Andre is unable to spend much time interacting with kids directly, making it difficult to form strong bonds with individual kids, the brief hugging displays can signal to kids that one of the club leaders recognizes and appreciates them. From a child's perspective, the physical affirmation from a respected adult while in the company of the child's peers may constitute a meaningful marker of an emotional tie.

Unfortunately, societal concerns about adult males' potential misbehavior have cast a dark shadow over men's relations with children in a variety of organizational settings. The Boy Scouts of America, for instance, developed a detailed policy to protect youth from the unwanted advances of men while camping, and to protect the adults from false accusations.[6] One policy goes so far as to prohibit one-on-one contact between adults and youth members on trips and outings. The policy can be interpreted as a responsible, proactive step to protect young boys from the rare instance of adult abuse, but it unintentionally constrains the mentoring process. Although there is no explicit policy forbidding physical affection, the cultural climate of the Boy Scouts appears to discourage it. Yet, at the end of an evening when I attended a Boy Scout meeting, a few of the adult leaders and all members of the troop huddled in a circle. Those who wanted to share a special saying, poem, aphorism, or whatever could do so. After that, Jeff, the scout master, asked that the brightest lights be turned off in the semimodernized log cabin. They recited something from the Boy Scout oath and placed their right hand on the left shoulder of the person to their right and then the left hand on the right shoulder of the person to the left. Later, Jeff mentioned that this is a common way of expressing fellowship. In some respects, the group ritual, with its physical bonding component, is not unlike what commonly takes place with athletic teams.

Boy Scouts culture has also been affected by the explicit and controversial policy excluding as members and leaders youth and men who are homosexual. Although the motivation for the sexual orientation policy can be viewed separately from the policy prohibiting unsupervised one-on-one interaction, both policies are perceived by some as "protecting" young boys from either abuse or immoral conduct that may originate from primarily male leaders.

The Boy Scouts' approach stands in stark contrast to the Big Brothers Big Sisters philosophy, which encourages mentors to carve out opportunities to have one-on-one time with the child and not to discriminate on the basis of sexual orientation. During their training, Big Brothers are discouraged from getting too involved with the child's family. Rather, the adult mentors are encouraged to focus their social and emotional support on the individual boy himself. The organization celebrates the power of the one-on-one mentoring relationship, meeting the needs for protection of the youth by means of in-house training and modest oversight.

Cognitive Expressions

For many men, one of the most comfortable ways to interact with kids involves their doing a task requiring them to communicate ideas or instructions about how something can be accomplished (e.g., helping with homework, building a mechanical device, teaching an athletic skill). Sometimes it is the kid who assumes the teacher role and instructs the adult (e.g., playing a video or board game). In either form, cognitive work connected to a specific activity can be a very successful source of bonding, and it is often interlaced with emotional and spiritual expressions as well. Though a man and child may undertake a task in a matter-of-fact way, the flow of the activity can provide them the emotional space to have an intimate talk. Thus, what began as a mundane shared activity is transformed by a dose of emotional energy.

Alan and Dwight both value the time they've spent teaching kids basic carpentry and painting skills when they've been supervising kids working on community projects. Each feels that these informal teaching experiences enhance their relationships with the kids. One of the biggest joys for Dwight occurred when he got involved with a residential facility for females who have recently been released from prison. Using his carpentry and painting skills, he organized some of the kids at his alternative school to help renovate a house for the facility in a nearby neighborhood. He was incredibly moved by the kids' volunteer spirit once they got started, seeing it as a beautiful thing. Although some kids were reluctant to do volunteer work, after they got going, many enjoyed it and would even ask Dwight enthusiastically when they were next going to go over to the house and work. The kids took a lot of pride in helping others and in their handiwork. Dwight was able to teach them practical skills they could take with them once they left school. By working with the kids on such a project, Dwight tries to inspire them to develop a desire to give back to the community. He wants them to think beyond themselves, and if that happens, he feels he is accomplishing something. In his mind, Dwight was able to pull something out of the kids without their even knowing they had it inside them. By helping kids in this way, Dwight takes them on a kind of self-discovery venture.

Spiritual Expressions

Men of faith often promote a related venture for kids. Many times, the overriding purpose of men's interaction with kids is to inculcate in them particular religious convictions and values. During the past century, women have probably devoted more time to children in faith-based teaching environments than have men, but these settings provide men ample opportunities to form interpersonal bonds with youngsters. Although the fact that these relationships can sometimes turn abusive grabbed extensive media coverage with the revelations of gross misconduct by Catholic priests, the much more numerous and seldom-publicized instances of male religious leaders building bonds with youth should be celebrated. To the extent that men are involved in these organizations and related programs, they increasingly will have unique opportunities to reach out to kids and establish meaningful relationships grounded in shared religious beliefs. The youth ministers I interviewed are clearly devoting lots of time and energy trying to offer youth life lessons about compassion, discipline, and self-respect.

RITUALS

One way to think about how the behavioral, emotional, cognitive, and spiritual aspects of bonds are expressed and intertwined is to look closely at culture, in particular, situations' ritual qualities. Because the world is socially constructed, sociologist Ann Swidler suggests that culture is best viewed as a tool kit filled with what she calls "symbolic forms."[7] These cultural tools are resources that enable people to express emotion and meaning in their lives. Rituals, a form of patterned social activity, are central to this view. Men and youth use rituals to form and sustain certain types of social bonds with one another. The social activities are symbolic of how we value special relationships. Although formal and informal rituals are central to how fathers bond with their children, rituals are also part of the social bonds developed between men and unrelated youth. They are occasions in which men and young people can have fun, develop individual and interpersonal skills, and build a sense of self-confidence.

Some rituals are an established feature of how an organization accomplishes specific tasks, such as teachers' imparting knowledge, coaches' honing players' skills, and religious leaders' training their young followers to understand and put into practice particular faith beliefs. The norms and memories collectively shared by the participants in these settings help perpetuate the rituals. Other rituals are more casual in nature, stylized routines of everyday life that people craft and share. For Ron and his Little Brother, Sunday afternoons have come to mean time together playing video games, going to a movie, or doing some other shared activity. Although rituals, either formal or informal, can occur in one-on-one settings, most formal rituals involve groups. This holds true for men's activities with kids.

Generally speaking, rituals provide an emotional bonding experience and a chance to experience a sense of group membership and belonging.[8] Membership may be to a formal group, say, a sports team or neighborhood Boys & Girls Club, or simply a friendship. Examples of activities that solidify the bonds men and youth form and which may become ritualized, include team sports, activities as part of a Boy Scout function, a summer camp activity, sharing a winter hunting cabin, spending Wednesday afternoons in a tutoring session at school, and attending the Jewish bar and bat mitzvah training. Men and youth can each enjoy these activities and feel more connected to the group because they participated. For Big Brothers and Little Brothers, participating in a group constitutes having a clearly defined one-on-one friendship. Several Big Brothers confirmed how their shared activities had fostered their pride in creating a paired identity. The Big Brothers also noted that the boys had said things to their mothers and teachers that conveyed how special it made them feel to have a Big Brother.

Men sometimes create rituals, either deliberately or out of habit, that communicate particular messages to kids while providing them opportunities to grow. The messages may influence the nature of the bonds kids develop with one another and with the men in charge. For example, organizing a soccer league as an all-boy, all-girl, or mixed-gender arrangement can influence boys' and girls' experiences. In an all-boy league, masculinity themes may be featured more prominently, such that the boys are more apt to identify with their coach(es) as a man among males. Through their actions and talk, the coach and players may remind each other of their shared identity as males, with the boys looking to the man for guidance in constructing their own sense of masculinity.

Masculinity themes may be displayed less consciously when a man coaches girls in an all-girls league as compared to a mixed league. In an all-girls league, girls will probably define their relationship with the coach as girls, rather than as "not boys." In a mixed league, boys will be exposed to adult men as they instruct, encourage, judge, and discipline girls as well as boys in a competitive sports environment. Observing those exchanges may affect how the boys perceive and treat girls and may influence how they relate to the coach, who may be less likely to stress masculinity norms in his interactions with his players than he would in an all-boys league.

Rites of passage are a specific, and relatively rare, subset of rituals that help young persons make the transition from one phase of life to another, in most cases from adolescence to adulthood. Take the example of bar and bat mitzvah for Jewish boys and girls. A rabbi and other male (and sometimes female) religious figures play significant roles in the time-honored ritual, viewed by many as an adolescent's symbolic transformation from child to adult in the eyes of the Jewish community. Though practices vary, men often provide Jewish kids intensive instruction in the faith and in Hebrew as preparation for this cherished ritual. Unlike most rabbis, though, Jacob tries to downplay the bar mitzvah experience because he does not want kids to see it as the ultimate moment in their Jewish life but as "only one step of many steps that they take in their life." He adds:

> I like it to be focused on a sense of achievement and involvement in the religious community as opposed to what it becomes in many places, in most places really, . . . a rite of passage because you become 13, like a sweet 16 party.

Part of Jacob's novel rabbinical approach is developing more long-term relationships with the kids by getting to know them once they start attending religious school on Sundays. Unlike most rabbis, he personally attends the preparation sessions and leads the students in prayer while sitting on the floor. He also regularly visits the other Sunday school classes. Having been involved almost continuously with Sunday school teaching since he was 15 years old, Jacob feels at home in this setting. So, even though he deemphasizes the bar mitzvah ritual as a rite of passage, he stresses the bonding opportunities that arise from the weekly rituals he and the kids participate in on Sunday mornings.

In a more secular context, rites of passage have been much discussed because of their implications for how men relate to boys. Some writers in recent decades, like poet Robert Bly, have expressed considerable concern about adolescent boys' lack of exposure to well-articulated rites of passage.[9] Bly laments that the indus-

trial age has stripped young boys of valuable opportunities to mingle construc-
tively with male elders, and he points out that Western societies have few rituals
to assist boys in their transition from boyhood to manhood. He asserts that boys
today are far less likely to be involved in male-run hunting parties or to share
work with older men on farms or elsewhere. For Bly, many problems boys face
today can be traced to the way Western industrialized cultures have largely abandoned boys in their quest for manhood. He sees men as having shirked their responsibility for initiating young males into adulthood. A number of feminist
writers have adeptly challenged Bly's misguided historical analysis of boys' troubles and faulty assessment of the contemporary "soft male."[10] But his sense that
rituals and rites of passage are valuable still resonates with some who believe
that men can do more to help young boys manage their transition to responsible
manhood.

A compelling question will need to be addressed: How can men responsibly
use cultural practices to guide youth through adolescence while promoting gender equity for boys and girls? Few would disagree that contemporary youth can
benefit from establishing healthy relationships with adults other than their parents during their journey from childhood to adulthood. Whether instituting
gender-oriented rites of passage, as are found in various nonwestern cultures, is
the answer is another matter.[11] Moreover, because women with adequate resources are quite capable of rearing healthy, well-adjusted boys and girls, it is an
open question whether male youth workers tend to make unique contributions
relative to what women offer in rites of passage.

Anthropologist David Gilmore describes a wide range of physically demanding rituals peoples around the world practice to test boys' initial claim to adult
male status. Although the specifics of these transition-to-manhood rituals vary
among societies, they often entail adolescent boys' being subjected to painful
bloodletting practices involving circumcision, whippings, or scarring. A common
feature of these rites of passage is that male elders play a prominent role in coor-
dinating and overseeing the ritual. Thus, older males, including male relatives in
some cases, are essential to male youths' quest for masculine standing within the
community. Male youth and the male elders of the community may establish a
close bond with the youths based on behavioral, emotional, cognitive, and spiritual ties. Meanwhile, the male elders have little, if any, role to play in activities that
help adolescent girls transition to womanhood. Where there are equivalent rituals for the girls, they are overseen by adult women in the community.

In the United States, interest in less physically gruesome rites of passage rituals is found among African Americans who promote the benefits of all-male

black schools. Although these schools have received mixed reviews from African American and other leaders, they have received a fair amount of support.[12] To varying degrees, these schools follow an Afrocentric curriculum designed to provide young boys with manhood training. A small but significant number of schools throughout the country have experimented with different versions of African-style rites of passage, to encourage African American boys to rethink their identity as black males in contemporary society. According to Richard Majors, cofounder of the National Council of African American Men, these programs teach some or all of the following:

> African history and culture; appropriate roles for fathers, husbands, brothers, and sons; respect for elder people; how to develop positive male/female relationships and adopt appropriate sexual roles; how to make positive contributions to one's family and community; and how to resist peer pressure and to make personal decisions.[13]

Notice that a premium is placed on encouraging young African American males to develop healthy ways of relating to others. Once the students finish the assigned activities, exercises, and tasks, they are eligible to participate in an African-style rite of passage ceremony that takes on different forms, in which drumming and the wearing of African garb are commonplace.

An important aspect of these programs is the emphasis on incorporating African American men into the education process as teachers within the schools or as mentors who serve as a bridge to the community and workplace. The rationale is to provide the primarily urban African American boys, many of whom lack the active presence of a father in their lives, opportunities to establish meaningful bonds and rituals with successful black men, ideally ones with established roots in the local community.

MANAGING BORDERS WITH KIDS AND PARENTS

As they build relationships, participate in rituals, and manage youths' behavior, men must negotiate interpersonal borders between them and the kids. How do men want the youngsters with whom they work or volunteer to perceive them? Do they want to be seen only as an authority figure, or are they comfortable sharing some type of friendship with kids as well? And if friendship is possible, what type of friendship? How should they spend time with the kids? What types of issues are men willing to discuss with children, with adolescents? Are they willing to let kids talk to them about personal matters in confidence, or do they sometimes feel compelled to tell the kids' parents about something the child has revealed? Prior to making decisions involving a child, to what extent do men consult the child's parents or take them into account?

It appears that a man's personality, personal history with kids, and aspects of the specific setting shape how he orients himself toward youth. Compared to reserved men, those who are gregarious and high energy appear more willing to explore the possibility of developing a closer bond with kids. Those with a history of keeping in touch with kids who have since moved on may be more apt to think that building a friendship is possible. Being a Big Brother is predicated on forming a one-to-one mentoring relationship with a boy, whereas Boy Scouting deemphasizes one-on-one relationships and it would not be appropriate for a probation officer to anticipate or strive to develop a genuine friendship with a kid on probation.

The way some men manage their relations with kids is anchored in those men's perceptions of how parents think children (and parents) should be treated. But how and to what extent does it matter to men that they have responsibilities for other people's children? More specifically, how much do they take into account parental authority and preferences when working with kids in diverse settings, including those settings where kids have little or no contact with their parents? Finally, how do men juggle the potentially competing interests of kids and parents in situations where those interests seem to clash?

Because I generally didn't ask the men I interviewed to comment on what they thought parents expected of them, my understanding of the men's views is pieced together from remarks they made as they told stories about their interactions with parents. The men varied considerably in how much contact they had with parents and how much thought they had given to how the parents affected their interactions with kids.

Scott, a Boys & Girls Club director, provides one example of acknowledging parents' perspective: "Their most prized possession is their child, and yeah, I understand that it's the most important thing in the world to them most of the time, and, I'm gonna find out what kind of things . . . they want to go on." Scott believes parents may have constructive ideas that can help him provide a more positive experience for their kids at the club. Tony, speaking of why he and his friends valued the responsibility during their teen years of being soccer coaches for young kids in a recreational league, offers another rendition of a man's sensitivity to the parental perspective: "The fact that . . . these parents were allowing us to work with their kids, and . . . teach them, whether it was lessons about sports, or just being fair on the field, and whatever." Because Tony regularly saw the parents at games, practices, and picnics, he implicitly was reminded that the parents were entrusting their kids to him and his buddies, assuming all the time that they were good role models. My sense is that those men who have the most contact with parents tend to appreciate most the idea that parents place faith in them to take good care of their children.

Yet, because youth work takes on many forms with diverse objectives, it is to be expected that men process differently parents' input about the men's relationships with their kids and certain decisions they make affecting the youths. Andrew's description of his coaching experience highlights a few competing ways men react to parents. Commenting on one way he used to take his cue from parents to determine how he interacted with young kids on his basketball teams, Andrew says:

> If the parents were very cold and stiff, I would typically not be as physical or touchy as with a kid that I saw parents hugging and so forth. [With the latter,] I was probably more intuitive, and I would tend to feel more comfortable, being more, um, tactile, that's the word, touching and grabbing and so forth.

But when deciding how he should talk about a player's abilities or make decisions about a player's participation on the team, Andrew resists parents' persuasion:

> Typically, parents have a biased view of their child's skills and so forth. I worked very hard to be very, very honest with parents. . . . I've seen in the past some coaches or teachers tell the parents what they want to hear. And I can be gentle but . . . if somebody asks me a question about why Johnny isn't playing or what do you think of Johnny as a player, I'll give a very honest answer. And many times, a couple of parents didn't really like the feedback that I gave. So I don't want my behavior to be modified . . . how I treat the kids, because somebody's parents [are] there. Could be a prestigious parent or important parent or a rich parent or a parent who's a real pain and you don't want to get him upset; again I was pretty defiant that I was going to treat the kids as I was going to treat the kids, irrespective of parental desires.

Being fair to his players is the central issue for Andrew, so he asserts his moral authority to make decisions about other people's kids that may not sit well with the parents. The compelling question of how much moral or practical authority men have when directing the activities of other people's children is relevant to school teachers, juvenile detention officers, youth ministers, childcare workers, and men in other positions involving youth.

Of particular interest to how youth workers manage interpersonal borders with kids and with their parents is how men perceive norms of discretion regarding private talks with kids. When and why do men feel obligated to keep kids' secrets or share what they've learned with parents, guardians, or authorities? In Chapter 7, I explore men's willingness to build social capital for kids indirectly by being an ally to parents. In the final chapter, I revisit this general topic by describing how men's candid commentary about parental shortcomings can shape initiatives to enhance men's youth work.

As we saw earlier, men often strive to gain youth's trust; they want kids to feel comfortable confiding in them and seeking guidance on personal issues. Acting as an adult confidant has its benefits for kids, but men often realize they have obligations as well to keep parents informed about their child's experiences, especially when they involve serious issues. Most men recognize this as a sensitive matter and feel they handle it reasonably well. Charles, the director of a neighborhood Boys & Girls Club serving African Americans almost exclusively, reports that youth as well as parents often confide in him. He appears to take these conversations seriously.

> I mean, it's private. And unless they give me permission to share, I don't share, because in our community, and in our race, if you ever breach that trust, you not only lost that person, but you lost that entire community. And I would not dare risk, I would not gamble that. You know, integrity is more important to me than anything else.

When he's struggling with how to deal with sensitive disclosures about drugs, sex, and the like, Charles says:

> I talk with them [the kids] and ask, "Look, would you like for me to find you some other help?" And at that time, if they say yea, then I do what . . . you know. And there's also policies and procedures on different things. Now if there's something that happened to a kid . . . something beyond abuse or to the point where they're gonna be hurt, or harmed in any way, any danger, then I have an obligation to call abuse or call Children and Families [government protective agency]. And I have made that call. Those are difficult calls, because in our culture, family is so important, family continuity, and being together as a family. And sometimes these kids have to be separated from family.

Under the most dreaded circumstances, Charles feels compelled to confront the issue head-on even if it means disrupting a child's life.

On a less serious note, the youth minister Ben describes how he initially had a candid chat with a teenage girl frustrated by what she perceived to be her domineering mother's attempts to choose her friends. He then spontaneously raised the issue in private with the mother soon thereafter, allowing her to talk about her fears that her daughter hated her. Ben also mentions having suspicions that some girls in his congregation were struggling with eating disorders and deciding to give a general talk about the subject to a support group of parents, including the girls' mothers. Without naming the girls, he was able to raise parents' awareness of the issue. In both instances, Ben chose to share information in order to help kids and parents while trying to protect privacy, to ensure that others view him as a man of integrity.

Another youth minister, Carlos, expresses his desire to be a trustworthy and supportive faith advisor and confidant to his young parishioners. In those instances when abuse is present, he acts decisively to protect the child, in other situations he struggles to find a way to help the kid without alienating him or her from the parent(s). He explains:

> If it's a lifestyle thing, and it's just, dysfunction in a parent, what I always try
> to do, is I never want to turn a kid against his mom and dad, even if it's a
> bad situation, so I always protect the parent as best I can. I never want to
> just jump on a kid's bandwagon and say, "Yeah, your parents, your dad and
> mom, they are jerks," you know [laughs]. I don't want to ever do that; they
> feel bad enough. I always want to try to enforce what the Bible says, to
> honor your mother and father. Now, honoring them doesn't mean that you
> fully support or take everything that they dish out; it means just having a
> right attitude towards them. And that's what I try to put in the young peo-
> ple. It's like, "Hey, yeah, your mom might be a lush, a drunk, but man, just
> honor her. You know, don't . . . allow yourself to hate them and, and develop
> a negative mindset. Try to see, man, your mom's probably like that 'cause of
> something she went through as a kid."

As men like Carlos gain more experience working with kids and their parents, they tend to grow more comfortable negotiating delicate situations in which they try to balance the youth's best interests with those of the parents.

Not surprisingly, as we look specifically and more closely at men's relations with kids, what we find in real life is that different men manage those relationships quite differently. Some, like Frank, are more apt to keep their distance. He describes in a matter-of-fact way how he relates to kids at the Boys & Girls Club: "I don't try to connect with them; I just be me, that's my approach. I believe in being firm and being fair." Later, he adds:

> I don't try to be everybody['s] friend; I never been like that. . . . Because, you know, you'll go wrong if you try to be everybody['s] friend, especially kids, because then when you want to get tough and discipline them, then they gonna think that you just joking or you playing, so it's good to keep a difference, you know, a boundary, on what you're allowed to be doing and what you won't allow them to do.

Whereas Frank is careful to keep kids at arm's length, Mark, who mentors several young men, is more inclined to work at developing a strong friendship that covers not only mentoring about school and work but casual talk, sometimes over a meal. But Mark asserts that he also has limits. Although he is willing to buy college books, pay for eye exams, and chat about many topics, he doesn't want kids to approach him in certain ways. In his words, "Their ultra private lives are theirs, and if there's anything they want to share with me as far as go buy me some beer or did you get laid last night or whatever, we just don't even go there." Despite his giving nature and willingness to go to great lengths to help kids succeed, he sets his boundaries and is not afraid to be candid with the young men he mentors. Mark illustrates his perspective by describing how he responded to one kid who tried to tell him how he "chewed out" the police officer who had his car towed:

> so when he started to tell me about what he said, I said, "You know what, guess what, I don't want to hear that shit. I don't want to hear it. I'm promoting you as a positive college kid, intelligent, with it; and so all the gangster punk stuff, you just save it for somebody else, because I don't want to hear it."

Although Mark never explicitly describes himself as a friend to any of the boys he has mentioned, some of the aspects of friendship are present. By contrast, Ben, in his capacity as a youth minister, uses the language of friendship to capture some of his experiences with his young parishioners. He initially describes his relationship with kids by alluding to how he has been willing to allow kids to see him in a different light away from the church and his formal attire. Ben talks about the kids spending time with him side by side on a working mission trip refurbishing people's homes in another state.

When they see me here [at church], I'm often times still dressed up. And it's inter-
esting just how much [effect] dress can have as far as their interpretation of me
goes. . . . They see me in my robe, but then in group, you know I'm always very—
I speak like this, you know I'm casual, I'm off the cuff, I say stupid things a lot. So
they know my personality, but when they were living with me for a week, they see
me in shorts and covered in paint and dirt and dust and, you know, acting a fool
with the rest of 'em, it equalizes us again. And it creates what I attempt to estab-
lish in the beginning of the year with my adult volunteers, a faithful adult friend.
Faithful in that they know much of the context of the church. I'm an adult, I'm
not their parent, but I am a grown-up, and I'm their friend.

In addition to describing his goal of becoming a "faithful adult friend" to kids in
his youth ministry, Ben goes further and explains how the family demographics
of the kids affect his perspective of what the kids need from him.

The boys I see, in my opinion, often times need more of a male role model, a
friend, you know a buddy, and someone to tell them what it means to be a
man. Because a lot of these guys are living just with their moms and assume
too much and can be real arrogant jerks as a result. And the girls, it's just a
matter of trying to be a positive example of what a man is or what a man can
be, through the example of me being a father to my kids. But also as being
someone who is not going to sexualize them or do anything that would estab-
lish failure or the concept of . . . them being a lesser than. Again pushing that
underlying theme of total equality for everyone.

It appears, then, that Ben has a much more fluid interpretation of the interpersonal borders that differentiate him from the kids. Even though he recognizes
that he is the adult in charge, he stresses equality as much as possible. With this
perspective guiding him, Ben is willing to talk to kids about his personal life, including his youthful indiscretions, if he feels that doing so will enable him to direct a kid to make healthy decisions.

Whether the men want the kids to consider them friends or not, most want
kids to feel comfortable enough to approach them with some of their problems.
Although some men may be a bit hesitant to deal with the kids' personal issues,
many want to appear accessible and willing to help. They want to make a difference in kids' lives.

Clearly, men can affect young people's development through the bonds they
establish while relating to them. Men's orientation to youths continues to be affected by the structural features of our patriarchal and postindustrial society

which are perpetuated in both blatant and subtle ways: homophobia, a gender-segregated labor market with dramatic pay differentials for "women's" work involving children, impoverished and dangerous inner-city urban areas, a corporate culture that is neither family- nor father-friendly, and media-generated negative images of men as exploiters of children. These and other social conditions shape the messages men receive as boys. As we saw in Chapter 4, experiences during the formative years, though by no means a sign of destiny, can influence men's motivation for and style of interacting with kids. Consequently, men's opportunities and approach to building bonds with youths can be traced, in part, to their own childhoods and how they came to define their life priorities, their approach to caregiving, and their views of children and adolescents. Being mindful of those early experiences can help men as they try to make a difference in kids' lives.

CHAPTER 6

MANAGING KIDS

"So, this is what 'scruffin'' looks like," I thought to myself as I stepped through the back door of the community center that housed a special program for boys and onto a grassy area late one afternoon in early May. There, in 90-degree heat and under sunny skies, I saw several at-risk teenage boys doing jumping jacks in unison. A staff member firmly directed the boys in their exercises while lecturing them about the value of projecting a positive attitude and respecting others. The boys were being disciplined, apparently because they were disrespectful to their peers and staff. Over the next few hours I saw several other boys escorted to this area and told to do push-ups, sit-ups, and other exercises because they had misbehaved. One boy was "asked" to carry a thick, heavy log back and forth along a sidewalk. The kids seemed familiar with the routine, complying without vocal or visible complaint. Aside from the log-carrying "exercise," the activities were comparable in style to, though less intense than, workouts my coaches and PE instructors had put me through in years past. The male staff appeared intent on using the method, unconventional for youth work settings, to send a message to the boys that undesirable consequences would follow if they were disrespectful and uncooperative.

I had anticipated seeing the staff apply the "scruffing" or "smoking" technique because I had heard Derek enthusiastically label and describe his program's paramilitary philosophy when I interviewed him the previous summer. With parents' written permission, Derek and other staff are free to apply this technique to boys who get out of line. Derek jokingly comments, "me being [ex]army helps out. . . . I know exactly how a drill sergeant scruffs and how to . . .

motivate a guy. . . . I can hurt you without putting my hands on you." He continues, saying:

> Basically, wherever they mess up, that's where we get 'em. If they mess up at
> home, and we have to come out to their house, basically we smoke them right
> there at their house. Like I said, we even smoked a guy in his front yard before,
> and the neighbors'd come out with lawn chairs and clap their hands, and eat
> popcorn, thinkin' it's a matinee or something. So it's basically just physical ac-
> tivity, kinda get them tired, get their mind right, and of course we talk to them
> afterwards and see how we can avoid this problem again.

Derek's description accurately depicts much of what I saw months later on that May afternoon. The scruffing experience is designed to shame kids into recognizing that they have done something wrong. In addition, it is supposed to force kids to reflect on their misbehavior and to think about how they can treat others with more respect in the future. Though currently a staple of a larger program targeting at-risk boys, the technique, Derek believes, may be dropped or altered drastically in the near future because of the tragic incident that occurred at the juvenile boot camp in Panama City, Florida, in early January 2006. Although the exact cause of death was contested, a 14-year-old boy died one day after being roughed up by guards for being uncooperative; he was then given ammonia capsules to keep him conscious—a scene captured on videotape.[1]

Scruffing is one of the many strategies men use to manage and direct kids' thinking and behavior. Some strategies are implemented before any bad behavior, while others are used after a misstep. In general, much can be learned about men's orientation toward youth by studying the ways they work with kids, including kids who pose special challenges due to their disruptive behavior. We saw in the previous chapter how several themes colored what men had to say about the way they related to youth, including their efforts at leveling; inviting comfort, contact, and trust; using touch; expressing bonds; and engaging in rituals. Admittedly, it is often difficult to distinguish between what passes as relating to youths versus managing them. But whether in relating to or managing kids, men's efforts reveal a common desire to make a positive difference in kids' lives.

Looking closely at how men manage kids, we must also consider the diversity of circumstances in which men interact with youth. A man's tactics for managing a youth in a one-on-one mentoring relationship may be quite different from what he uses when dealing with a large group of kids. Whether the mentoring is formal or informal may affect a man's approach, as will aspects of the groups themselves. Someone working with at-risk kids in an alternative high school or diversion program for juvenile offenders may see his work situation quite differently than does a man teaching kids in a regular school setting or coaching an athletic team. The most important element is whether or not the kids are participating in the activity by choice; this affects how both the men and the kids perceive the situation and treat each other. The extent to which a man's involvement with kids includes his interactions with parents and other authority figures can affect how he tries to coordinate his involvement with particular kids. A man who has personal experience relevant to working with kids in a particular setting is likely to deal with kids differently than someone new to the setting. Finally, the age and gender of the young people may lead a man to practice his youth work differently.

Men with extensive experience doing youth work with boys as well as girls tend to see gender differences in the intensity of the challenges kids confront, their personalities, and how they behave. Numerous men recognize that girls face some distinct and difficult circumstances—experiences rooted in the male-dominated social structure and gender norms. Extrapolating from his experience as director of a Boys & Girls Club located in a low-income neighborhood, Charles explains:

> Girls face a lot of the same challenges as the boys, but I think they have it harder. . . . They face challenges such as rape, and they have challenges of abuse, and society kind of pushes it under the carpet. And they kinda—a boy's only gonna be abused for so long before he stands up and fights back. Sometimes girls go through these things, and they feel like . . . everybody treats them like they were wrong. And even though they were the victim, people say, "Oh, you caused it . . . yourself," or they have to hold stuff in and can't express themselves about it, because they feel like they're gonna be judged. I have some young ladies that are members of this club, they've been victims of rape by their mama's boyfriend. And they try to tell mom, and mom says, "Oh, you're lying. He would never do that" or "You're just fast; you really want him or you don't want me to be with him," because that's mama's hang-up of trying to cling on because she doesn't want to lose another man.

Continuing, Charles emphasizes how some young girls confront the day-to-day challenges of raising their own children and many others are given extensive household duties by the adults responsible for them.

These girls, they carry that around every day, you know, with the peer pressure of being teen moms . . . haven't even developed the parenting skills but now they're thrust into parenthood. . . . We ask them when they leave . . . their communities, to go to school or to participate in youth groups, to be a child. But then when they come home, the families, or the lack of family, thrusts them into the role of being an adult. . . . Once you cross that threshold of adulthood, how do you turn that off? How do you learn to be a child and en-joy child things when your mom is telling you, "You need to get a job, you need to help with these bills around here" or "You need to take care of these kids, or you need to cook dinner" or "It's not important for you to go there, because I need you to do this." So now a kid's set up in a situation where they have to be an adult at home. So, I mean, that's a big challenge. You send them into every other aspect of their lives and they're expected to be a child and be submissive, and to be respectful of adults and authority, and learn this and learn that, but then back at home they're playing the role of an adult.

Charles's distress about what's happening to some of the girls he works with reflects in part the idealistic notion that childhood should be a sacred and protected developmental period with limited family responsibilities. In ad-dition, even though significant household responsibilities are sometimes thrust onto boys, Charles and other men tend to believe that girls are more of-ten subjected to these demands, particularly in families with limited re-sources.

Consistent with popular stereotypes and the developmental literature, men tend to perceive girls, compared to boys, as being more mature, future-oriented, relationship-focused, cooperative, better listeners, and emotionally sensitive—particularly in response to critical comments. As a result, some men find themselves treating boys and girls a bit differently. Overall, my sense is that the men tend to believe they have an easier time relating to boys on a masculine, activity-oriented level. But they also have a more difficult time managing boys, whom they perceive to be more confrontational and not as communicative at times.

Referring to the kids he works with at his alternative high school, Dwight says:

dealing with the boys, usually I'm a little bit more firm . . . , at least starting out, until you get a grip on what's going on. . . . Girls, I guess [I] give them a little more slack sometimes, just because I don't really fully understand all that may be going on with them in their lives.

Dwight speaks for numerous men involved with young and older teenagers who admit they assert a firmer, stricter approach when dealing with boys. Their rationale is based in part on perceiving boys as being more disruptive, in greater need of discipline, and more willing to test authority than girls. So too, men believe that girls are less likely to respond well if they use a firm approach. After declaring that as a coach and student counselor he tends to treat boys and girls similarly, Steve confesses, "I can't imagine yelling at a girl like I do some of my players, because if a girl ever started crying, I would just be, you know, I'm sorry. [Laughs.] I couldn't take it." Steve suspects that part of his fear of girls' reactions stems from his lack of experience raising a daughter.

Additionally, men's concerns about public scrutiny and being the target for false accusations prompts some to be more careful around girls. Usually this means avoiding certain types of situations completely or at least altering their behavior. Kevin, because his church stresses that males should largely provide ministerial care to boys while women should do the same for girls, and because of his own common sense understanding of people's perceptions of relationships, says: "I'm probably closer to the guys, just 'cause it's easier for me to, you know, I can take a guy out to lunch, say, 'Hey, let's go have lunch.' . . . I'm not gonna take a, a 17-year-old girl out to lunch. I just, you know, I think it's inappropriate." As a result, Kevin refrains from providing girls with the same type of activity-based, one-on-one talk time. He recognizes that he is less accessible to girls, but he does not see this as a problem, because the female religious leaders at the church can reach out and be available to the girls.

Some men are particularly cautious around girls in settings with a high proportion of at-risk youth. Nick, for example, referring to his job working with troubled youth in a residential facility remarks: "A lot of these kids been sexually abused, so a hug to them can mean something different . . . especially with the females. You don't wanna ever put yourself in that predicament, to hug one of these females." Given his concerns about girls' abuse histories and their possible reactions to his innocent gestures, Nick curtails using playful or affectionate touch to bond with girls.

Nick's comments highlight men's heightened vigilance around girls, which is generated either by worries about public scrutiny or a desire to protect the girls' emotional state. In the latter case, heterosexual men typically want to avoid misleading teenage girls they believe to be susceptible to developing romantic crushes or emotional longings for a father figure.

With a few exceptions, men's management of their interpersonal borders with girls includes distancing themselves from issues pertaining to girls' bodies, particularly menstruation. A number of the men immediately call upon female coworkers, whether in schools, camps, or church settings, to help with such "girl issues" when they arise. Men's typical awkward reaction probably parallels most girls' feeling more comfortable seeking advice from a woman about these matters. If men are insensitive to girls' emotions and deal poorly with questions about menstruation, they might cause girls to feel ashamed or to view their bodies as dirty. This outcome could be accentuated in coach-athlete relationships in which men are responsible for training girls' bodies. For many men, the roots of their discomfort can be traced back to early experiences with the boy code and the informal lesson to disdain anything feminine or having to do with girls. Boys' inability or unwillingness to deal with aspects of femininity as youth can resurface later to affect adult men's reactions to girls. Some male coaches and other men whose youth work involves girls are able to convey a comfortable attitude that allows some girls to talk to them about these subjects.[2]

Although the men clearly adjust their behavior by gender in some settings, only a few describe a dramatic difference in how they treat boys and girls. Some do assert, as we saw with Ben in the previous chapter, that their approach to boys is shaped in part by their knowledge that many boys need a "male role model" or "a buddy," whereas girls are more likely to be seeking a surrogate father.

With this in mind, I illustrate how men define their relationships with youth and why, therefore, they try to help youth. In addition to the various ways men relate to kids mentioned earlier, the men share accounts of how they orient themselves toward kids in their work and volunteering. Letting kids know they matter, making an effort to be candid and honest, and being ready to respond in useful ways help men define their approach to managing kids.

LETTING KIDS KNOW THEY MATTER

In recent years, the parent-education industry repeatedly has advised parents to let their children know explicitly that they love and care about them. The message is consistent with research showing that parents who are emotionally supportive and actively monitor their children tend to raise kids who are better-adjusted and more successful.[3] A similar logic seems to apply to men's work with unrelated kids. Some men believe it is critical for youth to realize that the adults care about them and have their best interests at heart. Presumably, kids want to feel as though they matter and are valued.

Because I did not interview the kids, I can only speculate on how they feel about the men's involvement. Having heard the men's stories and seen some of them interact with kids, I believe that many of the kids are aware that the men are trying to help them. Some of the kids, of course, may be annoyed at the time with what the men expect of them and how they are treated. However, as personal experience reminds us all, the passage of time and maturity often usher in a new perspective. We come to value more deeply what others were trying to do for us when we were much younger. So, even some of the youth who were not particularly pleased with how the men treated them at the time may learn later in life to cherish the attention they received as kids.

Nick, reflecting on his delinquent adolescent years, has fond memories of how a police officer who walked a beat in his childhood neighborhood counseled him one-on-one and advocated for him in the courts. He says, the man

> snatched me off the streets at a very early age. Basically, it was because of him that I went to a program that I went to. He seen something in me that I guess I didn't see in myself that was worth saving. And, what he did was . . . he went to court with me. My parents never showed up to court. . . . He pretty much pleaded my case in front of the judge, said basically if something wouldn't happen for me at that time, I'd probably end up dead or hurting somebody, doing something that I wouldn't be able to reverse. So, the judge put me in a program in Pennsylvania and I was there for four years.

Continuing, Nick explains how this man took a special interest in him, going beyond the call of duty trying to turn him toward a different life course.

> He'd come by the house, make sure I was okay. . . . I mean, actually, he took a lot of his personal time and, I think, made sure I wasn't on the street, and if I was he would direct me back to where I should be. And, like I said, I think about him every now and then, I was talking . . . about him to the kids the other day, how people influence your life, that you don't even realize it until way into your life when you look back and, you know, reflect in your life and you see certain steps and certain things that . . . really makes your life what it is today.

Given Nick's abusive home life, the detention center, though problematic in its own right, may have been the best option available to him. Had the police officer not intervened, Nick may have ended up dead or in prison for a long time. Although it appears that Nick's deep appreciation for what the man did for him emerged only with the benefit of hindsight, the officer's caring nature left a lasting and positive mark. Getting youth in their formative years to appreciate and cooperate with well-meaning adults is often difficult, but it is well worth the effort, especially when kids are not receiving positive attention, emotional support, and thoughtful guidance at home.

When kids trust particular male youth workers and perceive them as being willing to help them, they are more likely to respond with a cooperative spirit. Some youth workers find that daily exchanges can help forge this trust and make it much easier to guide a kid. Hernando, a 38-year-old Hispanic minister, shares this sentiment. He observes that if you can make a child "understand that you are looking out for his best interests, then things are going to have a better impact. You create that [understanding] with a relationship, because they see in you that interest, that love."

Ben, also a pastor, perceptively builds on the idea that a key to men's relating well to kids involves their reassuring the kids that they matter. Recollecting his interactions with kids at his summer camp, Ben stresses how important validating kids is to the mentoring process.

> When you interact with a 9-year-old who is away from his parents, doesn't have a TV, or Coke, or chocolate to turn to, and you have a conversation with him, it's a real conversation. It's not some bullshit two second, "Hey Billy, how are you?" You know. It's like, "Hey Billy, what's going on? Did you see the stars last night?" "Oh, yeah!" And you validate that. I was always validated in my experiences, my interactions with people. And as result, I always do my best to validate whomever I'm working with.

When men like Ben let kids know they matter, the kids grow more self-confident and willing to seek adult advice. By paying attention and affirming or validating kids, adults convey the message that they are engaged in the kids' moments, stories, and lives. Mentoring, as we'll see in Chapter 8, becomes a whole lot easier when kids are convinced that the adult is truly committed to helping them improve their lives.

Getting youth to embrace specific messages requires some finesse at times. Adults need to choose wisely among various strategies depending on kids' needs and other circumstances. Sometimes, an effective strategy may call for a man to share information with a kid in the company of the parents. Hernando quickly points out that he has intentionally directed encouraging and affirming remarks to kids while their parents were next to them. In broken English, he explains:

> If I were to give encouragement to a kid, say, she saw me talking to her mother or her father about something they had to do or something they not doing good. So, that's something they need, I believe [it] is important for them. And,

it's not just for [reprimanding]; part is to participate in encouraging and con-gratulating, too, when they something, they've done something good. And at the same time, it is something to be improved. I want the parents to be in-volved too, to be part of the game, to participate in the encouragement, so it's accomplished. [I] say, "Hey, he's not making the big effort. I mean, he's a per-fect guy. Look at him, look at him. He's marvelous, but at the same time, I be-lieve he is making lazy mistakes. So he needs to put up more effort." So I tell them in front of parents so that they know I am serious about it.

By talking about kids and directing his comments to them while the parents are present, Hernando accentuates the need to make sure kids perceive that they are being treated in an honest and balanced way. Kids are likely to see an adult's mo-tives as genuine and supportive if they hear that their positive traits as well as their shortcomings are being acknowledged.

The realization that kids want to feel valued hit home profoundly for Kevin when he made an extra effort for a young man only marginally involved in his church's youth group. Kevin went to watch Zachary play in a high school football game. After waving to Zachary on the sideline, Kevin shot some video, including close ups of Zachary playing during the game. Then he made a highlight video of the evening and showed it at the youth group meeting the following week. Af-ter that, Zachary came to the meetings faithfully. Once Zachary graduated, he surprised Kevin by choosing to stay with the youth group as a leader. Over a lunchtime chat sometime later, Zachary revealed to Kevin that the reason he started to attend the youth group regularly was because Kevin had gone to his football game and compiled the video. Reflecting on that conversation, Kevin de-scribes the importance of

finding a way to connect with them, finding a way to let them know that you care about what's important to them, no matter what it is. I mean, I've had to, you know . . . skateboarding, that's not my cup of tea. And music . . . I'm a R&B kinda music guy, but man since then I've . . . when a kid's in youth group [and] trying to start a rock band, well, I'm going to watch them scream and yell. So yeah, country music, rap music, I've embraced it all in the name of God. [Laughs.]

Kevin's story shows that men can reach out to kids by attending special events or just showing an interest in what the kids are doing. Some of the men commented on how they try to ask kids questions about their music, video games, and activities to demonstrate their desire to better understand the kids' lives and personalities. Vince, a 42-year-old ex-military man shares how his experiences as a juvenile detention officer and now as a team leader for an alternative school have taught him the practical value of demonstrating to kids that he is listening to them. "I guess a lot of them . . . they'll be talking, and to get them to know that you are listening to them, what I do, once they say something, I'll repeat what they said so that they know that I am listening to them, so that's how I go about doing it."

Whether a man is validating a kid's comments, or talking positively about a kid in front of his or her parents, or demonstrating an interest in the kid's special activities, a key to getting a kid to act appropriately and perform well is relationship-building skills. This is the wisdom 48-year-old Tom offers while discussing what he has come to see as the most important lesson he has learned about managing kids in various settings. Talking specifically about how he was able to teach kids effectively at an alternative school, Tom explains:

> I had to establish a relationship. I had to gain their respect by showing them respect; you know, do unto others as you would have them do unto you. And it's proven true, that it works, that if you show kids who are—no matter where they come from—you show them a sense of respect, they are always going to show you respect and be the way you want them to be. . . . the respect that I am showing them is respecting who they are. Not agreeing with everything they say and do, but respecting the fact that they have an opinion, they have thoughts, they have beliefs about certain things in life. In my position, in trying to establish a relationship [it] is not to bring . . . , not to talk about condemnation or judgment or right or wrongness, it is simply to hear what they have to say, and [their] knowing that they can say what they have to say. And plus it's to my advantage because it allows me to see inside them, who they are, what makes them tick or function, what motivates them, plus something about their life, their history, what has caused them to be who they are today, what life experiences, what things have buffered them along the way, that has brought this person to this point in their life, to act and respond or do the things they do.

Tom admits that this process took time in that situation and it wasn't always easy, but for him it was the key. In short, part of letting kids know they matter is showing them genuine respect, and part of being respectful is taking the time to listen well.

KEEPING IT REAL

Kids of all ages and types find themselves in the company of men whose responsibility it is to teach, coach, mentor, nurture, or supervise them. Although some kids may prefer to have the men in their lives paint a rosy picture for them, irrespective of how well it jibes with reality, some of the men believe they owe it to the kids to be candid and to "keep it real" or "tell it like it is." Just as some men are more inclined than others to find a way to relate to kids on their level, some men interpret the need for truthfulness more rigidly than others: they feel they need to be blatantly honest with kids. For most, it is a struggle to strike a balance between creating dreams for kids and being realistic with them. Many men want kids to feel that they can accomplish anything if they put their mind to it; however, they also believe it is vital to provide kids with a realistic assessment of what they can achieve based on the actual circumstances at hand or in light of their current attitude and behavior.

Given what we've learned about Nick to this point, it should come as no surprise that he thrives on being candid with kids. He is quick to say:

> I'm a realist. I look at it and tell it how it is. I'm not gonna pull no punches with them. I'm not gonna lie to 'em. I'm not gonna deceive 'em. I'm gonna tell exactly what they're doing and why they're doing it.

Calvin considers himself a realist whose role in working with kids is to be candid with those he's trying to help. He describes a vivid experience advising an ROTC student who wanted to apply to one of the military academies. Calvin initially describes the young man as having some self-doubt about his ability to "make that cut." Commenting on his response to this one kid, while also generalizing to other ROTC students he's helped, Calvin says, "I tried to . . . shoot straight with him and not . . . lie to them." He encourages kids to recognize that they have a "level of integrity and accountability and responsibility and that they need to accept those kinds of things whether they are in the military or not." Calvin reveals his straight-shooting style by sharing his perceptions about what kids want and how they are often treated.

> My experience is that kids are not afraid to have you hold their feet to the fire. I think too many times they get coddled and we think we are doing them a favor. I don't believe that, I believe kids need to be challenged.

The challenge for adults working with youth is to be firm and tell them things they may not necessarily want to hear and to ask them questions that require them to be more honest with themselves than they usually are.

Among probation officers, candor with youth is especially valued because the stakes for a failed relationship with a kid are high. Helping a kid find a new and honorable path when he or she has already gotten mixed up with crime requires solid and honest communication. Grady believes that his previous experience as a school teacher helps him to be a more effective probation officer for kids because he has an insider's perspective on how school bureaucracies work. His experience enables him to be direct with kids by asking the right questions.

> I think asking certain questions that teachers ask . . . I've drawn upon those things, cutting through all of the film, going right to the heart of the matter: "What did you do here, why," and, you know, "Do you have a planner that says you have homework?" "Yeah." "Well, why didn't you look at it?" You know, little things like that. And they try to pull the wool over your eyes and think you don't know what's going on. But, when you worked at a school, you know how school works and what type of measures they have in place to make sure everybody's accountable.

Ben also extends his comments about validating kids to accentuate the value of candor. He shares his views by referring to the exchanges he has with the teenagers participating in his youth ministry.

> I think the high school kids like me because I don't, soften anything. Like, if they say something stupid, I'm going to tell 'em that they're acting stupid. Or if they say something profound, I'll say, "Wow, that's profound." I try not to classify them as being kids per say. But I just recognize them as fellow human beings on this planet who I can probably learn something from.

Thus, Ben doesn't feel as though he has to sugar-coat the truth or his opinions when talking to kids. In some respects, he perceives that he and teenagers can relate on a level of parity; thus, it makes sense to talk to them openly and honestly.

In fact, the week of the interview, Ben was confronted by a situation (one of "his girls" was grounded by her parents for hanging out with a friend who had been holding cocaine straws) in which an open, honest discussion was particularly valuable.

She can only come to church and go to school. And, you know, she says, "That sucks." And I said, "Well yeah, you know, I agree. That does suck. But what do you expect? . . . Try to approach it with an open mind and recognizing that your parents have their best, your best interest at heart. You might not agree with that, but you at least need to validate them." So that, I think, is one example. I could have freaked out over hearing that her friends are doing coke. And I could have lectured her on why drug use is bad, but instead I just tried to hear what her emotions were in the situation, what her feelings were, validate her feelings, and then hopefully help her reconceptualize her world view so that she can feel better about herself, better about her relationship with her parents. And then maybe even reconsider finding new friends or finding a different approach to a social life.

Ben makes the most of his opportunities as a youth minister and informal counselor to "get real" with kids and talk to them about their joys, problems, and critical decisions. Other men also, in their capacities as Big Brothers, coaches, teachers, youth interventionalist specialists, and so forth, value having meaningful conversations with kids without pulling punches. Just as they stress the importance of kids' being honest, as I'll discuss in the next chapter, they realize they must deliver the same themselves. One thing that Nick, Calvin, Ben, and others find to be true is that building a relationship anchored in trust requires people to present themselves in genuine, credible ways. Being tactful but candid goes hand in hand with establishing credibility with kids, enabling one to earn kids' respect. Securing kids' respect in turn improves the chances of working with kids in a cooperative manner.

BEING READY: IT CAN HAPPEN ANY TIME

Much of what men do with kids involves spontaneous remarks and decision-making. Youth workers make seemingly inconsequential decisions as well as important ones during the flow of their everyday activities with kids. Several of the men explicitly emphasize, and I suspect many realize, that significant moments can happen when least expected. Thus, if men are to manage kids effectively and ideally position themselves to make a real difference in kids' lives, they should be mindful constantly that they can inadvertently but profoundly affect how kids think, feel, and act. When a local Boys & Girls Club staff member is approached by a 16-year-old girl seeking advice on how to deal with her two-month-old pregnancy, the staff member will sense that this is a big moment. Likewise,

if a 12-year-old boy mentions to his Big Brother that he is upset and scared because his mother is always drinking, taking drugs, and sometimes doesn't come
home at night, the Big Brother will realize the weight of the issue that has been
raised. But many far less dramatic moments fly beneath the radar men use
when monitoring kids. These moments may be just as important, though, if
they help a kid develop the confidence to do something special or enable a kid to
feel comfortable enough to ask others for help that may change his or her life
forever.

The Big Brothers Big Sisters slogan and the title of a 2004 book about the organization, *Little Moments, Big Magic,*[4] reminds us that even a seemingly inconsequential event can affect a person profoundly. It can come in the form of a
question, a short response, a physical expression, or an everyday activity. The
event can generate emotional magic as well as practical benefit. Alternatively, a
brief encounter handled poorly may result in loss of an opportune moment to
reach and help a kid or, worse yet, it may inadvertently leave a lasting emotional
scar on a young person.

Ben is one man who understands fully the importance of being attentive to
every moment, especially when working with kids. Pondering how he strives to
pay attention to kids' needs in all sorts of critical as well as mundane settings,
Ben refers to how he once sought to connect with an emotionally troubled boy at
his summer camp. The boy was struggling with family problems.

> I would grab him after a meal. I'd say, "Hey, Bobby, what's up? Can I talk to
> you for a minute?" Then we'd just go walk off on the hill somewhere. It's inter-
> esting, because I've always said that at camp I get to do pastoral care on a
> spontaneous basis. Which is one of the best things about camp for me. I'm
> able to literally do ministry, as far as my context of understanding it is, on a
> spontaneous basis. Super cool. Because you can have a real life impact in a
> heart beat. And it can take place over marshmallows, or it can take place after
> a meal, or, you know, after Billy's just hit a home run, something like that.

As mentioned earlier, a man often does not realize until months or many
years later that he made a significant impression on a kid. Thus, a man's devo-
tion to working with kids should not be contingent on being able to see immediate results. His chances for making a difference are more promising if he is
aware that *any* time he interacts with a kid he could make a difference.

A director at a Boys & Girls Club, Scott, elaborates on the importance of men
being prepared to deal with kids' concerns, irrespective of how important or

unimportant they may seem at the time. Listening to kids, he notes, opens doors. Kids will be more likely to discuss issues with a youth worker if they feel that the person has taken the time to pay attention to them. Reiterating what he shares with his staff, Scott says:

> If a child comes up and tells you something, it may be the most ridiculous thing. You could have a 6-year-old child come up and tell you, "Last night my tooth fell out and my dog ate it." And you may think it's the funniest story, but what I tell them is, if this child picked you, out of everybody to come tell, then you must mean something to this child. To this child, this is a tragedy. I mean, to a 6-year-old, how much do they go through? Their dog ate their tooth, and all they're thinking is, "I could have put that tooth—that was, that's money!" Under the pillow type thing, and [I] tell them that, you know, the kids come here [to the club] for what's going on, but the kids are coming here because [of] who's here. . . . And in the past, I would be the person, where, okay, like the example I gave earlier with the little kid losing the tooth. I would have told a kid early on "Yeah, whatever" type thing. But now I realize—I mean, a lot of it's with maturity—that kid's never gonna come tell me anything again, because I sat there and, they had some big tragedy or something big in their life happen, and I pretty much told them "I care less."

Scott's commentary shows that, while it is useful for individual men to realize how particular moments can take on major significance, the ability to teach that perspective to other adults will increase the likelihood that more of them will pay closer attention to kids' needs. A key part of men's efforts to manage kids effectively, then, is to figure out what they need to tell others when they train them. Major problems can be circumvented with conscientious training.

MANAGING DIFFICULT KIDS

Even though most of the men see kids as basically good, they recognize that some are disrespectful and present significant behavioral challenges. Youth workers' exposure to disruptive kids varies considerably. Some may have little if any contact with disruptive youth. Others may deal with a range of verbal insults while volunteering or on the job. And some may tangle with youth who wield weapons or who punch, scratch, kick, bite, and spit. An indication of a volatile environment is a high level of unpredictability. In potentially dangerous settings, adults are never sure what they will encounter when spending time with kids.

Men who work with kids involved in the juvenile justice system, residential facilities for emotionally troubled youth, diversion programs, alternative schooling and aftercare programs for at-risk youth, child and adolescent psychiatric wards, and similar facilities routinely handle difficult kids. They often learn to anticipate problems and adopt tactics to prevent them from happening. When a problem does arise, they are more likely to be familiar with specific techniques for de-escalating the situation and minimizing the damage.

Whereas some of the men I talked to had been exposed to rough, abusive behavior during their own childhood and adolescent years, others were sheltered as kids from this type of bad behavior. The latter type of adults are likely to find working with a disruptive population of youth eye opening. This was the case for Joseph, who grew up in a disciplined household and school setting where kids did not mouth off or physically lash out at adults. Joseph was also accustomed to working as a martial arts instructor for a bunch of friendly kids and adults who were respectful and appreciative. The owner of the martial arts school and the instructors created a familylike ambiance, organizing festive outings at the beach for the kids and their parents. However, Joseph's world suddenly changed when he was in his early twenties after he accepted an invitation to sample a preliminary job training session at a wilderness camp for troubled kids ages 10 to 17. Joseph recalls his surprise during his first training session for the job he eventually accepted.

> I really enjoyed it. . . . it was really neat. And it was the first time I had ever experienced seeing a child just yelling at an adult and use profanity. . . . I remember coming home . . . my parents asked me, "What was it like, what were they doing out there?" "It was really weird, Mom. These kids were cussing out the adults and these adults were having to break up fights and stuff between these kids, and they were having to put them on the ground and hold them down until they got calm, and they were getting dirt in their mouth, and it was just, everyone was just rolling around on the ground and it was crazy. It was raining outside and everybody's out in the rain, just being bad! . . . It's a lot like working at the bar, you know, as a bouncer, and yet these guys are a lot smaller and they were sober." . . . But that was my first experience, and I have not left working with that population of at-risk youth since then.

Over the years, Joseph has replaced his naïveté with a wealth of experience managing badly behaving youth. Offering an insider's view of the world for a select group of youth workers who must confront such challenges, Joseph vividly describes a precarious encounter in which he was alone on a baseball field with a group of kids when a fight broke out between the biggest two. He prefaces this story by noting that the 12- to 13-year-old boys were well over 250 pounds each and almost six and a half feet tall, "just enormous," and Joseph weighed only about 185–190 pounds at the time.

> An argument started, and the two biggest kids that were out there . . . were threatening each other, with all the other kids calling them on. One of them was holding the equipment, the bag that was full of baseball bats. And, they each grabbed—one grabbed [a bat] and threw the bag down; the other one went after [a bat]. I was faced with—we didn't have radios—and it was either run back to school calling for help or go out there and try to stop this. And the kids saw me come out there and just walk up to the bigger of the two kids . . . , and grab his bat and push him against the fence and tell him very sternly I wasn't gonna let him do this, that it was either gonna be him and me in the altercation or he was gonna get right and we were gonna settle down and talk about it. And, I was able to do that without somebody getting hurt, luckily [without] me getting hurt. . . . There's a lot of kids that remember that; [it] made a big impression on them that, you know, I wasn't doing that because I was the one being threatened [but because] I didn't want to see anybody get hurt, and I was standing up for the other kid, [who] regularly cussed me out and threatened me, but yet I was trying to keep from getting hurt or anybody. So, it made a big difference for them.

Faced with this predicament, Joseph had little time to react. Fortunately, his calculated risk turned out for the best. He feels he gained substantial respect from the other kids by rescuing someone everyone knew had verbally abused him repeatedly. The kids probably felt that if this guy mattered in Joseph's eyes, he must be concerned about the well-being of all of them. Once again, the importance of kids' feeling that they matter comes into play in how men can connect with individual kids.

Over the years, Joseph has received extensive training in therapeutic crisis intervention techniques designed to minimize the need to use physical force. Since learning the techniques, he spends a fair amount of time teaching them to others. Much of his recent work is helping others learn how to manage kids more efficiently without resorting to physical force.

Joseph and other men speak about a wide range of strategies they use to deal with kids' negative behavior. Like the kids in Tony's program for students expelled from other schools, the boys Derek deals with as a youth intervention specialist are struggling with their school and family lives, but Derek's kids are not currently being monitored by the juvenile justice system. Elaborating on the scruffing technique described earlier, Derek talks about how he incorporates parents and teachers into the program so a kid feels as though his entire circle of adults is on board with the program.

> *Sometimes we get calls from moms saying simple stuff, as, "He won't clean his room and I told him five times, he won't clean his room. I'm getting back talk." So I get on the phone, I try to talk to him, if I'm not satisfied with what he's saying, then . . . we get in the van and, like five or six staff members, and we'll all jump out and we'll be there just to smoke that one kid, scruff that one kid. And we've done it at school. . . . I think being scruffed in front of your friends will straighten an attitude quick. I mean, I scruffed a guy in front of the whole class before . . . right there on the spot, I'll scruff him in front of his friends, and I'll tell you, I haven't had a problem with that guy since. . . . I've seen like parents come out and whip their kids, . . . back in the day . . . in the middle of class; they'll come sit right next to their kid in class . . . I'm talking about mom would come out with the hair rollers and everything . . . embarrass the crap out of these kids. . . . I kinda did the same thing, and I mean, it works, it really works. This guy get scruffed in front of his parents and being embarrassed in front of his friends works more wonders than anything I've seen.*

In recent years, because of greater public scrutiny of adults' behavior with kids and a lower tolerance for sanctioning kids through physical punishments and shaming, adults have increasingly backed away from the "old school" methods Derek uses to get kids' attention and to punish them. Nonetheless, paramilitary strategies and adolescent boot camps have not been shelved entirely.

Derek is fond of his approach, given his military training and because some kids have come back to him the next day or sometime thereafter and apologized or acknowledged that they had screwed up. Obviously, this sort of practice is only going to be tolerated in certain settings, and parental consent seems a must. I also suspect that men are reluctant to apply this approach to girls, though adult females might use the technique with girls and young women in select settings.

Earning at-risk youths' respect is often no easy task because many have been physically abused, yelled at constantly, and neglected by those closest to them—their family members. Tony understands this all too well because of his work at an alternative school program sponsored by the Department of Juvenile Justice. One of his primary management strategies is to remain as calm as possible at all times, because he feels that the kids quickly disengage and are perhaps acutely annoyed when adults get angry with them because they have been yelled at so much and abused at home. Tony believes they turn a deaf ear when staff members raise their voices to reprimand them. Thinking about his Boys & Girls Club kids, Charles echoes Tony's logic.

You gotta be calm, cool, and collected. The calmer you are, the better the situation works out. When I was younger, you think raising your voice, and yelling yada yada yada, you think that's the best, but that's not the best way. The best way is sometimes the louder they get, the softer I get. And that kinda, that's when they get scared cuz they're like, "What is he thinking now? What is he really going to do now?" I teach the kids you can't sweat the small things and everything is small. You take life and you go through life enjoying it. You know, don't get hung up. If you get hung up on something, then life passes you by.

In addition to Tony and Charles, a number of the other men emphasize the value of maintaining order by remaining calm amidst chaos. Several share Tony's way of remaining calm: they avoid personalizing the kids' rage. They realize that most of the kids have difficult lives and are unhappy. Most are struggling with some combination of household and neighborhood poverty; family, school, and street violence; parents with alcohol and drug problems; learning disabilities; and truncated life dreams. The men do their best to place things in perspective, cutting the kids slack at times while making sure they still follow the program rules. Tony preaches the value of patience and understanding in the face of kids' anger. Most of the time, he feels, the kids "are not mad or angry at me or at my staff, they're angry at everything else that is going on around them, the family environment."

Similarly, Grady's previous experience working as an officer in a juvenile detention center taught him to be more reserved in approaching kids who are acting out. Though a probation officer now, he recalls that when he worked on the inside he was careful about exerting his authority. He tried his best to manage kids in a way that did not require him to resort to calling upon his ultimate authority as an officer to initiate a physical takedown or retract key privileges.

We ultimately have the power to do what we want to, but you know, sometimes it's better not to go, don't pull the trump card out yet. You want to stay back from that, 'cause once you use that card, you don't have anything else to use, so, you wanna let the situation . . . , if it doesn't dictate using that trump card, don't use it . . .'cause you got 'em for a period of time, you're not just done with them in one day.

His willingness to lay back and not play the "trump card" was partly a reflection of his ability to be patient and appreciate the complexity of kids' lives.

Like Tony, Grady tries not to take things personally, because he sees the bigger picture. To illustrate, Grady uses a particular incident in which he did not confront a boy who was giving him a fair amount of trouble one day. The situation would not have resolved as well, he believes,

> if I had gotten in his face, or put him in confinement for disrespect—and there is times it does warrant it, you know, and that's what you have to be the judge of when you work at a place like that. Is there other surrounding circumstances that's causing this young person to do that or is it just him being defiant? And of course, there are times when you have to assert your authority to make it a good place to work. You can't let them have control of the situation ultimately; you can let [them] perceive that they may have a little bit of control at a certain point, but then always remind them I get to go home at night, you stay here.

By referring to "surrounding circumstances," Grady suggests that he was willing to consider how a wide range of potentially mitigating conditions could affect detainees' attitudes and behavior. He felt it made sense to foster an ambiance that allowed the kids to feel as though they had some control over their affairs inside the detention center, so long as they understood the limits of their power.

Nick, about a foot taller and 125 pounds heavier than Tony, also tries to present a tranquil, friendly image, as a "big teddy bear." He is proud of how he manages the recurrent volatile outbursts at the residential facility for emotionally troubled youth where he works.

> When I see a kid escalated that high that I feel like they need to have hands put on them or be restrained, automatically my first thing is this, is to get the situation as quiet as possible, remove either them from the situation or remove the other kids out of that situation. When kids have a show, when they have a floor, an audience, they're gonna react. They're gonna get loud. They're gonna get aggressive. They're gonna make a point that they're not afraid. So, what I try to do is make it as quiet as possible, isolate the child from the situation and try to go one on one, soft tone. . . . I look at 'em, I say, "Am I yelling at you? Why you yelling at me?" The level drops about half the distance of what it was. . . . And, you gotta do somethin', automatically to break that ice with them, let them know you're not a threat. I never stand in a threatenin' manner. I always either put my hands behind my head or . . . I put my hand against the wall, I lean against the wall, . . . but I never give them the

opportunity to see that I'm willing and ready to grab if I have to. . . . It's the setting, it's the tone. If you got four or five guys standin' there yelling at a kid, boy, you gonna get a lot of yellin' back. Because when that staff is arguing with a child and being in a manner, the kid's arguing with him, he arguing with the kid, trying to get them to see the point. You're not gonna see the point. When a person's mad, you don't see no point. The only thing you see is what's in front of you, and that's somebody you don't like. So let's get that person out of the picture, put a new face there and say, "Now, what's the problem." . . . So, that decreases the whole volume of the situation at least ten levels down.

At the juvenile detention center, one of Grady's primary goals was to manage situations so as to avoid any physical confrontations. Though he felt threatened at times, especially when dealing with the bigger kids, he knew how to calm them down:

I could use my verbal and I could take them right down to my level again 'cause I just knew how to react to them. When somebody's in a confronta- tional mode, even though I have the power, the authority to deal with it, sometimes I would back off a little bit, to get the situation down; but once I gained their . . . , once the volatileness of the whole situation came down, then I can go back and deal with it properly, rather than having to wrestle with a kid, 'cause that doesn't do anybody good, them or me.

Another approach men use when working with difficult kids is to direct their interest. This strategy is designed to win kids over by getting them interested in a basic idea or task at hand in order to solicit their involvement. Frank grasps this concept. He describes what he does to enlist kids' help in taking care of the Boys & Girls Club facilities.

You get the roughest one, that's the one I like to deal with. That's the one I'll talk to. The one who think they bad, or who like to fight and all that. Because then all the other kids'll fall in line. That's kinda my strategy, what I've learned, you know, through juvenile justice and all that. . . .'Cause kids, some- times they'll listen to their peers faster than they'll listen to you.

Thus, men like Frank can gain a strategic edge by securing a commitment to their objectives from one kid who is respected and perhaps feared by the others.

When a youth worker first meets a kid who has been labeled a troublemaker or poor achiever because of past behavior, he has a chance to approach the kid with a more positive attitude. Tony speaks of this when describing how important it is for him and his staff to figure out a way to help a kid experience early success.

> *It's my job, it's what I delegate to my staff to do—is that when we get a kid here, . . . this kid has got to see some type of success early on to know that this is real. Which makes everything so much better, so much easier, when a kid starts seeing that they can be successful early on—"Oh! I can get out of this program!" Usually, the communication with that kid is a lot more effective as well because they have had early success, there has been a positive connection with the program, myself, my staff, so that really gets that kid off to a . . . off to a good start.*

First impressions make a difference in how communication flows and relationships evolve between people. Consequently, men should be encouraged to make every effort when interacting with kids, or training others, to be aware of how adults' initial responses can set the stage for youths' reactions, including cooperation. Men's attention to basic principles of motivational psychology in whatever setting can promote stronger ties with youths early on, improving the chances that the kids will develop a positive attitude and behave accordingly.

One of my observational trips took me to a small school cafeteria on a Monday night to see how Joseph establishes an "understanding" with kids at the first group session of his ten-week diversion program. Participants included seventeen kids, mostly boys, ages 7 to 17, and family members. The kids sat on benches next to their family members. Joseph had met separately with each participant and his or her family representative in his office two weeks earlier. There the kids signed a contract agreeing to a set of ground rules, including attendance at the once-a-week sessions, abiding by a 6:00 p.m. curfew, respecting parents and grandparents, doing what parents requested without incident, drafting an apology letter and developing a plan for restitution if a victim was involved in their offensive behavior, and making arrangements for and completing a set number of community service hours. Kids were sent to this program because of such behaviors as stealing, vandalism, fighting, and carrying a weapon onto school property.

Though technically not a probation officer, Joseph functions like one, given his considerable leverage over the youth in his program. In the second half of the opening session, using a tough-love tone, he tells the kids they will be dropped from the program if they break the rules. He also admonishes them not to cry if they are forced to go to the juvenile detention center for failing to complete the program—it will be their own fault.

166   MEN ON A MISSION

During the session, when directing comments to both the kids and their parents, Jospeh emphasizes the value of respect. Consistent with Tom's emphasis on establishing relationships, he tries to develop rapport with the kids and their parents or grandparents. On the one hand, Joseph appears as the strict disciplinarian who tells the kids they are in the program to earn a second chance, not a fifth or sixth one. On the other hand, he portrays himself as approachable by memorizing all of the kids' names. From the outset, he calls on kids by their first names as he asks them to update him on what is going on in their lives. The unspoken, subtle message here is that Joseph cares about the kids and their families; he wants to improve family communication while helping the kids get back on track. He builds on this message at the end of the evening with a fun, interactive communication exercise intended to demonstrate that there are different ways to communicate and accomplish tasks effectively while being respectful. The exercise illustrates that life tasks are not always presented in an easy format, so ingenuity may be required to get things done. Joseph informs the participants that they will get to know each other better over the coming weeks and will work together to break down barriers, dance together, hold hands, and even hug. By developing this type of rapport with the participants from the beginning, Joseph expects to retain the kids in the program, teach parents and kids how to "click" in their relationships, and get all participants to respect others more.

Ten weeks later, while attending the program's graduation session and celebratory pot-luck supper, I detect that many of the kids (and parents) have grown to appreciate Joseph's efforts on their behalf. Fourteen of the seventeen kids have made it through the diversion program. Most of the kids, after shuffling, strolling, or scurrying to the front of the room, look Joseph squarely in the eye as they shake his hand and accept the piece of paper acknowledging their hard-earned completion of the program. Three other male facilitators, including Tom and Malik, who have worked with Joseph on this project for several years, stand side by side, extending their hands and congratulations to the kids as they are showered with supportive applause by the entire group.

Earlier in the evening, the kids and families listened as each of the program's leaders shared a clever, inspirational message. In general, they highlighted the value of kids' making wise choices and maximizing the social support available to them. Joseph remarked that, just like the outfitters who provide mountain climbers and hikers with equipment and advice to help them navigate the obstacles of the natural world, he and his facilitators try to equip these young people and their families with resources that will enable them to anticipate, avoid, or handle all sorts of problems. In one instance, a tall African American man raised locally mentioned how he had overcome a troubled, disruptive childhood in which he had left every school he had ever attended. He eventually got his life in gear and was now honored to work with kids to help them avoid making the same mistakes. Seeing the men interact with the kids, talking to them informally throughout the evening, and recalling my sit-down interviews with them, I was struck by their genuine commitment to making a difference in kids' lives. They were all prepared to do the hard work of helping troubled kids and advocating for them, once the kids demonstrated their willingness get on a productive path.

CHAPTER 7

MAKING A DIFFERENCE

Sandy, a 4-H Club professional, began to describe to me an innovative clowning program he once used as a self-development tool for kids and adults. "What a marvelous idea," I thought to myself. As with Derek's moving childhood story about watching his father leaving his family, I felt a rush of intensity as I listened to Sandy describe his program, but this time my mood was joyful. Sandy's initial remarks set the tone.

> Teaching kids how to put on make-up, develop a character, how to perform
> in public, how to communicate one on one. You can see immense changes in
> kids, and adults for that matter. After a period of time, when you perform
> and do things, eventually it is sort of like you are doing it not in make-up,
> and you are not even realizing it. You see kids going from very severe intro-
> verts to extroverts by the time they have been in clowning for a couple of
> years.

Before he even had a chance to elaborate on his clowning project, I was imagining how exciting his program must have been—could be again. As a social psychologist and gender scholar, I understood the potential value of Sandy's program. Much good could come from creating a clown troupe with boys and girls of varying ages, each engrossed in his or her own self-discovery project, each enjoying the camaraderie of belonging to a program that encouraged them to help others construct their characters and costumes. Learning to perform for a wide range of audiences, large and small, could enhance kids' self-esteem and communication skills. The project was surely even more promising with a leader like

Sandy, a family man with three kids of his own, who transformed himself into the attentive, nurturing lead clown.

> Whenever I worked with them I always worked in character, in costume, even when I was teaching . . . because it would help me as well. I was now Sammy; I was no longer Sandy, I was Sammy. I think it helped them in terms of them relating to me as well, because here is this dude out there in costume and the whole bit, breaking up every once in awhile, goofing off and having fun, so I think that helped a great deal.

Although Sandy did not scientifically study the beneficial effects of kids participating in his clowning programs either when he was in Minnesota or after he moved to Florida, he is certain they made a difference in the kids' lives, and in his own. His confidence stems from his own observations as well as the many testimonies he received from kids and parents.

> Kids that are quiet, it is a great way to build self-esteem, because if you can develop a character, and if you can make people laugh and smile, that feeds you. It makes you feel like you are important. That starts to carry out [in] the rest of your life. I can see that in kids that would come into the program that were very quiet, very unsure of themselves. . . . One of the kids had a speaking handicap, and we worked on building that into her character. I could really tell the difference after a couple of years, doing the clowning with her, she was no longer aware of it. You could just tell that she was more outgoing, more willing to take on stuff. Then I had one other boy that was really hyper, not doing well in school. His mother was a university professor in psychiatry, did not know what to do with him. So she got him into the clowning program. She said within a year she could tell some major differences. Just because it slows him down a little bit and made him more aware of himself and gave him a better feeling for himself because he could do it.

Sandy's clowning program offers a glimpse into why it is useful to consider the meaning, value, and practical aspects of men's diverse approaches to working with youth. It also stirs interest in exploring the ways men's investment of time, energy, and sometimes money can benefit kids in the public arena. The assorted stories men share illustrate the wide range of settings in which they construct meaningful bonds with kids while contributing to their healthy development.

Because the interpersonal bonds and their consequences do not evolve in a social or cultural vacuum, they are best viewed against the backdrop of the larger context in which adults and youth are defined and manage their interactions with one another. This cultural and social dynamic is illustrated by Sandy's suspension of the clowning program. "The county commission was making a fuss about it," he recounts. In the eyes of the county commission, the program was an arts and crafts project, not an educational program. From Sandy's perspective, the county government objected to his 4-H program because they didn't understand what the program was about—helping kids develop self-confidence and communication skills in a creative environment. Sandy's novel program is an intriguing idea that deserves to be revived sometime, somewhere.

Filling out the portrait of men's involvement with kids means looking more closely at how men perceive kids' personal strengths and weaknesses. In addition, it requires us to explore how men try to make a difference in kids' lives by sharing life lessons, creating opportunities, and developing cooperative ties to other adults who can help kids. Sandy's hands-on style of teaching kids clowning and of performing alongside them is but one among many innovative approaches men have used. To name but several, they have taught magic to kids at summer camp, used puppets to secure kids' attention and put them at ease, participated in week-long "high adventure" hiking trips with teenage boys, and monitored kids on all sorts of mission trips around the world. And then there are the more everyday yet effective ways.

Whether men interact with kids doing something more or less unique, those who make a difference typically spend time with the kids over a period of weeks, months, sometimes years. But men also occasionally leave their mark on kids during even a brief episode. For example, Robby, a 23-year-old former camp counselor, believes that some of his short hospital visits as a volunteer leave a favorable and perhaps lasting impression on children. He shares one vivid experience about making decorative hats out of construction paper with kids and their parents in a hospital waiting room. Before he could finish one particular boy's hat, the child was called away to see the doctor and began to cry. Robby finished the hat while the boy was away and proudly describes that, upon the boy's return,

> there was this sense of overwhelming happiness when the hat looked great. And so that, I remember as being impactful on my life, because it wasn't just about interacting with kids, it was bringing the smiles, bringing the happiness and the joy to them and really being able to make a difference just through visiting kids you don't know well and will probably never see again.

Waxing philosophical, Robby assigns significant meaning to this experience, for both the kid and himself:

> It was one of those life changing moment(s), sort of like rain drops . . . they make an impact as soon as they hit, but then it's a limited impact until the next raindrop hits. Likewise, these were isolated raindrops where I select memories where raindrops fell from the heavens, and for even a moment isolated in time, made a difference in these people's lives. But in terms of how that impact affected the overall puddle over the long term, I couldn't tell you because I wasn't there to see the growth. But there was, if you want to call it short-term or momentary, there was momentary growth in some sense in me and in them. Making a kid cry out of happiness—"Oh my god, someone cares about me."

In an emotional and reflective tone, he concludes: "That really hits you when you realize that it doesn't take necessarily a long amount of time to impact someone. It takes the right amount of action." Obviously, the right amount of action will vary depending on all sorts of conditions. Men with more opportunities to interact and work with kids are more likely to make a difference, whether through their strategic planning or by accident. So too, those interacting with kids who are more receptive to new ideas and persuasion will be more likely to make a difference. Sometimes the right type of action at the right moment is the key.

PERCEPTIONS OF KIDS

During most of my interviews, I asked the men separate questions about what they admire most about kids, followed by what they find most unappealing and frustrating. Asking men to talk about kids' admirable traits typically provokes a reflective, appreciative glance—sometimes a smile. Apparently, the men experienced my questioning as an invitation to pool their abstract images and sentiments about kids, an exercise most of them find pleasurable. Focusing on positive images helps men frame their thinking about their time with youth. With few exceptions, the men responded quickly and confidently; many listed and enthusiastically described several traits they enjoy when they see them in kids. Compared to their quick responses when asked about when they admire kids, the men tended to struggle a bit when identifying what bothers them about kids. However, almost all of the men shared something they find frustrating. As one might imagine, men's standpoints on kids are influenced by the context in which they interact with them. So too, men who are raising or have raised their own children have a special vantage point from which to think about other youth, a topic I take up in Chapter 9.

The men's appreciations for and frustrations with kids seem to center on the following themes: willingness to work hard, resiliency and persistence, honesty, curiosity and wonder, compassion for and helpfulness to others, joyful innocence, and respect.

Two themes identified most often in some fashion tend to be linked—a strong work ethic and resiliency. Kids perceived to be hard working and capable of overcoming their difficult situation are greatly admired. Tony, recalling his experiences with students he's taught, soccer players he's coached, and at-risk kids he's monitored and counseled, labels one trait the "trying factor." Tony values kids who "don't stop"; they are "always looking for something more." The men speak about kids' determined state of mind and their willingness to do whatever it takes to overcome their unfortunate circumstances. These kids are not disabled by self-pity or self-doubt; rather, they make a conscientious effort to better themselves. The value of youth's persistence is amplified when their unfavorable living conditions are taken into account. Derek embraces this view, focusing on the disadvantaged kids with whom he works. He admires their "never say die attitude. That 'Yeah, I want to do this, or I want to do that, and you can't tell me that I can't do it.'" Others think of persistence more generally, without referring to any specific set of circumstances kids face; they focus on kids' passionate "motivation" or "zeal" in pursuing their dreams. When these kids lock onto a goal, big or small, they invest their heart and soul into achieving it.

In our gendered world, it is not surprising that the men often embrace the "trying factor" and resiliency as valuable traits for kids—apparently boys and girls alike. Though the men come from diverse family, social, and economic backgrounds, most appear to have had some exposure as boys or as men to the pervasive theme that quitting is unmanly. Laziness and giving up easily are inconsistent with most traditional and even more progressive images of masculinity.

Honesty is one of the themes numerous men find appealing. It may be no coincidence that the two active Boy Scout leaders, Matthew and Jeff, immediately mention honesty. Matthew observes that it is "easy for kids to [do] what I call *rounders*. To round it, not be direct with you." Recognizing that many kids do otherwise, Matthew values kids' being precisely honest, without pulling punches or fudging the truth. Jeff conveys a hopeful view of kids' natural tendencies but cautions that the social and cultural environment affects kids, making it difficult for them to be honest.

*You give them enough experience with what is right and what is wrong. Kids
are great and they want to be good. It is just when you let them, when you give
them the wrong environment, you got the wrong environment. It is leadership
by example. They get the wrong example, they are going to follow it. I really
believe that all the kids are really great. But the biggest thing we are doing
wrong, between what they see on TV, what their parents don't talk to them
about. You just got to sit down with them: "What are you thinking about?"*

Jeff sees kids as basically good but malleable; they will lean toward being honest
if those most important to them guide them in that direction, but they also are
susceptible to more negative forces that devalue honesty.

Grady, the probation officer, highlights how kids are usually willing to be hon-
est or candid with him about why they did something illegal. In these exchanges,
Grady feels, kids engage in a useful form of self-assessment and self-disclosure.
As he sees it, being honest means being honest with others, and with oneself.

Other men mention how younger kids can display honesty. Speaking of the
kids attending his Boys & Girls Club, Andre notes with a smile:

*When a kid comes forward and tells the truth, that means a lot to me, too,
and I have a lot of kids here that have done stuff they shouldn't do. But they
feel—they have a conscience, or whatever it is—and they'll come up—I'm
talking little kids—and, you know, [say,] "I didn't mean to steal this peanut
butter and jelly sandwich" . . . stuff like that happens all the time.*

Although the issues differ in type and level of seriousness, the men's comments
reveal that being honest is honored.

Men working with kids in various settings also value kids' curiosity and eagerness to expand their knowledge, whether in relation to school or to life more
generally. Robby captures the latter image by sharing his admiration for kids
when they express a "voracious interest in absorbing everything," while Greg ap-
plauds kids' "thirst for knowledge." Sidney, referring to his elementary school
students as well as other kids he's worked with over the years, stresses his similar excitement: "When the kids wanna learn and they're excited about something
and they just have that bright-eyed look and they wanna know more, they're crav-
ing as much as you can give 'em." In a couple of cases, men's perceptions of kids
changed once they began working with youngsters. They now realize that kids
are much brighter and more savvy than many adults seem to think.

Some of the men highlight the "exuberance" and "wonder" of youth when
they talk about admirable traits kids display. Thinking along these lines, the men

emphasize a perceived qualitative difference between childhood and adulthood experiences, between kids and grownups. They view some of the kids as being steeped in an enchanted phase of life, free from adult worries. Ramón, a school teacher with twelve years' experience mostly at the high school level, clarifies his fondness for kids' innocence by saying "some kids are not as tainted as others. When we get to adulthood sometimes we're more affected by society, by society's problems." He believes that kids in their middle teen years "can still be molded." Using clichés as well as their own words, the men share their views on youth's joyful innocence. For Reggie it is the "twinkle in their eye," for Alan the "new-ness of everything"; Ben speaks of kids' "wide-eyed brilliance," and John refers to kids' general "innocence" and that "they're not afraid to maybe ask about things they don't know." In short, some men cherish, perhaps idealize, the care-free and excitable approach to living life that is thought of as a characteristic of youth, even though many of the kids these men work with are not as able as oth-ers to experience it.

But some of the men, like Ramón, bemoan how youth's innocence is being forfeited too quickly these days. Many kids appear to be exposed earlier and more fully to the complexities and temptations of the adult world through media and friends. From Ramón's perspective, having taught successive cohorts of similarly aged kids for over a decade, the "innocence, little by little, is going away, year after year."

The men value kids' being respectful, especially to their elders, but also to other kids, and to themselves as well. As is seemingly true for every generation, some adults think that the current generation of youth is not as respectful as ear-lier cohorts were. Kids can show respect by speaking politely to adults, respond-ing well to authority, and treating others with kindness. Respect is closely related to another key trait the men admire, one best referred to as having a "good heart" and showing compassion for others. The men relate specific instances when youth treated other kids well, and they highlight a more general kind of al-truism, using phrases like "community service" and "social activism" that imply a commitment to more than an isolated person or small group of kids. Andre's words are direct: "When I see a kid who's compassionate and helps out his little brothers or little sisters, or other kids, that impresses me."

As might be expected, some of the men are quite vocal about kids disrespect-ing adults and being arrogant. Sandy explains that he particularly struggles with kids who are "disrespectful of everything and anybody." Distinguishing between behaviors and attitudes, he adds, "You can deal with behaviors but attitudes are a lot tougher to deal with, and when they have a bad attitude, that makes it a really difficult situation." Ben, the youth minister, relates this disrespectful attitude in some kids to arrogance. Quickly responding to my question, Ben identifies his biggest concern about kids.

> *Arrogance I suppose. Arrogance to the point of selfish arrogance, which is, which can be, just so cocky that they don't even have to listen to you. They don't even have to give you any respect or anything like that. I hate it when people do that. And that's not just kids.*

Their concerns about kids' disrespectful attitude is not confined to how kids treat adults. Kids' proclivity for bullying, teasing, and mistreating other kids is a recurrent concern. Bullying especially troubles Mark, an educator with over thirty years' experience in various school systems. What Mark finds striking is that girls are increasingly mistreating their peers, much as boys have done for years. He illustrates his point by recalling a recent incident.

> *I was talking to the bus driver at Fort Drexel [School], and a female, real pretty little girl, came up; and there [was also this] kid, suspended from the program, and he was coming up next to me: "Yes sir, no sir," really polite because he wanted back on that bus and back into the program. This girl came and hit him so hard that I could feel the wind from her hand where she slapped him. And he maintained his cool. . . . I probably would have knocked her over the bus. Then I went and watched her knock a kid off a bicycle, a boy, and actually stomp the spokes out of the bicycle, to render the bicycle totally unusable.*

Andre shares a similar story, showing his concern about how many kids, including girls, mistreat other kids.

> *There's a girl over at the Southeast Club . . . ; she's young, she's only about 12 or 13, but she's almost six feet tall and probably weighs close to 200 pounds. . . . She came running through the gym and just banged open the doors like that, almost hit me, and it just missed a little kid named Jacob, who's probably six. And I said, "First of all, you're not supposed to go running through the building; second of all, don't go barging through the doors because you coulda hit him, and it could have broke his nose, knocked his teeth out"; and she goes, "That've been his problem." And that's the attitude I see a lot, "If it doesn't affect me, who cares?"*

Notably, it was on the heels of talking about this incident that Andre described how moved he is when he sees youth express compassion toward other kids. It may be that these men who are in positions where they regularly see bullying, or witness it being displayed in dramatic ways, also grow more aware and appreciative of youth's potential for kindness. Phillip, a graduate student in school psychology, became more concerned about bullying after reading about it in one of his classes. He facilitated a couple of school programs to teach kids to recognize and deal with bullying individually and collectively. Phillip is alarmed by kids' bullying tendencies; he believes bullying is "difficult for teachers to deal with because a lot of times they don't see it or don't recognize an act of bullying as bullying. And I think it's happening all the time. And I think it has a negative impact on development. In fact, I'm quite certain that it does."

Sometimes it is hard to distinguish bullying from hurtful teasing. Typically, the latter is less likely to have physical domination associated with it, but bullying and teasing are both mean spirited and potentially damaging to youth. Ramón shares this view, forcefully asserting that teasing is "absolutely a pet peeve of mine. . . . [Teasing] really gets under my skin." He is so annoyed by it that when he sees teasing he violates his personal rule not to embarrass kids in front of their peers. Ramón admits, for example, that if a kid calls another kid "stupid" for receiving a bad test grade, he will "single out" the offender and chastise him or her.

The flip side of hard work and persistence is some youths' lack of motivation, or their shortsightedness. Just as men respect kids who do not let their circumstances impede them or get them down, some are frustrated or annoyed when they feel that kids are not living up to their potential. Charles describes his frustration with what is often a complex situation.

> When I know a kid can do better, and they give up, and they just give up. . . . Sometimes they give up on their own; sometimes they give up because everybody who they believe in or they trust have given up on them, or have told them, "You're not gonna be anything, you're not gonna be successful. You're dumb. You're handicap," whatever it is. Everybody who supposed to be protecting them, and loving them, and supporting them have turned their backs on them. And so that kid gives up. That's frustrating. And that's the thing I'm always fighting with, because, I mean, sometimes we work all week pumping a kid up, and Friday comes and the kid leaves here on a emotional high. And on Monday that kid comes back totally, just destroyed, because all weekend long somebody's just been badgering them and telling them all kinds of nonsense.

Here, Charles interprets the subtle reasons why he struggles with some kids who hang out at his club. He believes that some simply don't care; they give up on their own and have no serious interest in trying to better themselves. Apparently Charles holds these kids accountable for their life choices. Others, however, despite having the capacity to be motivated and improve themselves under the right circumstances, are brought down by a destructive home life. They possess some desire, but unfortunately, whatever desire they have is not sufficient to overcome the negative messages they receive from their intimate circle of family and friends.

The image of a child struggling against difficult circumstances is a classic theme in Hollywood depictions, which implies that it is an issue of interest to many people. The talented inner-city or rural child strives to succeed although surrounded by drug-using, poorly educated, violent, and unsupportive family members who ridicule the child's efforts. Of course, supportive persons also appear in these films, like the lone parent, supportive friend, teacher, or coach who takes pride in the child's determination to succeed against the odds. Charles sees himself has one of those supportive adults who can make a difference in a child's life if the kid is receptive to being helped.

Darnell, a teacher and high school coach, is disheartened by another inhibitor of hard work, what he perceives to be kids' sense of entitlement. Darnell believes that many of today's kids don't appreciate the value of working hard to achieve specific goals. At age 37, Darnell uses his generation as a point of comparison when he talks about kids in general and his own girls' basketball players more specifically. Sitting with me in his office inside the gym, which he has opened for a voluntary practice on this summer evening, Darnell disappointedly says,

> I just don't think they value life and . . . things that go on. Like, they don't value like we did. I know we valued a lot of stuff. There're kids now [who think] everything should be given to them. Like, right now you got [only] two or three varsity girls in the gym. All the others—you know, there's no excuse for that— they should all be there if they want to get better. But everybody thinks, "You owe me something," or something like that nowadays. I don't know where that's coming from but that's what I'm really beginning to dislike about kids. "We want it right here, right now," you know. It's gonna come but you have to work for it.

Some of the other men also use this generational comparison and share Darnell's sentiment that youth today are, on average, lazier and less willing to work for what they want than were previous generations of youth. From my perspective, each successive generation since World War II has cast similar aspersions on their immediate successors.

Kids who are motivated to achieve goals are able to focus beyond the present and visualize their future, but some kids, especially the types whom Grady regularly monitors as a probation officer, tend to live in the present without a clear sense of how their behavior today will affect their options later. Grady is particularly frustrated with kids' shortsightedness; he accentuates their counterproductive approach to life.

> A lot of them, I don't think, are thinking more than a day ahead. And, I'll ask them many times: "Do you realize that what you've done now may affect you for a year or more? You know, that $19 pair of earrings that you had to take is now; that $19 is gonna affect you for a year." I said, "You figure out how much that is over a period of a year, that $19 pair of earrings. How worthless is that?" I start putting it in perspective like that, 'cause a lot of times they know about money and they know about how much is good and how much is bad, a little bit and not a lot. . . . But, I put it in that perspective and, see, they have no concept of that. They live twelve hours ahead a time, right now. "Just make me feel good right now. I want those earrings right now." They don't consider, "This is gonna cost me a year of my freedom. How much is my freedom worth, $19?" It's amazing . . . how unprecious time is to them.

Grady's example reveals the absurdity of choosing to steal a piece of jewelry worth essentially five cents a day but costing them a year of probation restrictions.

In some cases, the men's views are mingled with their perceptions of the broader cultural climate. Calvin speaks for many men when he says:

> I have never been unwilling to say, "Yeah, I screwed up," 'cause we all make mistakes. Kids don't want to do that, and it is kind of a reflection [of] what you see in society. I think kids have picked up on that [e.g., sports celebrities acting poorly] and they are unwilling to accept responsibility and unwilling to be accountable for things, and that accountability might be to their grades, it might be to their job, it might be to whatever that they are required to do. . . . So I am very big in the integrity, accountability, responsibility issues. . . . When I see kids that are unwilling to accept their responsibility and when they make a mistake, they understand that there should be consequences. Too many parents are willing to give kids a free ride time after time.

As the men talk about the adverse cultural climate in the United States, parental shortcomings, and kids' limited sense of responsibility, many believe they face significant challenges in their quest to matter to kids.

TEACHING LIFE LESSONS

Much of the time men spend with kids involves doing practical tasks, such as, teaching a young person the finer points of camping, showing a kid how to throw a Frisbee, monitoring a youth's progress through phases of the juvenile justice system, and instructing a kid in how to make house repairs. For many men, everyday activities such as these also provide them a chance to teach broader life lessons through words and deeds. Although some lessons transcend specific settings—coaching, education, faith, mentoring—the life lessons are often tailored by the circumstances and the kids' ages. Lessons often overlap and are inspired by the men's images of kids—both good and bad. Among the more prominent of such lessons are the following virtues: trying new things and refining one's talents; working hard and overcoming obstacles; learning how to practice a religious faith in an everyday sense; respecting others; and making decisions in a more mindful, future-oriented way in which a person considers the consequences of his or her actions. In subtle and indirect ways, adults try to encourage kids to embrace a personal vision of hope while they enhance the young people's self-esteem and personal confidence. Finally, through their talk and actions men inspire boys and girls to reflect on the productive and destructive ways men express masculinity.

A number of the men shared how they push kids to apply themselves as students, employees, persons involved in recreational and athletic pursuits, and in other roles. The men often do this by "preaching" to kids the value of hard work or praising them when they focus on a project. Furthermore, they hope to make a difference with the kids by living their own lives in a principled way, offering the youths a chance to observe and emulate their dedication and hard work.

Men strive to make a difference for kids by being a creative resource; they seek to help kids teach themselves. The larger life lesson here involves encouraging kids to grow more comfortable with situations requiring them to step outside their comfort zone and take measured risks. Whether it's speaking in front of a large audience, taking a difficult course at school, learning a new hobby, or applying for a demanding job, the basic lesson is similar: people develop by learning that they can survive unusual circumstances even if they do not excel at the new experience.

The world of sports is one obvious arena where men capitalize on the competitive spirit to simulate life's hard realities. Calvin, a former competitive baseball player, explains his philosophy with kids by recounting a story from his experience coaching his son's baseball team. He initially describes how he takes exception with coaches like those in his son's league who instructed the worst hitters on their teams simply to bunt all the time, never try to get a hit. As Calvin sees it:

> What lesson are you learning about baseball and about life if every time you go to the plate [you bunt]? All you are reinforcing in that child is that "I am the worst hitter, so they are not going to allow me to do anything but to bunt the ball, even if there is nobody on base and there are two outs." That is pretty stupid, we had coaches that would do that. [My advice is to] go up there and take your hacks. You hit the ball, you hit the ball. You make an out, you make an out. You strike out, that's life you know, sometimes you strike out. You see a kid have some success, even if he hits a ground ball and the third baseman mops it and throws it away and he gets on base, he got a hit. [In] the scorebook, it is an E5 [error], but in their mind they got a hit, and they are going to run home and tell their moms they got a hit. They don't even know what a hit means other than they made contact with the ball with the bat.

Although Calvin told me he was quite competitive when he played, he was much more laid back coaching young kids. The youth league, for him, was a miniature life stage offering kids the chance to face adversity while exploring and expanding their personalities.

Elaborating on Calvin's thinking by extending it to school, Reggie explicitly integrates the lesson of hard work and dealing with adversity into his message to his fourth graders. He says, "I try to tell my kids in science, life is bigger than where we are right now." From Reggie's perspective, attitude is a key force that determines how well people move on to that "bigger part." He explains by way of example:

> How do you handle the fact that you might not be the best person in math? You can cry 'cause your grade wasn't higher than the other person, 'cause you're going to ask him what did he get. What are you going to do to get to where he's at or she's at? Are you going to try hard? That's probably what you need to do. That's the lesson. . . . I want kids to understand that life is not al-

*ways going to be so straightforward. There's going to be some bumps in the
road. How do you handle those bumps, no matter how big they are? And we
have this dialogue, my kids and I. How are you going to handle life when you
come to those bumps in the road? Are you going to stop and go back? Are you
going to try to figure out how you're going to get around or over those bumps?*

Though they use different metaphors, Calvin and Reggie want kids to develop a
"can-do" mentality. They feel that youth should confront whatever obstacles they
now face—whether it is hitting a baseball or learning math—so they will be better prepared later on to handle life's more serious obstacles. As Calvin suggests,
bunting should not be a kid's first option all the time; all kids should be encouraged to recognize that facing adversity is part of a life lived well.

The overlap between some men's style of managing difficult kids and their
desire to teach the "can-do" life lesson is apparent in Ray's description of how he
approaches boys in his role as director of an after-school program for at-risk
teenagers. A product himself of a relatively difficult childhood, Ray firmly states
that he has no sympathy for the kids. If he did, he says, he wouldn't show it to
them, because he doesn't want them to use it as a crutch. He doesn't tolerate excuses. Elaborating on why he withholds sympathy from the kids, Ray offers a
sample of what he might say to a 14-year-old kid.

*If I can make it, you can make it. I don't want to give you that excuse, "Man, I
feel sorry for you 'cause you're on the east side of town, you don't get the opportunities that people on the other side of town. . . . No, I ain't gonna give
you that because you have opportunities just like they got opportunities. They
go sit in the classrooms, you go sit your butt down in the classroom. I took advantage . . . , I might not have been the smartest one in the classroom but I sat
by the smartest ones.*

Oddly, despite his deterministic religious philosophy, Ray appears to see kids
as having an enormous amount of freedom in choosing their own life path.
Consistent with those social scientists championing "human agency," Ray em-
phatically believes that individual choice rather than social and economic circumstances associated with family and community ultimately determine what
people achieve. Ray asserts that he acquired his "no excuses" philosophy by ad-
miring the tenacity of one of his high school teachers. Old, sick, and visibly in
discomfort, she did her best to teach her classes, sometimes using a hand mi-
crophone to amplify her weak voice. Ray strives to emulate his teacher and believes today's kids should do the same.

Helping kids learn how to put their faith into practice in the everyday world is an important life lesson for the men who work with kids in faith-based environments. Earlier, I described the value some men place on inspiring kids to want to give back to their communities. This sentiment is consistent with how some ministers and lay professionals who teach religious studies try to help youth. They think it is important for religious people to have more than a general knowledge of their faith; they wish to motivate kids to see and treat others in ways informed by their faith. Ben acknowledges that he wants to provide a moral framework for kids so they will feel comfortable praying, reading the Bible, and using their faith as a resource to guide their lives. He asserts, "Most importantly I think that the best lessons that I taught anyone was putting your faith into action. And that was through the weekly work trips that we would do." Work trips melded abstract notions of faith with the concrete, get-your-hands-dirty practice of giving to others by sharing your time and manual labor.

Kevin sees his ministry as an opportunity to help kids, "make sense" of the Bible while "making it relative in their life, whatever they're going through, whatever time or season that they're in. Just making it real, instead [of] fake and religious, just giving it some substance and making it apply to them in everyday situations." Kevin was particularly vocal about teaching kids how to draw upon the principles of their faith to navigate situations involving peers or parents. Earlier in his career, when he was initially finding his place in his church, he and his wife had an opportunity to be youth leaders for a group of teenagers. It was in this context, working as a team, that Kevin felt he was able to give youth faith-based guidance as they faced the challenges of being upset or disappointed with their friends, romantic partners, and parents.

Similarly, Paul, an experienced lay teacher of religious studies, says that for the past fifteen years he has been trying to help kids in a faith-based environment develop "relationship skills." He recognizes that his ability to share life lessons in this area is fueled by his curiosity about how kids learn "the art and the science of relating to one another." He describes three broad areas that intrigue him in this regard. Paul frames his concerns by posing a series of questions directed at youth about listening, loyalty, and ecology.

How well do you deal with relating to the world around you, . . . ? One side of that is . . . do you have the necessary listening, communication skills. Another side of that is, do you relate, to use the church word . . . , ethically, do you do it justly, . . . in teenagers' term, are you loyal, you know, to your friends, that's another one of my concerns. . . . I can talk about that here [at church] freely.

The other is, how do you relate to . . . those bigger notions of community and the world, and some of that has to do with, ecology, sensitivity to the environment? How do you relate to groups of people? Do you hate being with vegans, can you not stand conservatives, liberals, either side of the coin, whatever it is?

Like Ben and Kevin, Paul is not merely interested in teaching young people standard messages about biblical verses, ideological dogma, or religious rituals. Each of these men, as well as others, want to help youth translate the larger lessons of faith into such behaviors as kindness, tolerance, understanding, and forgiveness to their everyday life.

I suspect that Rabbi Jacob's objective in teaching kids to appreciate how their special heritage should influence their daily living is comparable to how many other rabbis respond to Jewish youth. When helping Jewish kids understand how their minority status may affect them socially because they live among a population largely ignorant of Judaism, Jacob says:

I let them feel, let them find their place within the history of Jews, that they have a place within that history, that is a continuous history going back thousands of years. . . . I try and give them a special message . . . their tradition has teachings and a richness and a fabric to it that can enhance their life and make their life special and give some kind of special texture to life.

Here Jacob speaks of his role as a spiritual guide: helping kids see the significance of embracing their religious and cultural heritage as a means to interpret and manage their social affairs. Importantly, his philosophy is grounded in the sentiment he feels for how several rabbis mentored him when he was a kid.

They wanted to present a certain way of living life and a certain authenticity that I found very attractive in a way of inculcating a kind of sincerity in their work that really had a, you know, I think had a huge effect on me in terms of seeing this kind of total dedication to community and to Jewish values and to Judaism. So that was something I really admired and looked up to.

Though only some men couch their lessons explicitly in the language of faith, others, like Boy Scout leaders Jeff and Matthew, sometimes talk about helping kids discover a "moral compass" and building "character." More frequently, men encourage kids to show their elders and peers proper respect. Sometimes they directly tie learning the value of respecting others to developing self-respect.

In trying to convey values, numerous men target the fashion and music styles perpetuated by hip-hop culture. The men express how they confront youth about these behaviors, challenging them to abandon their disheveled, sexualized, and sometimes gangster look. They hound boys to tuck their shirt tails in, wear belts, pull their pants up, and to wear their hats straight or do without them. Some also discourage girls from wearing revealing clothes. Joseph illustrates how he confronts the clothing issue with teenagers who participate in his diversionary program. The program caters to youth who are referred by the courts due to their involvement in criminal activity as well as to youth whose parents perceive them to be on the verge of slipping into trouble. Joseph enforces a dress code for program outings, like the jail tour, and when they attend his classes. He admits to spending more time dealing with dress code issues for girls, explaining that he has to "go into the specifics" about the "type of provocative clothing," including items like "short shorts" and "little tight baby doll shirts" as well as the reasons why they shouldn't be wearing that type of clothing. Referring to his Monday night classes, Joseph continues:

> I'm the first person that they see when they walk in and I'm the one that says go back to your vehicle and find something to cover up with or you can go home. And they only get one class that they can miss. If they miss a second class then they're back in court. So, I said I don't care if you go out there and put on dad's shirt, whatever it's gonna take, you find some tube socks that come all the way up to the bottom of those shorts, but you're gonna need to put some more clothes on.

Joseph says he is not embarrassed giving this advice, but he is frustrated when girls continually violate the code despite his candid instructions. Part of his annoyance stems from the parents' ignoring his policy. He describes how, when he is speaking to a girl in front of her parents, he is also speaking indirectly to the parents, as if to say,

> "What are you thinking having your daughter come here dressed like a prostitute when I've clearly outlined what the dress code is and while you clearly have a daughter that is starting to get in trouble? And why in the world would you allow this to happen when obviously you were there when she left the house; you drove her here with your eyes wide open?" And they just expect [me] to do everything. So, I mean, I put it back on the parents a lot of times.

Joseph attempts to reinforce the life lesson he shares with kids by reminding the parents of the lesson as well. Even when interacting with kids in public settings without the parents' being directly involved, school teachers, coaches, youth ministers, after-school professionals, and other adult authority figures working with kids often try to remind parents in various ways how important it is for kids to embrace certain life messages.

Men's concerns about respect for others and self-respect also surface when they complain about how hip-hop culture, particularly the music industry, adversely affects youth's perceptions and treatment of women. For instance, Reggie encourages his fourth graders to discuss topics like rap music during their "morning meetings" and to consider how "certain aspects of the hip-hop culture" can be "demeaning" towards females. Imagine twenty mostly African American kids sitting comfortably on a carpeted floor in a circle, with the gregarious Reggie positioned on a small chair with his back against the wall, wedged into the circle of students. He asks the students to relate the lyrics of hip-hop music to their own family relationships and experiences. During our interview, Reggie reenacts for my benefit one of his lively morning sessions with the kids.

> The boys hear the [lyrics of the] music, so their assumption is that's the way they should treat women or talk to women or girls. And the first thing I say to them, I say this: "What did you think about how certain rappers talk about women?" "Man, they're just rapping, you know how it goes." I go, "But you use it, right?" "Umm." They're not going to let me know that they actually say those words that they hear. "I listen to it." So I say, "How would you feel if they talked about your momma like that?" "Uh uh. Nobody talk about my momma." "But that's females. Is your mom a man or a woman?" "She's a woman." "So what you're telling me is that you appreciate what those rappers are saying about your momma." Then the thinking starts and we take it from there. "So then, why do you say all those things those rappers say? Because they're very, . . . part of rap is demeaning to women. So your mom is now a hoe [whore]." "My mom ain't no . . ." "No, no, no. But you say that when you're rapping. Your momma's not b [bitch], right?" "No, my momma's not a b. My sister's not a b." "But you rejoice in those songs when those rappers start singing them." . . . So we have a lot of conversation about that, just me and my boys. So now, all of a sudden, my girls, we start talking. "So now, . . . you're a hoe now." "No. I ain't no hoe." "But that's what you listen to. That's what the songs are talking about." "But they're not talking about me." "Well, who are they talking about then, if you're a female?" So now they're thinking. "I don't like him no more 'cause he be

*calling . . ." "Are you still buying the music, or are you asking your momma
to buy you that music?" "No, Mr. Reggie. I don't ask her to do that. My
momma don't even let me watch him anymore." So now we have them
thinking about what they are listening to. . . . It's just a bunch of junk that
they out just to sell you something. And [these kids] are buying it, hook, line,
and sinker.*

Reggie also gives examples of how he forces kids to think about rap artists'
comments about killing cops and using the word "nigger." According to Reggie's
rendition of his exchanges with students, he presses both boys and girls to think
critically about the music and videos they consume. Although his story illustrates that he directs boys to respect others, and he encourages girls to look inward to manage their own self-respect, his messages also provide boys the
incentive to look inward. For Reggie, then, getting kids to appreciate and respect
women is a life lesson every bit as valuable as the math and science curriculum
he teaches.

Closely linked to self-respect is self-esteem and personal confidence. Learning how to face unique challenges while dealing with the harsh realities of life
can help kids develop a stronger self concept. Men like Barry understand this
notion and stress the need to help kids improve their self-esteem. Referring to
his work in an after-school program for young kids, especially those who come
from disadvantaged backgrounds like his own, Barry says:

*I want to show these kids that they can make it. And I've been trying to teach
self-esteem. And that's something that I'm big on, 'cause some of these kids
have so many reasons to, to be down and out, and to give up.*

I heard a similar message when visiting the after-school program for middle
and high school boys where Derek works. One day, while in Derek's company at
the community youth center, I stood next to several African American staff as
they directed an impromptu, spirited lesson at Jeremy, a regular program participant. The staff stressed the importance that Jeremy learn how to carry himself
more confidently. They pointed to a slightly younger boy the staff admired; they
encouraged Jeremy to look closely at the kid, at his self-assuredness. Challenging
Jeremy to develop the type of self-confidence and leadership qualities the other
boy possesses, they told Jeremy he should strive to become a leader at the community center the coming year. Although I can only speculate on what Jeremy
was thinking during this talk, he appeared to listen attentively to the staff members' suggestions.

A common lesson the men try to share with kids is that there are consequences associated with behavior. The lesson, one familiar to parents who struggle to teach their own children to think before they act, is viewed as important by many adults involved in mentoring, transmitting a religious model to frame decisionmaking, instilling a code of ethics like that of the Boys Scouts, molding young athletes, and so forth. Matthew, the Boy Scout leader who cherishes kids' honesty, is probably the participant who most explicitly and forcefully drives this message home with his words.

> One of the things I'm probably very frustrated with is kids that, they'll do something wrong and they'll go, "Eh, it's no big deal." They don't see the impact it had, not only on their life, but the people around them. There's consequences, you know. One of the first words my [own] kids learned to speak when they were little, truly, was the word "consequences," 'cause there's good consequences and there're bad consequences, but there's always consequences. Everything you do will have an effect, a consequence. And a lot of times kids will do things as if there are no consequences, because we societally tend to [say] "Oh, it's okay, it's all right. You screwed up; it's okay." Well, no, it's not. What are you going to do with knowledge that you screwed up? Are you going to do better next time? What did you learn from this? If you're doing something for the second wrong, . . . why didn't you learn it the first time? What can I do to help you learn so you don't do it a third time? So that sense of "Oh, it doesn't matter. Yeah, I screwed up, but it's okay." . . . That lack of ownership is very frustrating. . . . And I think that's probably the biggest thing that scouting does is it teaches boys, first of all, to step up, but with that, teaches you, gives you the tools to understand what you're supposed to do when you're stepping up to your responsibility.

As his words clearly show, part of Matthew's personal mission in working with kids is to teach them accountability. In his case, his perception of the Boy Scout philosophy and mission are consistent with his own. As a result, the organizational mission helps shape what he does with the boys in his troop.

A general lifestyle lesson men offer to kids involves their representation of masculinity. Men vary considerably in how conscious they seem to be of their opportunity to reveal the many faces of masculinity to boys and girls. Some try to show kids healthy images of manhood in practice through their hard work, generosity, and support. Others seek to challenge the debilitating consequences of versions of masculinity commonly displayed by abusive, disrespectful, and inat tentive boys and men who, in their lives as boyfriends/husbands, fathers, peers, and strangers treat others poorly. As men, the youth workers are uniquely positioned to show kids how men can relate in constructive ways to their own family and friends, coworkers, and to kids themselves. They can demonstrate firsthand that it is okay for men to hug one another, for a father to incorporate his child into youth group activities in a loving way, for a man to act like a gentleman toward his wife or girlfriend, for a male to demonstrate impeccable respect toward female coworkers, and for a man to teach girls to demand respect from their boyfriends. Some men put forth a conscious effort to make a difference in how kids define and respond to different types of masculine norms.

CREATING CHANCES AND CHALLENGES

The difference men can make for youth depends in part on their options for creating opportunities for kids to explore aspects of the world while tapping into their passions and talents. The ideas Charles put into play at his Boys & Girls Club illustrate the basic sentiment running through much of the men's thinking about creating opportunities for kids to grow into productive adults. Taking a broad view, he focuses on the need to mobilize youth's untapped potential.

A lot of people have the belief that kids are bad. I don't believe in bad kids; I believe in bored kids. Kids get bored, so you have to challenge them. And that's what this society is all about, it's about creating challenges. People wonder why [kids] get caught up in the video games; it's because it provides them with a challenge. It's always, get to the next level in the game, defeat the next person, and that's what it's about, I mean, that's why they're into it. It's always about being better, striving to be better.

Building on his many years of experience as a 4-H agent, Sandy extends Charles's sentiment regarding kids' potential:

I think all kids have an innate sense of kindness and wanting to please and wanting to be a good person. I find that exhilarating at times, especially just to get into their degree of excitement. They are going to do something and they are really excited about it. . . . I really think that is in every child, that can be tapped. Once you can find that, that is what makes the kids grow. Because you can open the door to them, to develop a relationship with them to help them grow. Because no kid likes to be knocked down, they like to be told that they are a good person. Of course sometimes it is hard to find the good in them.

But it is always there. I have never met a kid yet that didn't have some good in them.

By finding the things that excite particular youth, Sandy feels that adults can open kids' eyes to wonderful growth opportunities.

The notion that adults need to create meaningful situations for kids to discover and experience life is reflected in many of the male youth workers' accounts of what they are attempting to accomplish. In Charles's case, his passion for helping kids experience different situations is rooted in his belief that kids shape their self-concept through the stories they can share. But to share good stories, kids must do fun, exciting, or productive things. That's why Charles sometimes gives money to the poor kids who frequent his recreation center. Building on his comment that he recently gave money to a boy to go to a summer camp, Charles explains his reasoning:

Because I want the kid to enjoy it, and I don't want the kid's peers to find out, because kids are cruel. And kids judge or are socially accepted based on, basically, participation. . . . When kids [return from summer vacation] it's not gonna be about the clothes that they come back to school with and all, it's gonna be about the stories. Because the first question the kid's gonna be faced with, "What did you do this summer?" And it's all about bragging rights, the kids want to know, well, one kid's gonna say "I spent the time with my father, and I went to the beach, and we went . . ." Now here you got another kid over here, who comes from a single-parent home, who . . . nobody spent any time with. What is his story about? So now, from day one of school, he's kind of pushed off to the side. So that's why, in my current position, I try to make sure there's activities that these kids can get stories from, educational things, take field trips. . . . That kid gets back, he's bubbling, he's happy and he can compare his stories and say "Hey, well you know maybe I didn't do that with my father, but I went to Mr. Flowers and we did this, this, and this." And that is what the kids really like.

Men often figure out ways to create challenges for the kids within their circle of influence. Sometimes the challenges are shared with individual kids; other times kids are offered a chance to do something as part of an organized team or informal group. The principle of promoting challenges is well known and common in the world of sports, but it touches kids in other settings as well. For example, men with connections to Boy Scouts, 4-H Clubs, school classrooms, alternative schooling environments, after-school programs, and church youth groups frequently ask kids to deal with new and challenging circumstances. The specific types of challenges may vary, but the basic principle is similar. They push the kids to experiment with unfamiliar activities or to reach for lofty goals as a way of inspiring them to clarify their sense of purpose and develop their human potential.

Jeff, the avid Boy Scout troop leader, talks about the value of providing his scouts with experiences he refers to as occasions of "controlled failure" or the "discovery method." In other words, boys are given the chance to experiment with a meaningful activity in a somewhat controlled environment. Failure is possible, and the consequences are real and unpleasant, but failure will not lead to disastrous results. Jeff describes how he gives his scouts the chance to speak on their own to the entire group of scouts and deal with their "mic fright." He comments that although they initially are all "scared," and

> they don't make good eye contact, they don't speak bold, before you know it they are up there all the time, second nature. So they become much more adapted to having their own family some day, their own jobs; and when they figure that out and the parents see it happen—wow, it is not just Babysitters of America, the parents know that it is a good thing, they get more involved and the kids really do well. They want to do well.

Part of the mission of the Boy Scouts is to give boys the opportunity to test themselves and develop leadership qualities while being supervised by adults, mostly men, though an increasing number of female leaders and helpers have gotten involved in recent years. Jeff also notes that the logic of this approach can be jeopardized if others step in too quickly to relieve boys of the negative consequences associated with their poor choices. For example, more mothers are now going on camping trips with his troop, and he laments that some mothers are apt to pamper their sons. Left to his own devices to set up his tent, a boy may quickly learn that he is more likely to get wet if he doesn't pay attention to detail. However, if the boy's mother comes prepared with a fresh set of dry clothes, the learning process may be short circuited.

In pick-up football games at an after-school program for elementary school children, Barry makes an effort to incorporate both girls and boys into the games. He notes that, "some of these boys will never give these girls a chance if I don't." Barry even makes a point of allowing a girl to sometimes quarterback the team despite many of the boys' initial objections. As a result, Barry feels he has altered somewhat how boys think about gender.

*I'll simply say, "She's a girl and she can do it because I said so." You know,
and they'll leave it at that. And then, I think the kids grasp the concept, because I'll listen to the kids when they think I'm not. And they'll say, "Okay.
Well, you know,"—my name is BT so they call me Mr. BT—so they say, "Well,
Mr. BT thinks she can play. So she's a girl, let her play," you know. I think
they grasp it.*

Other men also see that encouraging girls to play sports is a unique way to
help girls grow and expand their confidence. Drawing on his extensive experience as a camp counselor and now director at a Boys & Girls Club, Scott notes
that only about a third of the kids at the club are girls and that "girls always have
the stereotype, as far as with athletics, [that] they're not as good as boys." Last
year, moved by his uneasiness with this negative perception, Scott organized a
club basketball team of 11- and 12-year-old girls. He also gave the team the choice
of either playing in the county girls league, in which they had won the champi-
onship the previous year, or playing against boys. Scott's face beams when he recounts how they eagerly decided to play against boys and then played quite well
during the season, overcoming negative comments shared by parents and other
spectators, who complained, "Oh, what are they trying to prove; they've got a
bunch of girls playing against boys; they're gonna get 'um killed." As it turned
out, reports Scott, "First game out, we won; it was 24–2." Having one of the
younger teams, with relatively few players, and aware that girls are stereotyped
as inferior to boys athletically, Scott admits to rooting for girls as a matter of
habit, and he shares that they have a "special place in my heart." Scott's team of
girls recognize his support and probably try harder as a result of it. Kids are
more willing to accept challenges, to reach beyond their comfort zone to explore
new aspects of their worlds and personalities, if they are confident they can trust
the men who are pushing them.

Sometimes, to help kids identify and arrange opportunities to broaden their
horizons, the men spend time talking to kids. Much of what men do to help kids
realize their dreams they do through conversation. And sometimes the men
work behind the scenes to make things happen. Ray, for example, spent time
helping one shy boy acknowledge that he wanted to become a pilot. He
promised the boy that he would help him learn to fly if the kid did well in the
after-school program and graduated from high school, and Ray honored his
agreement by negotiating a deal with a flight school. Ray paid $65 out of his own
pocket for a flying lesson for the boy. As Ray tells it, the boy had a marvelous
time flying around the area with a flight instructor. Whether this introductory

lesson will inspire him to pursue his dream is yet to be determined, but Ray's effort was appreciated either way.

BUILDING SOCIAL CAPITAL

An important way a man can make a difference in a kid's life is by contributing to a collective effort to expand his or her social capital. Although scholars have recently explored how fathers enhance their own children's family-based and community-based social capital,[1] much less has been written about how men contribute to the community-based social capital of children who are not their own. Social capital in this context refers to social relations that provide kids resources that enhance their cognitive and social development.[2] When multiple adults take a genuine interest in a young person, they can more easily share information about his or her needs, moods, and experiences while supervising the kid's actions more closely. In addition, the kid may gain access to an expanded set of intangible human resources and desirable community opportunities. The resources may provide social, educational, and job-related options that can enhance a youngster's well-being and effective transition to adulthood.[3]

Men's potential involvement in creating social capital for youth in our society can be appreciated most fully by revisiting the historical context outlined in Chapter 2. As sociologist James Coleman argues:

> The loss of social capital, inside and outside the family, has extensive implications for the structure of American childrearing. In effect, raising children once took place informally, as a by-product of other activities, in social institutions—the household, the extended family, and neighborhood-based organizations—that were held in place by these activities. As the locus of the other activities has changed, the institutions have crumbled, and the by-product, childrearing, has crumbled along with them. The institutions that have replaced them (the offices and factories that have replaced households or neighborhoods as workplaces, the shopping malls and catalogs that have replaced neighborhood stores as places to shop, the cocktail parties and rock concerts that have replaced gatherings of extended families as leisure settings) are inhospitable to the relations between adults and children that constitute social capital for the children's growth.[4]

Although Coleman's depiction of institutions as having "crumbled" appears to overstate the case in some instances, child-relevant institutions have surely been transformed, forcing adults and children to navigate a significantly different—and many would say less supportive—social landscape. There are, as Coleman recognizes, dangers and opportunities with the new social arrangement. In an earlier era, the public committed itself to investing in mass public schools as a response to one of the major consequences of industrialization— men's daily departure from the home for paid work. More recently, concerns have centered on how to assist children at a time in which an increasing proportion of mothers are also working outside the home. Coleman warns that the erosion of earlier institutions should encourage us to be vigilant about the declining provision of the "essential qualities" that children require: "attention, personal interest and intensity of involvement, some persistence and continuity over time, and a certain degree of intimacy."[5] These qualities cannot be replaced simply by providing more "school-like resources." Rather, institutional initiatives will need to ensure that youth have access to essential qualities that offer them the best chance to develop a healthy and secure sense of self—qualities that complement those provided by schools.

How men participate in building social capital for kids is likely to be shaped by various issues, including what's happening in their lives during their child and adolescent development, and their personal needs. Some of the needs are related to gender, family structure, and the physical and social characteristics of the particular community and interaction site. For example, young children are likely to need less community monitoring than adolescents because they are less mobile and spend less time out of the house. Meanwhile, middle and older teens will be more suitable candidates for pursuing job openings in the community. Men can help neighborhood youth find alternatives to inner-city street crime; in suburban neighborhoods, they may simply want to offer kids a part-time job to make extra money. Social capital is being leveraged if the men are able to offer kids information about legitimate jobs that they might otherwise not have heard about. Men's connections to information streams and their willingness to share that information with youth are examples of how social capital developed outside of families can benefit youth.

Derek's involvement with the youth program serving at-risk boys is a prime example of how men can enhance kids' social capital through their formal involvement with schools. By interacting with teachers, school administrators, school security guards, parents, and kids, Derek monitors particular youth and acts as an advocate if need be. When I visited a middle school with him, we headed directly to the student detention room, where Derek spoke openly to administrators about two boys, a pair of brothers, who had been suspended that day in separate incidents, one for allegedly stealing a purse and the other for verbally threatening a teacher. As a representative of the program, Derek has parental permission to access students' confidential records, and officials are encouraged to speak freely to him. Derek also has detailed class schedules for all the boys who participate in the program. Thus, he is free to drop by classrooms unannounced to check up on particular kids, as we did later that day.

Beyond the school setting, Derek also keeps in contact with parents and sometimes acts as a mediator. On this day, I listened to him speak candidly to the two boys' mother about her sons' predicaments, while she was at work. He did so by cell phone after arriving at her house to inquire about the boys' situation. The mother gave Derek permission to take the boys away from their home, where they were unsupervised, and to transport them to the community youth club. Witnessing Derek's personable style with school officials and parents underscored for me how persons like him are assets to kids. The productive relationships he has forged with school staff and with parents enable him to reach out to, monitor, and mentor kids in unique ways, because he can integrate information from various persons when working with the kids.

While riding in the van after Derek picked up several students from school to take them to the program, I saw how his work style ideally situated him to share information and build social capital in meaningful ways. On that May afternoon, he asked the students about their day in school and how much more time they had in classes before summer break. He initiated this conversation by referring to our earlier interactions that day with a couple of teachers who spoke openly about counting down the days to the end of school. He cautioned the kids that students and teachers were both anxious to get out of school, which probably leads to more school problems: teachers had a shorter fuse and kids were acting out.

Mark's recent mentoring of several young men he first met when they were in high school illustrates precisely how a man can make a difference in kids' lives by building social capital for them. One of the ways he has helped these guys is by introducing them to well-respected professionals in the city who should be able to help them later on. He has also helped at least one of them find a job, searched for opportunities for others, and continues to provide them with guidance about professional skills and demeanor. Referring to one of the young men and his experiences in a new job, Mark describes in detail how he would take the young man aside to polish his professional development. In one instance, he references candid advice he gave because the young man was laughing and joking immaturely in professional settings.

"You've got to stop doing that. . . . You're now in a different world. And I know you're still young, and I'm not saying don't be cool, but when you're in front of these kids or when you're in front of some of these big shots at [the Police Department] who have the power to keep you or let you go . . ." See, there's unwritten rules of poverty, and this kid, never was in poverty, but when you move into the middle class, those unwritten rules change. And the big question is, who tells you you're now in a whole different gig?

Mark continues, explaining that on another occasion,

I called the kid one day about something, and his whole message was rap: "And I don't know who you issss, I don't know where my phone issss," and he ends it up with this big bloodcurdling scream. So I scoop him up one day and I think I took him down to [restaurant]. . . . I said, "You got to change that answering machine. I want you to be cool, and I want you to be popular, but you now, again, have entered into a different realm. The [police] superintendent is on your resume. What if he calls you? . . . That answering machine just totally puts you at a level that you don't want to be put with the superintendent."

Mark's overriding objective is to impress upon the kids the importance of having adults take them seriously when they enter the work world. He believes he's well positioned to educate the young men on the finer points of dressing and acting professionally. As Mark sees it, he's giving them tips on how to navigate middle-class respectability. From his point of view, this is necessary because the kids do not circulate among people from whom they would naturally learn these lessons. This arrangement has been successful, in part because the kids have accepted and even solicited Mark's advice. Mimicking what the young men have said to him when he asks them if they want his help, Mark says:

[In] every one of those instances [they say,] "Yes, I want to know. I want to know, I want to do better, I want to do what's right. Yes, you tell me." And you just sort of get honest with them and say, "I know I may tick you off by what I'm saying but you know where my heart is." And they usually respond to the positive.

While shadowing Derek on the job, I had the pleasure of spending time with Ray, the director of a community program for at-risk boys and one of the young men whom Mark persuaded to act more professionally. Ray worked alongside Derek as well as independently of him, so I saw several sides to his personality and witnessed his ability to relate to kids over the course of a day. I saw a confident, mature, and respectful young man passionate about helping at-risk boys find and stay true to a productive path. My formal interview with Ray a few weeks later confirmed my initial observations; it appears that Mark's mentoring has made a difference.

As a youth specialist for an employment agency, Calvin sometimes, like Mark, plays a direct role with young people, but sometimes his role is more as an intermediary. He spends a fair amount of time talking to school guidance counselors to share and coordinate information on kids. For example, Calvin went to a high school counselor once to advocate for a boy who was struggling in school and at work because his best friend had recently been killed in a car accident. Calvin recognized that the boy's dramatic dip in grades was most likely due to this emotional trauma. In this instance, Calvin's willingness to share information about the kid with the school counselor provided the school's counseling staff useful information about the boy and enabled them to interpret and respond to his needs accordingly.

Another way men can get involved in providing social capital to kids is tied to their efforts to make neighborhoods safer. Neighborhoods perceived to be unsafe provide men chances to take it upon themselves to patrol the streets, perhaps becoming part of a proactive neighborhood watch group. Although none of the men I interviewed spoke directly about being involved in formal neighborhood watch groups, men can assume a protective posture in the community by creating activist groups.[6]

These days, it cannot be assumed that people recognize social capital as a valued good or believe that children will fare better if they are cared for and monitored by lots of people within a community. Scholars have lamented the loss of the community ethos of shared parenting that used to be so prevalent in many established, often ethnic, neighborhoods. In these settings, adults were more likely to know and trust one another. They also accepted some responsibility for other people's children because they experienced life as part of a loosely defined enclave of neighborly, social support. Helping neighbors was the right and natural thing to do, and watching out for the neighborhood kids was part of the unwritten social contract. For example, 42-year-old Vince reminisces about being raised in a country neighborhood in which his friends' parents had the "right" to reprimand him forcefully if he stepped out of line. Sometimes this meant getting a "whooping" from an adult neighbor, who would then tell Vince's parents, which then led to a second whooping or other punishment when he returned home. Viewed in this way, social capital is a product of families, communities, and the connection between the two.[7]

A number of the men are distinctly aware of either a self-imposed expectation or social pressure to create supportive relations with kids, especially boys living in single-mother homes, and also with parents. Some of the men involved with schools, churches, and youth-oriented organizations clearly recognize that becoming a supportive parent ally, both philosophically and pragmatically, can prove beneficial for kids. This nonfamily support can be particularly helpful for the kids, and perhaps the parents too, when parents are struggling for whatever reason to care adequately for their children's needs.

The men function as parent allies in various ways and to varying degrees. First, as we saw with Derek, men can act as a liaison between parents or kids and various organizations, particularly schools. For example, parents of many of the kids who belong to Charles's Boys & Girls Club ask him to help them navigate school bureaucracies, and Grady and Joseph help parents and kids manage the complexities of the criminal justice system. Second, men do helpful practical tasks for kids and their parents, sometimes as part of an outreach effort. For instance, after receiving parental and school approval, Richard initiated a practice of picking up assignments directly from teachers for the kids staying at his day-care/aftercare center. He and his staff can now better monitor the kids' homework and give parents a detailed account of what their children's teachers expect. Brandon, the middle-school science teacher, pays out of his own pocket for a web-based grade reporting system that enhances his communication with parents and allows them to stay up-to-date on their child's daily assignments and academic progress. Third, men may help parents and their kids improve their joint communication. Some formally step forward, like the youth minister doing group or private counseling sessions with parents and kids or the director of a family-based diversion program conducting parent-child communication workshops. Others casually help kids and parents talk to and empathize with each other during spontaneous exchanges. Fourth, men complement parents' efforts when they try to teach or model specific parental values, morals, manners, discipline, and interpersonal or practical skills. Some do this actively, by talking to youth about parents' expectations, others encourage kids more tacitly to adopt certain traits and behavior patterns. One might also argue, broadly speaking, that men act as parental allies when they in good faith try to compensate for parents' deficiencies or inattention. Men can express themselves as parental allies in each of these four ways by focusing on either a particular parent-child pairing or a collection of parents and youth.

As I discuss more fully in the next chapter, some parents are particularly intrigued with the prospects of having an unrelated man serve as a male role

model for their children. For instance, as a long-time staff member of a Boys &
Girls Club, Scott can develop relationships with kids extending over a period of
years. He regularly forges enduring ties with kids. Sometimes parents even
nudge him to take a more active role in their children's lives. Highlighting his
interactions with single moms, he notes that there are some things "you're a lot
more comfortable hearing . . . from dad, or from another male than, than from
your mom. So . . . I've had different mothers come and ask 'Well, could you kind
of talk to . . . my son about this or that.'"

Scott also takes the initiative to build social capital, or on occasion it occurs
largely by accident. For instance, he describes how the mother of one 8-year-old
girl sought him out at the club to say thank you the day after he had consoled her
daughter. In tears, the girl had sought Scott's comfort in the form of a hug after
she told him that her father was in prison and that she only got to talk to him on
the phone for her birthday and Christmas. Scott mentions that he told the girl,
"'Well, I'm sure he still loves you,' this and that." Referring to the mother's remarks to him the following day, Scott says:

> She said that meant so much, . . . "You're the first person that she's talked to
> about this other than me . . ." And, she said, "It was nice because . . . anytime
> we talk to her, I mean, we know the situation, and, . . . not rightfully so, but
> we're judgmental, because we know dad, and we know what he's done. . . . she
> obviously feels comfortable with you." And she says, "For me as a mother,
> knowing that my daughter's coming here, and you're not just here just to baby
> sit her, that it's even more than that, that you're sitting and you're listening to
> her and, not so much just even giving her advice, but a shoulder to cry on."

By having this conversation with the mother, Scott enhanced his understanding
of the difficult situation the 8-year-old was facing and his potential role in helping the girl and her mother navigate it.

In addition to working with individual families, much can be gained by getting in touch with local community sentiment about youth clubs, youth and family social services, and mentorship issues. Developing an understanding of how
a local culture can affect the direction of youth work resonates with Paul. His
previous administrative position with the Catholic Church in Wisconsin six
years earlier led him to work with an enclave of Hmong immigrants the church
had relocated from Vietnam. While spearheading an initiative to develop a community center for the Hmong kids, particularly those in gangs, and also training
local Hmong adults to provide others with parent education, Paul was reminded

of how important it is to experience kids, parents, and the larger community first-hand. As he recollects:

> *I wasn't working in a parish or a church like this [current position], so I wasn't local, I was regional at the time, but every once in a while I would volunteer to just be with them on the ground floor so that I can meet them one-on-one on the street. There's nothing to replace the street, all of this fancy stuff doesn't get you anywhere unless you're out on the street.*

To make headway in helping the Hmong youth, Paul felt he and his colleagues had to learn how to navigate a "radically different [cultural] system" and earn community trust to "alleviate the feeling of suspicion." Although he was viewed skeptically at first because he was a white man unfamiliar with their language, the Hmong eventually came to see him as more "reliable" once they saw over time how invested he was in helping the kids and adults access community resources.

Asserting that men can help children build community-based social capital that is likely to affect them in positive ways is one thing; saying that individuals within a community will attempt to promote these types of relationships or recognize their value is quite another. Not everyone to whom a man may offer assistance sees capital in the general social system as desirable. Thus, the value of men's contributions to youths' social capital is likely to be higher in communities that appreciate this form of involvement from unrelated family members and that hold mentoring in high regard.

CHAPTER 8

MEN AND MENTORING

Mark shares his definition of mentoring while reflecting on thirty-five years of working with kids as a history teacher and several years as a designated mentor

The essence of mentoring would be to create a mutual association, relation-ship or whatever, based upon trust and support for whatever the goal is.
My goal in those pictures [photos of Mark with three teenage boys] was that cap and gown [high school graduation regalia]. My goal now with those same kids, now they're 22, is to turn them into positive middle-class profes-sionals, again based upon trust, support, a little bit of love, or a lot of love or whatever. You don't want to sound freaky about it, but there is a lot of love there.

As we sit in his office early one morning, Mark freely shares his sentiments about several of his favorite and relatively recent high school students. His con-viction he brings to mentoring is etched in his words and demeanor. He points repeatedly to photos prominently displayed on his office wall of young men whom he has taught and mentored. In one instance, Mark, white and 58 years old, points to a photo of him standing next to two tall African American teenage boys. With a wide smile and a touch of laughter, he recalls how one of the kids displayed his platonic affection for Mark by walking around an amusement park much of one day with his arm resting on Mark's shoulder. The photos are vivid reminders of the loving pride he feels for these young men. Without question, making a difference in their lives matters greatly to Mark.

Though men have many options for making a difference in young people's lives, the mentoring relationship is a special and potentially powerful bond. Earlier, we saw how the youth minister Carlos had taken great pleasure in initiating a fruitful mentoring relationship with Malik, who, following in his mentor's footsteps, now channels his creative energies into mentoring youth in church and school settings. By any account, the journey Carlos and Malik have shared epitomizes the very best mentoring has to offer. In addition to their high regard for each other, they speak passionately about the emotional and spiritual gifts they offer and receive in mentoring youth.

Focusing on the state of mentoring in our society broadens our previous exploration of men's relations with kids and their efforts to manage them. I begin by exploring scholars' views about the distinctive attributes and value of mentoring and then I turn to insights shared by the men I interviewed. Mentoring's potential can be appreciated best by looking at how the larger cultural context has shaped the mentoring movement to date and how it's likely to affect men's future experiences working with kids in this fashion.

WHAT IS MENTORING?

Although aspects of the mentoring concept have been part of our cultural landscape for centuries—its roots traceable at least to ancient Greece—the term itself only recently gained widespread usage in the United States.[1] Mentoring received special attention in the 1980s when President George H. W. Bush was promoting volunteerism with his "thousand points of light" slogan.

Uri Bronfenbrenner, a noted child psychologist, defines the mentoring process as involving a developmentally oriented one-on-one relationship between unrelated individuals. In his words, a mentor is "an older, more experienced person who seeks to further the development of character and competence in a younger person."[2] Mentoring involves a "special bond of mutual commitment" and "an emotional character of respect, loyalty, and identification." Though some level of mutual commitment should exist in a mentoring relationship, in reality one person may be more committed than the other to the relationship. Other commentators suggest that a mentor tends to "help children build the skills, develop the strengths, and rally the resources they need to stay strong when adversity threatens to overwhelm."[3] In specific mentoring relationships, the process incorporates some or all of the key bonds (behavioral, cognitive, emotional, and spiritual) described in Chapter 5 that men form with kids through their various formal and informal activities. Of course, the intensity of the bonds which mentors and youth forge varies, and mentors differ in how well they supply youth with what are perceived to be, or turn out to be, usable skills, social support, and other resources. But mentors, by definition, intend to make a positive difference in kids' lives.

In everyday life, men may seldom call themselves mentors; they are more likely to identify themselves as teachers, coaches, counselors, friends, or buddies. However, even when the mentor label is not used explicitly, the elements of how men relate to a young person often fit the spirit of the mentor definition. Blake, the young 4-H agent, illustrates some of the muddiness of the "mentor" label.

> I, myself, wouldn't call myself a mentor. I would call myself a friend. But if you were to go ask these various ladies that I've worked with their sons, to them I'm a mentor to their kids and even to the other 4-H-ers; but that's because I don't, again, I don't put myself as a mentor, or even a teacher-student type relationship. I put myself on the same level. So, I mean, obviously, as I said, if you look back in retrospect, the little things have mattered to people and I've come to realize that maybe it was, you know, it did matter and all that.

Blake's hesitancy to adopt the mentor label contrasts with how he suspects others see him, but he realizes that he probably has made a difference in kids' lives and that others recognize his contributions.

Those who study mentoring differentiate between "natural" and "arranged" nonparental mentors, though the distinction is sometimes fuzzy. Some mentors come into contact with youth through the natural course of organized activities; these include teachers, coachs, and juvenile probation officers. Others, like neighbors, extended family members, parents' friends, may form a significant bond with particular kids simply because their paths cross and they take a liking to each other. In each of the first two sets of scenarios, an adult does not typically sign up to be a mentor; the relationship just emerges from the interaction. On the other hand, arranged mentoring relationships like those set up by the Big Brothers Big Sisters organization occur when an individual adult has volunteered explicitly to be paired with an individual youngster. I'm interested in both natural and arranged mentors. Although some of the men I interviewed were mentors to extended kin, the stories I focus on here involve men who have mentored kids who are not related to them.

Although the arranged mentoring relationships men build with youth can turn out to be important, they represent a modest proportion of all mentoring and only a small portion of the numerous situations in which men associate with kids in the public domain. Most mentoring men do occurs naturally as they volunteer in youth-oriented programs or do a little extra as part of their regular employment. Men interact with unrelated youth all the time in youth-oriented programs or in their regular work, play, religious, or other activity, but their involvement does not usually rise to the level of a full-fledged mentoring relationship. Being a coach, teacher, or having some similar status does not in and of itself mean that an adult will be a mentor. A man who has professional relationships with young people may serve as a mentor for some but not others. For example, the teachers who spoke with me often did not think of themselves as mentors to all their students, but they had all singled out some students for special attention. In his career as a high school teacher before working with at-risk youth specifically, Tony took it upon himself to focus some extra attention on one boy he describes as a "very Gothic kind of figure, at a school sitting out in the middle of sugar cane and cattle." This boy, he felt, was "just looking for a way to scream out" and needed support, in part because he had lost his father in a car accident when he was much younger. Tony recalls saying to the school's principal, "Hey, listen, I don't want to overstep my bounds in being a teacher, but this is a kid I'd like to spend some time with, and I don't want to offend anybody, you know. Do you mind?" After listening to Tony's intentions, the principal approved; so Tony proceeded to share time with the boy, going to lunch, sitting for hours doing jigsaw puzzles, and doing chores together.

Obviously, a teacher can't devote that kind of time with every student, but some of the men, like Nick, are in a position to mentor all of the kids with whom they work.

> As far as being mentors to these kids, I am a mentor to every one of them because they know they can come to me at any time and talk to me about anything and without any doors being shut. . . . Anybody's gonna work with kids should be willing to be a mentor to any kid, not just a certain kid.

Irrespective of whether a man looks to mentor one or many kids, being involved with youth professionally gives him the opportunity to earn a young person's trust and respect and the potential for a mentoring relationship arises.

Partly because of my study design and partly because men are more apt in their jobs and volunteering to focus on boys, my participants talked disproportionately about mentoring boys rather than girls. Yet, some men also have significant opportunities to mentor girls. Calvin, for instance, who is a retired naval officer, began mentoring relationships with numerous female cadets during his days running high school ROTC programs. Some of his mentoring relationships, with both boys and girls, have lasted for ten to fifteen years; the young people have sought his counsel on matters about education, military career options, and the like but also on personal issues, including teen pregnancy, physical abuse, and finances. Reflecting on his relationship with one woman he has stayed in close contact with over the years Calvin says:

> I can remember getting phone calls from her, ten, twelve years after she graduated, talking about that [unfavorable academic review by a military board].
> So, I think in terms of her military career and her personal life, I was a mentor for her for a long, long time. I think that everybody needs one. We called them the "sea daddy" when we were in the Navy. Everybody needs a sea daddy whether you are a kid or a teen or an adult. Everybody needs somebody to help them out.

Once he begins his storytelling, Calvin quickly recounts an extensive repertoire of stories about how he performed the "sea daddy" role for current and former cadets. In his mind, some of the girls and young women saw him as a father figure as well as a mentor. After establishing his credibility with his female cadets as both a man and former naval officer, he made sure they realized that it's "not just a man's world anymore" and that opportunities were available to them. No doubt Calvin's gender and the paramilitary ambiance of ROTC facilitated his mentoring girls about pursuits traditionally defined as masculine, but he also apparently was adept at offering more fatherly advice on a wide range of issues.

Listening to Calvin, we can begin to move beyond academic definitions of mentoring to explore how men in youth work settings assign meanings to mentoring, both in the abstract and for them personally. In my interviews, if the men did not bring up the topic on their own, I specifically asked them to define mentoring by sharing what they perceived to be its essential or key properties. Overall, they mentioned plenty of elements, but five themes dominate their comments—guidance, respect, listening, emotional support, and being a steady presence.

The most common message they express is that mentoring involves one person guiding or directing another along a path. Sidney, an elementary school teacher, succinctly describes a mentor as "somebody who teaches you things, who opens your eyes to new things, gives you guidance, advice." Asked to identify the "essential properties of good mentorship," 60-year-old Calvin stresses exposing kids to options:

Listening. Guiding. Not so much advice but advice when asked for. Because I think you can give too much advice. Showing lots of options, because a lot of times, when they begin to think about a problem or a situation they only see one path. They don't see a variety of options, different directions that they might go. So, providing alternate paths that they might take. That is something that I didn't get from my dad.

The youth minister Kevin's vision of mentoring reflects his desire to be a spiritual guide for young people.

Mentoring I guess is giving someone guidelines and opportunities to grow in their giftings, their talents, their abilities, helping shape their identity. And we all have a common thread here, and our common thread is our faith in Jesus Christ, so, I guess I'm sort of mentoring and facilitating that relationship. It's not necessarily their relationship with me as much as I'm trying to foster that relationship with Jesus, getting better and stronger, and you know, making sense of it, becoming real instead of some religious, stupid thing that we do.

Kevin looks at mentoring as a way for him to encourage kids to embrace a faith-based philosophy, personified by the religious figure Jesus. He implicitly stresses the importance of helping kids adopt positive values while they mature and construct their identity.

Andrew, who has volunteered much of his spare time to coaching kids, offers a more general and elaborate analysis, explicitly highlighting values.

Mentoring would be helping to guide somebody who may not have their own values and principles fully owned. And attempting to have them, first of all, reflect on what's important to them, how they're gonna lead their lives, so they do it purposefully. And although I don't want to completely ingrain my values on them, I want them to come to their own conclusions, but I think helping to guide them with my values and so forth—I think they're healthy values—and I think that by sharing that or at least explaining as to why do I behave the way I do, why do I hold certain opinions about things, at least intellectually, gives someone the chance to understand why you think in this way. Right answer is "I've thought about this, I've experienced this, and I've come to this conclusion." Wrong answer is, "That's what my parents told me to do." I think you need to be authentic, in terms of your maturity and how you think through things. And sadly . . . there's too many people that don't have authentic ideas and principles. They borrow from somebody else, and I think that makes you vulnerable to following, sort of, the idea of the day.

One facet of guidance that the men enunciate is helping kids identify their goals, a process enriched by getting youth to understand their full range of life options. Directing kids to set goals is, in turn, part of the larger process of helping them become better decisionmakers. Becoming a more mature decisionmaker requires learning to appreciate more fully how behavior produces short- and long-term consequences. Andrew implies that youth stand a better chance of becoming good decisionmakers if they are well grounded in their values; they should know what is important to them and why. Andrew asserts his willingness to explain his own life philosophy and the decisions he makes, to illustrate what it means to live life purposively. In the end, however, he realizes that he must step back and allow kids to make their own decisions. Ideally, he wants them to claim their own values and reasoning instead of clinging to or adopting someone else's.

Because kids, especially teenagers, are often disparagingly stereotyped as self-proclaimed "know-it-alls"—sometimes for good reason—it is no easy task for a man to establish his credibility with teenagers, so that his guidance is sought, appreciated, and followed. Many men realize that being an effective mentor requires that kids "look up to" you and respect you. Dwight puts it simply when describing a mentor as "someone that has to kind of just live his life in a fashion that makes other people kinda look at you and say, 'Well you know, he's all right.'" Setting an example by deed as well as word is critical because kids may observe a potential mentor at any time. As Nick says, "You're the book. They're reading you. They're learning from you." Many times a man may not even be aware that he is being "read." Ricardo, a 44-year-old Latino man who devotes time every Sunday morning to teaching catechism to Catholic kids, remarks: "I try to be a mentor and teach everywhere. I see everywhere I go, to a supermarket, I go to [places] around the neighborhood; I know they're watching me, and I just try to project the positive. Not just in the classroom, but everywhere." Ricardo knows that kids do watch him when they see him, so he tries to conduct himself appropriately.

Another key aspect of how men define mentoring emphasizes kids' perception of whether adults are willing to listen. In varied ways, the men talk about how critical it is for kids to feel comfortable enough to approach someone capable of guiding and supporting them. As we saw in Chapter 5, male youth workers tend to value their ability to have kids trust and reach out to them. When given the chance, then, men who mentor must listen closely to the messages springing from kids' minds and hearts, all the while managing the borders of power and friendship. Generally speaking, men recognize that accentuating the trust associated with being a confidant pays bigger dividends than pushing the authority button. Reflecting on how he has mentored troubled kids over the years, Nick demonstrates his astute understanding of this principle.

A mentor to me is giving life experiences, you know, as much as you can; being free to let them be free; be their self; express their self, but show 'em where they're making wrong decisions in a nonthreatening manner, because once you become threatening, to a child especially, the mentorism part is gone. You're not a mentor no more. You become an authority figure.

Closely tied to men's awareness that listening is vital is their desire to support kids emotionally with their struggles while encouraging them to pursue their dreams. Although the men do not suggest that strings should be attached to the emotional support they offer, some point out that as mentors they need to be real with the kids. In Paul's words, the ideal is to be "affirming yet challenging."

The final issue a number of the men raise involves mentors' willingness to stay the course and be a steady presence in kids' lives. Men working with kids who have spent years in disruptive and unpredictable home environments are especially attuned to the value of being dependable. Tony, who works with kids who have been expelled from multiple schools, stresses this aspect of mentoring:

I don't just mean having the time for it, I mean making yourself available for what that kid is needing. . . . I think a good mentor is someone who's got . . . there's got to be an element of dedication in there somewhere, I mean, there just has to be.

The men who carry their own negative memories of distant fathers, mothers, and other adults seem particularly mindful of how their reliability may imprint youth. For these men, the payoff for being reliable is that kids are more likely to believe that one has good intentions and is committed to helping them. Reliability may be appreciated most fully when the mentor is not getting paid. While Tony stresses the value of a mentor's "availability," he quickly extends his comment. In Tony's eyes, being dedicated to figuring out what kids need should go hand in hand with making oneself available. Being available, of course, increases a youth worker's chances of figuring out what a youngster needs.

Taken together, then, the men echo much of what those in academic settings suggest is important about mentoring. Men believe they can be good mentors when they act as a reliable and respectable guide for youth, helping them grow more comfortable identifying and pursuing life goals. Having the interpersonal skills to be both a good listener and emotionally supportive are also key to mentoring kids effectively.

My discussions with the men unearthed a few other noteworthy observations highlighting the nuances of how mentoring is perceived. Some of the men's comments suggest additional criteria for mentors. Like Gerald, some refer to mentors as essentially role models. Drawing on his Big Brother experience, Gerald says "I associate mentor [as] being a positive role model to someone." But not all role models are mentors. Ben, a full-time youth minister and summer camp counselor, distinguishes between role models and mentors.

> As far as I can tell I have two maybe three mentors in my life. And they are men, but it's different. It's not just a male role model; I've got a ton of male role models. As far as [an] actual mentor is concerned, that implies close relationship, it implies [a] similar life context, I suppose, to an extent. But also it implies intentional pilgrimage, intentional journey together. For me, mentor signifies an intentional relationship.

Ben's notion that mentoring involves two people sharing an "intentional journey" means that two people are consciously moving toward something together. Being a role model is typically part of the mentoring package, but it is not by itself a sufficient condition. Ben's thinking seems consistent with Bronfenbrenner's scholarly definition, that for a man to be a mentor he must have a tight, one-on-one relationship with the person being mentored. I also suspect that Ben applies a higher threshold than Gerald, Nick, and some of the other men when considering how intense a relationship has to be for it to qualify as one of mentoring.

For most of the men, mentoring is seen as a way to leave a lasting imprint on kids, even if the kids may not recognize the benefit of the mentoring experience immediately. Because men who mentor typically try to encourage kids to identify, pursue, and achieve meaningful goals, as well as develop a responsible decision-making style, they are likely to evaluate their mentor status based on whether they believe they have affected the kids, or will affect them, in the long run. Fostering that sort of difference is generally more likely when men spend an extended period of time with individual kids, watching them wrestle with multiple life challenges and mature. Men in longstanding mentoring relationships are likely to see their roles change over time; as kids age, their needs for attention and advice change. Mark, for instance, has seen his mentoring roles change as the young men he first started mentoring as high school teenagers have graduated and moved on to jobs and community college. His initial role was to motivate them to do well in school and to stay out of trouble. More recently, he has been trying to help them find jobs and develop a more professional demeanor.

Finally, though similar in some respects, teaching others to become mentors within a particular setting, say, a church youth group differs from mentoring younger kids directly. Being a step removed, men who assume the formal arrangement as a mentor of mentors may incorporate more of a friendly and collegial dimension into their relationships with their understudies. Men in these arrangements are likely to work at managing the borders of acting like friends and sharing secrets with youth who may be on the verge of adulthood and want to be treated accordingly. Though much of this training occurs informally, some is folded into routine training exercises. The impact of training others to be good mentors, when done well, is noteworthy because men can extend their reach in passing on the messages they deem important.

THE MENTORING MOVEMENT

Marc Freedman's *The Kindness of Strangers*[4] compellingly analyzes how various social developments in recent decades facilitated the growth of the modern mentoring movement. Citing some of the key social conditions and activities of recent decades, Freedman provides a backdrop against which to consider how men act as mentors to youth and their prospects for doing so. He also draws attention to viable initiatives for recruiting men into mentoring while enhancing their options to interact with kids in diverse settings.

Mentoring has taken on characteristics of a social movement, largely targeting the needs of disadvantaged or at-risk youth. Understanding the evolution of the mentoring movement to date requires an appreciation for how it is affected by two basic obstacles: availability of volunteers and the infrastructure and resources to support mentoring programs.[5] Although a few scholars have addressed these issues for men specifically, most have talked about mentors more generally. I focus on how these two obstacles relate to men's experiences—or lack there of—with volunteering and working with kids, as both natural and arranged mentors.

The two obstacles are embedded in our larger social system, which has, from a sociohistorical perspective, been shaped by a number of interrelated trends associated with family, work, education, neighborhoods, and the economy. How these factors have shaped the mentoring movement, and the contours of children's lives more specifically, also can be viewed through a lens sensitive to race, ethnicity, and gender concerns. Freedman found the impetus for the mentoring movement to be rooted in several factors: "dire circumstances of disadvantaged youth, the yearning and frustration felt by many middle-class adults, the current crisis in education and social policy, and mentoring's inherent qualities as a mechanism [for child and adolescent development], so evident in its long history."[6]

Changes in the Inner City

Taking a broad view, some commentators have lamented the transition to a more individualistic society in which neighborhood cohesiveness has declined and people have grown to feel more isolated.[7] Two decades ago, sociologist James Coleman warned that children from diverse social class backgrounds were suffering because they had less access to social capital—"the norms, the social networks, and the relationships between adults and children that are of value for the child's growing up."[8] It was true then, and now, that kids living in poverty are the most likely to be harmed by the changing nature of neighborhoods and families. Whereas more affluent parents have the financial means to purchase opportunities for other adults to invest in their children, through activities such as child care, private lessons, coaching, magnet school opportunities, summer camps, and therapy, poor parents are ill-equipped to expose their children to these resources.

As described in Chapter 2, a large proportion of American youth face significant daily challenges and pursue risky behaviors related to drugs, alcohol, sex, and violence. Many young people live a portion or all of their childhood and adolescence in single-parent homes, many of which can be defined as fragile families living in poverty.[9] In fragile families, limited options exist for providing supervision for kids while parents are at work and the household environment often is not conducive to promoting young people's commitment to school and academic achievement. Moreover, many kids live in impoverished, abandoned, and dangerous neighborhoods not conducive to building strong social ties between their inhabitants. Faced with traumatizing experiences from living in violence-riddled neighborhoods,[10] many youth struggle to find help and others have trouble accepting it when it's offered.[11] Lots of kids walk away from the kindness of mentors, as did a young man who abruptly turned his back on Kenny, his mentor. A business owner, Kenny gave the youth a job. Despite Kenny's generous efforts to share friendship, time, wisdom, and business resources with this kid, the disadvantaged young man never quite embraced the value of having a mentor. He quit the job shortly after taking it, and did so without giving notice.

The plight of urban youth, and their families, is seen by some to be at the core of the most recent surge of interest in mentoring. According to various observers of the urban world, one dramatic consequence of deindustrialization was the loss of blue-collar jobs and the declining presence of the middle class in urban areas.[12] Most notably, the gainfully employed family man is now in short supply. With the flight of the middle class from cities came a corresponding erosion of the physical and social spaces based on residential neighborhoods that had defined urban life. Revitalized sections of the urban landscape aside, much of inner-city living space is unsafe, or at least perceived to be so.[13] Public space is contested, the threat or use of violence often dictating individuals' mundane decisions about if, when, where, and how they traverse urban neighborhoods, streets, and subways. Symbolically, the shift in perspective is aptly captured by the vernacular "hood"—the word of choice for inner-city youth and many others when referring to the physical and symbolic space they claim as home. Notably lacking "neighbor," the "hood" turf has been stripped of its neighborly vitality, leaving its residents far more isolated from each other and from those living in the surrounding suburbs.

Recent ethnographers offer an intimate portrait of the stress, pessimism, and fear permeating inner-city people's daily lives.[14] Elija Anderson describes how the physical surroundings and local culture in one section of Philadelphia has undergone radical change because the "old heads," community leaders, many of whom are male, have retreated or been pushed to the background of public life. According to Anderson, for generations, old heads provided youth with role models of the working and family man as well as the community man with status, someone committed to helping the neighborhood thrive. In their roles as ministers, police officers, small store entrepreneurs, coaches, and the like, the old heads grabbed youths' attention and respect. They were natural mentors directly and indirectly helping youth, especially boys, navigate their poor, yet manageable surroundings. It was understood that they were "to teach, support, encourage, and in effect socialize young men to meet their responsibilities regarding work, family, the law, and common decency."[15] They provided youngsters with social capital and a vital service by connecting them to places and jobs outside the inner city. In short, they were pillars of responsibility, surrogate fathers in some cases, and messengers of hope.

Increasing economic poverty and the rise of the new urban gangster have fostered a cultural and physical environment in which old heads are less valued by those who live in the community. Many old heads left the area; others retreated to a more isolated existence to avoid the street conflicts. Previously able to share their folk wisdom and practical advice in public spaces, they now fear their neighbors and the "new heads"—the drug dealers and gang bangers who roam and control the dangerous city streets. Viewed as irrelevant, old heads are dismissed or mocked for their "outdated" philosophy and traditional tips for success. In short, old heads lost much of their standing and ability to persuade youth in the neighborhood

> due to the erosion of the values they embody—of responsibility, restraint, deferred gratification—in the larger American culture. In the immediate environment, the old head's salience is undercut by the loss of meaningful employment in the inner cities. Their teachings carry far less weight and make less intuitive sense in the context of little opportunity, as the means through which they established themselves is no longer visible or available to the next generation.[16]

The old heads have been replaced with a new breed of angry young men that rules the street by intimidation, sporting a "cool pose" all the while.[17] Immersed in the violent, sexually raw, "bling-bling" arm of hip-hop culture, the new urban power brokers of the street live life moment to moment, showing little interest in education, paid employment, the church, or establishing a two-parent family. To be sure, gangs and violent elements have always dotted the urban landscape, but their significance was offset by those more committed to the values and institutions associated with mainstream culture.

Drawing on his ethnographic fieldwork in inner-city Chicago, Mitchell Duneier offers a critical reading of this type of recent scholarly and journalistic portrait of race and city life, which relies heavily on the role model concept. The concept is central to explanations of the processes relating to African Americans, middle- and upper-working-class migration from inner cities, and contemporary urban poverty and culture. As alluded to earlier, the logic of the role model perspective suggests that, in the absence of individuals to use as socially acceptable exemplars of how life should be lived, individuals often lose their way or search for alternative models outside the mainstream. Duneier finds William Julius Wilson's census-based, structural analysis and Anderson's ethnographic interpretations misleading in some respects. Most notably, Duneier questions their assumptions about how much contact there was between the financially well-off and poor African Americans in the "old-time black neighborhoods." To make his case, Duneier cites W. E. B. Du Bois's classic work on Philadelphia in the late 1800s:

> They [middle and affluent class] teach the masses to a very small extent, mingle with them but little, do not largely hire their labor. Instead then of social classes held together by strong ties of mutual interest, we have in the case of the Negroes, classes who have much to keep them apart, and only community of blood and color prejudice to bind them together.[18]

Although there is room to debate how important middle-class blacks were to the way lower-income blacks lived their lives during the past 100 plus years, this uncertainty does not negate what middle- and upper-working-class African Americans might contribute today and in the immediate future.

Arguing that conventional descriptions are based largely on anecdotal materials, Duneier also suggests that mainstream images and discussion of social class of blacks is often organized around a crude dichotomy of middle class and underclass; the working class and working poor, along with their moral values, are left largely invisible. This dichotomy, says Duneier, has

> resulted in a tendency to associate any "respectable" behavioral characteristics in black people with a middle-class orientation. . . . The prevalent imagery of the black class structure renders the most effective agents of social control in the black community irrelevant in the debate over the future of their own people.[19]

In other words, the working class and working poor, men and women alike, are mostly ignored by many who tackle urban problems, including problems directly related to children.

One potential shortcoming of overemphasizing the role model concept is that it tends to deemphasize how much those in the inner city are isolated from mainstream values.[20] As Duneier argues:

> What distinguishes the poor from other members of society is not that they are isolated from mainstream values, but that they do not have the standard of living to buffer them from the destructive effects of the permissiveness, freedom, and spontaneity of American life.[21]

Consequently, the difficulties some minority youth face, for instance, teenage pregnancy, are perceived as largely African American issues rather than as part of larger cultural shifts in the public's perceptions and experiences related to sex, relationships, and single parenthood.[22]

Focusing on Kids

In many ways this profile of urban enclaves in recent decades stands in stark contrast to that of working- and middle-class neighborhoods in the suburbs. Ironically though, unique common ground emerged over recent years as middle-class and suburban parents increasingly felt the pressure of finding the time, money, and social support to care for their children in a manner consistent with their expectations, the same pressure poor inner-city parents had been feeling for years. Although their situation is patently better than those living in the inner city, parents residing outside urban poverty may have become more attuned than their counterparts from earlier decades to the difficulties poor children face—at least in the abstract.[23]

As the public became more sensitive to poor children's plight it also came to recognize more fully that the economically gutted inner-city infrastructure, most notably the school systems and local businesses, was incapable of addressing children's developmental needs efficiently. Notwithstanding the unresolved debate about how processes tied to race and social class have altered the social dynamics in poor inner-city areas, most would agree that things have gotten worse.

The mentoring movement emerged out of the public's unease with standing idle as poor children were subjected to unusual suffering, sometimes ending in needless deaths. According to Freedman, mentoring was an attractive outlet for those who wanted to help because it is simple, direct, sympathetic, legitimate, bounded, and plastic. Individuals can reduce a major social problem to a manageable situation. Having a one-on-one relationship with an at-risk young person puts a face on the problem, personalizing it to those willing to volunteer. Mentors can do something more or less immediately; they need not deal with the cumbersome political process. They can get involved directly by helping a child learn to read, write, do math, or simply have a bit of fun. Mentoring is a valued experience; it can be a personally satisfying accomplishment that wins praise from others as well. For adults, it has social legitimacy; it enables them to be involved with unrelated children in socially acceptable ways. Generally speaking, adults need not worry about interfering with parents' prerogatives, as mentors are merely helpers. Whatever level of involvement mentoring entails, it is loosely bounded in the amount of time, energy, emotion, and money it demands. In other words, mentors are not expected to be full-time caregivers or surrogate parents attentive to a youth's needs 24/7. They negotiate a place in a kid's life as an adult friend or guide with an understanding that they have limited responsibilities. Finally, individuals can choose and shape their mentoring opportunities in various ways to favor whatever attributes they care to express. They may wish to teach kids particular skills, provide emotional support, or make opportunities available to youth that they would otherwise not have. For some mentors, experiencing a deeper or lost sense of community and attachment to others may be sufficient incentive for them to invest in a child's life. To varying degrees, all of the attributes that make mentoring attractive surfaced in the stories told by the Big Brothers and other men I interviewed who volunteered as mentors for kids.

Finally, amidst the larger mentoring movement, 100 Black Men of America, Inc. emerged as an important national organization in 1986, targeting much of its effort on young African Americans. The roots for this organization go back to the early 1960s when the One Hundred Men organization was founded in New York.[24] As of 2006, there were 106 chapters in the United States with over 10,000 members, largely successful professionals in diverse fields, including business, medicine, law, education, politics, and entertainment. Intent on improving educational and economic opportunities for all African Americans, part of its mission is to "serve as a beacon of leadership by utilizing our diverse talents to create environments where our children are motivated to achieve."[25] In 1994, the organization initiated a plan to channel resources into four critical areas: mentoring, education, health and wellness, and economic development. Mentoring it describes as "the cornerstone of what the organization brings to the community by guiding youth in life experiences, fostering a positive self-perception and self-respect, encouraging excellence in education, and the pursuit of positive life-long goals." In his book, *The Miracles of Mentoring*, past president of the organization, Thomas W. Dortch, Jr., provides a detailed practical guide to "mentoring the 100 way" while sharing some of the personal and organizational success stories from around the country.

Over 120,000 youth participate annually in the organization's activities; most are involved with one of two mentoring programs, Mentoring the 100 Way and Collegiate 100. Adult men involved in the former are trained to be mentors, advocates, and role models for youth ages 8–18. Using one-on-one, group, and tag team mentoring, the holistic program addresses the social, emotional, and cultural needs of African American youth. Mentors work with youth to build skills necessary for productive citizenship, addressing topics relating to identity development, moral character, work ethic, and life skills. The latter program, Collegiate 100, enlists college students as mentors, tutors, and positive role models for kids. Students are sponsored by an advisor trained and active in a local chapter of 100 Black Men.

MENTORING PROGRAMS: PRACTICE AND VALUE

No one knows precisely how many young people across the country believe they have either an arranged or natural mentor outside their immediate family, but an informed guess is that perhaps 50–60 percent do.[26] According to one estimate, three million American kids are active in some sort of formal mentoring relationship, roughly 300,000 of those through Big Brothers Big Sisters (BBBS) programs.[27]

In some instances, arranged mentors must submit to a careful screening process prior to being matched with a young person. Big Brothers Big Sisters uses one of the most rigorous screening procedures; it includes a criminal background check, personal interview, references check, psychological testing, and a home assessment.[28] Although this screening process has many positive consequences, it may also deter some men from participating because they do not want to submit to a criminal background check. In some instances, then, men's transgressions during their own youth or young adulthood preclude them from volunteering for one-on-one mentoring. This policy is likely to have a disproportionate effect on African American men raised in inner cities, because they are more likely than whites to be arrested and convicted of drug related offenses, even though self-reported data suggest that whites use and sell drugs at higher rates.[29] In addition, the policy eliminates from becoming Big Brothers men who could say to at-risk youth: "I can relate to where you're coming from because I was there too. I made mistakes, but I turned my life around, and so can you." My interviews and observations suggest that these types of interpersonal connections in other youth work settings can be valuable.

A fairly common practice in mentoring programs is a prerelationship training workshop or orientation session for mentors. Unfortunately, due to financial and time constraints, programs are less likely to provide ongoing training for mentors.[30] Big Brothers Big Sisters provides a type of ongoing training by supplying a staff member called a Match Support Specialist, who is available to help mentors and youth adjust to their match. Some believe this training is an essential reason why this particular mentoring program produces positive results.

In recent years, researchers have begun to develop a clearer picture of what types of programs benefit kids, what types of youth are better off after being involved with arranged mentors, the limitations of mentoring, and the difficulties of recruiting mentors (both male and female). One review of fifty-five youth-mentoring programs conducted between 1970 and 1998, not taking into account

mentors' gender, concludes that there are significant, though relatively small, benefits for the average young person who participates.[31] Kids exposed to conditions
of "environment risk and disadvantage" are most likely to benefit from being involved in a mentoring program. Being raised in a family with low socioeconomic
status also raises youths' chances for experiencing a positive change.

Programs organized around key theoretical principles and "best practices"
tend to have a higher chance of producing positive results. The practices include
"ongoing training for mentors, structured activities for mentors and youth as
well as expectations for frequency of contact, mechanisms for support and involvement of parents, and monitoring of overall program implementation."[32]
Unfortunately, some of the best practice strategies require a significant funding
stream, and those are in short supply.

Although we know little about how men actually influence youths' lives
through mentoring, one rigorous eight-city experiment involving the Big Brothers Big Sisters program shows that youth can be affected positively in various
ways by a systematically implemented mentoring intervention.[33] Data from an
eighteen-month follow-up showed that Little Brothers and Little Sisters aged
10–16 who were involved in a one-on-one mentoring relationship were significantly less likely, compared to controls, to initiate drug or alcohol use, hit someone, or skip school. Compared to controls, they also felt more competent in their
schoolwork, showed modest improvement in their grades, and experienced improved relations with their parents and peers.

That mentors tend to differ in their relationship styles is likely to affect
whether relationships continue for a significant length of time or end prematurely. In a study of urban kids who had applied to the BBBS program, adult volunteers who had more money tended to stay in their mentoring relationship
longer than those who were less well-off.[34] This pattern is consistent with the
finding noted earlier that more affluent individuals are also more likely to do volunteer work in the first place. Married mentors between 26 and 30 years of age
were the most likely to end their match early; however, the researchers did not
report whether being married for a certain period of time made more of a difference for males or females. Extended mentoring relationships are more likely to
contribute something positive to kids. The most dramatic increase in positive
outcomes was found in relationships that lasted for over a year. Most of the one-
on-one mentoring arrangements men reported to me lasted less than a year,
with the notable exceptions of Michael, Mark, and several others. Consistent
with the findings in the literature, those men who sustained longer-term relationships were more likely to believe they made a bigger difference for the kids.

Even though the BBBS study indicated that early termination was related to negative outcomes for the kids, it is not clear whether mentors involved in prematurely terminated relationships experience any negative consequences, but it is possible. Several of the men I interviewed, for example, were disappointed that their mentoring relationships ended relatively quickly, though none reported being significantly distraught because of it.

RECRUITING MEN

Recruiting adults to serve as mentors for youth is quite challenging. Getting males to participate is especially difficult, and as more mentoring programs have been launched across the country, competition for mentors has increased. The intensity of the recruitment challenge accentuates the value of work by social scientists,[35] marketing specialists,[36] and mentoring experts[37] analyzing the difficulties associated with attracting volunteers and mentors for community programs, including those addressing children's needs.

Despite their positive reputation[38] and documented success, even Big Brothers Big Sisters programs throughout the country struggle to recruit adequate numbers of adult mentors, especially males, for the large waiting list of youth and families. In community-based mentoring, the main BBBS program, adults are asked to spend as little as an hour a week with their Little Brother or Sister, sharing activities and stories in community and residential settings. Participants in the school-based program meet in schools, libraries, and community centers once a week for primarily fun and friendship, and sometimes a bit of tutoring.[39] National figures for BBBS show that boys, especially African American males, wait a long time to be matched, and some never are.[40] One study of initial inquiries from potential mentors at eight BBBS sites across the country in 1993 found that only 42 percent were from males. Men with at least some college education were much more likely to inquire about mentoring, apply, and then be matched.[41]

The five broad types of reasons men get involved with youth discussed in Chapter 4 apply to Big Brothers' motives. Though men may have additional motives for pursuing one-on-one mentoring in particular, the Big Brothers I interviewed recognize the value of giving back to others, helping kids expand their options, passing along values and experiences to a younger generation, feeling good, and being able to see the results of their mentoring efforts.

Why are men less likely than women to volunteer for mentoring programs? Lacking rigorous research, informed speculation offers the best thinking.

Michael Garringer, editor of the National Mentoring Center bulletin, and Stephanie Blackman, a former National Service Fellow who prepared a guide for recruiting male volunteers based on interviews with volunteer coordinators and volunteers in the northwestern states, offer possible explanations for men's limited involvement.[42] In general, men are thought to value volunteering much less than paid work and to have less available time than women, often because of their paid work schedules. As to volunteering with children, men are thought to regard it as a feminine activity (especially work with very young children), to feel scared or lack confidence, fear allegations of abuse, be unaware of the need for mentoring, and have little knowledge of how particular programs work.

In addition, programs may be poorly marketed to men, because some do not take into account local or regional differences in how men think, feel, and act. Marketing strategies may be oriented, consciously or unconsciously, toward women or may be ineffective at appealing to contemporary men's personalities, preferences, and needs because they rely on traditional, sometimes outdated, male stereotypes. Yet, some of the common impressions about men's limited involvement implicitly acknowledge that the traditional gender norms that have influenced males' and females' perceptions of relationships in the workplace and families continue to hold sway. They may still affect men's perceptions of what they are likely to gain or lose by being involved with youth. Throughout its 100-year history, BBBS, in consultation with marketing specialists in recent years, has attempted to incorporate masculine representations as part of its recruitment messages, taking into account dominant masculine gender myths and emerging variations.[43] The myths have focused on themes such as men as authority figures, winners, warriors, father substitutes, and buddies. Thus, while those responsible for recruiting men must be prepared to take into account how traditional gender norms affect men's willingness or opportunities to participate, they must also demonstrate an ability to think in fresh ways about men in order to develop effective recruitment strategies.

Because men have diverse sociocultural backgrounds, it is useful to explore how life experiences and conditions due to social class, race, ethnicity, and gender combine to influence men's perceptions, motivations, availability, and decisions regarding mentoring youth. For example, middle-class men may anticipate that they will have little in common with disadvantaged youth, particularly those from different racial or ethnic backgrounds.[44] Even Mark, who has established a successful long-term mentoring relationship with several African American young men, feels he is limited in some ways in reaching black youth because he is white. To address this self-perceived limitation, he has his sights set on incorporating a few black men into the kids' lives to help round out their experiences and opportunities.

In more extreme cases, men may feel awkward, unable to relate to kids whose living circumstances are very different from their own or from anything they have witnessed first-hand. For middle-class white men, the combination of distinct generational, social class, and cultural differences may test their ability to adapt, forcing them to look creatively for common ground to develop a meaningful relationship with individual kids. Some may turn to a mutual interest in sports or a passion for a hobby, for example, playing music. Playing and watching sports together can be a masculinity-validating and bonding experience for men and boys. However, despite wonderful stories profiling how well some white men and kids from different racial backgrounds relate through sports and other activities, a large percentage of relationships end quickly because the men and the youths do not bond. An inability to bridge the generation gap may thwart some relationships, while others falter because the men and the kids don't succeed in bridging the cultural divide between them.

Issues involving social class discrepancies are not confined to white men trying to mentor poor African American or Hispanic kids. Middle-class African American and Hispanic men must grapple with their own unique challenges. Despite a common racial or ethnic heritage, they may wonder whether they can relate to and inspire less advantaged inner-city youth if they have inherited their comfortable class position and followed a conventional educational and work path to sustain it. Unlike their counterparts raised in poverty who later escaped, these men may not be "streetwise"[45] because they have little or no intimate understanding of inner-city life's daily rhythms and the insidious, debilitating problems poor youth face. While whites may see middle-class men's dark skin color as code for inner-city status, urban youth, the real insiders, are likely to question professional men's legitimacy because of their "white" lifestyle and values. Just as the old heads in Anderson's Philadelphia study were seen as irrelevant, professional men trying to help kids must overcome many youths' perceptions of them as intrusive, clueless outsiders. Inner-city youth may be more forgiving of the professional athlete or hip-hop entertainer who returns to the "hood," but the middle-class doctor, lawyer, or legitimate businessman is often seen as having sold out to the "other" side. Thus, middle-class men of color—like many of the members of 100 Black Men—who want to mentor at-risk urban youth must walk a fine line. They must feel secure enough with their privileged class standing and related values—responsibility, education, work ethic, civility—to convince kids teetering on the brink of self-destruction that there is a better way to get by and to succeed. At the same time, their chance for success may be enhanced if they identify emotionally with youth based on their lived experiences as persons of color, even if they haven't suffered directly from poverty.

Kenny, the highly successful middle-aged African American business owner and mentor mentioned above, experienced poverty as a child—though he was largely unaware of it at the time. He recalls his efforts to bridge the social class gap between him and a black male high school student he once mentored for part of a school year. Given his own modest family beginnings, Kenny tried to draw upon his personal experiences to show how someone, irrespective of racial background and economic resources, can succeed. Referring to the student, Kenny summarizes:

> He would sometimes, occasionally, say things that would make me believe that he felt that he was at a disadvantage, that he was not going to be able to succeed because he was black. [He seemed to think that his] father is in jail because he was black; his mother is not at home because she is black. That people in his neighborhood are doing whatever they are doing because they cannot succeed because [of] what society is not going to allow them. We would have those conversations that you can succeed, you just have [to] want to do so, and you have to come up with a plan how to do that. Yeah it is going to be tough. . . . I remember telling him I had it tough, we had it tough, we didn't know it was tough, but our teachers always said, "The only way you are going to survive is you learn as much as you possibly can and become educated." I didn't have white teachers; one of the differences: black teachers were truly, truly dedicated in talking a language to us and say[ing], "You better learn this, you better pay attention, because when you get out of here, it is a different world." White teachers would not necessarily say that. That is my impression. So we would have, I would try to share with him, the differences today as opposed to when I was growing up and what my teachers meant to me. He has got to do a lot of it on his own, you have got to be your own motivator, you have got to decide. . . . You may not do it now; one day, hopefully you will wake up before it is too late. It may be ten years, it may be five years, but you will think back on this thing and say, "If I am going to get out of the rut that I am in, it is up to me." Nobody else. You can't blame society, you cannot blame other people, it is up to you. Nobody is going to physically chain you down.

Despite providing the teenager a job at his company and counseling him on how to manage his personal finances, Kenny's mentoring efforts came to a close when the kid abruptly quit his job and went on his way.

It is surprising to me that only a few of the African American men, Kenny among them, explicitly discussed race issues with the kids they personally mentored; most of the black professionals and college students either never raised the subject or mentioned it only in passing. The same was true of white men mentoring African American kids. Race typically was not a big issue for the men in their relationships with kids. Of course, these men represent those most motivated to work with youth; they have actually taken steps to get involved. Other men may be standing on the sidelines because they doubt their ability to relate to kids different from them in race, social class, culture, and perhaps sexual orientation.

Volunteer coordinators need to develop strategies to minimize men's sundry concerns about becoming mentors for youth. Creative strategies that ease men's and youths' discomfort about how to manage perceptions of physical and social spaces are clearly warranted. Programs such as Outward Bound that provide inner-city kids opportunities to travel outside their physical and cultural space to interact with mentors in different settings may be worthwhile. Although such programs are encumbered by logistical challenges, including transportation for the attendees, the concept should be explored.

Ironically, the men most likely to volunteer—those with at least some college education—may face the biggest problems in relating to at-risk youth, whether they are of a similar or different racial background. Consequently, volunteer coordinators should expand their efforts to secure working-class men's participation in mentoring programs. Some observe that the "most successful mentors are commonly individuals who have weathered 'hard lives,' growing up in the same way as the youth, often coming from the same neighborhoods and able to talk to them in their own language."[46] Derek, the home-grown self-proclaimed "thug" turned police officer, illustrates this principle perfectly. Working-class men may actually have a more "privileged" life than many of the kids living in the inner-city, but these men are likely to have similar class-based experiences. Many men in blue-collar jobs already make valuable contributions to youth through their involvement in coaching recreational sports.

Even though numerous men (professional and working-class) are comfortable volunteering their time to coach a group of youth in a recreational sport, especially if they have a son or daughter participating, the same men may feel uncomfortable forging a one-on-one mentoring relationship outside a group setting—the type popularized by BBBS.[47] Part of the explanation for why there are disproportionately more well-educated BBBS mentors may be that working-class men feel less comfortable forming a one-on-one mentoring relationship. History shows, however, that it was quite common in the 1800s and even early 1900s for blue-collar and semiskilled workers to take an interest in training an individual boy or young man in a trade, treating him as an apprentice even if there was no formal apprentice contract.[48] Far fewer relationships of this sort exist today because of economic and social changes, but this need not mean an end to the relationships. Arrangements matching an adult worker, or a small crew of workers with a less advantaged young person could emphasize the value of mentoring vis-à-vis a wide range of work experiences.

Apprenticeships, formal and informal, represent a viable option for incorporating at-risk kids and even more privileged youth, into situations that foster a broad form of mentoring. Such arrangements vary considerably in how they are structured, but most are designed as opportunities for young people to gain more than technical knowledge. Successful apprenticeships enable youth to learn fundamental worker virtues associated with punctuality, diligence, responsibility, and openness to supervision. Youth may also develop social skills that will enable them to work with diverse coworkers and customers while acquiring higher-order cognitive skills so they can learn new information more efficiently and solve problems. In essence, young people experientially learn some of the basic lessons of adulthood while being exposed to aspects of work life.

After studying the elaborate and highly effective German apprenticeship system, Stephen Hamilton, who studies human development, has proposed a creative vision of an American apprentice system.[49] Many of the reforms he outlines would require leaders of schools, businesses, and communities to make significant changes, but he also notes that various elements of apprenticeship already exist in the United States. He highlights a few successful apprentice programs (e.g., Job Corps, targeting 16–24-year-olds) that have an important mentoring component. Hamilton identifies four key features of any apprenticeship system: (a) workplaces and other community settings are exploited as learning environments; (b) work experience is linked to academic training; (c) youth are simultaneously workers with real responsibilities and learners; and (d) close relationships are fostered between youth and adult mentors. In this type of apprenticeship system, not all adults working with apprentices become their mentors, and not all mentors have apprentices. However, youth workers who do an apprenticeship are placed in a setting where they have a realistic chance of being mentored in ways that go beyond being taught technical skills.

Anyone wanting to develop or modify a mentoring program for teenagers should explore ways to establish partnerships with the labor market, integrating individual, family, school, and community resources. Given men's dominant presence in many labor market sectors and their general commitment to the work world, men will be key players in making mentoring a vital element to any apprenticeship system. Strategies need to be flexible, so that kids from poor neighborhoods can be linked to options in communities with an adequate economic infrastructure. Rebuilding the infrastructure in the poorest urban areas to make local apprenticeships more viable is an obvious need, though a challenging policy path.

Several authors have provided useful insights and practical tips on how social service providers can get more men to volunteer in community programs in general,[50] or mentoring[51] and early childhood development programs[52] in particular. Focusing on mentoring issues, I selectively draw from these practical guides to elaborate on my earlier comments about how gender, race, ethnicity, fathering, and community issues relate to men's involvement with unrelated youth.

Among the challenges volunteer coordinators face is that many men continue to view certain forms of involvement with youth as women's work. Developing and sustaining personal, one-on-one relationships appears to be one such area. Despite changing views about gender, plenty of men still see the world through homophobic and anti-feminine lenses. Generally speaking, men's self-perceptions are affected by how they believe others, especially other men, judge their manliness in various areas. Recruiters should therefore make a specific effort to include men as recruiters and represent volunteer work with kids as an activity suitable for all sorts of men. Once a program secures a few men (perhaps even only one man) whom most men are likely to respect, recruiters can capitalize on that to legitimize volunteering with youth.

Some situations may require recruiters to clarify for potential volunteers how the skills they could teach youth would probably produce economic and social impacts in the real world. Although some men may be comfortable with the thought of developing a nurturing relationship with a young person, they will be motivated more by the knowledge that they could help a person achieve a particular, measurable result (e.g., better grades, a job). It makes sense, then, to develop a recruitment pitch for some men that highlights what concrete outcomes are possible and what men can do to make them happen. While recruiters should project an honest assessment of the potential benefits of men's involvement, they also should be careful not to inadvertently portray the tasks at hand as daunting.

Strategies like creative packaging and using the right spokesperson(s) will help organizations involve men in productive and appealing ways. One possibility is to promote mentoring by buddies, in which two male friends share responsibility for being involved with a particular young person.[53] This approach can minimize the overall investment required of either man while providing each with an added incentive to continue the mentoring relationship. Men who might otherwise not be inclined to volunteer for a mentoring program might be attracted to this arrangement for logistical as well as interpersonal reasons. Kids who participate may acquire even more social capital if their relationship is with two mentors who are friends with each other. Marketing this option as part of a competition or challenge between groups of men (e.g., fraternity brothers, men who work together, men who play on competing recreational sports teams) may generate some interest, though adequate screening is necessary to ensure that the mentoring teams are dedicated enough to pursue a mentoring relationship for an extended period of time. Ideally, mentoring will involve men who truly want to be involved with youth, for reasons other than winning a bet or trying to win a volunteerism contest. Perhaps the best strategy for securing and maintaining men's involvement is to appeal to both groups and individuals, using an approach like that initiated by the 100 Black Men organization.

Recruiters should also strive to identify and recruit men through the significant women in their lives, most notably their romantic partner. Obviously, those men on reasonably good terms with their romantic partner are more likely to be susceptible to a partner's enthusiastic support of their involvement. Recruiters and program personnel might consider developing options whereby committed couples, like the male buddies noted above, can volunteer as a team. Recruiting these couples through churches and other civic organizations seems feasible. Depending on the gender of the person being mentored, the male or female could be designated as the primary contact. The male-female team mentoring approach expands the gender-matching theme by offering the youth a chance to be mentored by both a male and a female. Derek in particular, but other men as well, reports that he was mentored effectively by women. Even if few men pursue this approach, providing men creative options for structuring their mentoring experience should result in more men becoming volunteers.

Unfortunately, the cultural climate responsible for perpetuating the "bad guy" and "dubious guy" stereotypes has tainted the process of recruiting men to mentor youth in settings emphasizing the building of close friendships. Though it is unclear how many men are affected, some male volunteers and those contemplating mentoring admit to being concerned about being falsely accused of acting inappropriately toward kids.[54] Whereas men's involvement with youth in certain types of group settings (e.g., recreational sports) seldom raises red flags about men's motivation or behavior, men feel more vulnerable to the public's and youth's misperceptions if they pursue the one-on-one mentoring option. The magnitude of this concern is mirrored in the fairly standard organizational practice of matching mentors and youth based on gender. Due diligence requires mentoring organizations to implement rigorous screening procedures, to help protect children from truly bad men, but organizations also need to clarify for other men what the real chances are that they might be falsely accused. Organizations should also articulate what procedures are in place for processing complaints.[55] For some men, the team mentoring approach might alleviate or reduce their worries about false child abuse accusations, especially if their teammate is a woman.

Volunteer coordinators believe that many men shy away from mentoring because they feel pressed for time due to work and family commitments.[56] For example, only a small percentage of Big Brothers have children of their own, particularly small children living at home. Ironically, fathers, given their extensive "on the job" training with their own kids, represent an untapped pool of potential volunteers for mentoring programs capable of accommodating them. Unfortunately, the current BBBS philosophy emphasizing the virtues of one-on-one mentoring may not be ideal for men who already have family commitments. But administrators and recruiters who are free to expand mentoring options can try to make them more appealing to those fathers who would like to get involved. Experimenting with options enabling men to incorporate their own families, at least to a limited extent, may prove useful. Securing a father's commitment to a time-consuming mentoring relationship might be more feasible if his personal investment might directly benefit his family. Some arrangements might produce a unique intergenerational family bonding experience. For instance, a man and his teenage child might jointly mentor a younger child. The father might become the primary mentor while his teenage son or daughter participated in a quasi-mentoring role, perhaps as a school tutor or instructor in a particular skill. By incorporating his teenage child into the program, the father may minimize that child's potential jealousy while opening a new channel for communicating with that child. The father could still spend some one-to-one time with the kid being mentored in addition to sharing time together that included his own child. Some fathers may see this type of arrangement as a meaningful opportunity to teach their own children the value of caring for others.

EVOLVING RELATIONSHIPS

Mentoring programs must help men build healthy mentoring relationships that last. Several studies sponsored by Public/Private Ventures, a Philadelphia-based nonprofit research, public policy, and program development organization, offer insights about the joys and struggles adult mentors and youth experience in their relationships with one another. Because most mentoring matches eventually end—at least as formal arrangements—studying how men and kids transition out of their relationships is also useful. Although research has not clearly distinguished between male and female mentors, the general findings may provide insights for thinking about male mentors.

The formal mentors I interviewed shared stories depicting a wide range of relationships in terms of depth, duration, and consequence. In a few cases men reported experiencing awkward or eventful transitions out of their mentoring relationship, but most men indicated that the transitions had not been unusual or difficult.

What has been learned from research targeting exclusively arranged mentoring relationships? One research initiative focused on four programs involving male and female mentors 55 years of age and older and at-risk youth aged 12 to 17.[57] A major finding of the small four-site study was that, when elders allowed "relationships to be youth-driven in their content and timing," mentors and youth tended to report satisfaction with the relationship.[58] Mentors in good relationships appeared to wait patiently for youth to express their needs and took their cue from the kid about when and how trust was established. Also, the adults were serious about the interests the youth expressed, asking the kid what activities he or she wanted to do and initiating plans with the youth's preferences in mind. Moreover, they worked to help the youngster in the area where he or she was most open to assistance. Relationships that turned out to be dissatisfying tended to involve adults who often made the decisions about when and how much time they spent with youth and didn't provide the kid a reasonable amount of say in what they did together. One of the biggest mistakes mentors made in dissatisfying relationships was to push the youth too quickly to reveal intimate, "emotionally challenging" details about his or her personal life (e.g., "poor school performance, criminal records, or dysfunctional or abusive family behaviors").[59] The Big Brothers and other formal mentors I interviewed seemed particularly sensitive to allowing kids to open up at their own pace. They realize that kids might not feel comfortable talking about certain things, so they try to show kids that they are willing to listen but try to avoid being too pushy.

One Big Brother, John, a 23-year-old Asian college student, provides an example of how a young man can pursue a two-year mentoring relationship with a Little Brother in a manner consistent with the "youth-driven" strategy. John describes how he got things rolling when he started to interact with his 6-year-old new friend. During their first year, he met his Little Brother at the kid's school.

> So, just getting to know him . . . it was just like "What do you like? . . . What kind of sports do you like? Do you like this kind of basketball player?" Or, you know, . . . maybe famous athletes. And, also, TV shows. . . . I remember we talked about, like, Sponge Bob Squarepants a lot. And . . . some other Nickelodeon shows. . . . I kinda wanted to do that and just, just sorta establish . . . kinda the things you're interested in, . . . that kind of stuff. . . . Maybe I would just ask, . . . "What do you want to be when you grow up?"

The types of questions John asked initially are designed to demonstrate that John is comfortable talking about things that presumably are of interest to the Little Brother. Consistent with the process of leveling discussed earlier, John displays his willingness to meet his Little Brother on the kid's turf.

Reggie, an elementary school teacher, also demonstrates patience in allowing his mentoring relationship with Devon, a fourth grade student he has known for several years, to evolve in a manner and at a pace Devon finds acceptable. Prior to becoming Devon's formal mentor as part of a school program, they had already formed a unique bond that seems to buffer Devon's experience of not having his mother or father living with him. As Reggie explains:

> He and I correspond in letters. He's always written letters to me. He brings me pictures. "Mr. Reggie, I got a picture for you." That's just his being affectionate with me, showing, telling me that he loves me. He did that in the second grade, third grade, he brought me pictures . . . every year. We just have a relationship. . . . And he says, "Mr. Reggie, I love you. I love Mr. Jerry [a teacher]. You two are the only ones that really understand me. You're always treating me nice and you're always telling me what I need to do." And I just love this kid, man. He's just wonderful to me. I see his potential. . . . And he always tells me, he loves wrestling; man, he is just crazy about it.

Because of Reggie's nurturing demeanor, Devon has opened up to him. As a result of their relationship, Reggie was able to help Devon's reading teacher inspire him to improve his reading performance, by letting her know that Devon would eagerly read books about wrestling.

Another intriguing area the four-site study addressed involved how mentors interacted with the youth's parents. Those in satisfying relationships tended to listen to parents when it seemed appropriate but were reluctant to engage the parents in lengthy, intimate conversations dealing with the youth. Thus, those mentors who guarded the confidences of the youth tended to fare better. Although this strategy makes sense on one level, it potentially limits the type and amount of social capital mentors can contribute to youth, because the mentors will be reluctant to coordinate and share protective and supervisory roles with the parents. Although it is not clear from the data whether the male mentors had unique types of exchanges with the child's mother, I suspect that the communication dynamics between a male mentor and the child's mother are likely to differ from those between a female mentor and the mother. A mother is probably less likely to feel threatened by a male mentor, who, because of his gender, can never truly replace her as mom. During my conversations with Big Brothers, I found that they generally try to tread lightly and avoid becoming deeply involved with the Little Brother's mom or other family members. They have casual conversations and exchange information at times, but the men report being relatively reserved with family members.

One qualitative study explored how forty-three Big Brothers and thirty-nine Big Sisters developed and managed their mentoring relationships with youth, providing additional insight into the types of relationships mentors and youth form.[60] Mentors tended to manage their relationships in one of two basic ways. The first, labeled developmental, is characterized by mentors focusing on building a relationship with the youngster. The focus on relationship-building translates into mentors doing things with the kid that are fun and being responsive to the kid's interests. Mentors in developmental relationships make sure their relationship evolves in a friendly, positive way. They are not set on fixing the kid or inclined to see the child as a project. Rather, they essentially see themselves as the kid's buddy. For the most part, the men who talked with me about their mentoring painted a self-portrait that mirrors the developmental style of relationship. Paul comments that mentoring involves "some of the aspects of being a friend. . . . The other aspect is somebody who listens to you," while Dwight candidly says, "You have to be their friend." That's not to say that these men or others do not see the youth's educational deficiencies and try to improve them, but they emphasize the value of their friendship first.

The other style of mentoring is described as the prescriptive approach. Mentors with this style see a child with whom they are matched as a challenge, as someone who needs to be transformed. These mentors view the kid as being too aggressive, not disciplined enough, too lackadaisical about school work, poorly mannered, not passionate enough about life, and the like. The mentors feel they have a mission to correct the youth's deficiencies in order to improve the youth's life chances. In these cases, the child is viewed as a project, something that needs to be fixed. They perceive themselves a having a teacher-student type of relationship. None of the men I interviewed depicted themselves in this manner, though some do pass judgment on their Little Brother's demeanor from time to time.

A brief gender analysis of Big Brother Big Sister matches reveals that whereas 74 percent of Big Brothers form developmental relationships, 54 percent of female matches are characterized this way.[61] This pattern is consistent with staff impressions and annual surveys of BBBS agencies, which indicate that, compared to female matches, male matches last longer and have fewer difficulties. Studies of other mentoring programs have found the opposite pattern.[62] Big Brothers may be more apt to form development relationships with kids because of differences between the boys and the girls who enter the program. The girls are perceived to have more difficulties with their mothers and are more likely to have been subjected to physical and sexual abuse. Whereas most boys are enrolled in the program because their mothers want to provide them a male role model, many of the girls are referred to the agency by a school or third party, and they tend to be dealing with more complex issues. Just like stereotypical adult same-gender friendships,[63] male matches tend to resemble "buddy" relationships in which doing activities together is emphasized and the female matches are like "girlfriends," who seek activities that permit talking and self-disclosure. This is consistent with the notion that males are more likely to form "side-by-side" friendships with other males—despite recent efforts to encourage men to have more nurturing relationships—whereas females are inclined to form "face-to-face" friendships with their female friends.[64]

Practical considerations of male mentoring relationships are also significant, because they can affect the connection between a man and a kid. For example, a biological father's presence or absence in a child's life may influence how the child and an unrelated man perceive each other and interact. The man's own family responsibilities can influence how much time, energy, and empathy he can expend on a kid outside his family. Characteristics associated with the physical and environmental context may facilitate or hinder certain types of exchanges. For instance, a man who lives in and interacts with kids in a dilapidated, dangerous inner-city slum may feel a self-imposed responsibility to monitor and protect them in the neighborhood. A man who lives outside this environment but interacts with a kid who calls this place home may be eager to help the kid move beyond this environment but may recognize that what he has to offer may not be able to compete with what the kid is experiencing. This is how one mentor in a program matching elderly adults with at-risk kids describes such a situation:

> You have to understand where they come from, these kids. The first time I took him home, there had to be twenty policemen at the entrance to the project. . . . Well, he thought it was very exciting, [that] it was a murder. [He wanted to] get out and watch this thing. . . . This goes on and on with this kind of life. So the next time I took him home, there was two men who were ab-solutely killing each other with fists and about fifty people were watching this. [So, I said] let's go home. But, oh, no, he wasn't going home. Oh, no way. When they see the police, they just follow the police, and it's just something that you see on TV. . . . The next time, [the police had] put two big gates on the back end of that project where he lives [before executing a drug raid]. But when they started to make the dope raid, the dopers took their big cars and went right through the gates with the cars, and the kids thought this was absolutely terrific. Well, this is what he lives with; and now, when he lives with this, how do I compete with this? Teach him how to read and write?[65]

Environments other than poor inner-city areas can also influence how men perceive their involvement with youth. If a man is interacting with a kid in a neighborhood blessed with bountiful physical and economic amenities, he may feel he should engage the kid in activities that maximize the local resources. In the man's eyes, it may be his responsibility to entertain the kid with local activi-ties requiring significant amounts of money and time. Finally, social similarity or dissimilarity between a man and a kid can affect the level of comfort between them as well as the type and intensity of the bond they develop.

Based more on their gut feelings than on an extensive body of rigorous re-search, the public and the social service community continue to stress the value of adult men as mentors and role models for at-risk youth and especially for any kid who, for whatever reason, does not have an involved father.[66] The main mes-sage is that men can help monitor youth and keep them out of trouble. Addi-tionally, men can foster youths' personal development by exposing them to new and healthy opportunities, increasing their community-based social capital, and providing them with educational support and an adult friend. Helping kids de-velop resiliency—the capacity to deal with adversity effectively—is considered a critical benefit of men's greater involvement in the mentoring process.[67]

Greater perspective on men's involvement in mentoring will be achieved as more insights are gained into the types of bonds men and youth forge, how males' personalities can affect their preferred relationship styles, and how fathering experiences can help mentors and youth build relationships. Further examination of the ethic of generativity, the nurturing spirit connecting persons from different generations, which is central to both fathering and mentoring, will expand our understanding of these relationships.

CHAPTER 9

PUBLIC AND PRIVATE LIVES

Although this book focuses on why, how, and with what effect men devote much of their time and energy to helping unrelated kids, men also have lives away from these youths to whom they devote some of themselves. They are husbands, partners, friends, neighbors, students, sons, grandsons, and so forth. Many also are fathers, grandfathers, and uncles. Although many youth workers get paid to work with kids, others hold jobs that have nothing to do with youth. So what are the implications of men's overlapping public and private lives?

Exploring how men define and navigate the borders between their youth work activities and their personal lives, especially family, helps expand and deepen the story about male youth workers. To achieve this broader view we must look at how and to what extent men encourage, or at least permit, overlap between their two life worlds, with and away from these kids. Men's approach to managing these worlds is sometimes affected by the reactions they receive from romantic partners, children, friends, and others about their youth work. I explore two fundamental questions: How does working with kids influence men's desire to become fathers and their approach to fathering? And, how do men's experiences as fathers affect the way they see and treat unrelated kids in public settings?

Answering these questions well requires an appreciation for the cultural landscape of fathering. I showed in Chapter 2 that understanding the public's perceptions of men's work and volunteering with youth must take into account larger social and cultural forces. Prevailing ideologies and cultural representations of good fathering are of particular interest when studying men's perceptions of and experiences with youth outside a family setting.

Since the nation's founding, fathers in the United States have been exposed to a cultural ideology emphasizing their responsibility to provide financially for their children, as well as other family members in many instances.[1] Similarly, fathers have been expected to protect their children from physical harm by outsiders, even while encouraging their children to take risks and to absorb the non-life-threatening bumps and bruises that come with an active childhood.[2] In addition, depending on the era and the subculture, fathers have been expected to contribute emotional support, monitoring and discipline, skill development, gender socialization, and spiritual guidance to their children to varying degrees.[3] For the most part, though, men have assumed little "community-based responsibility" for children. According to sociologist Andrea Doucet, community-based childrearing involves parents' sharing "responsibility for their children with others who take on caring practices— caregivers, other parents, neighbours, kin, childcare experts, nurses and doctors, teachers, librarians, music teachers, soccer coaches and so on."[4] The enterprise includes attempts to plan and manage activities between households as well as between the household and other social institutions, like the state, schools, and work.

However, some expectation of an adult male role model or quasi-fathering duty has also existed in the cultural conversation about men and youth. Pervasive in American culture, this ethos warns that youth—particularly boys—can experience difficulties when they are without a positive male role model in their lives. Thus, the ethos predicts that youth with a positive adult male role model are more likely to develop in healthy ways. In the public's eye, the ideal male role model has been the devoted, hardworking, loving, and law-abiding father. When this sort of man is not living in the home, the public has called on men outside the home to pick up the slack. Since the early 1900s, segments of the public have challenged men to step forward when children's fathers have been unavailable or unwilling to be involved. Irrespective of fathers' availability, men have also been urged to monitor boys in sports, Boy Scout activities, and when they enter the criminal justice system. Historically, the quasi-fathering ethos has been fueled by such patterns as high rates of young men dropping out of school or failing military physical exams, elevated juvenile delinquency rates, concerns about a perceived increase in gay or "soft" men, and similar demographic fluctuations. Irrespective of its impetus or value, the male role model ethos reminds us that understanding men's orientation toward unrelated children is tied to public perceptions about the value and level of involvement of either active fathers or adult male role models.

BLENDED VERSUS SEPARATE LIVES

Although men who do youth work differ in how much time they spend engaged in activities with kids, all of them must navigate the borders between their youth work and their personal time. Whereas some enjoy blending the two, others merely tolerate an overlap, and the rest do their best to separate their youth work from their personal lives.

In practical terms, these men make numerous decisions affecting how they organize their lives according to the dictates of time and place. With or without much thought, they essentially ask themselves: Should I give out my cell and home phone numbers and my e-mail address to the kids (and parents)? Should I invite kids to my home or encourage them to participate in activities with my friends and family? To what extent should I spend time with kids away from the designated sites for interacting with them? What should I tell my friends and family about my youth work activities? How should I balance the time I spend with youth versus my family? Should I seek others' advice about improving my relations with kids?

In talking to men about such matters, I discovered that they differ considerably in how they manage their life worlds. Family circumstances, personality traits, work conditions, and professional philosophy help set the tone for how men organize their lives. Because men's involvement with kids outside the family is often time-consuming and sometimes emotionally intense, examining how men manage the time and spatial borders of their youth work and family life is revealing.

Although both Richard and Tom do their youth work with members of their family, they have chosen different ways to blend youth work and family life successfully. Since convincing his wife to open a small daycare business five years ago and leaving his managerial position at a retail store, Richard has learned to organize his life in a new way. Most recently, he has incorporated his teenage daughter into the day-to-day operations of the daycare facility. He explains: "In the past, I'm used to working away from my family, you know, go to work away from my family for years. But then now, it seems like all of us are working together towards the same goal. And that common goal is to make sure we provide for these children." Richard goes on to describe how he, his wife, and daughter combine, yet separate, their family and business roles as they go about their daily routines in the same physical workspace. They respect each other's duties in the business setting and act accordingly. Richard also notes that the kids' parents sometimes call him and his wife at home on days when the facility is closed, because the children want to say hello, and Richard does not discourage this intermingling of daycare and home life.

Tom's case illustrates a slightly different pattern. Despite his long history of working with kids as a youth minister, coach, and school teacher, it was Tom's wife who mentored him while he trained to become a certified behavior analyst for youth. His wife has taken the lead in their developing a business together that caters to kids with special needs. Currently, they each have individual clients but consult one another frequently on specific cases. Even though Tom's youth work and family life are integrated to some extent, he and his wife agreed to segment their work and family lives by operating their business out of a separate building—a house in which they used to live—and they have agreed not to bring paperwork to their present home.

Other men talk about the fluid borders between their youth work and family life, though they technically do not merge their lives to the extent that Richard and Tom do. For example, Jeff, age 50, and a Boy Scout troop leader for fifteen years, frankly asserts:

> Scouting doesn't have fixed hours; . . . scouting is like raising kids. Scouting is really being a scoutmaster, you get kids, it isn't an eight to five. They tell you that to be an effective leader it takes one hour a week, and that is a joke; it is [more] like you have one hour left. Over the years you learn how to balance that out and it all melds together.

Similarly, Kevin says, "the ministry, it's not like a job. It's not an eight to five job. It's more or less, it's my life. Thus the phone calls throughout the day and night."

As these men, and others like them, get more invested in their work, the boundaries between their youth work and family grow increasingly blurred, though they may try to clarify them at times. Both Jeff and Kevin illustrate how cell and e-mail technology is increasingly expanding the temporal and spatial dimensions of youth work. Jeff feels that his scouts need him beyond the scheduled time he spends with them in troop functions. Because he sees them as part of his larger family, they have certain claims on his time—not quite as much as his wife—but strong claims nonetheless. All the scouts have his cell phone number, and they make liberal use of it. Jeff is essentially on-call throughout the day and week, an arrangement made possible by his flexible work schedule as an engineer. Recently, he even took several calls from scouts when he was away with his wife on an anniversary weekend! Thus, with a cell phone by his side and being willing to take calls from scouts, Jeff functions as a scout master even when he is physically not with his scouts.

Though Jeff and Kevin accept most calls, both admit to some monitoring. Kevin's feeling is:

If I'm on a date with my wife, I won't, I try not to answer my phone. They can leave a message. If I'm reading to my boys at night [I won't answer], for the most [part] I'm probably always accessible, but, you know there's moments that, I purposely try not to answer my cell phone.

Despite his efforts to protect some of his family time, Kevin quickly clarifies that he is committed to being as responsive as possible to youth's needs.

Let me [give an] example: Somebody's in the hospital, some kid's having his appendix taken out, I mean, I'll get a call at midnight and I'm out the door to the hospital to be with that young man. And that family, the parents are there as well. . . . and my wife understands that, we're in the ministry together; I'm the one that just, pretty much, has the office . . . but we try to balance it out. I mean, we try to make sure—vacations with our family, that's our family time. But all of our three sons, they all understand the ministry. There's huge rewards for them too, though, as much as there is sacrifice, when I take the youth group on a ski trip, all my sons love that part of the ministry because they get to come with us. So there's challenges to the schedule but, I mean, like I said, it's a life.

Sometimes calls to Kevin refer to medical emergencies or family or personal crises, or simply difficulties with honoring a scheduled appointment. Other times, kids simply want to contact him because they want to share their excitement and receive recognition. Kevin mentions that kids call him when they "made the state tournament, or just qualified for the state track meet. Or they just got a job, or they just got a raise, or . . . a car."

Although men like Jeff and Kevin are still more accessible to their own children in certain ways, they display an unwavering commitment to the kids they see outside their family. They are fortunate, because their children appreciate their dedication to their youth work. In Kevin's case, he is also able to incorporate his own children into some of his ministerial work by taking them on trips. By doing so, he is able to merge his responsibilities as a minister and a father, providing both unrelated youth and his own children a chance to benefit from his attention, energy, and time. Other men also speak of integrating their own children into age-appropriate youth activities like clowning, tutoring, sports, and Boy Scouts.

Indirectly, men blend personal life and youth work by talking about the kids to their family and friends away from the physical site where they interact with the youth. This talking can serve to relieve stress, get help solving a problem, or simply to share their joy. Because very few men actually do youth work side-by-side with their wives or partners, when the men discuss the kids with them it is typically without the kids being physically present. By discussing matters in this way, the men express their continuing awareness of the kids while away from the places where they are usually with them. Their inclination to have these discussions reflects how mindful they are of the kids. Just as parents often think about their children when they are not with them, youth workers do the same with unrelated kids. Some of that time may be spent contemplating solutions to specific problems or devising plans to secure resources to help youth. Vince, not a minister by profession, notes that the kids are in his thoughts regularly, saying, "I pray for the kids every night."

Wives and female companions who endorse men's youth work contribute in their own ways, offering insight and informal counseling. Several of the men stress how women have helped them look at kids, especially adolescent girls, from a different perspective. Getting the inside scoop from women about the types of things young girls experience while growing up enables men to feel more comfortable approaching girls and helping them cope with life. At times, the women in men's lives also help them to understand more fully how kids are influenced by their larger family context, while emphasizing the parents' perspective as well. For instance, Hernando is indebted to his wife, a child psychiatrist, because she helps him execute his duties more effectively as a youth minister. Referring to the kids at his church, Hernando shares:

> Some of them start doing [some behavior] that they never did before. Where that came from? How is that, how that perfect kid, he was gentle and nice and stuff, he starts beating other kids, suddenly. Something is wrong, that you notice a change in their mood. So, yep. My wife gave me a lot of advice about what can be happening in many of the situations: . . . there are issues in their homes and they are influenced . . . their parents are going through a divorce or worse or something like that, and that creates a lot of distress in the kids. . . . So sometimes you identify that and you talk to the parents to see what's going on. So, or you create situations where people can open up and tell you what's going on.

Hernando feels blessed because his wife has the professional expertise and is generous enough to offer him "good feedback" when discussing issues affecting his kids at church. By providing a fresh and informed perspective, Hernando's wife offers an invaluable resource to supplement Hernando's ministerial work.

Another youth minister, Ben, sees his wife as a critical asset because she helps him curtail unhelpful personal tendencies. "Sometimes if I'm too cocky or something like that she can help reel me in, or encourage me not [to] give a particular kid such a hard time. I'm a tough love kind of guy." It appears that women in the mold of Hernando's and Ben's wives can improve the quality of their men's youth work in various ways.

Having friends who do youth work can also provide a man a convenient network for sharing ideas about kids and reinforcing their commitment to working with them. Malik marvels at his good fortune in being paid "for just being who I am and doing me." He celebrates that most of his friends work in fields similar to his own, because their shared passion guides the conversations he has with his friends while they're hanging out, away from formal work responsibilities.

> That's all our conversation is focused on most of the time, is how can we do what we do even better? How can we take what we're doing to another level? How can we have more of an impact? "This is what I did." Hey man, "I really like the way you, I saw you, what you guys were doing the other day at that outreach event. I really liked how you guys were doing this."

Consequently, Malik spends much of his day either working directly with kids or talking about them to others.

Sometimes men talk to others about kids without seeking advice; they simply do so for fun or as a sign of friendship. They bond with others by sharing a part of themselves and often do so regularly. Spending time with young children inspires some men to tell funny, endearing, or emotional stories. Jackson's volunteering in recent years at a preschool, elementary school, and a "cuddler program" in which adults hold babies in the hospital has given him unique and meaningful experiences to share with his girlfriend and others. Most recently, Jackson, who describes himself as "very pro-life," has enjoyed sharing stories about the cuddler program with a fellow Christian at work, a mother of three. He mimics how he excitedly tells her, "I saw the babies today. . . . they're so small, and their little heartbeats." To Jackson, sharing stories about his warm feelings helps him convey a part of himself to others.

In addition to sharing stories for fun, men on occasion talk about their activities with kids to others because they want them to get involved. For example, Robby describes his efforts to convince people to invest their time, energy, and money in helping kids, especially the seriously ill being treated in hospitals.

Asked if he ever motivates others to visit children in hospitals or to help kids in some other way, he proudly asserts:

All the time. All the time. I mean, I certainly, I do that. It's part of my job, every day. I sell people on things. So I think I'm pretty effective in that sense . . . at least I'm told I'm a fairly good story teller, good motivator, and all the time I get people to join causes and go volunteer and seek out kids and make an impact in a way that they can't through their classes and through their everyday interactions.

Robby explains how he has refined his storytelling style by interjecting personal accounts of visiting sick kids. He confesses that he uses emotional stories to "hopefully instill an unquenchable thirst for these people to know more, to feel more, to experience more" and ultimately to be more involved in what he firmly believes is a worthwhile cause.

In addition to managing time with kids and talking about them, adults doing youth work must make decisions about whether to associate with the kids in physical spaces they deem personal, or whether they should introduce aspects of their personal lives into the kids' physical orbits. For example, when men spend time with kids going out to lunch; entertaining them at their homes; traveling from place to place in a car, bus, or airplane; going to movies, sporting events, or camping; or spending time on mission trips, they extend the physical borders within which they do youth work beyond the conventional, formal sites. These ventures give men the chance to navigate the rules and borders governing the use of physical space. Spending time with youth like this is common for Big Brothers, but coaches, teachers, ministers, Boy Scout leaders, 4-H leaders, and others occasionally spend time this way as well.

In a couple of cases, the men even allowed kids to live with them in their homes, decisions that produced mixed results. Carlos had relatively successful experiences when on separate occasions he and a former housemate took in a few younger guys who were trying to escape gang life. Unfortunately, things did not go as well for Michael when he stepped beyond the protocol for Big Brothers by letting his Little Brother live with him for an extended period of time because the boy was having a very difficult time in his own home. The boy broke the house rules Michael had established to keep the kid's friends from coming over when Michael was not at home, and then lied about doing so. Irrespective of the outcomes, though, men's willingness to take on the responsibility of opening their homes to kids speaks volumes about some men's commitment to helping kids find their way in life.

Not surprisingly, some men are much more careful about allowing their involvement with kids away from home to encroach on their family time and space. These men make sure they are not compromising their responsibilities as devoted partners and fathers. Some compartmentalize their lives because they have seen how kids suffer from inadequate parental attention. Dwight pulls no punches expressing how he tries his best when he comes home at the end of the day to forget about his work responsibilities at an alternative school for at-risk youth. His reasoning:

> because I have a family of my own to take care [of] and my son is 6 years old, and he needs me as much as I can give. Work is important, I enjoy work but, you know, I gotta make sure I take care of my family first. And I need to kinda be all ears to just listen to [my son], or help with homework, or we going out and play ball, or whatever. And same with my wife I mean I need to be there for her . . . open to and [willing to] listen to her when she wants to talk.

Although Dwight is not alone in strictly dividing his work and family life along these lines, most men are willing to share things with those close to them and at times to incorporate family members into their youth work activities, a choice I address a bit later. Men who mirror Dwight's approach, sustaining a separate and healthy personal life away from kids, may feel that it enhances their ability to work effectively when they are with them.

While blurring the borders between men's work-related and personal interactions with kids, cell phone and e-mail technologies provide young people opportunities to establish contact more easily with men who are currently involved or were involved in their lives. Lots of the men interviewed acknowledge that, with the advent of e-mail, once their formal relationship ends with students, players, campers, and Little Brothers, the kids (and the men) are much better equipped and willing to stay in contact. Thinking about the many campers and several exchange students he has worked with over the years, Brandon confirms:

> With e-mail, I find myself writing longer letters and I find myself receiving longer letters and longer communications back and forth. And it really amazes me. Like, one of the exchange students that we [he and former wife] had is 27 now. And he'll sit down and instant message from France for two or three hours.

Brandon also believes that the content of the e-mail messages he gets from kids has become more personal because youth feel more comfortable sharing their thoughts and asking for advice from a slight distance compared to when they are face-to-face with him.

With this increase in volume, intimacy, and longevity of youths' communicating, these men's ability to influence kids is extending beyond their formal involvement, even into the young adult years. When the relationship lasts into adulthood, this means, as we saw in Chapter 6, that the men must figure out how to negotiate becoming more of a friend rather than an authority figure—perhaps even father figure—or role model.

Single men, especially those without family responsibilities, have fewer restrictions when deciding to compartmentalize or mix their youth work and personal lives. In contrast, men with partners, and especially those with children, are much more likely to have others affect how they manage their youth work and make decisions about it. Whether it is receiving helpful advice, having partners actively participate in and share aspects of the youth work, or simply knowing that their partners are supportive of the time, energy, and money they devote to kids outside the home, having supportive loved ones enhances men's ability to feel comfortable with their commitment to youth. The men convey a shared sentiment—their partners typically appreciate their involvement with kids—although the challenges may have increased because of the penetration of cellular and e-mail technology into everyday life. It appears, though, that some men nurture their partners' understanding by circumventing potential conflicts between youth work and family commitments before they arise. Expressing a cooperative spirit, these men self-monitor their activities in order to protect their families from unwanted intrusions on their time and energies.

THE CULTURE OF FATHERHOOD

In academic circles, a distinction is sometimes made between the culture of fatherhood and the conduct of fatherhood.[5] Dissecting this distinction enables us to think more systematically about men's activities with youth in public settings. It also highlights the potential overlap between men's public and private lives.

At the cultural level, fatherhood is represented by the values, norms, institutional arrangements, and symbolic meanings associated with fathering in a given society or community. Individuals are exposed to cultural messages about fatherhood through numerous channels, including communications media, literature, religious doctrine, law, and social policies. Though specific mainstream images may prevail at any given time, the messages can vary by subcultural group and are often politicized. Moreover, in class-stratified cultures where childcare is marginalized and generally viewed as women's work, most boys and men have general impressions about fathering but they do not learn the particulars about early childcare until they become fathers.[6] Several men I talked to fell outside this normative pattern, because they had either worked or volunteered in daycare centers caring for young children when they were teenagers. A few are still actively involved in that setting.

Fatherhood discourses both stem from and foster the culture of fatherhood; they are produced and disseminated by those working in various disciplines, including science, medicine and public health, and the social sciences.[7] In general, discourses can be thought of as the ways people and groups represent experiences and ideas through various forms of verbal, written, or visual communication. Expert knowledge systems help establish what is viewed as acceptable or unacceptable, healthy or unhealthy, and productive or unproductive behavior. Discourses are disseminated through magazines, newspapers, books, film, television, and in conversation. They are experienced as part of social relations and how we experience and express ourselves as persons with distinct physical bodies and traits. At any given period in time, prevailing discourses help shape how people think, talk about, and react to aspects of their surroundings. Depending on one's perspective, discourses can either enhance or restrict how individuals see reality and behave. All of these forces together decide what is thought of as good fathering.

In contrast, the conduct or practice of fathering refers to fathers' actual behaviors that may or may not be consistent with the cultural images and discourses. These behaviors may involve children directly (e.g., playing with them) or indirectly (e.g., discussing childrearing with the child's mother). Over the years the relative emphasis on different aspects of good fathering has varied in the United States, though breadwinning has continued to be a key marker of how responsible fathers are defined and judged.[8]

When fatherhood is viewed as a sociocultural phenomenon,[9] interpretations of both the culture of fatherhood and conduct of fatherhood are fused. Fatherhood is not seen as something distinct or separate from society and culture per se. Rather, fatherhood is conceptualized as being expressed through the seemingly more abstract social and cultural processes that connect people's lives in a family setting as they define and negotiate aspects of fathering.

One way the culture and conduct of fatherhood are linked is in public and personal perceptions about who can claim a father status. Despite Americans' tendency to privilege biology when thinking about fatherhood (or motherhood), there appears to be a gradual shift toward a broader interpretation that does not make father status dependent on genetic paternity. This emerging flexibility is played out in everyday life as men who are not biologically related to particular children interact with them in fatherly ways—making breakfast, carpooling for soccer practice, buying clothes, making play dates, and telling bedtime stories. Meanings are assigned to these activities based on the cultural discourse, imagery, and institutional norms that define the larger context for "social fathering."

Paying attention to fathering is critical to this discussion because the cultural context within which men define and negotiate their involvement with unrelated children outside a family setting is connected to the prevailing ideologies and cultural representations of fatherhood. Although fathers in most societies are typically designated as playing important roles in their own children's lives, in some societies unrelated men are granted liberal opportunities and a great deal of responsibility for monitoring, instructing, and caring for youth. For example, in nonindustrialized societies (foraging, farming, or pastoral) men typically learn about and practice childcare long before they themselves become fathers.[10] They learn through their experiences as relatives to young children living in their extended family or they are around others caring for children who are growing up in their immediate surroundings. By observing and practicing basic childcare tasks, these men learn to be at ease in physical and social spaces where children's physical and emotional needs are addressed.

Historically, fatherhood images in the United Status represent expectations about how involved fathers should be with their children, and these expectations are likely to color social views about men and youth more generally. Unfortunately, the recent historical scholarship on fatherhood[11] has not been supplemented with parallel study of the level, nature, and consequences of men's involvement with youth outside the family.

Today, the antithetical images of the involved father versus the irresponsible "deadbeat dad" help frame the meaning of the positive and negative relations between men and kids more generally. The discourses of fathering offer a kind of cultural standard against which to evaluate other men's place and purpose in youths' lives. The general public and social service providers often claim that young boys living in single-parent families without an involved father need a positive male role model or mentor to help them develop their gender identity and transition from childhood to adulthood, from boyhood to manhood. Even though expectations of a male role model or mentor are more modest than those associated with fathering, they are the same as some of the qualities linked to good fathering: being there, conscientiously monitoring, being a thoughtful conveyor of advice, and acting as an ethical guide for responsible behavior.

The most common departure from the expectations of good fathering is that men are not expected to financially support children who are not their offspring. When they do invest in them financially, others take note and admire it—though people are often unaware of such financial contributions to children, for the men prefer to make them privately. A lot of the men who spoke with me mentioned that it is not uncommon for them to spend their own money on needy kids for entertainment, health care, and basic needs like clothing. For instance, referring to one of the kids who attends the alternative school where he works as a teacher's aide, Dwight relates:

Just yesterday I bought a young man a jacket. You know, he didn't have a jacket. I didn't really have the money to do it for him, but I felt like I would be okay. But I hate the thought of this child going home without a jacket. It's kinda cool and the cold weather just kinda came up all of the sudden.

The culture of fatherhood is tied to some extent to prevailing social constructions of masculinity, and adult manhood in particular. The connection is captured most vividly by how the meaning of nurturance is framed by the culture of fatherhood and conventional images of masculinity. Our language has evolved so that the terms "mothering" or "motherly" are used loosely to depict people's nurturing orientation to others, family or not, but "fathering" and "fatherly" have not (yet) achieved a comparable meaning beyond (or even within) the family context. "Fatherly" has, however, increasingly been used to capture what many stepfathers or other social fathers do. Despite the gender bias in labeling, the experiential learning that comes from being a father, stepfather, or social father, particularly an active one, is likely to shape how a man treats unrelated children in the public realm.

In modern times, direct care of children has been assigned typically to the feminine domain; put simply, mothers' or women's work.[12] Viewed through a gender lens, conventional family norms have seldom called for fathers to be vigilant about their children's emotional or practical needs other than financial sustenance and protection. Fathers have been encouraged to care about their kids and to help out, of course, but when push comes to shove, mothers have been cast as the emotional stewards and managers of family and household routines. Any casual perusal of parenting materials in the form of books, magazines, videos, Internet sites, and workshops documents the extent to which moms remain the principal target audience.

Manhood images offer men guidance on how they should express themselves as fathers, but practical realities of everyday life, struggles among family members over their respective responsibilities, and changing norms about fathers' and mothers' behavior have expanded how men, on average, perceive and conduct family labor, including childcare. In recent years, many people have opened their eyes to a broader definition of manhood and fathering. They are convinced that men can and should be more nurturing and emotionally supportive of their children. Greater public recognition is also being given to the fathers who have already demonstrated their willingness to nurture their children.

The culture of fatherhood includes categories of paternal identities assigned to and embraced by men. Although the criteria for membership in a category may shift from time to time, men are granted or negotiate their status as biological, step-, adoptive, or social fathers. They make sense of their lives as fathers by managing the rights, privileges, and obligations that go along with each respective designation. Men may be further defined as married/divorced/never married, resident/nonresident, or single/coparent. The common thread: men perceive that they have, or should have, some type of familylike relationship with the child or children. Even though they configure their identities in unique ways depending on their precise relationship to the child (and mother), they build their identity using a family template.

In recent decades, scholars have stressed the diversity of ways biological fathers and stepfathers "do fathering" while noting several general categories of fatherly involvement.[13] Three of the basic forms of fathering are labeled engagement, accessibility, and responsibility. Fathers who are engaged with their children are directly involved in some sort of activity or communication. Play is the most obvious activity, though fathers can also be engaged with their children when they feed, dress, do homework together, talk about discipline issues, and so forth. Accessibility captures those times when fathers are available for their children but are not actively engaged with them. They can be summoned if necessary and are generally close by. Fatherly involvement is described as responsibility when the fathers are serving a managerial role for their kids by helping anticipate their needs (e.g., food, clothes, shelter, health care) or are making specific arrangements to have those needs met (e.g., calling another parent about carpooling, making a doctor's appointment).

The term "father" provides men a well-known device that homogenizes their self-perceptions to some extent. Men who interact with kids in public settings do not have a comparable label to unify their identities. I use the convenient phrase "youth worker" to refer to the many men who volunteer and work with kids, but the men do not regularly use this label in referring to themselves and each other. Granted, male youth workers may see commonalities among themselves based on their membership in a distinct professional category, such as teachers, coaches, or daycare workers, but these identities do not bridge the gap between the various positions. In contrast, even though individual men may define and experience their lives as fathers somewhat diversely, fathers and others recognize that fatherhood is a distinct position imbued with certain privileges and obligations. Being a father provides men a common thread to establish, express, and talk about their paternal identities. Thus, one significant way male youth workers actually experience a common perspective is by recognizing that, usually, they are *not* fathers to the children they serve. In acknowledging this, they internalize the broad cultural message outlining the limitations of how men can legitimately interact with kids other than their own children.

The controversial issue of adults touching kids provides a powerful illustration of these boundaries. Cognizant of the public scrutiny of how adults interact with youth, men realize that friendly or affectionate touching is risky and should be avoided in most cases, and hands-on physical punishment is typically not condoned. In both instances the norms are predicated on men not having standing as legitimate father figures. On the other hand, fathers today are often encouraged to shower their kids with verbal and physical affection while still retaining the right to discipline them by spanking, so long as it is not abusive.

For men not yet fathers, the experience of working with kids in public settings may affect their desire to have children and their sense of competence should they be fathers someday. They may more readily form images of their "possible selves," as men who do or do not want to have their own children.[14] Meanwhile, working with kids in public settings can provide fathers unique opportunities to orient themselves toward their own children. Men who interact with diverse youth may be better equipped to recognize the value of treating different offspring differently. In other words, having extensive public experience working with kids may lead some men to recognize that the rigid, one-template-fits-all style of childrearing is limited.

In sum, my approach to studying men acknowledges that public perceptions of how men should relate to children are separate from, yet related to, the rich tradition of ideas about fathering I introduced in Chapter 4 dealing with generativity,[15] and Erik Erikson's[16] life span model of psychosocial development, which sees generativity as various forms of caring, both inside and outside a family, that contribute to the spirit of future generations.

YOUTH WORK AS TRAINING FOR FATHERING

For men who have not yet fathered a child, the various chances to work with youth in public settings offer them a unique opportunity to learn about kids and develop their skills for relating to and managing them. Some men may anticipate their youth work experience will benefit them in the future whereas others may not realize until sometime later how it primed them to want to become fathers or prepared them to handle the day-to-day tasks of being a dad.

Intrigued by the possible overlap between men's involvement with youth and men's family life, I asked fathers to consider how working with unrelated kids had affected their desire to have children prior to their becoming fathers, and I asked men who were not fathers to share their future plans regarding paternity. The responses suggest that working with youth does not inspire men to want to have their own kids; the vast majority of men already have a fairly clear sense that, circumstances permitting, they want to have kids of their own. However, a few of the men who had had no serious plans to have children felt that their involvement with kids had confirmed the soundness of their decision to avoid the full-time responsibility of fatherhood. Drawing particularly on his experiences coaching basketball with kids in the United States and Europe, Andrew summarizes his thinking about becoming a father:

> I think I probably also recognize the incredible effort that it takes to really raise a child well. And perhaps to a degree since I recognize the effort to raise a kid, based on my limited exposure with coaching and so forth, probably made me a little more reluctant or maybe more thoroughly thought through the obligation that goes along with having children. [My wife and I] recognize that it's a big responsibility to do it well. And perhaps at this stage of my life [age 44], I don't want to have that much responsibility for my own child. And that's probably one reason why I do want to spend more [time in] mentoring relationships, be it coaching or other things, with kids, because I feel I have a lot to give, but I guess I want to give it on my terms versus 24/7.

In contrast to Andrew, Barry's take on his involvement with kids in camps and after-school care settings has led him to reassess his position on becoming a father. At age 27, Barry has more time than Andrew to make a final decision. As of today, Barry's thinking is:

A few years ago, I never envisioned or just thought about having kids when I got older. And, after dealing with the different types of kids, I think, I would like to have kids. I think I would be able to deal with them. I mean, there's nothing like, you know, having your own kids. But knowing the different personalities and the different things that kids do, I think it said to me or helped me see that it won't be as difficult as I thought it would be, you know, to raise a child or something. I'm patient.

Now that Barry feels more comfortable around kids, the prospects of becoming a dad are much more realistic and appealing.

Working with youth typically gives men who already want kids more confidence to see themselves as being good fathers someday. Thirty-two-year-old Charles, like most men, has his mind set on starting a family once he gets married. He believes the time he's spent with kids from his Boys & Girls Club has taught him to be patient and to "not take anything for granted." Speaking in sweeping terms, he adds:

I think it's preparing me to be a better father, to be a good father, whenever I have kids. 'Cause it's kinda like a blueprint of if you learn to work with kids, so now you learn how to be a better father. Learn how to listen, 'cause the kids told you. Kids tell you really. If you want to know how to be a good parent, learn how to be a good teacher, listen to the kids. They'll tell you how to do it.

For Charles, a key feature of the fathering blueprint is paying attention to what kids truly want and need. He emphasizes the value of spending time together, of being there for one's children. Ever the optimist, Charles even suggests that kids are more likely to appreciate their parent taking the day off of work to spend time with them on their birthday than they would be if the parent spent $300 on "something crazy."

Being active with kids in diverse settings has also helped Malik feel more comfortable with the prospects of fathering; he feels he understands guys better and is more sensitive to young girls' emotional needs. In an animated voice, he emphasizes how his abstinence programs and extensive youth ministry work with at-risk youth have prepared him to see the value of showering his future son or daughter with genuine verbal and physical affection. As he says,

I wanna be able to be there just to be able to hug my son and say, "Hey you know what man, I love you. I care about you." "Come on Dad, stop hugging me." "You know I love you though, right?" "Yeah, geez." I want him to be able to know. Not to where they have to question it. . . . I [also] can't wait for my daughter to be able to understand the words "You're beautiful." So I'll be the first man to tell her that, and it's genuine. . . . Some of these girls have lived with mom and just different boyfriends that come in and out their whole lives, and they've never heard the words a guy . . . looked them in the eye and said, "Girl, you're beautiful. You're looking good today." And even though it's game, even though it's false, that these guys are saying to these girls, these girls they want that affection, so that they'll give that guy whatever he wants to get that kind of emotional attention that gratifies them. . . . And I know the importance of that. I've seen what happens when kids go without it, so I wanna be the kind of dad that can look my daughter in the eyes and say "Girl you are so beautiful; I love you so much" and be able to give her a clear, understandable example . . . and what it feels like, and for her to know what it isn't, so that when the false stuff comes around and these guys are just, "Hey girl, what's up, show me that number, what you doin' this weekend," all that stupid nonsense, she'll say, "Pfft, you better get out of my face, man, what you talking about?"

Malik's visions about fathering his own son and daughter someday are also shaped by his memories of being raised in a single-mother household after his parents divorced when he was four, and of his father being only minimally involved thereafter. Thus, the combination of his early life experience and more recent interactions with youth accentuates his desire to become a hands-on, nurturing father.

Sidney, currently a novice elementary school teacher with plenty of experience working with youth in other settings, projects that his diverse experiences provide him invaluable insights for relating to his future children. He focuses on how his experience will improve his ability to communicate with his own children someday.

Hopefully I'll be able to have a relationship where I can talk to them closely and not feel uncomfortable about talking to them about any different situation that might come up, 'cause I've talked to kids about almost every situation you can think of in my other jobs, any situation I can think of. So it'll

*make it a little bit easier when broaching subjects such as sex, drugs, alcohol
with my kids.*

Sidney is banking on his belief that his extensive talks with kids about a wide
range of topics will put him at ease when he talks to his children and lead to productive exchanges.

Blake shares how experiences as a 22-year-old 4-H agent give him instruc-
tive opportunities to observe how other professionals and parents work with
teenagers. His observations teach him invaluable lessons about people and the
most effective ways to manage young kids.

> *So it helped me at that point because I try to watch people so later in life I
> learned from their problems as far as my kids, so I won't have to suffer and
> they [his own kids] won't have to suffer through what could be totally
> avoided . . . little things like that I notice that some of these adults just blow
> their stack over it and get so mad over these little things that it's just like, it
> teaches me, how to interact with the kid and get the kid to do what they're
> supposed to do or what I deem is what they're supposed to do without, you
> know, having to scream and yell.*

Though Blake also mentions how he learns directly from kids, here he emphasizes how he can gather insights about communication styles that will improve
his ability to be a parent someday.

Together, the men's accounts illustrate that the benefits of youth work experience can transcend the moment and the people immediately involved. When developing their patience, willingness and ability to listen, and their sense of
confidence in managing kids men are likely to consider the prospects of becoming a father using a different mindset than they might have had without that experience.

While Barry, Charles, Malik, Sidney, and Blake relate stories about their work
with groups of kids in their respective positions, Ron, a Big Brother, tells how he
has been gathering insights throughout the course of his one-on-one relationship with his Little Brother, learning lessons about how he might communicate
with kids—including his own some day. Ron incorporates his wife into some of
the things he does with his Little Brother, but not often, because he senses that
her presence alters the dynamics. As he sees it, when he and his Little Brother
are alone, they are able to relate to each other as males—Ron's wife does not like
video games or science fiction movies. During such one-on-one times, Ron and

the boy can have private talks. Although Ron does not believe their conversations are particularly intimate, they allow him to develop insights about communicating with kids that are likely to influence his experiences as a father sometime down the road.

> Maybe I'm learning a little bit more about how to be able to talk to kids in a comfortable way. . . . I mean whenever you're growing up, you don't really want to talk to your parents about things sometimes. . . . Some people have those types of relationships with their family where they think they can, they feel like they can talk about anything. . . . I feel like maybe I'm learning the other side of . . . how a kid maybe wishes their parent would talk to them, or relate to them, as opposed to how parents traditionally do. . . . What parents have to do is be [the] disciplinarian and have to get them to do their schoolwork and get them to clean up at home, and things like that. But on the other side, [I'm] learning what are the other things that [kids] need or want in their life besides just somebody that tells them what to do.

Even though Ron and the other Big Brothers don't incorporate their wives or girlfriends regularly into outings with their Little Brothers, when they do, they acquire a sense of what it might be like to coparent.

HOW YOUTH WORK AFFECTS FATHERING

The life histories I used to prepare this book illustrate men moving into, out of, and between diverse opportunities for working and volunteering with youth. Although most of the men were interacting with kids in one or more of these settings prior to having their own children, some became fathers first. Every father I spoke with is currently involved with kids outside the home. The men's stories reveal that past as well as current experiences with kids can affect how fathers perceive and treat their own children. Although most of the men point to how their time with kids in public settings has positively affected them—in terms of becoming more focused, attentive, patient, discerning, confident, caring, and approachable fathers—several also mention that the ill effects of working with disruptive and emotionally demanding kids sometimes seep into their family life.[17]

Kevin, a father of three sons, clearly sees the positive connection between his youth work and his fathering. He feels that his youth ministry experience has been invaluable because it gave him a vision of what he should be doing as a father before he journeyed down that path. In his words:

> It gave me a vision that I could help see where I'm trying to take my child to, what he's going through, so working in youth ministry was huge, and to this day I think it's the best parenting class for anybody. . . . just come work in youth ministry for a little while and deal with kids, and you can see, at least help map out where you're trying to take your kids instead of just raising them randomly and hoping they all turn out well.

By working with kids in his church, Kevin became more aware of how he wanted to help the kids and what he could do to accomplish his goals. After having his own kids, he realized he could apply the same logic to them. Kevin clearly sees his youth ministry experience as invaluable because it has set him up to succeed as a father by being more focused.

Another minister, Ben, has two toddler children, so he hasn't yet had a chance to see how his youth work may affect his fathering, but he anticipates it will. He jokingly talks about the stereotypical connection people make about how a minister's work indirectly affects his or her kids while he highlights the value of incorporating other adults into a child's life.

> Well you've always heard about a preacher's kid, right? That's my biggest fear. But . . . I don't see myself as a classic definition of a minister. I see myself as just me being me and the fact that I'm an ordained minister is part of the package. I'm gonna have a couple of preacher's kids on my hands. But at the same time I know what a kid's eyes look like after he's smoked a joint. And I'll be like, "Boy! What are you doing?" . . . And my perspective on my relationship, like camp [he's a summer camp director], has I think or will give me the opportunity to trust in other adults to shape the lives of my children in positive ways, maybe even in negative ways, too.

As he completes this thought, Ben alludes to being a staff member and director of a boys' summer camp. He believes that both his ministry and his camp time provide a solid basis for learning how to trust other adults to play an important role in shaping his children. Thus, he may be more attuned to how these processes unfold and be in a better position to know how he can support his children's healthy relationships with other adults while curbing the negative ones.

Working with kids, especially those exhibiting bad behavior due in part to troubled family backgrounds, can also motivate men to be more attentive to their own children. Earlier we learned that Dwight compartmentalizes his work and family life to make sure he spends quality time with his son and wife. Here he describes more explicitly why working with kids in an alternative school has prompted him to be attentive to his son.

> Because kids need a lot of time and attention and I see a lot of the young men that come through here. A lot of the things they get caught up in is because they didn't have that father figure in the house with them or somebody close by who kinda kept their grip on. . . . This job, I think it has helped me to realize the things that I need to do, and I need to be there for my son. We try to spend a lot of time together: Cub Scouts, he likes to sing, church, or whatever. Something at the school, PTA, I'm involved in that. I'll be there. And I realize, like I said, it's quality time that's important with a lot of these kids.

Earlier, I described how a number of men believe that their youth work experience has helped teach them to be more patient. Sandy's 4-H experience affected him this way, paying dividends in the way he treated his own children.

> I think a lot of the parenting skills that I learned in 4-H I was able to apply directly as a parent. You know, again, working with a group of kids and volunteers requires a lot of patience and tolerance. Because you have people that don't have to be there if they don't want to. So to a certain extent your kids don't have to be there unless they want to. They can tune you out real easy so I think learning how to do that [be patient and tolerant] was very optimal around children.

Over the years, Sandy's job afforded him countless occasions to work with kids and adults that taught him how to be more accepting of kids, a lesson that carried over to how he treated his own children.

The ways in which their youth work has enabled the men to relate to their sons and daughters more easily depend on the nature of the men's experiences with kids outside the home. Ramón describes how his years of experience teaching kids in several school systems has made him a better father.

> I've learned a lot about . . . classroom settings and peer influences and the whole variety of people that the children come across, the good and bad influences. So

knowing that, yes, that gives me a lot of information about what to share with my son. So, sure, I give my son advice all the time about situations and people, etc., based on my own experience with my students.

Because Ramón has an insider's view of how kids get into trouble in school, even though they may not be wrong, he mentions later how he tries to help his son avoid the negative consequences that often come with mishandling particular types of situations.

Gaining knowledge on the job is something Carlos also points to when considering how his more than ten years of experience as a youth minister have prepared him to be a good father. As he notes, working with kids has given him greater security to face the challenges of fathering.

I feel like I've had a lot of practice. I feel like through the years I've fathered a lot of kids, and so as I look at my own kids, it gives me more security that I can do this [be a good father]. I'm gonna have some answers for [my son] when he gets older, because I've already had to find them for somebody else.

The value of Carlos's experience as a youth minister is heightened by his willingness to stay abreast of how youth culture affects kids' values, desires, and behavior. Carlos is one of numerous men who see that keeping pace with the rapid changes in youth culture is made easier by their active involvement with kids in schools, churches, and other youth programs. If they are attentive, their observations of kids and impromptu exchanges with them about hip-hop culture can be highly informative. Being exposed to the latest in music, fashion, youth lingo, and communication technology gives them a bit of an edge in trying to understand and stay in touch with their own children, even though they, like most adults, seem to lag behind.

Depending on the type of youth work the men do, some are also able to appreciate their own kids more and encourage them to consider how fortunate they are. Working with kids in a juvenile detention center and now at an alternative school for kids with a history of poor conduct at other schools, Vince sees his experience as a valuable resource for his own fathering.

I can tell them [his children] about what I go through every day with some of the kids. I tell them all the time, "Be thankful for what you've got because some kids that I work with don't have what y'all had growin' up. Y'all got a mama and a daddy; most of these kids that we have out here are from single-parent homes." So I just tell them, "Just be thankful for what you've got. Don't

*take anything for granted, 'cause y'all are doing, and did, a lot better than a
lot of the kids we have out here."*

Of course, parents who do not work with youth can also lecture their children
on how well off they are, but getting their children's attention may be easier
when they have a wealth of personal experience and anecdotes to support their
position. Alternatively, the men themselves may recognize how good they have it
as parents; they may appreciate more fully that their kids are well-adjusted. Tom
says that his youth work with kids who have made poor decisions has encouraged him to be more "gracious" in dealing with his own children's occasional
poor choices.

For the most part, the men see their youth work activities as having a positive influence on their own fathering, but a few acknowledge that their lives as
youth workers can create problems at home as well. This is evident in 51-year-
old Grady's observation about his time working in a juvenile detention center.

*I was trying to run my family like at work, you know, be kinda harsh and
harsher on my kids and talking to them in an abrupt way and try to be the
same way. I kinda bring it home with me. And, my wife quickly pointed it out
to me: "What's going on here. You're talking to us a little harsh here." So, I
had to consciously, you know, when I walk through that door, change it, 'cause
if you don't watch it you'll kinda wanta run your house like a detention center
and that don't work.*

Grady's difficulty illustrates the possible spillover effect of work stress affecting family life. Some men, like Grady, try to put a buffer between their
work and families because they have learned through unpleasant personal experiences; others have avoided bad experiences and are adamant that they
want to avoid bringing their youth work home with them. Even if they do not
bring their work home with them, those who work with troubled kids are
sometimes reminded that their own children's behavioral shortcomings may
not be all that bad.

HOW FATHERING AFFECTS YOUTH WORK

Although a man's involvement with his own children may not always affect
how he perceives or treats other kids, being a father, especially one who takes an
interest in his child, is often a life-altering adventure. As an active father accu-

mulates fathering experience, he learns various lessons about child development and raising children while becoming more sensitive to children's practical and emotional needs. A father with multiple offspring, particularly both sons and daughters, may come to appreciate more fully the varied personalities that young people express. Navigating interactions with diverse offspring can provide a training ground for interacting more effectively as a teacher, coach, counselor, or mentor with all sorts of children in different public venues. The fathers in my study talk about such things as becoming more sensitive to kids' well-being and emotions, being concerned about kids' family circumstances and the roles that parents play, learning how to predict and manage kids' behavior, becoming more comfortable talking to kids, and developing a better understanding of different aspects of youth culture.

Experiencing the joys and struggles of fathering firsthand, then, provides men a unique window into understanding and appreciating other kids and their parents. An attentive father of a 10-year-old boy and 7-year-old daughter, Santiago believes he has learned quite a bit about kids since becoming a dad. After debating with himself momentarily whether it is because he has matured with age or because he became a father, he asserts that he has indeed become more sensitive to kids' feelings because he's a father. "Maybe you feel more the fear of a boy, more the wish. You feel more the feelings, also, of the kid. You try not to hurt them, you hope to be more careful with them." Adding to Santiago's comments, Carlos says, that being a father

> changes your heart, and I believe makes you a better man in many respects because of the selflessness that you have to have to be an effective father. . . .
> That kind of a selfless living I don't think people experience until you have kids. The enjoyment you get from giving, I think it just really changes your heart and your perspective, and I know that it's done that for me, and in turn it's caused me to, have a greater heart towards the young people.

One way a man can experience a "greater heart" is to become more tolerant of kids' creative efforts to differentiate themselves from mainstream culture. Indoctrinated by nearly thirty years of military service, Calvin received guidance from his youngest son, who has pushed him during the past ten years to reassess how he judges people based on their physical appearance, to become more accepting of "alternative lifestyles," and to "deal with kids" differently. Explaining how his son exposed him to all sorts of kids, Calvin sets the stage by referring initially to one of his son's friends:

*To see a child who has twenty-nine earrings in this ear and black lipstick and it is
a female. Immediately you think she is some kind of a weirdo slut, when in fact
she is a real sweet kid and bright and whatever. My younger [son] brought all of
those home . . . everybody was his friend, everybody. Having to deal with a lot of
his friends, and dealing with the different lifestyles, and whatever. . . . Here was
my military son, who lived on a military base, and he is a skateboarder. All of the
things you might think of, whatever your conceptions are of skateboarders, they
all came to our house, or he went off with them. You know there are certain subjects about skateboarders, that they are bad kids, they are into drugs and yada
yada; well, not the case. Having him bring all of these just live, rowdy group of
kids through our house for years and years. It certainly made me more tolerant.*

Reggie shares a similar sentiment showing how his experiences as a father of
an 11-year-old daughter and 14-year-old son have encouraged him to see kids differently. Reggie notes that being a dad has

*taught me how to, I guess, see things from their perspective a little more. . . .
It helps me to understand that I should not be so judgmental as far as their
lives and the way they see things at a certain point. I know now, even in my
conversations with my daughter, what I would think would be them just being
crazy about a certain dress, the way they dress, or a certain way they say
things.*

Having two adolescent children provides Reggie useful reference points that help
him relate to his fourth grade students. An earlier experience Reggie had with his
daughter helped him deal more comfortably with girls' puberty issues at school.
After noting that "girls are coming into a lot of things at that age" he adds:

*Their body odor changes as far as under the arm, and being tactful as far as
knowing when to say, "I want you to think about this, about being more aware
of your body odor." And I had to have that conversation with my daughter, I
had to. And now I know how to be tactful in a way, instead of saying, "Girl, you
need to check yourself under the arm." I didn't know how to pull a girl to the
side as far as, "Come here. I want you to be aware of this. Now that you're becoming a little older, you running around brings on a different smell on your
body." And that does happen. So as far as knowing that you have a child who's
been through that whole situation, it always brings you to be a little more
thoughtful as far as speed in saying things, your awareness of where you are
when you say things, your awareness of how you say things. That has to be because I have a child.*

Being the father of a daughter has helped Reggie become more knowledge-able and sensitive when it comes to dealing with his female students. Knowing the subtleties of how a man can best build rapport with young girls and ap-proach them about sensitive issues may be every bit as important as knowing specific bits of information. Being an active and caring father may be the most efficient way to acquire this type of sensitivity.

Ironically, even though Grady notes that his extended stint working in the ju-venile detention center posed problems for him as a father and husband at one time, he believes his experience with his own three kids enabled him to be a much better guard. Reflecting on how his fathering experience mattered to him, he drew conclusions about himself as well as the other guards who were fathers.

> You know, there's no substitute for having a child and being a father. You learn so much about kids by what making them tick, and how I interact with them, how they interact with me. . . . I'm more accepting. I think I'm ready for some-thing when they do it. I say, oh, I knew that was coming, I could tell that. And certain way that kids do, the way, their mannerisms, you'll see that coming, you know, you'll see anger coming, you'll see silliness coming, things such as that, that I don't think if you weren't a father you wouldn't know about stuff like that.

When working at the detention center, being able to read teenagers' behavior prior to its getting out of hand was critical. Grady felt that being able to defuse situations with a regular pitched voice and without becoming confrontational was less common in guards who were not fathers. As we saw in Chapter 5, being able to manage kids effectively is critical to many men's youth work, especially with kids who are emotionally troubled or have violent tendencies. Effective techniques for relating to and managing kids are valuable in other set-tings as well.

Fathers may also have more empathy with parents than men who are not themselves parents, and that enables them to handle the dynamics that can emerge between parents, kids, and the adults who care for the kids. A number of the men emphasize this point. Joseph, a father of four, admits, "I'm a little more sympathetic with parents, knowing . . . what it takes to control, supervise, attend to children along with having a job, running a house, and everything else." Sandy shares a similar attitude toward parents while also noting how his fathering experience has helped him interact with kids directly.

Since I was watching my own kids grow and the frustrations that I would go through as a father, it helped . . . in terms of understanding how other parents were doing with their children. It also helped me in dealing with other children. I knew the importance of patience and understanding and those types of things. You know, getting angry never helped, at least it never did with my kids. So, I just made that assumption that it wouldn't help with other kids either and if you were upset, there were certain ways that you could show being upset without being angry or raising your voice or things like that.

If we look more closely at Sandy's life as a youth worker, we find that his involvement with his clowning program provides a unique example of how youth work and family life can be mutually reinforcing. Sandy's youth work greatly affected his experiences as a family man. He, his wife, and their three kids would sometimes do the clowning activity together in various settings, like entertaining elderly persons in retirement homes. According to Sandy, this venture strengthened the interpersonal bonds in all directions in his family. He witnessed the same thing happening for some other families as well. On the flip side, by taking his children with him to meetings and programs, Sandy enabled other parents to see him as an approachable guy who loved kids. By blending his two life worlds, Sandy made it much easier for the kids and their parents to trust him and enthusiastically participate in his programs.

Sandy's example illustrates quite well how some men's youth work and fathering affect each other. Because some of the men organize their lives with a great deal of overlap between what they do with youth in public and their own children, it is tricky to sort out how each domain affects the other.

For some men, being a father is one of the motivating forces pushing them into the world of youth work, often as the volunteer coach for a son's or daughter's athletic team. Many fathers involved in youth work have coached their own children, and most indicate that they enjoy it immensely. The overlap between men's roles as dad and coach establishes unique opportunities for men to interact with their own kids and other youth in the same setting, and at times in the men's personal space, including their homes. Santiago believes his experiences coaching his 10-year-old son's baseball and soccer teams the past few years have enabled him and his son to become tighter, because they have a new turf to share and topics to discuss. It offers them personal and special everyday rituals for bonding. Santiago speculates that being involved with kids has made him a more sensitive father and man. He is able to be attentive to how kids feel and is able to see the pros and cons of various situations. By seeing the kids on the teams change for the better or worse during the course of a season, he is able to look at his own son differently. His discussions with his son are enhanced because he knows more about what can affect kids in the wrong way.

Santiago also talks about how his dual roles as coach and father are sometimes hard on his son. The arrangement sometimes produces awkward situations in which he and his son may be viewing the situation differently; consequently, he believes, the arrangement is harder for his son than it is for him. Santiago explains:

> Sometimes you give him bad reactions, or you give him a reaction as a coach, and he's expecting a reaction as a father, and it's not gonna work. It doesn't work sometimes. But, yeah, it's been hard. . . . And you have to push him more than the other ones, of course. If you don't want ones complaining, you have to push your son more than the other ones.

He adds that his son

> doesn't like it at all. He complains to me and all that, but I tell him, "I have to, because I am the coach. And you are the coach's son, so I have to. I cannot give you any advantage, 'cause they are gonna think, "Ah! Of course, that the coach's son!"

As Santiago's situation illustrates, coaching your own child's team can be a bumpy ride for a man, because he feels awkward navigating the borders between being a coach and being a dad. These fathers must learn how to juggle their respective identities and relationships. For instance, when Matthew tried his hand at coaching his daughters' teams, he found that he sometimes blurred the line between coaching and parenting. He felt that coaching affected his fathering because the distinction between the two is often muddled.

> Yeah. I think I learned; it taught me how to turn [coaching] off. You're not always a coach, but you're always a father. So when you're done coaching, you're done coaching. When you're done for the day, you're done for the day. You don't go home and make your kids work harder once you get home. See that's—as I said, the kids can't—it's blurred. . . . it became a blurred line when I was a coach and when I was a dad and I had to understand I was always a dad and only occasionally a coach. . . . I need to compartmentalize my coaching—this is the time when we're coaching, we'll coach here, but all the time I'm a dad and I need to

understand that. That's probably what it helped me do, be able to understand that my responsibility is first and foremost [to being a dad], and as a coach secondary.

While Santiago and Matthew both got involved in coaching kids sports because they wanted to be involved with their own children, men sometimes are already involved in coaching or some other type of youth activity then invite their children to participate, as we saw with Sandy, who involved his kids in clowning. In either case, mixing youth work and fathering opens up opportunities for men to learn more about their children, other kids, and themselves. Most men appear to enjoy managing their dual involvement with unrelated youth and their own children.

FAMILY BUILDING AND CLAIMING

Some male youth workers, especially those involved with kids in a group setting, such as a school, coaching, Boys & Girls Club, daycare facility, or residential facility for troubled youth, develop special bonds with individual kids. Watching men on numerous occasions interact with youths in these types of settings showed me how comfortable some men are forming strong emotional bonds with certain kids in public settings.

The men's language sometimes reveals a strong affinity with the kids they work with, sometimes claiming them as their "own." Though they may not expressly refer to kids as family members per se, they use specific words and phrases that convey a familial tone. In addition, their language asserts their willingness to assume responsibility for the kids in some manner. A sampling of comments illustrates this sentiment.

I have to follow the policies and procedures, because my ultimate responsibility is to protect my babies. And I can't let anyone or anything hurt them. (Charles, 32, Boys & Girls Club director)

You create that identity. And I've sort of been criticized by friends of mine who are not educators, when I call these guys my guys, or my boys, or my posse, or my dogs, whatever. "You sound like they're possessions!" But see they don't understand. (Mark, 58, educator and mentor)

I dedicate most of my time to them. I love them just like they're mine. Most of our time is surrounded with these children, and I love it, simply because it's very challenging, it's the love, that you see from these children. . . .

It's not that I'm taking them away from their biological parents, but I know that deep down all I'm doing for them is, just the family, I mean, the father. (Richard, 47, owner childcare facility)

And to build that relationship with someone or child and to still see them from time to time and see what they've grown into, I mean, it' just like being a father. (Dwight, 36, teacher's aide)

My kids are my kids. I feel responsible for, I have been successful by default. It just worked, it has happened so many times, I just got a big family out there. (Jeff, 50, Boy Scout troop leader)

Whether a man refers affectionately to kids at a community club as "my babies," or invokes a hip-hop vernacular to describe kids in a mentoring program as "my boys, my posse," or asserts that he loves the kids at his daycare facility "just like they're mine," he sends an emotionally laden message: I have a special affinity with these kids and they matter to me.

The feelings men develop for kids do not emerge in a vacuum but as part of two-way relationships. A number of the men remark that they either know or suspect that kids cast them as father figures. Some kids actually use familial language (e.g., dad, daddy), expressing these perceptions and feelings plainly. One young boy approached Barry in after-school care and said, "Oh, I want you to be my dad. Can you be my father?" When Barry asked the boy why, he simply said, "Because I like you," and then repeated his initial request. After the boy told him his father was in jail, Barry went along with the boy's name game for the entire year. The boy's twin was in the program, too. The staff had placed the two boys in different groups to minimize conduct problems, but Barry made a point of occasionally spending time with both simultaneously. For my benefit, he recreates an exchange where he was sitting with the boy who first asked him to be his dad and the other twin came and sat next to Barry. The first boy said, "Get away from my daddy." And the second would say, "Well, he's my daddy, too." Naming rituals also surface with teenagers. Vince, a team leader working mostly with teenagers at an alternative school, plays along with the kids (primarily girls) who use familial terms for him. "Most of these kids out here call me Daddy, yeah a lot of them, 'My daddy right there,' and I get respect from most of them." He interprets this naming convention as indicating that these kids are comfortable talking to and seeking advice from him.

Family building also occurs when a male youth worker who is not planning on becoming a biological father sees his youth work as a way to feel connected to children. Alan's eagerness to work with the kids in his church youth group is flavored with a blend of motives, one of them being his situation as a gay man with no children of his own. He defines his youth work as

> my way of giving something to society as you would with your, through your kids. I can do it through others. And a lot of the families here tell me they're like my surrogate kids, you know, 'cause they're that attached. But yeah, . . . this kind of makes up for that void, the not having kids. I would have loved to have been a parent.

Without children of his own, Alan looks to nurture other people's kids as a way to experience the generative spirit of contributing to his social world. In turn, he has enjoyed indirectly the self-satisfaction and warm feelings parenting can produce. As noted earlier, the men—both fathers and those without kids—mention that they value this generative spirit. Thus, working with kids offers men opportunities to achieve a sense of belonging to a family while experiencing personal growth and giving to the next generation.

Men can also be involved in building family sentiments in settings away from a formal organizational site. Among the Big Brothers, Michael probably came closest to establishing familylike rituals with a Little Brother who was being raised in a single-mother household. Michael's description of this period in his life looks at events largely through his Little Brother's eyes, but I sense that Michael appreciated aspects of the quasi-family experience as well. After commenting that the boy felt at home in Michael's house and with his dog, Michael explains further:

> . . . the time he spent with my girlfriend and I and Stella [girlfriend's daughter], because we would do things together, like all four of us go to the Springs, go out for pizza . . . I think it made him kinda feel like a little bit of a family, 'cause we had kinda a little bit of like family thing going. . . . I think he enjoyed that, and then he couldn't always just interact with me, he could interact with my girlfriend and her child. And she was a pretty cool woman, so . . . and he liked her. So I think that those things, maybe a sense of seeing like—not that my girlfriend and I were normal in every way—but for the time that he knew us, we seemed that way . . . that was the best part of our relationship, those years, so he got to experience that and I guess have some sense of what it's like to have a relationship with a woman and be normal and have like a family and have kids and responsibilities and do stuff and have fun.

Michael's story also offers a glimpse of how everyday activities with unrelated kids can incorporate men's partners too. His story is a more complex version of what some young men probably feel if they help their girlfriend babysit.

The setting that may provide men the best chance to experience a sense of family with youth is coaching competitive team sports. In the amateur and professional worlds of sports, a longstanding history exists of using "family" as a metaphor to symbolize team chemistry and loyalty. Team sports offer an opportunity both to solidify bonds with individual players while promoting team trust and camaraderie. Working to create a sense of "we-ness," coaches pit "our family" against other teams and their obnoxious fans, as they pursue a competitive goal. Sharing the pain of demanding workouts, as well as the "thrill of victory and the agony of defeat," are ritual practices a coach uses to forge a family identity among his players. One high school basketball coach, Steve, talks about this bonding when he reflects on how he helped a team he coached deal with one of its players collapsing and dying on the court during a game.

> And I think that will always be there. I mean, I still hear from a couple of those kids today. When you go through something like that together . . . I always talk to our players as we're a family, and this is your family for a large part of the year. And I think when you go through something like that as a family, it draws you closer.

Of course, men's involvement with youth typically does not involve dramatic stories on par with Steve's, but men often encounter subtle reminders that they can nurture emotional and effective ties with kids, sometimes with long-term consequences. The family-type bonds, social exchanges, and practical routines men experience with youth can enhance the personal development of men and youth alike.

CHAPTER 10

PERSONAL GROWTH

Let us return to Steve's story, which comes from roughly ten years ago, when he was a 31-year-old assistant basketball coach. We find him sitting on the bench during a high school game with five minutes remaining in the second quarter. Suddenly, one of his players drops to the floor; he is having a heart attack. Steve performs CPR, as do paramedics, but the 17-year-old boy is pronounced dead a few minutes after being transported to the hospital. About a month later, the team learns that another player has contracted spinal meningitis; that boy is hospitalized and almost dies.

The unforeseen events that season altered Steve's life perspective. With vivid images of his player's tragic death in mind, Steve reflects on how he was affected.

You think as a coach, "I'm prepared for everything. Down two with one second to go, I've got a play, or whatever the situation is, I've got a plan or a play," but that was something that I don't think anybody was ever prepared for. And that was a big point in my life, just because . . . a couple of things happened. Number one, his parents weren't even at the game, because they couldn't afford to come. The kid was such a great kid. And it was just gut wrenching to see that happen. Then, counseling the other kids on the team and dealing with that whole thing was a good learning experience. And to be honest with you, I had never been to a funeral, and then they asked me to speak at the funeral.

Prior to the player's untimely death, Steve had spent much of his energy teaching kids the finer points of basketball and the value of team play. Basketball was and continues to be a sport Steve loves dearly and knows exceptionally well. He feels at home with his players on the court and in the locker room. However, on that shocking evening and in the weeks to follow, he found himself in foreign space. His new challenge called him to expand his coaching role to helping his players first mourn the death of their teammate and friend, then manage their fears as another fellow player lay deathly ill in a hospital bed. Steve guided them as they sought a fresh perspective on life, death, and living. He describes his conscientious efforts throughout the season to reach out and support his players.

> I tried to talk to each of them individually at one point in time and let them know I was there for them. Anytime, if they needed to call me; I'd come over if they felt like they were losing it or whatever. And, you know, just tried to be strong for them. And let them know it was okay to cry and show emotion, that kind of thing. I think sometimes, with male bravado, sometimes kids think that, "Well I'm not really supposed to cry." And just let them know it's okay, that's the way you grieve.

Although the boy code undoubtedly complicated Steve's efforts to comfort his players entrenched in the world of boys' high school sports, he confidently remarks, "It taught me, and it taught the kids, a lot about—there's a lot more important things in life than a basketball game." For his part, Steve developed a keener sense of how he, as an adult man and coach, could affect his players on and off the court when confronted with an unusual set of circumstances. Though nervous, he felt privileged to speak on behalf of this "great kid" to his family, teammates, friends, and others at his first funeral service. Ultimately, by being there for his players when they needed him most, Steve gained self-confidence in his leadership qualities and interpersonal skills.

The typical way to think about the significance of men's involvement with youth is to consider how kids' lives are affected. But Steve, like many other men, illustrates that time spent working and volunteering with youth can change the personalities, knowledge, self-perceptions, and life perspectives of the men as well. Granted, men may not be able to sort out exactly how much of their personal development can be attributed directly to their involvement with kids compared to their natural maturation, but some men are certain their youth work has made them a different, and usually better, person. As detailed earlier, some men explicitly say that their motivation to work with kids is partly due to the benefits they receive, most notably the sense of nurturing a younger generation and making a difference in kids' lives.[1] Also, fathers describe how working with kids affects the way they perceive and react to their own children. Becoming a more attentive, understanding, and skilled father is clearly an area in which men believe they experience personal growth by being with unrelated kids in public settings.[2] For some men, their personal growth extends beyond these types of changes.

Prior to our interview, many of the men had not thought seriously about how their involvement with youth had altered their way of seeing the world, themselves, and others. Even some of those who had thought about these matters previously, began to see their experiences more clearly once I asked them to think about a wide range of issues. In the process of sharing their stories, insights once ignored or only vaguely appreciated began to take on new meaning. For example, Ray, a 22-year-old who has worked with at-risk kids in an afterschool program for a little less than two years, initially indicated that he did not feel as though he had "picked up any new [personality] traits" from working with kids. However, when I separately inquire about patience and listening skills, Ray immediately indicates that he has experienced tremendous changes: "Two hundred percent more patient, man. . . . That's one thing I didn't have, was patience. I got all the patience in the world. . . . I don't know how it happened." He then adds, "Yeah, man, you learn to listen in detail, especially . . . it is law enforcement, community policing, you need to listen in detail." Obviously, that the men may not have thought about these issues in the past does not mean that their interactions with kids have had no impact. Youth work experiences can affect men's personalities and interaction styles in ways that go largely unnoticed—even by the men themselves. Many of the changes men experience alter the way they treat youth, but the men's personalities and approach to life may change without directly influencing kids.

The men describe an assortment of ways being involved with kids has mattered to them. I have distilled from their comments four general impressions concerning individual changes they experience: states and styles of feeling, powers of perception, self-perception, and life perspective. For simplicity's sake, I deal with each of these areas in turn while acknowledging that personal development does not occur in a neat, compartmentalized fashion; people may grow in related ways all at once.

EMOTIONAL STATES AND STYLES OF FEELING

As one might expect, spending lots of time around energetic kids, some of whom exhibit emotional and behavioral problems, as well as at-risk kids who are struggling with difficult circumstances, offers men unique opportunities to work through their own emotions. For some, dealing with these situations leads them to become more patient, caring, compassionate, and kind-hearted. Sandy's succinct self-assessment is similar to that expressed by a number of other men: "I think I am a fairly patient and tolerant person and that is [in] no small amount from the kids I work with." Brandon, who works with middle school students and older teenagers in a residential facility for emotionally troubled kids, gives a more nuanced explanation. Working with kids, he says, has

> made me more caring. . . . Kids are resilient but I think they're very fragile. And by the same token, I don't think they realize [that] a lot of what they say [to us] hurts. We're adults, so they don't imagine they can hurt us. And I think it's important to be able to communicate with them and express my feeling[s] with them, and let them know, you know, "Right now, I'm very disappointed in what you've done, okay." Before, I wouldn't do that. With adults, it's kinda like [I would say], "Aw, screw you." What do I have to . . . [talk about my reactions] for? So I think that working with kids has really helped my development, again, in ways that I just normally, you know, I probably would not have if I had just chosen to work in an adult field. . . . Working with kids has made me pay attention to the details.

Because Brandon realizes that kids are learning about life and themselves, he is more willing to be attentive to their frailties than he probably would be if he were dealing with adults. Consequently, he's more willing to express patience while showing them that he cares about their personal well-being and maturity and his relationship with them.

Patience is something that Eric also feels he has acquired much more of since he's started volunteering and working in preschool childcare programs. In addition, after noting that he now sees "things from a different perspective," Eric says that his work has

> allowed me to realize there's more important things than what I was seeing, like, I was pretty self-centered and just worried about myself before I started these jobs, and I feel like I have a lot more compassion; . . . like, before, I think, I wouldn't even get sad if I, like I wouldn't haven't had any emotions or anything if I saw a kid crying, I might feel a little bit of guilt or something. But now I actually feel sadness and, feels like I have more sympathy for [kids].

Pressed to comment on whether his compassion and sympathy extended to persons other than children, Eric believes his increased sensitivity extends only to kids.

Reggie, an elementary school teacher, also takes a reflective turn. He observes that working with young children, as well as the older kids he mentors through his church, has

> helped me develop as a more caring person, dealing with the youth and being a more compassionate, a little more helpful person, though I've always been that way from my earlier upbringing, through my mother, my grandmother being a caring, compassionate person. I think every step you take in life just maybe enhances it or contributes to it.

For Reggie and some of the other men, being helpful equates to expressing a "giving" personality; having certain feelings is important, but acting on those feelings in a productive fashion is critical too. As with Michael, for whom becoming a Big Brother pushed him to become "less selfish and a little more giving," working with youth often leads men to revamp their life perspective, as discussed below.

Though I did not ask the men to compare their style of feeling to how men who do not work with kids manage their emotions, I suspect many would say they have a more caring disposition, at least toward kids. They would reason that both their willingness to commit their time and energy to being involved in the first place plus the experiences they have had would make them more sensitive to kids' needs.

POWERS OF PERCEPTION

An important feature of compassion is being open-minded about other people's life circumstances. Thus, another impression I took from some of the men's comments—that working with kids has increased their powers of perception—is closely tied to their style of feeling. Compared to when they first began working with kids, the men believe that they are less inclined to pass judgment on others and increasingly eager to examine kids' behavior to assess what might be leading them to feel and act a certain way. Men who learn to perceive the youth world in this fashion polish the perspectives they use to make sense of kids' lives. Reflecting on his time working with kids at an alternative school, Dwight says it has taught him to be a "little more open minded . . . with the kids or everyday life." He explains how he has changed over the years:

> There was times when I ran into negative situations and I just said, "Well forget it," you know, "it can't be fixed." But working here . . . has made me just

*put forth a little more effort in getting to the bottom of things and trying to see
what's actually going on. Made me a little more aware of how people act, why
they act like they do, if they having a bad day or whatever. So it's just made
me, I guess, be a little bit more kind-hearted, I would say.*

Scott's work in various positions at a busy Boys & Girls Club has provided
him plenty of opportunities for over a decade to broaden and relax his perceptions of kids. He cautions that it is

*hard to judge someone until you've walked in their shoes. You can sit there and
chastise somebody and sit and say, "Well, I would have done it this way." But
you can't, and working with kids, so many of them, they go through different
things. I see them in a school year for 4 to 6 hours a day, in the summer I see
'em anywhere from 8 to 12 hours or so a day. But I don't know what goes on at
home. But while I have them I, what I say is I can't judge a lot of things that
go on with them. So as far as how it influenced my relationship, I'm a
listener . . . I'm not gonna judge.*

As Scott suggests, attentive listening—that critical interpersonal skill showcased
in the men's stories in earlier sections of this book—is a vital tool for appreciating kids. Scott is committed to listening so that he can better understand kids'
dilemmas.

Matthew's experience as a Boy Scout troop leader has influenced him in a
similar way, teaching him to meet kids "where they are."

*I'd say it's probably taught me more about the ability to ask questions and to
listen, and to really listen. . . . You either have the kid who will tell you everything, straight as an arrow. You know, "Why are you having a hard time?"
"Well, because mom and dad are getting a divorce." . . . But then you have
[the] kid on the other end, "Why are you having such a hard time?" "Well, I
don't know." So . . . you gotta be willing to go to where they are, find out what
their issues are. . . . you gotta be willing to invest more and more time into
that one who's wanting to hold the information back, but you also invest more
time in the one who's willing to give it to you, because he wants the details of
how to fix it.*

Over time, Matthew feels, he has become much better at figuring out how to listen and ask questions so that he can dig more deeply into what is going on in
kids' lives. In some sense, he has become a lay counselor.

Working with kids teaches people about the key conditions that influence their experiences: families, communities, schools, and friends. Over time, youth workers can accumulate a wealth of formal and anecdotal knowledge and, as a result, grow more confident in their ability to see the bigger picture and anticipate how they might help individual kids. Joseph believes his extensive experience working with at-risk youth in various settings, as well as his association with key youth organizations, has heightened his awareness about kids. It has also fostered his professional development.

> I think it has made me more aware of different society norms that a lot of people that are not in the area that I'm involved with aren't aware. Different things are going on within homes. I'm part of a multidisciplinary team that reviews abuse cases for [the county]. . . . It's just made a tremendous difference in a lot of what I do, a lot of how I think about . . . things at home, a lot of how I see working with parents.

The youth minister Kevin feels he is in a much better position because of his career choice to understand situations kids are in and contribute in a positive way to kids' lives. He avoids attending formal youth conferences, so his insights are gleaned primarily from his relationships.

> Over the years [relationships with kids] have certainly enriched my life. Getting to know all these different kids. . . . I mean, I've watched kids grow up, and the relationships certainly have added to who I am as a person. And I guess, the lessons, the tears, the joys, the failures, the ups, the downs, all those experiences, I mean, they're always there, and I can draw on them when I'm speaking to another kid or I'm speaking to a parent. I've had parents get onto me, and I've had parents sitting here telling me I've done this wrong, or, "Why are you doing this," "My kid said this." And you know, all those experiences have added to the person that I am. To understand, to . . . appreciate how I say things. To appreciate the, you know, the influence that I do have in some of these kids' lives, not to take it for granted.

As Kevin notes, the countless experiences he has had with kids and their parents over the years enhances his ability to be a better youth minister. His powers of perception are related to his ability to express himself carefully to the kids and parents who look to him for guidance. Knowing which messages have worked well and which have not allows Kevin to be more self-assured when talking to his parishioners.

Finally, being around girls enables some men to develop a deeper appreciation for the challenges girls experience growing up, as they negotiate puberty, their evolving identities, and their relations with girlfriends, boys, family members, and other adults. As mentioned earlier, some of the men raising daughters find the knowledge they develop from having a daughter helpful in their youth work.

Nick's experience in the residential facility for troubled youth provides an example of learning from the girls he monitors. He came to see girls' lives in a new light by listening to them and watching them interact with boys. Nick explains one lesson he's learned about gender relations from paying attention to the nuances of young girls' everyday realities:

> The girls want to be girls, but to a point they want to be a male because they want to be strong. They want to be able to defend themselves [here but] they don't have to. You know, every female on this floor out here thinks they have to be aggressive at times to get a point across. They have to attack the staff; they have to attack another client to prove a point. And, I'm like, "You guys don't have to do that; you're females first off. You don't have to be aggressive to get attention. You don't have to be like that." And, they're like, "Yeah we do." So, I ask one of them one time, I said, "Why do you feel the need to be aggressive?" And she looked at me and she said, "When I'm aggressive to a male or female they won't come in my space. But, if I talk like a female, they feel like I'm inviting them into my space." And, I kinda went, it's kinda interesting. . . . I start watching, and sure enough, when they talk like a female to the boys you see the boys get closer and closer and closer, like they're inviting 'em. But, when they're like "Look, you don't need to be coming around me," they back away. So it's a defensive mode, and it's good to have that defense, but you don't want to be so good to where you push everybody away from you. And, I try to tell them that.

Although Nick has developed a better understanding of why the girls act as they do, he is concerned that they will regret "draw[ing] the line" so rigidly because they eventually will "want a mate." Aware that the girls' aggressive stance has pushed the boys away, Nick encourages the boys to try a different approach to being friends with them, to go to the girls' wing of the facility: "Spend at least five or ten minutes over there, talk to 'em, just walk around, ask them questions about what they're doin'." Now that he has a better handle on what's going on with the kids, Nick, in his role as the mediator of gender distrust, tries to encourage both boys and girls to explore opportunities to see each other differently.

Malik's vision of youth and his understanding of girls have also evolved based on his everyday youth work in schools and church. He now believes he has a much better sense of what many girls have been lacking in recent decades.

> I've seen it so much, like in, especially teenage girls, the ones in our programs who, who are really sexually active. I mean, it's not because they want to be labeled a slut. It's not that they want everybody at school to say, "Oh she's a hoe," or "She's nasty," . . . they don't want that. It's that these kids are looking for attention.

Malik has incorporated his insights about girls into how he affirms his young nieces. He now also appreciates more fully how important it will be for him to provide positive feedback to his future daughters to help them build self-respect and feel secure.

SELF-PERCEPTIONS

Some of the men I interviewed have come to see themselves in different ways because of their interactions with youth. I already commented about men seeing themselves as becoming more patient, caring, compassionate, and more able to parent, now or in the future. In addition, men's positive experiences with kids sometimes leave them feeling more personally self-confident and feeling better about themselves. When men feel as though they have experienced generativity by mentoring kids, including getting them to adopt the philosophy of wanting to "pass it on" to others, then they tend to feel a sense of accomplishment. Of course, they still feel uneasy that they are unable to make a difference for other kids. Andre's mixed feelings illustrate this struggle.

> It depends which day you ask me. I mean, there're days where I'm, you know, . . . I go home and I'm happy and I feel like I've done something; but, you know, a lot of days I go home and I'm just, you know, depressed, and pulling what little hair I have out.

A brief sampling of things men say about how working with kids makes them feel about themselves underscores that the benefits of men's involvement with kids go beyond outcomes for the kids. Alan talks about how his general well-being has been enhanced by his involvement with kids in the church.

I had some depression problems in my high school years, and I think it's helped me deal better with that now. I don't feel so much, as, being a loner and stuff. I feel better about where our future's going . . . when I see some of these kids and knowing that they're so accepting of me and my lifestyle [being gay and cohabiting].

Scott, who has handled numerous positions at the same Boys & Girls Club he now directs, admits that working at the club

does wonders for your self-esteem. I mean, you realize that what you're doing is important. It makes you feel good about yourself that, when someone asks you "What do you do?" . . . "Well, I run a boys and girls club," "Well what do you do there?" . . . and you kinda describe what you do, and people are like "Oh, that's very, I mean, that you're spending your time with them, there's a lot of people that wouldn't have the patience" this or that. . . . I look at it as a reward, and, over the years, I've gotten so much more satisfaction from the kids I work with than I could ever give to the kids.

According to Scott, the listening skills he has developed from his youth work have also enabled him to improve how he relates to his girlfriend. "I'm a listener so, I listen to what she has to say, I'm not gonna judge." Consequently, he believes he can understand and appreciate his girlfriend more fully.

A teacher for thirty-five years and a formal and informal mentor for many kids, Mark echoes Scott's impression that working with kids has mattered to him a great deal. Indeed, he says working with kids has "totally molded my personality. I think that it's molded me in almost every facet of my life." Mark's comments can be interpreted in a positive light because he is content with his personality and his professional accomplishments.

Thomas highlights how his professional development is tied directly to the students in his first grade classes.

It's been my experience that I wanted to learn everything I could about how to be a teacher, to best accommodate the children that I work with. . . . It wasn't enough for me to go to school just to get my Bachelor's in elementary ed. I wanted a Master's, like I wanted to become a master teacher, and I still do, I'm still working towards that. . . . I just feel like what I do for them is exactly what they do for me, and it's kind of like its own machine, in that the more I help them learn, the more they help me learn. The more I help them grow, the more they help me grow. . . . My life is now dedicated to helping children in

whatever capacity I can, as far as their academics are concerned and life in
general.

In Thomas's life, the kids are the critical motivating force driving him to want to become a "master teacher."

Sometimes, their work with kids has caused men to examine their own behaviors and attitude toward themselves. They decide they must alter their ways in order to work with kids effectively. Such a decision by Ray, the African American 22-year-old who has mentored and worked with at-risk boys for a couple of years, illustrates how youth work can challenge men to self-reflect, and sometimes take the initiative to see and present themselves differently. Conscious of the power of first impressions, while he was still a teenager himself Ray became increasingly aware of the image he was projecting to both youth and adults. As an upper division student in high school, Ray ran a peer student mentoring program, which pressed him to open his eyes to how personal appearance influences others' reactions. Two practical consequences of this observation were that he eventually, as he puts it, started to pull his pants up over his butt, and he cut off his dreadlocks. In addition to wanting to set a good example for the younger guys, he reasoned that "it's easier to play the game." He recounts how he felt that school administrators looked at him and thought, "Oh, he's garbage, he ain't gonna be able to achieve it," even though many did not know much about him. His concern about others' perceptions was reinforced once he took his paid staff position working with at-risk male teenagers—almost all African American. Asked to reflect on whether his life and self-perception have changed because of his experience working with youth, Ray adamantly responds:

> *I've changed drastically, man. I gave you . . . my definition of mentoring and that's by walking, man, leading by example. Some of the stuff that I did . . . I don't do no more. Some of the clothes I used to wear, I don't wear no more. The places that I used to hang out, dope hole [place were drugs are used and sold], I don't hang out no more because some of those guys hang out, too. . . . And I can't ask them to do something, man, that I wouldn't do myself. I don't drive my car as much. I bought a new car. I've got a couple of cars with big rims and all that stuff, that's a perception that I don't want. You know, first appearance to people is everything, man, you only get one. And so for the guys that don't know me, I just don't need that biased attitude, man . . . and I had to cut some family off.*

Ray's personal transformation is complicated because, as he later told me, he still would prefer having long hair and he is attracted to some "bling bling" features of hip-hop culture. While he believes that hair, clothes, jewelry, cars, and the like should not define who a person really is, he realizes that those facets of a person's appearance often engender negative perceptions from others and project a negative example to "the guys" he is mentoring. Drawing from personal experience, Ray tells the boys how his outward changes have led to people's treating him "a lot differently . . . it's like night and day, man. People just respond to you in more of a positive way, man. And if they have an opinion about you, man, they're more of an optimist about it."

LIFE PERSPECTIVES

Being responsible for kids seems to inspire men to clarify their values and their approach to life, rethink their life priorities, and motivate them to try new things. Because the men work with kids representing various ages and backgrounds and do their youth work in diverse settings, it is not surprising that they change in different ways. Only a small proportion of men doing youth work actually provide formal hands-on childcare, such as, changing diapers, feeding, dressing, and physically assisting infants, toddlers, or kids with special needs. But caring for youth in this fashion may strengthen certain personality traits more than supervising teenagers in a juvenile detention center, though the latter may produce its own benefits.

The broadest and most fundamental way youth work can affect men is by prompting them to redefine their meaning of life, clarifying what is important to them. Andrew pulls together his thoughts about what coaching means to him by focusing on the relationships he's had and placing them into a larger life frame.

It's fun to go and see that enthusiasm that youth has, where they haven't been beaten down by life yet. Frankly, it inspires me, and I like to think that . . . I'm more enthusiastic in terms of what I do professionally with friends. Most clearly, from a teaching standpoint, you begin to realize what's really important in terms of relationships, and that fundamental principles matter, be it playing basketball or how you deal with people in business or how you deal with your wife. And so, this past year especially, while I was coaching, which was a huge time commitment, I was a better business person, I was a better husband. I was more conscious of the kind of decor, behavior, and issues that you need to do to be successful, in part because you're teaching it for two to three hours a day. It's inconsistent if you come back [from coaching] and . . . you don't work hard at your office or your job or your clients or treat your wife fairly.

Thus, the lesson Andrew has learned is not just about working with kids, it's about devoting oneself to the core principles that build and sustain strong relationships. Working with kids enables him to translate those principles into practice repeatedly, making him more aware of how critical they are to how he wants to be as a human being in all his endeavors. Coaching, then, becomes the medium for teaching the larger life lessons, to himself as well as the players. With time, Andrew's coaching experiences and self-reflection have led him to shift his priorities in teaching kids.

I probably have a better perspective now than I did twenty years ago. In terms of that, maybe twenty years ago, teaching this skill or that was sort of the dominant goal that I judged my self-success—did I help a kid get better in terms of their skills, specifically in athletics? Where now, I clearly want them to improve, but I really do have, probably, a broader philosophical reason as to why I'm doing it. . . . Whether his jump shot improved or he's a better dribbler doesn't matter nearly as much as is he learning that hard work and focused effort can result in positive results. That's very important, I think that's a life skill and a foundational principle that you can learn. As well, trying how to be unselfish.

Just as Andrew has learned by coaching kids for extended periods of time, men can also evolve as individuals based on isolated, serendipitous events. Robby describes in detail how one of his volunteer outings to a hospital left a lasting impression on him about the meaning of vulnerability in life and volunteering. He recalls visiting a teenage girl on a children's cancer ward. She was wearing a bunch of colored wristbands symbolizing her experience, intimate or indirect, with various cancer-related support groups. Robby's intense mental and emotional processing of this event is worth considering at length.

I asked her about her wristbands and gave her a teddy bear, and she started crying because she was just overwhelmed. She's 13, and she just was touched by someone caring about her. And I didn't understand. . . . Why was she crying? But it was overwhelming for a 13-year-old to have cancer, and it hit her. And it hit us, all of us, the three or four of us who were in that hospital room, because the wristbands weren't just wristbands. The reason they came about was because they had meaning behind them. And now you just see people wearing them as a fashion trend, but for this little girl to wear them, you understood what they really meant. It wasn't just a wristband, and it wasn't just a teddy bear. The wristband was for her, it was derived to be worn and to be understood, or to be representative of this little girl. And so seeing it, it clicked. Or living through that experience helped me grow and understand what volunteering was all about, what kind of values you need to have, and kind of the difference between societal . . . views on fashion, on trends and what's in, on what you want to do with your friends versus true meaning behind certain actions and true meaning behind certain cultural elements and where they really fit in society.

Though brief, Robby's experience with this young girl prompted him to reaffirm what really matters in life and how he can best contribute to others' happiness. As Robby struggles in his story to make sense of his emotional encounter, he appears to contrast the mentalities driving the commercial world of images with loving acts of kindness—the threads of connectedness that define wholesome features of the social world. After elaborating on his story he concludes by saying:

It just made me think about how we view things and where we put our importance as humans. Is it more important to put things in context? And then what happens when we take them out of context? How does that change our perspective on certain things that we hold true or put value on?

What I took from my longer conversation with Robby is that his regular excursions to visit kids in hospitals, as well as his efforts to advocate on their behalf by recruiting adult volunteers, offer him regular checkpoints to think about and solidify his life philosophy.

Though some men's youth work experience has inspired them to grapple with the heady questions of what is most important in life, some men are prompted to think about matters like staying young, having fun, and trying new things. At age 60, Calvin is apt to be viewed by many as middle-aged and approaching the late life stages. But Calvin believes his job at an employment-training center for youth, his earlier position as a high school teacher, and his wife's job as a kindergarten teacher have kept him and his wife young in spirit. He admits to feeling uncomfortable with many people his age, even referring to one former college classmate as an "old fart" because of the man's mindset. Calvin fears falling into this elderly mindset and feels fortunate.

*The stories that she [his wife] brings home and the stories that I bring home, I
just think that it keeps you in touch with, not only keeps you in touch with
what's going on with kids and parents, but it keeps you younger. I mean, you
can't . . . have one foot in the grave and go out dealing with these 14-, 15-, 16-
year-olds. I mean, they try to pull the wool over your eyes, and if you are not
up on the step and paying attention and understand where they're coming
from [problems will occur]. . . . That's a really big thing, it kind of keeps you in
life and what's going on with the young people and how they think and how
they act, how they dress and where they are coming from. That to me is really
important, 'cause my wife and I love children.*

Staying young is also seen as a benefit by 43-year-old Alan, who associates his
increasingly youthful orientation with the kids he mentors at his church. Alan
gets directly involved with the kids in some of their activities, especially on their
camping and missionary trips.

*I look at everything different. I look at things back through younger eyes
again. . . . As you get older, your routines tend to [fit] . . . into other people's
ideals of what that age should be and what you should be doing, and I
think . . . that ages you inside too, when you get into those kind of routines. By
working with these groups, it keeps me young at heart, and so it makes decisions on things I do maybe a little different, some of the things I might not do
because I feel I'm getting too old to do, I'll do, because I say, well, you know,
you're only as old as you feel.*

Alan is uncomfortable around water and does not consider himself to be a
risk-taker. He credits the teenagers at church for getting him to experiment with
highly physical activities like rafting, skiing, and rock climbing. They also made
him feel at ease in conversations about faith, so he now talks much more freely
about his religious beliefs. Other men also talk about how spending time with
kids has afforded them the opportunity to try new things or try things they
might not otherwise do at this point in their life, such as, public speaking, clowning, playing video games, and going camping. In Alan's case, he is quite grateful
that he has stretched his personality at the urging of these youths.

Even 22-year old Gerald, significantly younger than either Calvin or Alan,
stresses the value of having a younger, carefree outlook on life from time to time.
Gerald's venture into being a Big Brother has taken him to the lighter side of life.
A college student, Gerald finds himself frequently stressed about his school
work and job, but his mentoring experience enables him to appreciate the value

of relaxing and having fun. Gerald offers this advice, gathered from being around his Little Brother:

> *Have fun. Enjoy life. Enjoy what's out there and . . . everything doesn't have to be a job in a sense. You know, it's okay to have fun. It's okay to go to the arcade every now and then and to use that as, in a sense, as your escape tool. Get away from the other stresses.*

Gerald emphasizes the therapeutic value of working with kids. Though relatively young himself, Gerald's Big Brother experience has given him a legitimate excuse to slow down and relax.

On a more serious note, Gerald shares the experience described in Calvin's earlier comments about how being around his son's friends made him more tolerant of kids outside the mainstream. Gerald's Little Brother is also someone who has a "very diverse group of friends." Impressed with how easily the boy relates to his friends, Gerald feels his Little Brother has taught him an important life lesson.

> *I guess, his appreciation and his acceptance of other cultures has taught me to be the same. You know, it has me, I guess, more willin' to open up and to experience a variety, and I guess to interact with people of different cultures, different ethnicities, and backgrounds and so on.*

Usually the mentors are thought of as the ones passing on life lessons, but sometimes the kids set the example and do the teaching. Gerald's experience, like those of many, conveys a key message for those wanting to increase men's involvement in kids' lives: getting men to see more clearly the benefits they reap from doing youth work may be an important step in persuading men to increase their commitment to help kids.

CHAPTER 11

YOUTH WORK DOMAINS

For eighteen months I enjoyed talking to, watching, and learning from men in diverse settings who have for various reasons decided to work and volunteer with kids. My time with these men has exposed me to a fascinating insider's perspective. The detailed, sometimes emotionally riveting first-hand accounts they share have enriched my efforts to tell the big and multilayered story of men's youth work in the United States. Most importantly, the men's life histories impress upon me the passion many of them have for what they do with and for kids. Armed with a deeper appreciation for the various settings in which men interact with kids, I have sought to generate insights into how they treat diverse youth of all ages. Throughout this book I show how men transition into their youth work activities and how they adapt lessons they learn from one setting to the next as they assume new positions. I also dissect men's motives, interactive styles, mentoring philosophies, preferences for handling the overlap between their public and private lives, and their personal development.

Thus far, however, I have analyzed the men's stories by looking at critical points about the men themselves, with only minimal attention to the specific domain in which they were working. Now I shift my focus and separately discuss critical issues associated with five major domains, types of settings, in which men interact with kids: childcare, schools, monitoring and criminal justice programs, recreation, and faith-based organizations. These individual assessments will inform the broader, forward-looking comments I make in my final chapter.

CHILDCARE

Of all the public settings in which men may spend time with kids, they are most reluctant to work in daycare centers or after-school programs that serve young children. Though the percentages vary slightly, typically, less than 5 percent of childcare workers in facilities across Europe, North America, and Australia are men.[1] These rates have remained stable or increased only slightly in the past decade. Throughout the world, men's limited involvement in childcare services (as well as elementary education) produces a mixed response. Some people enthusiastically encourage more men to get involved; others are opposed to recruiting men for this work.[2] Much of the discussion about men doing childcare is laced with ideological and political overtones. Broadly speaking, two diverse discourses focusing on men in general help place in context the negative images of male childcare workers. Men are either victimized as scapegoats of gender stereotyping that portrays them as suspicious and potentially bad, or they are painted as members of a privileged class of persons—men—that has historically propagated a set of dominant masculine norms while also demonstrating a greater proclivity than women to harm children.[3] The public and academic debate as to whether and to what extent men and women are "essentially" different rages on. Do men and women express themselves in uniquely gendered ways, and if so, what are the consequences for kids?

Many in favor of men's greater involvement believe that kids respond to men and women differently; they also base their preference for more male childcare workers to varying degrees on one of three arguments.[4] First, some see male childcare workers serving a compensatory role for the large numbers of children who have limited, if any, contact with a father and may therefore be missing a close relationship with an adult male. Although those embracing this view may underestimate the amount of contact kids have with adult males in their family, my interviews reveal that some children clearly seek out and try to connect with men in what resembles a familial tie.

Second, a related argument emphasizes the value of having positive male role models for youth, especially boys. My participants typically share this sentiment. One image men can portray is that caring for others is consistent with manly behavior, although the literature exploring this possibility says little about how male childcare workers affect girls. Commentators sometimes point out that men may reinforce gender stereotypes in occupations typically dominated by women.[5]

Third, some observers assume that recruiting a sufficient number of men into the childcare industry would lead to greater gender equality in the workplace and generate cultural changes. Claire Cameron and Peter Moss, two researchers devoted to increasing men's involvement in childcare in Europe, argue that

> nurseries and other early childhood services are understood to be community institutions and public spaces which undertake projects of social and cultural significance, including the co-construction, by children and workers, of gender identity; and, as such, the gender mix of the staff is significant for this process of co-construction.[6]

Skeptics suspect, however, that if there were an increase in men working in the childcare sector, men would simply move into management positions in the sector at a disproportionate rate compared to females. Admittedly, this pattern is more likely to occur in the educational system than in childcare because the organizational structure for the latter tends to have a flat career structure with few opportunities for promotion.[7]

In any case, men's movement into the childcare profession tends to occur coincidently and is seldom men's first career choice. We saw this with Richard, the former retail manager and current owner and operator of a childcare facility. He entered childcare after experiencing the emotional turning point of finding and returning a kidnapped girl to her parents. One of the other men, Eric, drifted into the field because his mother asked him to help her when he was a teenager. Later, he confirmed that he enjoyed working with children, having started by babysitting for his nephew. Now he's studying to pursue a career in elementary education after which he will transition from childcare into a classroom as an art teacher for young children.

Some commentators stress that the public should be very leery of male childcare workers because they see men as having a greater tendency than women to be violent or abusive, toward children in particular.[8] Unfortunately, because we have transformed ourselves into a risk-conscious society in which individuals are increasingly anxious about all sorts of potential dangers, sober discussions about men's and women's relative threat to children in childcare facilities are few and far between. The formal and informal public scrutiny has resulted in men like Eric being subjected to unwritten rules concerning their access to children.[9] Most of the men with childcare experience recognize that different informal norms govern how they and their female counterparts can express themselves with kids. For example, men acknowledge that women are much freer than they are to have small children sit on their laps or show physical affection. Despite these disparities, the men who have worked with infants and young children report having enjoyed spending time with kids in childcare settings, even though some chose to pursue other forms of work later on.

Powerful comments by several of the men about holding vulnerable infants and attending to children in hospitals further underscore the penchant of some men for connecting with kids. For example, being around babies in the pediatric wing of a hospital and having them fall asleep in his arms was an emotional experience for Jackson, and it had long-lasting implications. He believes it led him to be much more tolerant of adults.

> I learned a little more about love. . . . A lot of children that I held, you know, some of them are gonna grow up to be racists. Some of them are gonna be agnostic. Who knows what they're gonna do in the future. But that's not gonna matter to me, 'cause, you know, I saw them at such an innocent stage. . . . That baby is still them in some ways.

If we are to continue to forge new meanings for the masculine code in this new century, we must strive to normalize boys and men's involvement in childcare facilities. Boys and men need to be encouraged to participate in childcare for fun, pay, or both. Unfortunately, unless the cultural stereotypes and pay scale are radically altered, recruiting men into this field will remain difficult. Creative partnerships between childcare providers and schools, religious organizations, and work sites can provide boys the chance to either volunteer or pursue a part-time job in the field.

SCHOOL

Although debates regarding men's participation in schools are somewhat similar to those pertaining to childcare, men's involvement in diverse educational settings raises separate issues as well. For starters, teaching environments are more diverse than childcare settings. Men's teaching experience with kids covers grades K–12, public and private educational environments, and standard schools as well as alternative sites targeting at-risk kids, many of whom have been expelled from regular schools. My conversations with men provide a sampling of how training and teaching of kids occur in a wide range of settings. But, given the relatively small number of current and former teachers I interviewed, I cannot offer detailed commentary on men's involvement with any particular level or type of teaching environment.

Various studies show that men shy away from pursuing a teaching career with kids for at least one of the following five reasons: low social status, low salary, perception of teaching as "women's work," concerns about potential complaints of child abuse, and the absence of a male peer group.[10] Consistent with other small-scale studies, the teachers I interviewed express concern about these issues to varying degrees. They all did, however, at least try their hand at teaching. A select group of men demonstrate how intensely committed some men are to teaching youth.

Among the most frequently cited reasons for increasing men's contributions to teaching, some argue, is that having more male teachers would balance the teaching styles presented in schools. Contemplating the possible merits of broadening teaching styles is timely, in light of recent public debates about boys' purported school performance problems and about whether boys and girls have different learning styles that affect the quality of their academic performance.

For at least a decade, commentators ranging from conservatives to progressives have raised awareness of the debate concerning school reform and boys' purported educational woes.[11] In 2006, media reports on the so-called "boy crisis" appeared in *Newsweek, New Republic,* and *Esquire,* and on a segment of the *Today* show.[12] Some commentators warn of dire consequences stemming from gender disparity in school performance. They advance a range of pet theories to explain the perceived and real gender gaps in achievement, including the view that schools increasingly have become feminized places that impede boys' learning. Although their form and intensity may have shifted, concerns about the feminization of school culture have been part of the public conversation since the early 1900s.[13]

A nuanced discussion of the debate exceeds my focus here,[14] however, Sara Mead, senior analyst at Education Sector (an independent education think tank) presents an informed analysis after reviewing several decades of national trend data from two major sources. Mead's balanced assessment—a refreshing reprieve from the slanted opinions served up by many leading commentators on this issue—is that boys, in general, are doing reasonably well at the elementary school level but their performance is declining somewhat in high school. In short, boys on average are improving but not as quickly as is the case for girls. Mead acknowledges that current schools are not working effectively with the disproportionately large number of boys who are diagnosed with learning and emotional disabilities, suspended from school, or who drop out. Some boys are clearly in trouble.

Sharing the view of some academics, Mead also raises concerns about whether observed gender differences in performance are due principally to disparities between boys and girls overall or whether those larger patterns mask differences due to individuals' racial and social class background.[15] She concludes that African American and Hispanic boys are particularly susceptible to poor educational outcomes but that their problems stem less from gender-related factors than from conditions associated with their race or ethnicity and social class. Although it is tricky to untangle the specific reasons why boys of color are vulnerable, the findings reveal that these boys experience unique risks. Is it possible that for these boys, highly accomplished men of color—like some of the men I interviewed—may offer a glimmer of hope? I tend to think so, as do the men I interviewed.

In addition to assessing the comparative data on boys and girls' academic performance, Mead highlights how a "growth industry of experts" advising educators on ways to make schools more "boy friendly" has developed recently. She warns that we should be

> skeptical of simplistic approaches aimed at fixing the boy crisis, such as expanding single-sex schooling, implementing gender-based instructional techniques, or funding new federal programs aimed at improving boys' achievement. The close relation between the difficulties facing some boys and complex educational challenges such as racial and economic achievement gaps, high school reform, and special education suggests that silver-bullet approaches are unlikely to solve the problems facing many boys. Each of these ideas may have a modicum of merit, but there is little sound research evidence for their effectiveness.[16]

Although she does not explicitly comment on the merit of recruiting more male teachers, recruitment efforts of this sort could be viewed as attempts to make schools more "boy friendly." Regardless of whether a "boy crisis" actually exists in schools, the call to get men more involved in grade school classrooms appears to have grown louder since the early 1990s.

Unfortunately, because my interviews focus on men's perceptions and experiences, I cannot assert whether elementary school boys, or boys in higher grades, benefit academically if they are taught by or associate with men in schools. Much probably depends on a host of conditions, including the types of men entering the teaching ranks, characteristics of the students themselves, features of particular school environments, and so forth. Actually, the very limited research on this topic is mixed. Some studies suggest that having men teach them does not help boys' motivation, engagement, or performance on standardized tests,[17] though boys may prefer to consult men teachers if they have personal or emotional issues.[18] Thomas Dee, an economist, constructs a different story, using the dated but unique 1988 National Education Longitudinal Survey of eighth graders, and two of each student's teachers in different subjects, from public and private schools. Summarizing his findings, Dee says:

> A teacher's gender does have large effects on student test performance, teacher perceptions of students, and students' engagement with academic material. Simply put, girls have better educational outcomes when taught by women and boys are better off when taught by men.[19]

Although Dee is unclear why gender interactions might matter in the classroom, it seems reasonable to assume that boys of color, particularly those living in the inner-city, might benefit in various ways from seeing and interacting with more men teachers and administrators who come from similar racial backgrounds. Educators tend to agree that students are likely to feel comfortable in their school environment and perform better if teachers are sensitive to their family and cultural life circumstances, and if students are more engaged in classroom activities.[20]

A great deal of discussion in academic circles and in the school trenches accentuates men's value as role models for youth. Perceptions of male role models' contributions influence recommendations to diversify teaching styles and incorporate more men into the classroom. Though many commentators, parents, teachers, and the men I interviewed invoke the "role model" term, it is often used quite loosely—appearing to refer to various unspecified attributes and behaviors.[21] Sometimes men's physical presence is sought in the classroom to provide youth with stereotypical examples of how men should behave responsibly, athletically, authoritatively, and in a disciplined way. Their presence is expected to alter the school culture and to defeminize it. They are viewed as the strong replacement figures for certain categories of kids, especially boys, who are perceived to be largely without a strong male presence in their lives.[22] Other times, men are called upon to display counter-stereotypical "male" beliefs and behaviors. Men are to show youth that they, as men, can be sensitive to students' emotional needs while convincing them to value learning in an orderly, school environment—in other words, that being a good student should not threaten boys' efforts to express their masculinity. Child psychologists Dan Kindlon and Michael Thompson conclude, based on a combined thirty-five years of experience working with boys in clinical and school settings, that:

Boys benefit from the presence of male teachers and authority figures as role models of academic leadership, scholarship, professional commitment, moral as well as athletic leadership, and emotional literacy. The presence of men can have a tremendously calming effect on boys. When boys feel full acceptance—when they feel that their normal development skills and behavior are normal and that others perceive them that way—they engage more meaningfully in the learning experience.[23]

So, whether the motivation is to broaden kids' learning opportunities or expose them to individuals with whom they may relate more easily, the underlying expectation is that kids will benefit by having more men to admire and emulate. In addition, having more men as teachers is likely to inspire boys to consider pursuing teaching as a career.[24]

Many who advocate social change simply call for more men to be recruited into teaching, hoping to achieve an arbitrary predetermined threshold, say, 20 percent in elementary school. But much is yet unknown about how the number or type of male teachers might affect youths' development in schools. Along these lines, indiscriminate demands for fathers to be more involved with their own children may produce mixed results overall. More involvement is not necessarily better, because much depends on how the fathers interact with their children. For example, when abusive fathers interact with their children more, they are likely to inflict more physical and emotional damage. Similarly, one can easily imagine that if recruitment efforts prove successful in attracting men with poor interpersonal and teaching skills into the teaching ranks, youth may have more to lose than if no special recruitment efforts targeting men were undertaken.

Discussion about recruiting more men as teachers should not be viewed as discrediting women's teaching abilities—either in general or with respect to reaching boys in particular. Rather, efforts to incorporate more men into our classrooms may help curtail the disruptive aspects of masculine culture while reaffirming the legitimacy of formal education in the eyes of at-risk boys. As the fourth grade teacher, Reggie, eloquently describes, the school setting is not just about teaching academic skills. It's a venue for teaching kids critical life lessons about interpersonal respect, hard work, and integrity. Because we live in a gendered and multicultural society, learning those lessons from a diverse set of teachers, men included, seems appropriate and appealing.

MONITORING SITES AND CRIMINAL JUSTICE

Alternative schools bridge the divide between typical educational facilities and those where monitoring, including aspects of the criminal justice system, comes more fully into play. Several men with extensive experience working in alternative schools impressed upon me the unique challenges men face working with kids in these settings. Their detailed accounts reveal that men must learn how to reach out to at-risk kids, many of whom have turned their backs on the possible benefits of formal schooling. Although behavior problems occur in regular school environments, they are far more prevalent in alternative schools. Thus, men must first learn how to manage kids' temperaments and aggressive behavior before they can help kids progress in the classroom and life.

A critical feature marking these facilities is that kids are usually pressured or forced to be there. Thus, the men working at alternative schools and criminal justice facilities are often confronted with distrusting and uncooperative kids. A juvenile detention facility housing kids who have been adjudicated through the criminal justice system is the most obvious example. Given the high rate of juvenile crime in the United States, men have plenty of opportunities to interact with kids who are being processed through the justice system. In their respective criminal justice positions, men typically come into contact with a larger number of disruptive kids than do youth workers in other settings. Moreover, because girls' involvement with the juvenile justice system increased 83 percent between 1985 and 2000, probation officers have also been asked to expand their expertise in dealing with girls.[25]

Although men face unique challenges working with kids in this type of setting compared to childcare and regular schools, their ability to interact with kids effectively is to some extent based on similar principles. For example, adults in each of these settings are likely to be more successful if they can convince kids they respect them and care about their well-being. Although getting this message across to youth in a residential facility is often quite challenging, the ability to connect with kids on some level and manage their behavior is a valuable asset. According to Grady, the juvenile probation officer who had worked previously in a detention center, officers with children of their own tend to be more sensitive to kids' moods. Fathering gives them an advantage in navigating relationships and managing kids in a lockdown facility. Displaying the poise of being firm but fair, disciplined yet understanding, is no easy task. At the same time, fathers may face more struggles at home if they allow the stress of working with troubled and disrespectful kids to affect their family life. Even though men in all sorts of youth work settings struggle to find a balance between their involvement with kids and their personal life, those who deal with the most difficult kids probably face the biggest hurdles.

Men's own childhood histories can provide them valuable insights about interacting with kids in a wide range of settings. Early life experiences may be most helpful to those working with at-risk youth. Men like Derek, Nick, Barry, Joseph, Ray, and others who have been affected by poverty, physical and emotional abuse, violent crime, drugs and alcohol, or neglectful parents are uniquely equipped to empathize with at-risk kids who are tormented by similar life histories. They are challenged to translate their personal misfortunes into messages that will inspire kids to choose a productive path. Organizations need to identify more systematic and effective ways to tap into the population of productive men who have ultimately beat the odds—sometimes profoundly turning their lives around—in order to recruit them to work with at-risk kids.

Treatment centers for kids with emotional, psychological, and behavioral problems represent another type of facility in which monitoring represents an important dimension. Several of the men describe these positions' intense emotional and physical demands—they are clearly not jobs for wimps. Although Nick continues to work in this type of setting after many years, job stress forced several of the men to move on to other forms of youth work.

In most cases, the men in monitoring and criminal justice programs work with kids away from the kids' families. However, as we see with Joseph's diversion program, there are times when men must manage relationships with both parents and their kids—often times when the kids have misbehaved or underachieved. I sense that, with or without their kids by their side, a number of parents feel at ease approaching Joseph. They chat openly with him about their struggles and the progress they have made with their kids. Some seem eager to seek his support and guidance in helping them become more effective parents.

Of course, men also have numerous opportunities to deal with discipline and monitoring outside settings designed to handle troubled youth. For instance, while shadowing Charles at his Boys & Girls Club on a Friday afternoon, I sat in on a meeting he arranged with a 13-year-old boy who had been creating problems at the club, his mother, and a few staff members. During the meeting, and in a subsequent conversation with Charles, I learned how he manages the potentially volatile interpersonal dynamics in these meetings. Charles always lets the kid speak first, as a way to secure the mother's (or father's) involvement and trust. Ideally, he wants to create an ally out of the parent. His style seemed to have its desired effect, because the mother was very supportive of the staff and was prepared to remove her son from the club for a week or more as a form of punishment and a wake-up call, though Charles didn't feel this was necessary. At the mother's request, a staff member in charge of a conflict resolution class agreed to use examples involving her son—while he was attending the class— and have the boy's peers suggest better ways of dealing with the problem. Charles chimed in to encourage the mother to put the boy in his place in front of his peers to challenge his attempts to put on his "cool image."

Key to Charles's handling of this situation was that he felt it was important to write up the complaints on the boy so that his mother would have detailed information on his behavior. Charles reasoned that she might be confronted in the future with similar accusations from teachers at school. This way she will be in a better position to see a pattern and realize that her son is in fact disrespecting others. Charles sees himself, and I suspect the mother concurs, as a valuable resource to the family, because he enhances the single mother's ability to monitor and discipline her child. He also perceives his approach as helping other agencies monitor this boy over time.

Because our society still operates in stereotypically gendered ways, the discipline and rigid monitoring aspects of youth work, especially in the criminal justice system, are widely perceived as men's turf. In other words, gender stereotypes depicting men as more suitable for controlling the most disruptive youth and dispensing discipline continue to define monitoring activity in youth work as largely men's work. Much of that activity occurs in the lockdown facilities and alternative schools housing kids who have behavioral issues, but men working in regular schools, recreational environments, and even faith-based organizations are often expected and asked to take charge of discipline issues.

It also seems reasonable to assume that men may have an edge over women in getting a kid's father, stepfather, or other male relative to take a more active role when the kid misbehaves. For some men, being "called-out" by another man rather than a woman may carry more weight.

RECREATION

As the men's stories reveal, men of every age are involved with kids in a wide range of recreational activities, in diverse settings, and in paid as well as volunteer capacities. Some activities are tied to school, criminal justice, or religious organizations, whereas others operate independently. Most involve sports, camping, or value-based, leadership, and adventure programs like the Boy Scouts of America, 4-H clubs, and Outward Bound. These activities, primarily perceived as fun, provide men the chance to make a difference in kids' lives. Helping kids have fun while teaching them the value of competition, cooperation, discipline, integrity, hard work, sacrifice, leadership, and other virtues— often as part of a team—are the basic objectives underlying many of these recreational activities.

An important aspect of recreational activity with kids involves helping them improve their knowledge and skills in some area. By teaching kids how to kick a soccer ball, operate a computer program, earn a Boy Scout merit badge, or develop a clown persona, men are placing themselves in a position to evaluate kids' progress. They can also help kids figure out a plan to improve, all while having fun! As the men indicate, one can grow personally by spending time with kids in recreational activities.

In Chapter 2 I briefly describe the historical roots of the Boy Scouts, 4-H Clubs, and Little League Baseball, three of the most visible recreational organizations in which men continue to play a vital role. Millions of youth participate in these and other organizations with a few million adult supervisors. Soccer leagues in particular have grown tremendously in recent years. The sheer volume of time men spend instructing, mentoring, and supervising kids in these recreational activities suggests that much of men's impact on kids (outside their own families) occurs in these settings.

Coaches are clearly visible in the lives of young people as they practice and play sports. Not surprisingly, then, when members of the general public initially think about men's involvement with youth in the community many are likely to imagine coaches—paid as well as volunteer. Thousands of men throughout the country earn their living teaching kids in team and individual sports, often in conjunction with schools. As noted earlier, coaches' ability to inspire young boys and girls while molding their character is celebrated in movie and documentary form. When done well, coaching leaves a mark on young people that can last a lifetime. Thirty-five-year-old Tony captures this sentiment beautifully with his touching story about his high school teacher and soccer coach.

After all those years, especially now, we go back . . . we do a thing on Thanksgiving . . . we call it the Turkey Bowl, where we go . . . [back to our hometown] and . . . play; and it's now . . . a very large thing, with players from not just our classes, but other classes as well. And Mr. Thompson's there, every year, just sitting in a chair and sipping on coffee, or, uh, probably a couple beers, and it's a great thing. We all get together, and a lot of people have kids now, they bring their kids. . . . I think it's something that he enjoys, just sitting there and watching, he affected the lives of, wow, I'd say probably fifty or sixty of us, and he loves just sitting there and hanging out . . . a wonderful man.

Just as it appears that coaching left an indelible impression on Mr. Thompson, we saw a similar type of process in Steve's emotional response to his player's death during the high school basketball game. As with Tony, a number of the men's own childhood coaches have profoundly affected them. These men's childhood coaches nurtured their personal growth and burned life lessons into their young minds. Ray, for example, began to believe in himself after one of his football coaches repeatedly showered him with praise. Though the lessons often were tied to an athletic objective, their value transcended sport to help the youth, now men, develop character and a healthier outlook on life.

Outside of school, a sizeable proportion of recreational coaches are drawn into working with kids because their sons and daughters are participating. The opportunities provide men the chance to navigate the delicate waters of being both father and coach. Most find it a rewarding experience. Some men also do nate time to help youth in recreational settings even if their own children are not involved. Whether as an employee, a father volunteer, or a man donating time to unrelated kids, men who coach kids are well-positioned to use sport to teach valuable life lessons.

As some of the men's stories reveal, one doesn't need to wait to become a grown man to work with kids through sports. Several of the men describe how they pursued coaching opportunities with younger kids when they themselves were teenagers. In some instances the experiences led them to pursue coaching careers later on in life. More commonly though, it gave them their first taste of what it's like to make a difference in kids' lives. Early coaching experiences often lead men to feel more eager and confident to pursue other paid and unpaid activities with kids. In other words, grounded in fun, early coaching is a valuable training ground and a way for young men to assess whether working with kids is something they would like to pursue more seriously. Presumably, creating more chances for teenagers to volunteer as coaches in recreational leagues could nurture men's desire to be involved with coaching.

Aside from these early coaching gigs, many men fondly describe their teenage experiences working at day and summer camps for kids. Some continue to speak enthusiastically as adults about spending time with youth at camp. In some instances, boys initially attend camps, then "graduate" from camper status to counselors. Introduced to the world of caring for kids, camp counselors typically supervise and teach youth about any number of activities—sports, nature, computers, magic, arts and crafts, music, religion. The relationship skills counselors develop with kids are based on their ability to help kids organize, learn, and perform activities, usually in a group context. At times, though, particularly in the quiet outdoor environment of camps, men are able to go beyond participating in activities and engage kids in meaningful conversations that might not happen in more formal, enclosed settings.

Men's recreation with kids today is almost always conducted in the company of other adults, because of the heightened public scrutiny of adults' relations with kids. One notable exception, as mentioned elsewhere, involves some of the time Big Brothers spend with their Little Brothers. Operating under a more flexible set of guidelines, Big Brothers have the unique chance to spend one-on-one time with their Little Brothers, sometimes completely out of the public eye. As the Big Brothers I interviewed suggest, bonding and mentoring in these settings can take on a much more personal quality. Despite significant age gaps friendships can emerge.

Although much of this recreational activity is with boys, men clearly have opportunities to be with both boys and girls (4-H Clubs, Boys & Girls Clubs) or even with girls exclusively (girls' athletic teams). As with men's involvement in the juvenile justice system, men in recent years are increasingly likely to be involved with girls in recreational settings, a pattern that can positively affect men, girls, and even boys.

FAITH-BASED SETTINGS

The men formally involved in some sort of faith-based organization appear to have, as a group, the keenest and deepest sense of how they want to affect kids' lives. Each has given considerable thought to what he wants to accomplish and how this can best be achieved.[26] Getting kids to understand how religious values can guide the practical decisions of everyday living is important to the religious leaders I interviewed. All are also aware that they are not immune to the public's concern for youth safety. In fact, some feel they are squarely in the public eye because of recent scandals involving the Catholic Church. None, however, has allowed the public scrutiny to derail his efforts.

Obviously, one can encourage religious leaders to commit themselves more fully to the needs of youth who belong to their organization. Many religious leaders already run active youth group programs in which they engage kids in conversations about a wide range of timely topics. If religious leaders expand their time commitment and the scope of youth group activities, they can become even more involved with kids. For example, religious leaders can impart important life lessons to youth by organizing mission trips and community work groups. The ministers I spoke with describe these ventures as ideal settings for bonding and developing community awareness. Rabbi Jacob is poised to initiate a new series of volunteer community support activities in the coming year for his youth group. In most cases, the activities men supervise take on a form of recreational work with the explicit purpose of helping others. These men appear well-equipped to devise and arrange experiential learning in a group context.

Mission trips and community projects provide the men working at a church or synagogue a chance to reach beyond the immediate borders of the congregation for ways to touch kids' lives. A complementary approach focuses on reaching out to kids who are not affiliated with the religious organization. This message is consistent with the work of Public/Private Ventures, which in 1998 launched the National Faith-Based Initiative for high-risk youth.[27] With sites in twelve cities, it attempts to foster partnerships between faith-based organizations and other community groups to provide mentoring, education, and employment readiness services to at-risk youth.

In Carlos's youth ministry he has successfully moved beyond his church walls to help kids. He developed a school-based mentoring program focusing on youth in the community, most of whom are not members of his church. The church also sponsors a youth summer basketball league. In these settings he does not preach the Bible or even explicitly talk about religion. Instead, he uses his energy and community ties to forge opportunities to inspire at-risk kids to get on course and stay out of trouble. The kids being served have an open invitation to attend his church services and religious youth group should they be interested.[28]

Faith-based environments provide ideal settings for training teenage and young adult youth mentors—male and female. These young people are generally conscientious leaders who help run the youth group and associated programs. Many men find supervising such kids particularly rewarding, both in terms of giving and receiving. With respect to the latter, the teenage and young adult youth leaders can pass along valuable information about youth culture to the men, thereby enhancing the men's sensitivity to what is going on in the "youth world." Mentoring these young people also expands men's opportunities to affect an even larger group of kids indirectly. At times, religious leaders like Carlos are able to witness the fruits of their labor as they watch those they have trained make a difference in children's lives. This is a powerful experience that fuels an adult's commitment to doing youth work. In Carlos's case, he has followed his mentoring efforts with Malik to their most recent highpoint—seeing Malik become a youth pastor.

Not surprisingly, compared to men in other youth work domains, men in religious settings appear more likely to mention potential opportunities for their youth work and family life to overlap. The men refer in passing to work-family stress, but, for the most part, they seem reasonably content with how they have come to manage the pressing demands at work and at home. This differs from findings based on a 1998 survey of 2,130 youth ministers who stressed their struggles with managing the time conflicts they experienced with work and family.[29]

The religious leaders in my study, compared to the other youth workers, appear to rely more heavily on their wives' direct and indirect contribution to their youth work. Sometimes the men incorporate their wives into carrying out their practical obligations to kids. Carlos and Kevin, for instance, look to their wives to counsel and console young girls facing difficult life challenges. The men also tend to include their wives at public gatherings and activities involving kids. Referring to his wife, Jacob explains:

> When I go to these youth group activities or we go to a team dance or whatever, she's always there with me and I specifically bring her because that's part of the role model that I'm presenting. It's, you know, the both of us are together, husband and wife.

Carlos echoes Jacob's sentiment by emphasizing how important he believes it is for youth to see him interacting in a healthy way with his wife and kids. In some instances, men recruit their wives and children to participate in activities at the church/synagogue, mission trips, and other community outings. They realize that if they are to present the "family man" image effectively, they must create opportunities for kids to see them interacting with their family in responsible, loving ways. Behind the scenes, most male religious leaders also turn to their wives for guidance on sermons, lesson plans, and strategies for advising kids. The men may wear the public face as the religious leader directing youth's spiritual journey, but they seek family input to help them shape their message.

Unlike the typical public image of ministers, priests, and rabbis as being largely out-of-touch with hip-hop and other youth cultures, the religious leaders I interviewed are relatively attentive to the commercial media influencing kids. They recognize they face an uphill battle in managing the competing messages of their faith and aspects of youth culture. To connect with kids, the men know they must develop some familiarity with the commercial messages that shape kids' lives today. In varied ways, the men try to stay abreast of what is happening in youth culture while making a concerted effort to convey their faith messages in a "down-to-earth" and accessible fashion. In short, they seek to navigate the borders of being a religious role model and a secular adult mentor.

Somewhat surprisingly, the religious leaders I interviewed who had the most direct contact with kids spend little time talking about youth issues to those holding similar positions in other faith-based organizations. Indeed, Jacob reports that during the past three years he does not recall ever talking about youth with the handful of ministers he meets for a monthly informal lunch. Ironically, though I was able to locate a number of religious leaders working with kids in the general vicinity, most of the men struggled to name peers who do similar work in other religious organizations. These religious youth leaders do little brainstorming or coordination of activities with their counterparts. If they came together, I suspect they could create numerous worthwhile opportunities for kids from different congregations to meet, talk, cooperate, and compete in recreational activities. Although there are surely advantages to having private, religiously segregated summer youth camps, faith-based camps might intentionally bring together kids of different faiths.

Most faith-based youth programs focus on kids away from their parents, but religious leaders are involved in a few activities that incorporate the larger family. Creating opportunities for families to act as a mentoring team could prove to be useful.

APPLYING LESSONS ACROSS DOMAINS

The youth workers I studied had diverse social backgrounds and work histories, but the vast majority have worked with kids in multiple domains (e.g., school and recreational activities) or varied settings within domains (e.g., elementary and middle school) over time. A fair number even work with kids in different domains and settings simultaneously. As mentioned previously, experiencing kids in one context influences one's perceptions of and work with youth in another.

Generally speaking, at least four potentially overlapping conditions or processes relevant to youth work influence how the men's earlier experiences informed their subsequent efforts. Granted, it may be difficult to discern when changes are simply the result of accrued experience and when the specific setting contributed a lesson. Nonetheless, the men clearly assimilated lessons from their youth work and applied them in new settings. Earlier experiences also have solidified some men's commitment to continue to work with kids in certain settings and domains.

First, men can gain insights—positive or negative—about kids because they work with kids who are distinctive in some way. For example, working with youth who are economically disadvantaged or belong to a particular race or ethnic group or are of a certain age or have special needs sometimes shapes how a man sees and treats kids in other settings. At least eight of the men had worked fairly closely with special needs youth at some point in their life and three were currently involved with them. Men spent time with youth suffering from Down syndrome, autism, mental disorders, cerebral palsy, and learning disabilities, trying to help them learn how to manage their daily lives and master basic life tasks. Collectively, the men who have worked with special needs kids have done so in all five youth work domains. Steve, the high school basketball coach, is trained to do individual assessments and develop learning programs for kids with learning disabilities. He believes his educational training pushes him to see individuals' unique qualities and to respond accordingly. Steve readily applies this training by tailoring individualized strategies to motivate his basketball players. Jacob spent four summers during his young adult years in the 1970s working as a camp counselor at a Jewish summer camp. There he closely supervised and taught a wide range of special needs children ages 12 to 18. Notably, he often spent concentrated blocks of time each day over an eight-week session teaching severely challenged children several words in preparation for their bar mitzvah. He notes, "I loved doing it and it was very fulfilling." Though men who are inclined to be more patient may in fact be more likely to choose youth work involving special needs kids, the men confirm that such work can sometimes deepen their patience with kids.

Second, time spent with kids in particular domains is likely to expose men to specialized knowledge or folk wisdom that can have cross-over advantages in other domains. For instance, men who learn techniques for therapeutic crisis intervention or prevention while working with emotionally, mentally, and physically challenged youth are apt to put that specialized knowledge to good use in other youth work settings, such as a regular classroom or coaching. Joseph is a case in point. He traded in working with kids in a high-stress environment to build his diversion program to help youth flagged by the criminal justice system. The skills he acquired working with difficult youth enable him to work more productively with the at-risk kids in his more recent program. In addition, his skills garner him credibility and respect among the facilitators in the program and the parents and kids. Likewise, Thomas, a first grade teacher, explicitly mentions how similar training has benefited him as a teacher.

> *I appreciated the training because it really, I think it prepared me for teaching. I mean, . . . how do you make requests: They were very adamant about saying, you say the child's name, you say please, and then you give them a [positive] direction. So, . . . "Nathan, please, tie your shoes immediately," as opposed to "Nathan, don't walk around with your shoes untied."*

Also, Grady believes his early first-hand experience as a school teacher has enabled him to be a more effective juvenile parole officer because he acquired intimate knowledge about school system bureaucracies. And Frank collected insights about getting hardcore kids in a juvenile detention center to buy into his expectations as a means to secure other youth's cooperation. This knowledge has served Frank well during his tenure as an administrative decisionmaker at his Boys & Girls Club.

Third, men can accumulate knowledge about and access to useful community contacts and resources over time as they move from one type of youth work to another or between domains. The youth minister Ben provides some of the boys who participate in his youth group at church opportunities to join him at his summer camp. His familiarity and comfort working with kids in these different domains mutually informs the way he relates to kids, especially boys. By working connections they have made, men can capitalize on opportunities to build social capital for kids.

Finally, as we saw in Chapter 10, men often experience personal growth by working with kids; they thus bring a richer personality to bear when they move to another youth work domain. Personal growth can allow men to express their emotions more fully, to perceive situations and people in more refined and mature ways, and to develop the self-confidence necessary to meet the challenges of youth work. Numerous men reported that their successful teenage and young adult experiences as camp counselors, religious youth group leaders, coaches, Big Brothers, and tutors signaled to them how much they enjoyed being around kids. They also discovered they were good at it. Moreover, men who experience personal growth in conjunction with interacting with certain types of youth sometimes adapt their new perspective to working with subsequent cohorts of kids. Men who learn in one setting to be less judgmental about kids' behavior can apply their greater tolerance to how they relate to and manage kids in other settings.

Clarifying how men view themselves, as well as how they interact with kids, highlights the unique and overlapping issues men face in childcare, schools, recreational venues, monitoring sites including the criminal justice system, and faith-based environments. Men's cultural commentary about the state of society and its children is a good place to begin to talk about possible initiatives to expand and improve men's involvement in kids' lives.

CHAPTER 12

MOVING FORWARD

Public interest in men's involvement with youth outside the home is neither new nor restricted to the United States. Since early in the twentieth century, sundry voices have called for men to get more involved with youth, both in and outside a family context. In the early 1900s incremental progress was achieved with the advent of organizations such as the Boy Scouts of America, 4-H Club, Big Brothers and the future Big Sisters, Boys Clubs (later Boys & Girls Clubs), and Little League Baseball and other youth sports. These and newer activities continue to provide men opportunities to interact with youth other than their own children. More recent initiatives targeting fathers have sought to increase fathers' involvement in public sites like schools, churches, and early childhood programs, such as, Headstart. In this book I focus primarily on men's interactions with unrelated kids, but I also show how the culture and conduct of fatherhood are intertwined with men's more general commitment to children.

Unfortunately, the contemporary storyline about men and kids, generally speaking, reveals that men remain drastically underrepresented in child-oriented jobs, such as childcare and teaching—especially in the lower grades. Also, men's rate of volunteering for youth-related activities is not ideal. Matters are complicated further because public scrutiny of men in their relationships with youths is at an all-time high, leaving far too many men reluctant to either get involved with kids or feeling frustrated sometimes by constraints when they do. But, despite the complexities, numerous men from diverse backgrounds are committed to making a difference in kids' lives. The men's stories I have presented illustrate that men who choose to work or volunteer with youth do not fit any particular pattern; individuals from all walks of life try to and succeed in en-hancing kids' well-being.

In recent years, Australia, Great Britain, Nordic and Scandinavian countries, New Zealand, and other nations have generated public debates about promoting youth work by men. This suggests a potentially powerful wave of international interest. In 1992, for example, the European Union's Equal Opportunities Pro-gramme stated:

> As regards responsibilities arising from the care and upbringing of children, it is recommended that member states should promote and encourage, with due re-spect for the freedom of the individual, increased participation by men.[1]

Worldwide, little has been documented about male youth workers' experi-ences, but information is slowly accumulating, and this book adds to that liter-ature.[2]

Public perceptions about what it means for men to take an active role in kids' lives affect men's decisions to do youth work. The low pay rate found in female-dominated professions, along with lingering perceptions of these jobs as "women's work," dissuade many men from pursuing this type of employment. Volunteer work, though viewed by many as noble, often conflicts with men's work commitments and precious leisure time. Furthermore, because fathers in recent years have become a bit more involved in the day-to-day affairs of family life, they may have less available time and feel obligated to spend that time with their own children rather than on other youth activities, especially those not in-volving their own children.

Looking at the cross-cultural evidence, we find that fathers and uncles in some foraging cultures are quite active and competent in providing infant child-care.[3] Although foraging societies are drastically different from our own postin-dustrial society, the Aka of the Central African Republic demonstrate that a culture can be highly supportive of men caring for children. Fathers in this African society spend roughly half of their day either holding or within arm's reach of their infant.[4] Yet, in the United States, diverse longstanding forces thwart efforts to establish a more pervasive pattern of egalitarian division of do-mestic labor and childcare. Nonetheless, it is within our reach to construct a phi-losophy of caring for children based on men's heightened investments as fathers and youth workers. Doing so will require an extended commitment from men and women alike.

Understanding how aspects of the cultural landscape, institutional settings, and men's life histories and personalities shape their orientation toward youth work is critical to crafting well-informed initiatives to encourage men to play a more active and productive role in kids' lives. Social scientists have described four major areas that influence fathers' involvement with their own children: motivation, skills and self-confidence, social support, and institutional practices.[5] These areas also represent useful guides in promoting men's greater involvement with youth outside a family context.

COMMENTS ON THE CULTURAL CLIMATE

Through their engaging storytelling and discerning commentary, the fifty-five men I interviewed have taken us deep into the settings where kids spend much of their time. They provide a reality check of what it's like to work and volunteer with kids in diverse settings. Their stories give a sampling of the men's passionate commitment to working with youth. Most importantly, their accounts offer us the means to think more clearly about how we can inspire other men to make a difference in kids' lives. Such thinking is timely, because national indicators of youth's well-being, as shown in Chapter 2, reveal that many kids are struggling and could use a helping hand.

It seems appropriate, then, to rely on the men's accumulated wisdom to help us forge a forward-looking agenda. I summarize several general observations the men make about how prevailing cultural patterns implicate their interactions with kids. On the one hand, valuable insights can be cultivated by exploring these stories detailing their personal experiences and observations of the social landscape. On the other hand, care must be taken when interpreting the stories. Even though some men may experience few difficulties in particular settings, the prevailing masculinity norms that historically have reinforced men's dominant position in society as a class of persons have undermined men's greater involvement with children. In other words, men, largely white men, influenced by the forces of industrialization and urbanization, are to be blamed—not women or feminist ideology, as some conservative thinkers argue—for sowing the seeds for men in recent centuries to be less involved with youth inside and outside the home compared to men in preindustrialized society.

In general, the men in my study recognize that the cultural landscape has undergone significant changes in recent years. For instance, many of the men are aware of and uncomfortable with the amount of public scrutiny they receive as males interacting with kids in public settings. Though conscious of the shadow of suspicion looming over them, relatively few are distinctly annoyed by it. Some say they are more careful in how they manage their space and show kids affection. For the most part, the men find the increased public scrutiny more of a nuisance that occasionally affects the quality of what they offer kids. For instance, Steve is largely unaffected by public scrutiny when dealing with his boys' basketball team, but he is more attentive when he's with a girls' team. Now that he is 40, he senses he is less vulnerable to misguided accusations, but he admits to being "careful" when coaching girls.

> I used to tell my wife all the time, you know, I said, "It's a shame but all it would take would be for one girl to just get pissed off at me and say, 'Oh well he tried to do something,' and even if I was found not to do it, like your reputation is gone." That's just the way society thinks.

Darnell, another high school teacher and coach, shares Steve's views while explicitly emphasizing the legal implications, adding that "everybody's trying to get easy money, quick money. . . . everything is a liability, which is pretty sad." A middle school teacher, Brandon, chimes in, saying, "Everybody is so worried . . . somebody's gonna turn around and sue you or say something or draw the media down on your school; that is what public school is like."

As I describe in previous chapters, it's not just school teachers and coaches who are concerned; men in all areas of youth work are aware of the cultural mood. Youth minister Carlos recognizes that public scrutiny has changed in recent years, making it essential that he and other adults avoid any appearance of impropriety. Having worked with kids in California and Florida, Carlos frames his perspective by commenting on the larger society:

> I think that is just so important, because people nowadays are so . . . suspicious about people that work [with] kids . . . because of all the junk that's gone on, and it's really a sad thing; but you can't blame 'em, because it seems that, you know, child molesters and people like that tend to go and get jobs where they're working around kids. And so what does that do for those of us who have a pure heart that are trying to work with kids; it casts a spotlight on us. . . . I think it's once a month, at least in this county, in this community, there is a story, at least once a month about teenagers involved in some kind of sex with an adult, and crime. We know the whole thing nationally with pedophiles and internet stuff, and man, they're facing a lot of stuff that just ten years ago when I got started with this, things weren't even to the level that they're at now.

Expressing his thoughts about the changing times, Carlos highlights how community and national concerns and news reports about child predators in a high-tech age combine to create a challenging set of circumstances for youth workers, especially males. Although observers can only speculate on the scope of the adverse effect, current circumstances apparently discourage some men from getting involved with youth in the first place.

Continuing with an assessment of the state of affairs for kids, Carlos underscores how the "drug problem" and the high divorce rate change "the kind of teenagers that are being produced in society." Consequently,

> it changes how we do youth work, because now more than ever, anybody that's mentoring a young person needs . . . [to] see that they're taking on more of a parental role, more of an authority in their lives. Where before, a mentor I think was a helper, now man, it's like, they could be the source of life, of positivity, of direction.

Carlos's comments flag another critical issue the men raise concerning changing family circumstances and kids' approach to living. As Carlos suggests, being the "source of life" or being a key caretaker is a very different position from being a "helper." Many of the men comment that parents are not as involved with their children as in previous generations, and when they are involved they are deemed to be less effective. Other men simply acknowledge that contemporary families are more likely to have two busy parents working outside the home, or to be run by a resident single parent with limited time because she or he is working—perhaps multiple jobs. Charles, relying on his talks with kids and their parents at the Boys & Girls Club he directs, offers a stinging indictment of how changing family life has negatively affected parenting quality.

> Families of today spend more time concentrating on providing for the kids the things that they didn't get, but they miss out on the things that they did get, which was the time, the quality time, with the family, the sense of religion, the sense of how important education is—how important discipline is, and respect, and how manners will get you places that money won't, and about giving back to your community, putting back into your community— not looking for this overnight success, that anything worth having is worth working for, don't look for the handout, having self-pride— . . . those types of qualities.

Because parents are spending less time teaching kids the types of values Charles cherishes, he believes he and his staff must expend more effort to control and direct the kids.

Some of the men perceive that the parents are not only less involved with their children directly, but that they are less involved in school or youth-oriented organizations targeting their kids. Kenny illustrates by noting parents' poor attendance at school PTO meetings. As a Big Brother, he feels he needs to pick up the slack through his volunteer efforts. From his vantage point, if parents did their job, there would not be a backlog of requests for Big Brothers. Andre, drawing on his extensive experience with kids in California and Florida, also expresses his frustration with how parents appear to become less involved with kids as they enter their teen years.

> What I see in the Hispanic community, and I see it a little bit in the African American community, and really in all kids, is parents are really supportive when they're 6 and 7, 8, but when they get to be about middle school age they just kind of blow it off and don't go to their games anymore. And I think that really, all of a sudden, a kid 12 or 13 years old, all of a sudden his parents just don't seem interested anymore. It's got to be hard to understand, hard to deal with. But I see that a lot here [Boys & Girls Club]. The younger kids' games will be packed with parents, the older kids won't be.

Andre voices his awareness of the larger context: "It's a challenge. Some of those parents have it rough, the amount of time they have to work and the number of kids they have and the conditions they live in." Continuing, Andre adds, "but for the most part, I didn't have a lot of sympathy for them. I know they could've done more." Other men express a bit of empathy for struggling parents if they sense their limited involvement is due to juggling multiple jobs to provide for their kids.

Nick is more direct in expressing his dissatisfaction with some parents who have dropped the ball by trying to shift responsibility for their children to others. Commenting on the parents of kids he works with at a residential facility, who have emotional and behavioral problems, he says:

> Parents don't feel any need to have to deal with their children anymore. They want everybody else to deal with their kids. . . . They want the system to deal with their kids, they want people like me to deal with their kids. . . . that's where they want the responsibility.

Nick sometimes finds himself exasperated, as he did a few days earlier when a teenager's mother criticized him for her daughter's poor behavior. Recreating their exchange, Nick describes challenging the woman in front of his boss:

"Ma'am, your daughter's been here four months." And, she's like, "Yeah and I don't know why you people cannot make her do." And I said, "Well ma'am, she's 15 years old. We had [her] for [a few] months. What happened to all the other years? Who's working those years?"

Though his boss was stunned by his reply, Nick felt compelled to be a "realist" by telling the woman he was not prepared to take full responsibility for her daughter's behavior.

As Hernando suggests, parental neglect can also affect the three-way interpersonal dynamics between youth workers, kids, and parents. In his youth ministry, Hernando finds that parents often sabotage his efforts to teach and discipline their children.

Most of the time, [if] parents who do not help or support you, is because they want to . . . show their kid that they are their friends, they are on their side. No matter what they are doing, I am your friend. And why do they do that? Because they know that they are not putting all the effort and all the attention into their kids. So they are, they sense, it is a feeling of guilty, in their part, and they can feel . . . "Hey, I've not been there for you. I've not been a good [parent] for you. But you know what? I gonna stand behind you against this teacher, so I show you that you have the support."

Hernando, like a number of other men, suggests that the larger cultural shifts influencing family life have increased the odds of parents' being less effective. He believes that parents today are more willing to take the "easy way," rather than do what is "right" for their child in the long run.

Many of Hernando's parishioners are relatively well-off, but other men are equally frustrated by low-income parents. In describing why he has a difficult job, Ray places some of the blame on the single mothers of the at-risk kids he works with in an after-school program.

They still want to date. They like Stella [movie character], they want their groove back. . . . Mama still hanging out at the club. Mama still chasing after that dope boy with all that money thinkin' he'll take care of them kids. The mama still lying about her income so she can get that $15 rent, you know, some way of living. Guys see that, man. There was a little boy walked up to me, about 7, the other day—I was speaking to a class, man—talking about how his mama get Food Stamps. He knew about WIC and what she can get on WIC and how she . . . gonna buy some crabs with her Food Stamp card and *sell them to get more money. That's crazy, man. That little kid shouldn't know stuff like that, man. So it starts at home.*

Ray also recognizes that many mothers have it rough because they are trying to raise children with inadequate help from inattentive fathers and in a society awash in "bling-bling" values. Ray's comments speak to the heated debate about who or what is to blame for some kids' doing less well than others.

Jackson, a veteran of several types of youth work, echoes a common sentiment that a large segment of men "aren't doing their roles as fathers" and deserve much of the blame for youth's difficulties.[6] He explains:

When men aren't around their daughters, . . . their daughters go out looking for boyfriends at age 14, end up getting pregnant. They end up having children, and their boyfriends aren't ready to be fathers, they're not fathers, so it just continues on and on and on. So if we, we had one generation of men who took fatherhood seriously, . . . Like I said, my father wasn't perfect, but at least he was around. I was scared, I feared my father. Discipline, if one generation of men took that up and said, "I'm gonna be a father to my children," we'd have so many less problems than we have today.

Variations of this view, widely asserted by social commentators for decades,[7] help frame many of the men's thoughts about why their involvement with kids might matter. One facet of the larger thesis is that in recent decades men have become increasingly more interested in satisfying their individual materialistic needs and less committed to assuming familial responsibilities.[8] Although the argument is sometimes used irrespective of men's social class standing, it is often code for patterns found among inner-city, low-income African Americans.

Yet, men's concerns about the inadequacies of contemporary parenting extend beyond any one racial, ethnic, or gender category. Eduardo's experiences with South American immigrants have led him to believe that mothers and fathers alike are susceptible to the powers of a highly commercialized, material age.

The parents, they both work, they have to work hours that are incredible. The kids are left at home, they are not given values. They, the parents, get contaminated with this society today. . . . It's not who you are but it's how much you have. . . . I think that society is making the project of raising a kid more difficult every year, for some reason. I mean, values and the things that the

parents . . . they need to have the latest model car and the big house and all
that and they don't realize that their greatest asset is their kids. So I think that
people . . . they neglect their responsibilities as parents.

Kids are even more vulnerable to commercial manipulation than are their parents. Hip-hop culture,[9] fueled by an ever-expanding and diverse commercial media, is viewed as offering kids a new but less productive way to spend their time, manage their self-images, and evaluate their personal worth. In various ways, the men express their distaste for facets of hip-hop culture perpetuated through video games, music videos, movies, and other outlets. Frank, an African American director of a Boys & Girls Club, leaves no doubt as to where he stands.

I'm not like the average brother. I don't like videos, BET, all that kinda stuff. I
don't like that. You know, that just me. My TV don't go up to BET, 'cause I
don't want my daughter watching it, 'cause it's garbage, it's not edifying any-
thing, it's not teaching the kids anything, you know, a bunch of rump shaking
on there and all that kinda stuff.

As mentioned previously, some of the men, including Frank—a rugged, no-nonsense kind of guy—expect the kids in their programs to conform to mainstream values by wearing their pants up, not wearing braids, or avoiding certain types of music. Some explicitly challenge kids to rethink why they watch music videos or listen to lyrics that degrade women and glorify conspicuous consumption and violence. Gerald describes hip-hop culture as a "little disappointing in a sense because [the] primary focus is on money, clothes, jewelry, women, and excessive violence." He subtly tries to shift kids' experiences by exposing them to other forms of music.

Although the men have plenty to say about the larger culture, their take home message is that kids today are growing up more quickly and with less supervision and love than in times past. Not surprisingly, the men tend to see contemporary kids, on average, as less focused and not as hardworking as earlier generations were. Many kids, as well as their parents, face difficult times, because family arrangements are more fluid and unpredictable. The men applaud energetic, highly invested parents who support their kids and are eager to challenge them to do better. The men also believe that many youth—sometimes in spite of the cultural forces—are bright, creative, idealistic, and eager to help others in need.

A VISION

In Western cultures, women have long been decidedly more willing than men to answer the call to care for kids—in public and at home. Today, with high rates of divorce, single parenting, and dual-earner families, the time is right to encourage more men to share with women the responsibility for mentoring, teaching, nurturing, monitoring, and supporting kids of all kinds, their own and other people's. If inspired and directed, most youth can be helped and are capable of helping others. Youth stand to benefit if we can persuade well-intentioned men to journey in greater numbers and with more passion into the world of youth work. Initiatives to assist men (and women) who are already involved with youth are vital, too. In short, the commonly recited mantra is simple yet profound: it takes a village to raise a child. Men must become more active members of the "village" by strengthening their commitment to the collective ethos of caring for our youth—in spirit and in deed.

Talk of a collective ethos is firmly grounded in an interventionist caregiving model. Beyond the direct benefits to many kids if more men were inspired to work and volunteer with youth, men's greater participation in youth work would foster positive cultural change, prompting men to be more vocal public advocates for kids. It is no coincidence that the society with the highest proportion of female politicians in the world—Sweden[10]—also has one of the most, if not the most, progressive social agendas for meeting children's needs.[11] Developing a stronger cultural message about male caregiving, and reinforcing the institutionalized processes encouraging men to be involved with kids, should produce a social climate in which key stakeholders are compelled to reorder spending priorities and more generously earmark monies for youth. The business community, in partnership with government at all levels, must invest convincingly and creatively to revitalize urban development via improved schools, effective job training programs, better family support services, and desirable jobs. Forward-thinking initiatives are needed if the inner cities (and poor rural areas) are to have any chance of encouraging more responsible family men to live in currently impoverished communities and to be involved productively with the kids who reside there. It seems only logical that such initiatives should be incorporated into any comprehensive strategy to enlist men's time and energies in support of our youth.

Obviously, the narratives I have used to tell the larger story about male youth workers should not be interpreted as fully capturing all men's experiences with kids in the inner cities, suburbs, or rural areas across the nation. Nonetheless, the story is nuanced, because the men I interviewed are a relatively eclectic bunch, owing to their varied social backgrounds, physical attributes, and personalities. They experience life through the eyes of different racial and ethnic identities, childhood family circumstances, and social classes and neighborhood environments; they are fathers and non-fathers and vary in many other defining markers of their personal life trajectories. Some, like Derek, Nick, and Ray, embody traditional features of the ultra-masculine physique, some live in average-size bodies, and others are relatively small in physical stature. The men's personalities cover a full spectrum from the "old school" hard-working tough disciplinarian to the laid back sensitive male—with most of them falling somewhere in between. Men like Alan, Eric, Greg, and Robby prove that gay men can be just as effective youth workers and role models as straight men.[12] Overall, this diverse sample of men is well-suited for sensitizing us to the many facets of men's involvements with youth.

We can learn more about the many aspects of men's youth work by viewing them through the prism of larger cultural forces. In the United States, as well as some other nations, men relate to kids in public settings in the context of a media-driven, postmodern society where public scrutiny of men has grown rampant in recent years. Men's youth work activities also occur alongside the ever-unfolding subplot of gender relations. That subplot accentuates feminist concerns about the gendered social conditions defining men's and women's private and public lives, their family work and paid work, and, importantly, their respective approaches to kids—their own as well as others.[13]

To sharpen our vision of what men are doing, could be doing, and should be doing for our children today and tomorrow, we must listen to what men say motivates them to get involved and stay involved with kids. This is especially true in light of the low pay and limited social status men receive when they do participate in certain forms of youth work. Though men enter the world of youth work for varied, sometimes idiosyncratic, reasons, their descriptions of their years of involvement are telling. When studied closely, men's descriptions about their motives implicate the skills and self-confidence men need to work effectively with kids.

For some men, their vision for their involvement with kids grows out of their own childhood memories. Having been deprived of adequate love, affection, healthy guidance, money, security, and the like as children, some emerge on the other side of adolescence inspired to provide such sustenance to children in their community or similar kids. Others come from more privileged families where love, guidance, and money flowed more freely, and they are motivated by a desire to give to others from the bounty they enjoyed. Whatever their path, men sometimes see the need to fill the debilitating gaps left by adults'—often parents'—inadequate investments in kids' mental, emotional, and physical health. Many youth are pessimistic about their life chances, having been essentially abandoned or set adrift into troubled waters, unable or unwilling to fashion dreams of a productive life. Some men, deeply moved by kids' dreamless state, travel to their side hoping to expand their horizons of possibilities. These men seek to open kids' minds to fresh and productive options for experiencing life.

Some youth work settings allow men to help kids develop synergy and a sense of team unity or family. Here, men try to get kids to define a common goal and cooperate to achieve it. The team-oriented journey can be fulfilling to men and kids alike. Although boys may be more receptive to this approach, given their greater fondness for group play, men can also capitalize on girls' cooperative spirit.[14]

Regardless of their other motives for getting involved, all of the men value kids. The "valued child" sentiment permeates the men's stories and actions in numerous ways. Men demonstrate that they value kids when they spend their own money to help a kid pay for eye glasses, clothes, food, camp fees, field trips, or other items. They value youth by treating them like family, sometimes even taking them into their homes on a temporary or extended basis. Kids are being valued when men go out of their way to create healthy opportunities for them or spend hours and hours of their free time by their side. And some men express their affinity for kids by finding ways to be a parental ally.

Generativity is a key motivator of men to spend time with youth. Sometimes emboldened by their religious convictions, sometimes without a faith perspective, many men strive to nurture and teach a younger generation by sharing their time, life lessons, and resources. Filled with the spirit of "passing it on," they search for ways to build kids' character and enhance their life chances by sharing value-laden messages about hard work, respect, integrity, trust, and commitment. The meaning of men passing on their legacy of skills, values, and wisdom has been transformed in recent eras by the dramatic decline in family-owned farms, shifts in family demography, and feminist advances challenging patriarchal privileges. As Andrew so eloquently expresses, his early conviction to teach kids about basketball as well as life was inspired by his desire to carry forward his father's legacy of nurturing meaningful human ties. More recently, as Andrew has matured into middle age, he wishes to share his life philosophy with youth. In bygone eras, Andrew might have been more likely to "pass on" his

message to youth in the context of a formal or informal apprenticeship relationship. Perhaps we need to explore more resourceful ways to recreate such
arrangements between men and youth.[15]

Altruistic virtues may motivate the men to look out for kids' best interests,
but most men are not blind to the intangible gifts they receive in return. Men engaged in youth work tend to realize that it feels good to contribute to kids' development because it also feeds their own personal growth while keeping them
young at heart. Similarly, though most men are not motivated to be with kids as
a way of enhancing their own reputation, they generally enjoy being appreciated
and recognized for their efforts. Whether it is formal or informal, immediate or
delayed, men are emotionally moved when kids or others recognize their efforts.
Though kudos are handed out to men for simply showing up in some settings,
men usually must make a sincere effort to bond with youth in order for kids to
acknowledge their efforts. As the men note, most kids are good at discerning
frauds.

How can men acquire the insights and skills relevant to working with kids?
Such things are gained through experiential learning and specific training when
a man participates in childcare, schooling, camping, tutoring, coaching, and so
forth. Granted, individuals with certain personality characteristics may be more
likely to wish to work with kids or pursue specific forms of youth work. They
may be "naturally" drawn to it and believe in advance that they will be good at it.
Some men see themselves as having been "kid persons" ever since they were
teenagers or young adults. But men without any "natural" inclination toward
kids may also grow more eager and confident about working with youth if they
have a chance to gain firsthand experience. They may discover they have a hidden passion or talent for working with kids, particularly if they receive social
support for their efforts.

Getting boys and men to try their hand at working with kids will be made easier if social support for such activities is increased. To foster that support we
must transform the social conditions shaping men's motives concerning kids,
dating, family, leisure, and work. Males, like females, operate in a gendered social world where their work and volunteering decisions are influenced, in part,
by what enhances social status and others' respect. In particular, heterosexual
boys and men want to secure girls' and women's favorable attention and, ultimately, their willingness to pursue some type of romantic union. Most boys and
men also seek validation of their manliness from other males. Judgments from
other boys and men are often the most consequential in shaping a man's self-
perceptions.[16]

Though males are not always fully aware of the processes constraining or fostering their inclination to do youth work, living in a gendered social world does matter. Some types of youth work (e.g., coaching boys' athletic teams, being a probation officer) are publicly portrayed as more appropriate for males than other activities (e.g., childcare, elementary school teaching). This cultural message is not lost on boys and adult men. They see, they hear, they know how guys are perceived and treated when they venture into the foreign terrain commonly viewed as women's work.

Early in the twenty-first century, economic breadwinning remains a critical marker for how a man is judged by women as well as other men. Today, women are increasingly likely to value a man's hands-on abilities as a father, but when looking for a serious romantic partner, women still tend to devalue a man who has a feminine gender-typed, low-paying job, including those involving kids.[17] In short, women appear more likely to look twice at a car mechanic or electrical engineer than a childcare worker or elementary school teacher. The message is clear: if a man is involved with kids in a low-paying "female-oriented" occupation, many women and men taper their respect, or worse, view him suspiciously.

These sentiments are reinforced by our gendered views of work and parenting, despite the influx of women, including mothers, into the labor force in the last sixty years. Men's social status is still disproportionately linked to money. Thus, the man who wishes to work with kids often has to navigate the formidable patriarchal landscape of our postindustrial society. Without significant structural and cultural changes, the recent movement toward a more equitable division of household labor is likely to be hindered. Similarly, if women do not in sufficient numbers alter their dating and mating criteria, men will continue to take the path of least resistance, shunning the chance to be more involved with kids at home or in public settings.

Ultimately, men will venture into the world of youth work more readily when incentives to do so are passed from men to men, men to boys, and boys to boys. Taking the long view, creative initiatives motivating boys to interact with younger kids should pay dividends. If program coordinators are to make youth work attractive to boys in schools and neighborhoods, they will do well to inspire high status boys to participate as volunteer helpers and mentors, as well as paid workers. Trusted adults must find ways to showcase the tangible and intangible rewards of interacting with and caring for younger kids, boys as well as girls. Once commitments are secured from adolescent male leaders, others will likely follow. Creative group rituals and routines can then perpetuate the process of getting other boys more involved.

Though leisure activities such as sports will pull many boys into coaching and mentoring roles, getting boys involved in other youth work activities, including childcare, tutoring, religious youth groups, working with special needs children, and so forth is ideal. A similar process of enlisting high-profile men in youth work activities in schools, churches, clubs, and neighborhoods can pave the way for other men to participate. The rhythms of the gendered social world reveal the power of the collective spirit. Promoting greater male involvement in youth work must tap into the pressures males feel to be affirmed by other males. In short, unless boys and men are directing clear and powerful incentives at other boys and men to become more child oriented, the cause of providing kids more attention and resources will be slow to advance.

Thus, part of the trick of persuading boys and men to see youth work as an appealing option is to expose more boys to situations that enable them to bond with younger kids and experience the joy of making a difference. Common sense says that creating opportunities for kids to learn about and polish certain skills at an early age should prove useful, especially since most positions in which teenagers and men interact with kids do not require an advanced degree or extensive training. In a related vein, programs facilitating the training of teenagers or young adults to help younger kids are particularly valuable. The "assistant" religious youth group leader, camp counselor, adolescent Boy Scout leader, or junior staff member at a Boys & Girls Club can get an early feel for the generative spirit as he or she reaches back to enrich a younger person's life. At the same time, this young leader is likely to learn something about responsibility, gain self-respect, and feel a sense of accomplishment. Ray, now several years out of high school, illustrates this logic by confirming how instrumental it was for him to be singled out as a high school volunteer mentor for younger kids. Mentoring launched him into his current paid position overseeing and molding at-risk boys' life views in a community boys club.

Any serious call for men to get more involved in kids' lives inevitably must confront our culture's increasingly pervasive "stranger danger" discourse. Even though research suggests that children today are probably no more likely—perhaps even less likely—than their counterparts in previous eras to be sexually abused,[18] the public largely ignores this reality. Media depictions of the seemingly ubiquitous "bad man" in the form of a child predator or sex offender have been emblazoned on the public consciousness. Many parents are quite anxious that their children will be abducted by a stranger and killed, even though a child age 14 or younger in the United States has roughly a one in a million chance of becoming a victim of a deadly kidnapping—most abductions are by disgruntled parents.[19]

Of course, violent and inappropriate acts toward children are disturbing and have detrimental, sometimes devastating, consequences for kids as well as their families and friends. There is little if any dispute that people who commit these heinous acts should be punished severely and that due diligence is called for in protecting youth. But we should also step back and listen closely to what dedicated men who work with kids say about the potentially stifling effects of excessive public scrutiny. For many, the rush to protect kids is at times overshadowing the need to support them emotionally. The commonsense wisdom rings true that "everybody needs a hug sometimes"—kids in particular. Social paranoia has also restricted opportunities for adults and kids to have private conversations. Youth can benefit from a wholesome one-on-one chat in which they have an adult's undivided attention. Opportunities for this experience between nonrelated adults and children are now rare and still declining.

Sadly, fears about the possibility of men's criminal touch have undermined what the late Jack Eckerd, founder in 1968 of the highly successful Eckerd Youth Alternatives (EYA) organization, recognized as the positive power of touch in helping troubled youth. One of the photographs symbolizing the EYA youth workers' dedication to helping at-risk kids was shot from behind and shows Jack walking with two boys on their way to a wilderness campsite. Eckerd, taller and situated in the middle, is resting his arms on the boys' shoulders while each boy's inside arm rests against his back and extends upwards so that each boy has a hand grasping one of Jack's shoulders. To me, the embrace signifies the potentially critical role touch can play in establishing and developing a supportive interpersonal bond between adults and youth. That symbolic pose is much like the playful and affectionate gestures I sometimes saw during my time with my participants as they interacted with kids. Hearing about, then seeing Mariano's playful and caring "hands-on" approach with his middle school students affirmed for me that well-meaning, age-appropriate, and gender-sensitive touch can generate an impressive chemistry that sharpens attentiveness and fosters the sharing of life lessons. Unfortunately, I also learned that the child protection campaign has made some men so self-conscious that they refuse even to shake kids' hands or show them *any* physical affection. That caring adults would opt for the excruciatingly "safe rather than sorry" route, even at the risk of turning away a child's offer of affection, speaks volumes about our pervasively suspicious and litigious cultural climate.

Derek's story, the first we heard, highlights a critical issue relevant to how neighborhood context relates to organized efforts to get men more involved with kids. Raised largely in a single-parent home in a housing project, Derek ran the streets as a teenage thug. As an adult, he traded in the life of poverty and crime for a middle-class, family-man respectability, complete with a house in a much nicer, safer neighborhood. Derek gives a great deal back to poor African American kids through his youth work, but the poor kids do not experience him as their reliable neighbor next door, or local business owner down the street. He is in their world, yet even though he came from it he is not part of it. He visits them on their turf but is able to escape to his own place miles away from the persistent danger and poverty of the street. Most of the time, the kids see him at their school or the boys community club. The youngsters respect Derek but he differs from the "old heads," the community elders who once lived among the youth in the inner cities. These were the men who lived in the community and were admired and emulated by the kids because they were wise and operated within the law to make the system work for them. Unfortunately, strategies that could bring those types of men permanently back to these neighborhoods involve impressive structural changes linked to political ideologies, economic policies, and corporate culture. Despite occasional rhetoric of urban renewal, wholesale fundamental changes capable of affecting inner-city youth work settings are unlikely to occur anytime soon.

By redirecting his life, Derek represents one model, a man who overcame difficult childhood circumstances and landed on his feet, firmly implanted in the middle class. Derek is able to relate to the kids because he grew up in the projects and intimately knows the "street game." A contrasting model is found in 100 Black Men of America, which draws upon civic and business leaders, some of whom have little or no experience with inner-city street life, to provide poor kids a chance to be mentored by successful African American men.

Such initiatives can either bring men into the inner city to be with kids or provide kids opportunities to travel outside their impoverished neighborhoods to experience the world, as Carlos has done by taking poor kids on mission trips to foreign countries when some had never stepped foot outside their own community. Ideally, of course, more structural changes will be made to rejuvenate the inner-city economic base, thereby attracting middle-class African American and Latino men and their families to work and live in revitalized neighborhoods. Youth will then share time and space with productive mentors throughout the course of their everyday lives. In their neighborhoods and at school, youth will encounter men who are their neighbors and who embrace their responsibility to contribute to the kids' healthy development.

In a truly generative society, family, friends, neighbors, and coworkers support men's efforts to work and volunteer with youth. Social support is most effective when it is formally incorporated into the larger society, as illustrated by the recent mentoring movement. The mentoring philosophy provides a sound rationale for men (and women) to take a more active interest in youth. Organizations like Big Brothers Big Sisters, often in conjunction with schools or the criminal justice system, provide the programmatic structure necessary to recruit, screen, match, and support men who will create productive bonds with kids. Recent attempts to get the corporate world to encourage employees to mentor youth may be one successful way to get more men involved with kids. Bringing such men into kids' everyday orbits is likely to enhance their social capital. When successful men enter kids' networks, they come equipped with useful community contacts and valuable resources, including information and opportunities. Securing these additional contacts is valuable because kids usually benefit when multiple adults watch out for them across different settings.

A number of the men I studied, particularly the ministers, illustrate how romantic partners are capable of benefiting their youth work. Partners can be supportive by giving men the space and time to devote their energies to volunteering, by interacting with kids alongside the men, and by offering fresh perspectives and advice about youth—especially girls. When partners provide this type of support, men are probably more apt to get involved, stay involved, be effective, and encourage others to pursue youth work.

One of the best sources of inspiration for men to engage in youth work is hearing from men who have enjoyed working with kids. When veteran youth workers talk about their own experiences, they facilitate similar productive activities by other individuals and by organizations. Thus, another sign of a generative society is that adults are more distinctly self-aware of their personal journey and their impact on youth. Prior to talking to me, most of the men had not systematically thought about how their commitment and ability to connect to kids had been shaped by their assorted interactions with youth and others over the years. I hope this book will nudge every man who works with kids to think more deeply about his life journey as a youth worker. Most importantly, adults who work with youth can benefit by reflecting on these basic questions:

- How did various aspects of my childhood motivate me to get involved with kids and how did they affect my current approach to youth work?
- What core principles and expectations shape how I relate to kids and try to affect their lives?
- How am I trying to make a difference in kids' lives?
- Over the course of my life, how have I adapted lessons from the different

settings in which I've interacted with kids (including my own children) to
my current work or volunteering with youth?

- How has working or volunteering with kids affected the way I think and
  feel about myself and treat others?
- What changes can I make to enhance my effectiveness in working with
  youth?
- To what extent have I tried to inspire others to get involved in youth work?

Thinking seriously about these and related questions should enable adults to develop a keener sense of their involvement with youth and a sharper self-image.

People with no experience working or volunteering with youth, and those who are no longer involved with kids, can also heighten their self-awareness by asking themselves poignant questions. Contemplating the following questions can enhance personal insights about why one is not more involved with kids:

- Why haven't I made the effort to get involved with kids in some way, or
  what changes in my life have altered my desire to work with kids?
- Are there formal or informal steps I would be willing to take to become involved more actively with kids?
- If I were to devote time and energy to being with kids, what types of activities would be most appealing to me?
- What life lessons would I want to share with kids?

This mental exercise might also help professionals frame their recruitment of men for different forms of youth work, such as, directors of Big Brothers Big Sisters organizations or school principals who are trying to attract men teachers to coach and mentor.

Generally speaking, strategies to get men more involved with kids in settings outside the home must be sensitive to the prevailing culture and conduct of fatherhood. To the extent that recent cohorts of fathers are expected to devote more time to their own children and domestic responsibilities, and are in fact doing so, innovative strategies, tied to schools, community organizations, and businesses, are needed to encourage fathers to also reach out to other youth.[20] Altering the image of good fathering to include an ethic of community investment, particularly spending constructive time with kids, will yield dividends for the community. Ultimately, to get more men involved with kids and to improve the efforts of the men already active, we need to build upon recent shifts in the culture of fatherhood. We need to encourage men to open their eyes to the social and personal benefits of being more concerned about youth both in and outside their families.

Efforts to heighten men's interest in doing youth work should not only seek to convince individual men to devote time and energy to kids. An equally important goal is to transform the larger cultural climate so that more men actively embrace a generative spirit and collective consciousness of valuing and fostering children's development. The mindset should promote men's spirited sense of responsibility to help raise, nurture, protect, and mentor youth in general.[21] Such a collective mindset will prove most beneficial if men, as well as women, recognize that it often takes a child-oriented network to raise a kid—one that builds bridges among youth workers and between youth workers and families. This view reflects what some researchers have documented in African American fathers' collective efforts to share strategies for protecting kids in violent neighborhoods.[22]

The generative message can best be channeled through the institutions of families, work, school, religion, and communications media. Men should be encouraged to see their involvement with kids as part of a larger project of helping kids find their way through childhood and adolescence. This could be viewed as extending men's traditional responsibility to keep their family safe. Shortly after reviewing a draft of this book, Ben noted that he had gained a better appreciation for the fact that he and the other men who work with kids in diverse settings occupy the same "battlefield." Even though no enemy exists in the traditional sense, many dangers to youth litter the path to adulthood. Men might be led to recognize that they are in a loose alliance committed to keeping kids out of danger and to promoting good mental, emotional, and physical health.

In sum, to make progress in strengthening men's generative spirit toward youth, our multi-pronged effort must target boys as well as men of all ages from varied walks of life. Our youth—the at-risk and the well-off, all races and ethnicities, boys and girls—are most likely to thrive when men individually and collectively become more equal partners with women on a mission to promote kids' healthy development.

In many ways, as we saw in the debates about male school teachers' possible contributions to students' academic performance, it remains unclear whether and to what extent men as youth workers, compared to their female counterparts, provide unique assets that enhance kids' well-being. Obviously, because my study focuses only on men, I cannot systematically compare how male and female youth workers perceive and treat kids or assess their potentially distinctive contributions to youth. Yet, if men increase their involvement with kids in public settings and women's level of involvement remains similar, youth will have at the very least access to more resources (e.g., financial, emotional, psychological, practical, social capital, instructional) in an aggregate sense.

My interviews and observations lead me to believe that youth can be affected distinctively by watching men's interactions with their families, coworkers, and kids. Although my study does not document the outcomes, I suspect that watching responsible, caring, attentive men treat others respectfully can provide kids healthy models to emulate. Boys and girls stand to benefit as they see firsthand what it means to be a "good" man who lives life in harmony with feminist principles and healthy versions of masculinity. Kids will learn to recognize, initiate, and demand respectful relations with others without resorting to homophobic or sexist behavior. Because the masculine norms and social pressures defining adolescent male culture are deeply entrenched, men, not women, are uniquely positioned to redirect boys' thinking, feeling, and behavior about certain matters. In particular, in order for boys to hear and embrace a message calling for a more compassionate and less violent brand of masculinity, men will most likely have to play a key role in delivering it. Women can do their part, but if men remain silent, many boys will turn a deaf ear.

Also, with family demographic patterns being what they are—and with no dramatic change in sight—the biological parent most absent from kids' daily lives will continue to be the father. Because more kids are without an active father than an active mother, kids may be inclined to view the unrelated men in their lives, more than unrelated women, as gender models and parental substitutes.

In addition, some of the major goals of a liberal feminist agenda can only be realized if men develop a stronger commitment to kids beyond the provider role. Men's increased involvement with youth in public settings would probably directly and indirectly lead to greater gender equity in and outside the home. For example, female-dominated occupations, such as elementary school teaching and childcare, are likely to grow in stature and pay if men take a greater interest in them.

A more powerful cultural endorsement of men's greater involvement with kids should invoke meaningful structural changes in the society. This message could be incorporated more fully into evolving versions of masculinity ideology. To some extent, this pattern has already taken root in the contemporary culture of fatherhood and newer images of the manly father. Ideally, if men become more active in youth work they will also assume more community-based responsibility for their own children, building more social capital for them.[23] More broadly, if men throughout their adolescent and adult years spend more time with kids, they will develop a greater sensitivity to children while solidifying their claim on a new legitimate form of masculinity.

Beyond forging an ideological partnership, men and women must learn to work more effectively side by side at the diverse sites where the everyday business of youth work happens. Much good can come from kids' seeing men and women from varied backgrounds respecting one another as they work and volunteer to help kids. Whether they view youth work as a mission, a calling, doing a job, or simply time well spent, the men profiled in this book should inspire us all to direct more of our time, energy, and resources to helping kids successfully navigate their formative years.

Appendix A

Reflections on Study Methodology and Future Research

Many readers of this book will be content with my brief explanation in Chapter 1 of the basic demographic profile of the male youth workers I interviewed, the general types of issues I addressed with them, and my efforts to observe the men in action. For those wanting to know more about my methods, I now offer a detailed description of my study's key methodological features: my strategies for recruiting men, the men's background characteristics, how I conducted the interviews and an assessment of their quality, my approach to analyzing the transcripts, my efforts to supplement my interviews with ethnographic observations, my analytic and literary approach to writing about the men's lives, and several methodological and substantive suggestions for future research.

When I launched my study, I was intent on casting a wide net to incorporate men from various backgrounds who worked and/or volunteered with kids in diverse settings. I primarily recruited participants through selective targeting of employment sites that involved youth (e.g., schools, churches, juvenile justice facilities) and youth organizations that use male volunteers (e.g., Big Brothers Big Sisters, Boy Scouts, 4-H Clubs, city recreational youth leagues). Referrals from various sources, including ones made by the men I interviewed, were valuable. I also distributed an advertisement through several local listserves sponsored by gay/lesbian or Latino organizations.

Typically, I first contacted the men by telephone or e-mail, although several men contacted me after seeing a flyer or an e-mail announcement. Generally speaking, men were quite receptive to participating once I described the study. I did not systematically record a response rate because I was uninterested in securing a statistically representative sample. However, during the entire data collection process, I recall only four or five instances in which I invited a man to do an interview but it didn't happen. In at least three of those cases, the interview did not occur because the prospective participant and I encountered scheduling problems. Two men did not return my phone or e-mail messages after they had agreed to participate. And one man and I concluded that he had limited volunteering experience with kids, so I interviewed one of his much more experienced referrals instead.

In technical terms, my sampling was purposive, in that I sought to secure a diverse sample according to men's type of work and/or volunteer experience, race and ethnicity, sexual orientation, and age. All but one had volunteered or worked with kids in at least two different settings, and most had done so in more settings during their lifetimes.

The sample is racially and ethnically diverse: 28 white, 16 African American, 8 Hispanic, 2 Native American Indian, and 1 Asian. As for financial status, 19 of the men reported a total household income equal to or less than $40,000, 22 from $40,001 to $80,000, 11 from $80,0001 to $175,000, and 3 $175,000 or more. All of the men have earned either a high school diploma or GED, and 37 have completed a college degree. Thirty-one of the men are currently married, and 27 of all participants have biological children; two reported being stepfathers. Although I did not explicitly ask the men about their sexual orientation, four of them revealed they are gay. All of the men are presently involved in paid work or volunteering with kids under age 19; some also work with young adults. With one exception, the men reside in Florida (Gainesville, Ocala, and Miami). One man had moved out of state within the previous year or so but was visiting Florida, where he had been raised. I paid the participants $30 cash to complete the interview. All the men finished the interview.

Given my recruitment strategies, it seems safe to assume that the men I ultimately interviewed probably represent a somewhat more motivated subset of male youth workers. Although the men shared plenty of examples of their struggles in trying to make a difference in kids' lives, they are particularly well positioned to offer insights about the positive aspects of youth work and the interpersonal processes associated with it. Thus, my analysis probably does a better job of capturing the experiences of the highly motivated than of those who are going through the motions of a job in which they incidentally interact with kids.

Another "limitation" of my study is that the men had all made a point of volunteering for or accepting paid work in job(s) that involved kids (many had held multiple paid youth work positions during their life). Given the nature of my sample, then, I am restricted in what I might incorporate about the reservations men may have about working with children. In short, my research design does not afford the opportunity to ask men who have not gotten involved with kids what has prevented them from doing so. I do raise the issue of men's motivations in several chapters, particularly when I take up mentoring, but some of my suggestions for promoting men's greater involvement are based on others' impressions, rather than my own data.

THE INTERVIEWS

I conducted fifty-five semistructured interviews lasting roughly ninety minutes on average, in either home (mine or theirs), office (mine or theirs), or a youth work facility. I conducted my first interview on May 11, 2005, and my final one on July 31, 2006.

With two exceptions, I did not know the men prior to the interview, and one of the two exceptions was only a casual acquaintance. Depending on the circumstances, including time constraints and my perception of the man's level of comfort, I briefly engaged in small talk with the participant prior to the interview. I also answered any questions he had about my research background or the nature of the study. After the participant had read and signed the consent form, I reminded him that I would be asking him to tell me stories about his experiences with kids throughout his life. I encouraged the men to offer as much detail as possible, while assuring them that I welcomed long answers. With only a few exceptions, the men were very cooperative and eager to narrate their life as a youth worker. Even the two or three men who provided relatively curt answers seemed interested in helping me to understand their interaction with kids. Although the interviews were somewhat conversational in style, I usually directed the lengthy questioning without interjecting my own thoughts or experiences. When asked pointed questions I answered them candidly.

In general, I organized the interviews according to a life history format. I began by asking the participants to describe their childhood experiences, with an emphasis on their relations with their families, friends, communities, and mentors. I was particularly interested in what types of life lessons they felt they had learned from their family and others who had affected their formative years. After exploring their childhood memories I encouraged the men to talk, largely chronologically, about their early youth work opportunities and then their current experiences working with kids. As the study evolved and I grew more comfortable covering my main substantive areas of interest while accommodating the individualized flow of the men's narratives, I became more flexible in how I ordered my questions and probes after the initial question.

The interviews typically covered the following issues:

- Description of childhood and youth
- Key men and women affecting childhood and youth development
- Life lessons taken from parents and mentors
- First involvement with kids
- Current involvement with kids
- Types of bonds, relations, and interactions with kids
- Kids' traits liked and disliked
- Differences in perceptions and treatment of boys versus girls
- Factors shaping personal youth work philosophy
- Definition of mentor
- Difference he had made in kids' lives (i.e., contributions to their development and well-being)
- Experiences working with others (family members, coworkers, workers in other agencies) on youth work issues
- Perceptions of and experiences with touching and safe-environment policies
- How youth work has affected personal life (including own personal development)
- Extent to which and how youth work and personal life overlap
- Connections between fathering and youth work; if without kids, to what extent and how youth work has affected desire to become a father and preparation for fathering
- Insights about self derived from doing the interview
- Suggestions for additional topics to cover in current research project

Although I tended to explore all these issues if they were relevant to the man I was interviewing, I also asked various follow-up questions to give him an opportunity to assume specific standpoints when describing his perceptions of and experiences with kids. For example, I consciously altered questions in order to ask about how the participant—as an African American man, a gay man, relatively new youth worker, physically large man, man with international experience working with kids, or a father—oriented himself toward youth or certain types of youth (boys/girls, kids of color)?

Consistent with conventional strategies of qualitative research, I conducted simultaneous data collection and analysis; this produced minor modifications to my interview guide as the study unfolded. For example, in my first three interviews I asked participants to talk about the key men who had affected them during their early years. Subsequently, after a participant spoke about the importance of a female mentor, I decided to ask them to comment on all mentors, male and female. Similarly, midway through my interviews, I switched from asking directly how working with kids had affected their personality or personal development and instead asked a more open-ended question, allowing more descriptive freedom. If participants did not speak specifically about personality changes, I probed to see if they felt they had experienced any. Although some men immediately mentioned things like becoming more patient or happier, few men raised issues on their own about the work/family connection. Yet, once I expanded on the question with examples, many were able to verify that they had made particular changes or they saw connections between their work and personal life.

FRAMING, INTERPRETING, AND JUDGING THE INTERVIEWS

In framing the interview portion of this qualitative study, and my interpretive analysis, I assumed that the men's lives include meaningful phenomena that are independent of their efforts to describe those realities in an interview setting. In one sense, I treat the phenomena as real or having an ontological status of their own. Put differently, I tried to represent the beliefs, attitudes, sentiments, and experiences that are part of the men's lived reality as being distinct from their attempts to share them with me. Yet, I recognize that characteristics of, for example, the interview setting, my description of the study, my personal attributes (including my own lack of formal youth work experience), the blending of the men's personalities with my own, how the men wanted to be perceived, and conditions defining the larger sociocultural context, contributed to how the men reconstructed their experiences and framed their narratives. Although intriguing ontological, epistemological, and methodological issues can be raised about the processes by which the men and I collaboratively produced their accounts, I do not examine those complicated concerns here because I tailored this book to appeal to a broad audience.[1]

Generally speaking, I believe the co-constructed nature of the interview experience, while important, does not fundamentally alter the meaning of the men's accounts of their everyday realities. My ethnographic observations helped confirm my assumptions. Thus, I treat language as a medium that enables me to capture reasonably well how the men described their social realities. Their storytelling allowed me to see their world through their eyes while I interpreted it through a mix of multidisciplinary social science lenses.

Five well-known theoretical perspectives shaped my interpretive frame: social constructionism, a gender lens including a masculinities perspective, symbolic interactionism, a life course perspective, and adult development/generativity. I also adapt themes from my situated fathering perspective,[2] as described in Chapter 3, to accentuate how physical and social attributes of space and place relate to men's involvement with youth.

Through the prism of social contructionism,[3] a sociological theory of knowledge that accentuates context, individuals are viewed as living in a fluid, socially constructed world. Shifting cultural and social processes influence how society is organized as well as how individuals define and negotiate their everyday lives. In turn, people are thought to be instrumental in shaping the circumstances and institutions affecting their thoughts, feelings, and actions. I use this perspective to highlight how cultural meanings and public discourses frame the perceived social realities surrounding men's interactions with kids in a community.

I complement my macroanalysis of how the cultural climate affects men's contact with kids by turning selectively to the broad field of gender studies, specifically the subfield of men and masculinities.[4] My pro-feminist perspective guides my discussion of men as men. I explore how aspects of the gendered social order and gendered institutions, as well as the process of "doing gender,"[5] affect men's level and type of involvement with youth in varied settings.

The symbolic interactionist perspective accentuates that how individuals come to see themselves is, in part, shaped by how they believe others see and treat them.[6] Further, individuals produce and express their self-images while immersed in diverse types of encounters and relationships. Men's relations with youth through volunteering and paid work provide all involved diverse opportunities to define situations and negotiate identities.

Viewed from the multidisciplinary life course perspective, men's interactions with kids are embedded within a larger historical and socioeconomic context and are sometimes linked to cultural scripts about adult manhood.[7] A key insight is that individuals are guided by commonly understood norms about the appropriate timing of life events and experiences such as education, marriage, work, childbearing and childrearing, and community involvement. People are exposed to cultural messages urging them to organize and live their lives in particular ways, including having kids of their own and being ready to act in a protective and instructional way toward other children. Ultimately, though, men are viewed largely as active agents who make choices about their involvement in social activities and relationships, including how they perceive and orient themselves towards working with kids in public settings.

Public perceptions of how men should relate to children are separate from, yet related to, the rich tradition of ideas associated with Erikson's lifespan model of psychosocial development.[8] In Chapters 4, 10, and 12, I draw from this theoretical tradition to highlight the value and challenges men experience as they mature and manage psychosocial tasks associated with adult development, most importantly, caring for younger generations—generativity.[9] I link men's experiences of personal development with their opportunities to contribute to the larger community.

These perspectives guided my research by encouraging me to ask the men particular questions. They also led me to isolate, interpret, and present the men's stories in specific ways. In order to accommodate the general reader, however, I typically avoid jargon while subtly incorporating the basic themes from these perspectives into the text. Ultimately, then, my book should be viewed as my theoretically guided interpretation of what these men described as their meaningful experiences working with kids.

I use several indices I've presented in previous work to organize my reflections about the quality of my interviews with the men.[10] Ultimately, there is no absolute "gold standard" by which interview quality can be determined, but the following comments and examples shed some light on the nature of the interviews.

Emotional Accessibility

With several exceptions, the men appeared relaxed and eager to talk at length about their own childhoods, relationships with kids, and youth work more generally. As I convey in numerous places in the book, the men generally did not appear emotionally inhibited; they seemed unfazed by the prospect that I might expect them to present a masculine self.[11] For example, Derek immediately revealed his willingness to express his vulnerability by talking about his vivid childhood memory of seeing his father physically leave his family with another woman. Dwight shed tears as he described how deeply saddened and angry he still feels about an incident involving one of his students and the boy's mother. Although the boy physically abused his mother, she continues to stand by her son's side. Another example is Thomas's story about his remorse over the young girl who got hurt on the amusement ride he was operating and how he went out of his way to develop and sustain a lifetime friendship with her. In short, the men's willingness to share their emotions and intimate stories about the struggles and joys of their youth work throughout their lives convinced me that I was able to establish sufficient rapport with the men to develop a deep appreciation for their emotional worlds.

Collaborative Behavior

I have a strong sense that the vast majority of the participants were quite interested in my project and eager to help me get a better sense of how they, and men more generally, relate to kids in various domains. In moments before, during, and after the interviews, the men conveyed in various ways a collaborative sentiment of wanting to assist me. Some commented that they didn't mind rearranging their schedule or driving out of their way for an interview because they sensed it was for a worthy cause. Sometimes without prompting, other times in response to my request for referrals, many were quick to suggest other men I might interview, explaining why they thought particular guys would be good for my study. During the interview itself, most of the men appeared to make an effort to clarify their personal experiences with kids and their views about youth work. They did so in a respectful way, seemingly acknowledging that it would be worthwhile for them to share insights that probably went beyond any work experience I might have had with youth.

Whenever I asked the men near the end of the interview to suggest topics I should cover with future participants, all seemed to ponder my request seriously, and in some instances identified issues they thought warranted future study. Robby, a gay man, took the initiative to offer advice by emphasizing his particular standpoint. He begins by jokingly saying, "Obviously I'm going to stay away from things that you haven't hit on that I don't want to talk about." But he then continues to raise a sensitive issue, signaling his willingness to work collaboratively with me.

> *Certainly you can dive down more into psyches depending on your subject and cover things about sexual feelings toward kids. You stayed away from, umm, you know, "Did you ever intentionally put yourself in situations to be around kids?"*

Robby goes on to answer this delicate question, noting, "I'm sure there were times I got close." But he also asserts that he has always been careful because he never wanted to perpetuate any negative stereotypes about gay men and their relations with kids.

At times, the men put forth an extra effort to clarify unique aspects of specific youth work domains and to make sure I understood their distinctive views and experiences. For instance, Ray and I had a revealing exchange as we worked together to clarify why he felt his approach to his youth work—given his belief in predetermination—was more consistent with it being referred to as a "calling" rather than a "mission."

Declarations of Comfort

During the interviews, and particularly afterwards, most of the verbal and nonverbal signals the men gave off suggested they were relaxed and comfortable with the interview process. As noted above, I interpreted their willingness to talk about their feelings as evidence that they were at ease during the interview. I built considerable rapport with the men; this is evidenced by their receptiveness to spontaneous joking. Some of the men also talked about how they enjoyed the experience of reflecting on their youth work history, something very few of them had done in any systematic way prior to the interview. Perhaps most telling was that all of the men I asked for permission to do ethnographic observations agreed. I suspect, too, that all or nearly all of the men would have allowed me to shadow them as they worked with kids—assuming their supervisors would have given their approval if necessary.

Detailed, Dense, Personal Information

Prior to each interview, I explicitly told the men that I was eager for them to share detailed stories about their specific experiences, especially with kids. I asked them to share personal stories to illustrate their points and assured them, "long answers are good." Out of the fifty-five participants, I would characterize only two or three as being relatively terse, and even those men provided detailed information about selected topics. Men who did not initially narrate a story with sufficient detail almost always accommodated my request that they delve more deeply into the story. Consistent with interviewing strategies designed to foster the men's openness, I frequently asked them to describe an event or situation before I asked them to talk about their feelings about it.[12]

The men provided rich, emotion-laden personal information. Some talked about being investigated for sexual harassment or their fear of showering in the same facilities as boys or being around kids at summer camps without being fully dressed. Some shared a personal history of being abused and neglected as a child or of committing crimes. They expressed their frustrations with how coworkers interacted with kids. The men also talked in considerable detail about the wonderful relationships they've had with their own mentors, parents, and grandparents, and about the youth they have served throughout their lives.

MAKING SENSE OF THE TRANSCRIPTS

Immediately after each interview, I prepared extensive memos logging my insights and impressions related to theoretical, methodological, and personal concerns. My memos highlighted how preexisting theoretical perspectives or frameworks (e.g., symbolic interactionism, life course, situated fathering) and concepts (e.g., boy code, gender practice, looking-glass self, social capital) guided the way I framed, coded, and interpreted the interview data. I made use of sensitizing concepts[13] from the literature (e.g., generativity) as well as from the men's narratives (e.g., leveling) to shape my approach to interviewing and analysis. Various research assistants transcribed all the interviews and assistants read most of my memos. Although it is tempting to offer a step-by-step guide to how I analyzed the data, coding did not proceed in distinct phases. Rather, the "picture slowly emerged as a patchwork mosaic."[14]

As I closely read the transcripts I used grounded theory methodology to assign tentative "open" codes to ideas, terms, phrases, and moods to capture the meaning of passages (ranging from short phrases to paragraphs), many of which appeared in multiple interviews.[15] My purpose during the open coding process was to develop a classification scheme to make sense of men's stories about their feelings, thoughts, and experiences directly or indirectly related to their lives as youth workers. I compared multiple examples of phenomena that particular men described and I compared examples between the men. As I labeled similarities in experience, patterns, and emergent themes, I created a vast code list to document the numerous categories. The codes helped me to interpret men's descriptions of their experiences of becoming and being youth workers, often in different settings over the course of their lives. I was able to identify key categories and their properties through this coding process. For example, I heard a number of men talk about various facets of how they relate to kids. Because one of these involves men's efforts to get on the same "level" as kids, I explored the distinct physical, emotional, and intellectual strategies men use to achieve this type of interpersonal bond with youth.

In developing the second level of "axial" coding I explored the relationship between concepts, for instance, the connection between the process of relating to kids and developing credibility. Men who felt they had been able to communicate with youth on the kids' level were more likely to feel as though the youngsters trusted them. In some instances, I also was able to compare themes relevant to youth work to those described in the fathering literature (e.g., generativity).

As the assistants read chapter drafts, I discussed and checked my coding scheme with their perceptions of how and what the men were sharing in their stories. Because of the diversity of the men's occupational and volunteer experiences, I do not attempt to arrive at an overall theory of how men become and behave as youth workers, although some threads pertaining to men's motives, ways of relating and managing kids, personal development, and connections between youth work and family appear to transcend any particular domain of youth work. My analytic approach highlights the distinct features of the most prominent aspects defining men's experiences and self-descriptions as youth workers.

I have tried to incorporate the student assistants' reflections into my project, but I was the only person to code the interviews systematically, so a cautionary note is in order about my data analysis: the dependability of the results rests largely on my interpretation.[16] Yet, I got valuable feedback from three of the men I interviewed and observed: Ben, Mariano, and Malik. Consistent with the strategy labeled "member-checking" in the qualitative literature,[17] I asked each to read and comment on various features of a complete manuscript draft and to pay particular attention to the sections where I incorporated material about them. Without exception, they agreed that I had captured the essence and complexity of their feelings as well as their actions.

ETHNOGRAPHIC OBSERVATIONS

My original research was conceptualized as an in-depth interview study of male youth workers. It wasn't until I had interviewed forty-seven men that I seriously contemplated supplementing my interviews with ethnographic observations. After contacting a future participant (Ricardo) living in Miami, I accepted his generous invitation to stay at his apartment for several days during my research trip in order to facilitate my securing other interviews in the Miami area. After the interview, conducted at his home late on the Saturday night I arrived, Ricardo encouraged me to watch him teach his Catholic Christian doctrine class the next morning.

On Sunday, nestled unobtrusively in the back of the classroom during that hour session, I observed Ricardo's attentive, caring, and patient interactions with twenty-five highly energetic, talkative kids. Although Ricardo the night before had painted a reasonably detailed picture of how rambunctious his students were, seeing him manage the situation in person was quite revealing. It was then, in the midst of watching him try to answer students' questions while other kids restlessly chatted in the background, that I decided to supplement my interview data with ethnographic observations of other men. I realized that this "deeper immersion"[18] in the men's worlds would sensitize me more fully to the richness and breadth of their experiences. One of my study goals in adopting a mixed-method approach was to increase the dependability and credibility of my interpretations of men's lives.

My approach to incorporating the ethnographic element into my project was guided by an interest in spending time with men in diverse settings, as well as by practical concerns. I tried to select a subsample of men (Charles, Derek, Joseph, Ben, Jeff, Reggie, Mariano, Malik, Ricardo, Jacob, Ray) to observe whose work represented a wide range of activities. For practical reasons, I did not, however, observe any childcare workers, one-on-one mentors, or men in residential facilities for troubled youth.

The men I selected all seemed highly motivated in their youth work activities, past and current. Because I spent all of my observational time with the individual men after I interviewed them, I went into the field with preconceived notions of how each man perceived and interacted with kids. I believe the rapport I built with the men during my interviews limited their need to put on a false or exaggerated front for me when they were with youth. Finally, although my study protocol did not allow me to ask the kids pointed questions about their experiences or perceptions of the men in charge, I was able to observe their reactions to the men.

I observed Charles, Ben, Joseph, Malik, and Ray for portions of two nonsequential days, and I spent time with the others on one day apiece. Because the men worked in diverse settings I made practical adjustments when conducting observations in response to situational contingencies. Sometimes I used different strategies with the same man. For example, I sometimes walked side-by-side with men like Ben, Derek, Malik, and Ray as they interacted with kids in church youth group sessions, after-school programs, and recreational activities. Other times with these same men, and others, I sat or remained standing in one place as I observed them while they taught, coached, played with, and supervised kids. Similarly, the men sometimes introduced me to the kids (collectively or one-on-one) by either telling the kids a visitor was present or describing me as someone (often a professor) writing a book about men and kids. There were times too that the men did not acknowledge me; they simply went about their business while I quietly observed. I also spent time with some of the men during transitional periods when they were not actively engaged with the kids or the kids were not even present. During a few of these periods, the men's coworkers were also available. Most of my conversations with the men were semiprofessional, focusing on kid-oriented issues; but the men, coworkers, and I also had more personal exchanges, often while sharing a meal. In all instances, I felt that the men and I built a casual rapport, one that may have accentuated at times a masculine bond of sorts based on sports and fathering histories.

In those settings where I sat and observed, I discreetly jotted short field notes to orient myself to the setting and to serve as triggers for my more reflective thinking once I left the site. For the most part, when I was moving around shadowing the men I kept my notepad hidden. Once I exited a site, however, I immediately used my jottings and/or memories to compile more thorough field notes.

The nature and level of detail of my note taking varied in relation to the setting in which I spent time. I tended to frame my descriptive and analytic observations by highlighting features of the physical site (old/new, natural/constructed, indoors/outdoors, size, visual details such as Martin Luther King poster, symbols of Boy Scouts, written guidelines for cooperative learning), properties of the interaction scenario (e.g., small group, mixed gender, coworkers' presence or absence), and men's style and strategies for interacting with kids and coworkers (e.g., humor, stern disciplinary tone, leveling, competitive).

THE WRITING

I had to make strategic decisions about how I could best use the men's stories and my observations of their activities with kids in diverse settings to help tell the big story about men's youth work. To my knowledge, no one has previously studied a sample of men who occupy such an eclectic array of youth-oriented jobs and volunteering positions. Thus, I make liberal use of the men's quoted remarks, while supplementing them with my first-hand observations, to sensitize others to how men from different backgrounds think, feel, and act in relation to kids in various public settings. The diversity of the sample treats readers to a cornucopia of views and often sentimental as well as realistic reflections on what it is like to work and volunteer with youth. Hearing directly from the men in the trenches helps bring to life the larger story.

I write about men's lives as I do because I want to reach a wide audience, including academics, educated lay readers, and youth workers. Consequently, I make ample use of extended quotes and exemplary cases to help readers visualize and empathize with the men. I want to capture readers' attention while accentuating the complexity and intimate dimensions to individual men's life histories and personal circumstances. My literary style is intended to encourage readers to feel as if they have met and know some of these men personally. I hope that other men working with kids in public settings will see snippets of themselves in the men I depict. As they read manuscript drafts, my student assistants and three participant reviewers enthusiastically and unanimously encouraged me to incorporate the men's detailed narratives extensively into the book.

In the literary style I adopted I try to help readers "see" the men whose stories I'm representing, to provide readers with selective cues about the possible standpoints or perspectives the men bring with them to their youth work experience. I incorporate descriptive information about the men, including their age, race or ethnicity, family of origin descriptors such as social class and family structure and size, markers of community and occasionally geographic residence, marital and fatherhood status, sexual orientation, and physical body type and personality characteristics. The potential danger of this approach, of course, is that readers, when presented with limited information, will process descriptive material through a rather narrow cognitive filter, filling in gaps by resorting to stereotypical thinking. In my view, this shortcoming is outweighed by the benefits of writing about the men in a fashion that motivates readers to imagine, empathize with, and remember the men.

I also contextualize men's comments and stories by describing the type of youth work they do or have done. Initially, to paint the big picture, I talk about youth workers in general as a way of delimiting my subject matter. But I comment specifically about some of the different types of involvements in the opening chapters and in various places throughout the book (e.g. when I describe in Chapter 3 the physical sites where men and kids interact). In Chapter 11, I clearly differentiate and separately discuss five major types of "youth work domains," noting that some men are involved with kids in childcare, schools, monitoring sites and criminal justice, recreation, or faith-based environments. That discussion highlights distinctive features related to those sites.

Because I'm creating more of a mosaic than a photo gallery of men and youth work and I have only a relatively small number of men in any one domain, I do not (and cannot) provide a detailed analysis of individuals in any particular arena, such as male youth ministers or male childcare workers. I realize that in some ways activities in these areas are not functional equivalents, but there are noteworthy similarities. Much depends on the level of analysis or abstraction one applies to the data. All the men are currently spending time with kids not their own in a public setting and I am convinced that they want to have a positive impact on those kids. Of course, some are more committed than others, but in one way or another they want to protect kids, help them find their way, and improve their well-being—even if their contribution might only represent a small advantage. So my approach to analyzing and writing about men's lives often reflects my sense that insights can be gleaned by highlighting common themes in the men's experiences in different types of youth work.

FUTURE RESEARCH

Future research should expand the type of sample I've used so that a data-driven explanation can be generated that will provide a deeper and broader analysis of the many forces that contribute to the tendency for men not to be as involved as women are in the daily lives and care of children. Collecting data from children and female youth workers could shed greater light on men's experiences as youth workers. Although kids may be somewhat limited in their ability to assess fully how men have affected their development, they are in a unique position to offer some intriguing ideas. They may, for instance, be capable of validating when, how, and why some men are able to gain their respect and trust. Such insights might be learned from short, focused interviews and focus groups that would complement ethnographic observations of men in particular settings.

Without a subsample of women youth workers for comparison, it is difficult to conclude how men, as men, uniquely contribute to kids' lives. I make some observations about what certain kinds of men might do for kids relative to other men, and I speculate on how men may bring something to youth's lives beyond what women typically do, but I am reluctant to stray too far beyond the data when writing about men's potential special contributions to kids.

Because we have limited knowledge about men's involvement with kids outside the home, an analysis focusing systematically on men irrespective of how much can be said confidently about their possible unique, gendered contribution is, I believe, a valuable contribution to the literatures exploring youth and men's involvement with them. Some of the findings might be equally relevant to women; we just don't know. Knowing more about the similarities and differences between men's and women's contributions is essential to pushing the literature even further.

Incorporating an ethnographic component into a study of male (and female) youth workers over an extended period of time could produce valuable results. Unfortunately, it is exceedingly difficult for one researcher to follow for months or years a significant number of study participants in different settings. A large research team would be required for such a project. Such a design could perhaps speak more powerfully to the social processes by which adult men and women develop and manage their connections to kids, while highlighting how youth work affects the kids and the adults alike.

Lastly, securing a larger sample of youth workers who are fathers to minor children, in addition to having a resident romantic partner, would foster opportunities to explore how men's public and family lives are connected. Such a sample would open up avenues for considering how men's specific responsibilities with kids outside the home affect their willingness and ability to embrace community-based responsibilities for their own children.[19] For example, what specific youth work conditions increase the chance that men will organize activities for their own children relating to school, work, clubs, athletics, birthday parties, baby sitting, and so on? Are men with certain types of experiences more likely to build social capital for their children? A sample including fathers with little or no youth work experience could offer other angles for studying how youth work experience affects men's willingness and ability to take on community-based responsibilities for their own children.

In addition, interviews with partners could generate significant insights into men's involvement with kids. Asking partners, as well as the men themselves, more extensive questions about possible overlap between youth work and family life could produce deeper understanding about how partners contribute to or constrain men's youth work. Under what conditions do partners offer their time, effort, advice, constructive criticism, moral support, and the like? When and with what effect do partners resist or discourage men's investment in youth work? Clearly, research efforts such as these would help scholars grasp more fully the complex web of relations affecting male youth workers' experiences with kids—their own as well as others.

Appendix B

Participant Profiles

Key

RECRUITING

BBBS = Big Brothers Big Sisters staff
Flyer 1 = school flyer
Flyer 2 = GLBT listserve
Flyer 3 = counseling center
Flyer 4 = Latin facility
Org = contacted organization directly
PC = personal contact
R-F = referral from friend
R-P (name) = referral from another
    study participant
R-S = referral from student

RACE & ETHNICITY

W = white
B = black (African American)
Bi = biracial
A = Asian
NAI = Native American Indian

H = Hispanic, ethnically:
    1. Cuba
    2. Mexico
    3. Nicaragua
    4. Colombia
    * = a native of

MARITAL STATUS

M = married
M, DR = married, divorced & remarried
S, NM = single, never married
S, D = single, divorced
S, LWP = single, living with partner

MONEY

P = poor
LBA = little below average
AVG = average
WO = well off

**ESTIMATED ANNUAL
HOUSEHOLD INCOME**

A = Under 20,000
B = 20,001–40,000
C = 40,001–60,000
D = 60,001–80,000
E = 80,001–125,000
F = 125,001–175,000
G = 175,001–250,000
H = Over 250,000

SCHOOL TYPE/POSITION

ES = elementary school
MS = middle school
HS = high school
PE = physical education
ESE = elementary special ed

Participant Profiles (Listed According to Interview Sequence)

Pseudonym	Recruiting Source	Age	Race	Occupation	Education	Financial Status	Marital Status	Age & Gender of Own & Step Kids	Context of Interaction with Kids
Andrew	PC	44	W	Financial planner	College degree	WO, E	M	–	Basketball coach, camp counselor
Charles	R-P Andre	32	B	Unit director of Boys & Girls Club	College degree	AVG, B	S, D	–	Youth minister, basketball & football coach, clergy, child-care worker, Big Brother, health care worker, counseling
Andre	Org	49	W	Executive director of Boys & Girls Clubs for county	Post-college degree	AVG, E	M	21F	Coach, camp counselor, police activities league
Scott	R-P Andre	32	W	Unit director of Boys & Girls Club	Post-college degree	AVG, B	S, LWP	–	Baseball, basketball, soccer & track coach, childcare worker, school teacher, camp counselor
Frank	R-P Andre	36	B	Asst. unit director of Boys & Girls Club	Some college	AVG, C	M	12F	Coach, clergy, juvenile probation officer, school teacher (ESE), Big Brother

Name	ID	Age	Race	Occupation	Education		M/S		Activities
Steve	R-P Scott	40	W	Special ed teacher, boys HS basketball coach	Post-college degree	AVG, D	M	12M 16M	Basketball coach, special education professional, camp counselor
David	Flyer 1	48	W	ESE paraprofessional, teacher's aide	AA degree	LBA, B	S, NM	—	School classroom, after-school programs, juvenile alternative service programs, public defenders office
Mark	R-P Charles	58	W	Educator	Post-college degree	WO, D	S, NM	—	Swimming coach, school teacher, mentoring program, tutoring program
Darnell	R-P Steve	37	B	Coach, PE teacher	College degree	AVG, C	M	16M 13F 11F	Basketball coach, camp counselor, juvenile probation officer, school teacher, Big Brother
Paul	R-S1	52	W	Director of religious education at a church	Post-college degree	AVG, C	M	26F 25M 22M	Coach, Sunday school teacher, school teacher, Cub Scouts, youth ministry
Calvin	R-F1	60	W	Youth specialist at community center	Post-college degree	WO, D	M	35M 30M	Baseball, basketball & soccer coach, juvenile justice officer, school teacher

(continued)

Participant Profiles

Pseudonym	Recruiting Source	Age	Race	Occupation	Education	Financial Status	Marital Status	Age & Gender of Own & Step Kids	Context of Interaction with Kids
Richard	R-P Calvin	47	B	Daycare business owner	College degree	WO, C	M	19F 14M	Childcare worker
John	BBBS	23	A	Graduate student	College degree	LBA, A	S, NM	–	Big Brother, informal tutor
Michael	BBBS	49	W	HS science teacher	Post-college degree	WO, C	S, D	–	Community college professor, HS math & science teacher, Big Brother, day camp worker, science camp
Derek	R-P Mark	29	B	Police officer, youth intervention specialist	Some college	AVG, E	M	2F	Youth interventionist in program for at-risk teenage boys, football & basketball coach
Ron	BBBS	26	W	PhD student (medical physics)	Post-college degree	AVG, C	M	–	Camp counselor, Big Brother

Name	Code	Age	Race	Occupation	Education		Marital	Children	Activities
Gerald	BBBS	22	B	Psychiatric aide	College degree	LBA, B	S, NM	—	Basketball coach, Sunday school teacher, Big Brother, Boys & Girls Club employee, president of youth ministry
Kenny	R-P Andre	58	B	Business owner	College degree	WO, H	M	—	Sunday school teacher, Big Brother, board member Boys Club, Rotary mentor
Blake	Org	22	W	Night manager at hotel	AA degree	LBA, B	S, NM	—	Camp counselor, 4-H Club, teen court
Donny	Org	34	W	Youth minister	Post-college degree	AVG, E	M	2M	Sunday school teacher, religious leader, school teacher, Big Brother
Sandy	R-F2	56	W	County extension agent	Post-college degree	AVG, E	M	35F 33M 32M	Softball coach, camp counselor, 4-H Club, Sunday school teacher, religious leader, Big Brother
Barry	PC	27	B	Activity leader after-school care	AA degree	P, A	S, NM	—	Basketball coach, camp counselor, childcare worker, teen pregnancy prevention worker, at-risk tester/counselor

(continued)

Participant Profiles

Pseudonym	Recruiting Source	Age	Race	Occupation	Education	Financial Status	Marital Status	Age & Gender of Own & Step Kids	Context of Interaction with Kids
Matthew	Org	48	W	Chief operating officer for medical device company	College degree	WO, F	M	19M 17M 25F 24F	Softball, baseball, soccer, football & basketball coach, Sunday school teacher, juvenile corrections, Boy Scouts, sports official
Kevin	Org	37	B	Youth minister	College degree	AVG, D	M	12M 10M 8M	Basketball coach, youth camp counselor, juvenile corrections, religious leader, substitute teacher, Big Brother
Joseph	R-S2	34	W	Program coordinator for at-risk youth	Some college	AVG, E	M	8M 7M 5M 4F	Soccer & T-ball coach, martial arts instructor, Sunday school teacher, juvenile corrections, school teacher, tech at psychiatric hospital

Name	Code	Age	Race	Occupation	Education			Marital	Children	Activities
Greg	Flyer 2	19	W	Student	Some college	WO, A	S, NM	—		Teacher's aide
Ben	R-F3	31	W	Associate minister	Post-college degree	AVG, D	M	3M 1F		Camp director, Sunday school teacher, after-school club, religious leader
Robby	Flyer 2	23	W	Banker	College degree	WO, C	S, NM	—		Camp counselor, tutor, volunteer at hospital
Jeff	R-P Matthew	50	W	Engineer	Post-college degree	WO, G	M	26F 21F 18F		Baseball, football & soccer coach, camp counselor, Boy Scout leader, substitute school teacher
Sidney	R-S1	28	W	2nd grade teacher	College degree	LBA, B	M	—		Camp counselor, childcare worker, school teacher, Sea World tour guide
Alan	R-P Ben	43	W	Carpenter	HS degree	AVG, B	S, LWP	—		Continuity person & church volunteer, HS program
Grady	R-F4	51	W	Juvenile probation officer	College degree	AVG, D	M	26M 12M 10F		Camp counselor, childcare worker, Sunday school teacher, juvenile corrections, Boy Scouts, ES teacher

(continued)

Participant Profiles

Pseudonym	Recruiting Source	Age	Race	Occupation	Education	Financial Status	Marital Status	Age & Gender of Own & Step Kids	Context of Interaction with Kids
Reggie	Org	45	B	4th grade teacher	College degree	AVG, B	S, D	11F 14M	Cub Scouts, country club kids, church youth group, school teacher
Mariano	Org	31	H 1	MS teacher	College degree	LBA, B –	M	–	Baseball, basketball & soccer coach, Sunday school teacher, religious leader, 7th grade teacher, mentor
Thomas	R-P Sidney	30	B	1st grade teacher	Post-college degree	AVG, B	M	–	Americorps, teacher's aide, camp counselor, after-school care, teacher, tech in children's psychiatric ward, church youth leader, mentor
Brandon	Org	41	NAI	MS science teacher	Post-college degree	AVG, D	S, D	21F 20M	Basketball, soccer & weight lifting coach, camp counselor, juvenile corrections, childcare worker, school teacher, wilderness camp director

Nick	R-P Brandon 49	NAI, W	Mental health assistant for overnight facility	HS GED, 9th grade	AVG, C	S, D	32F 29M 18M	Juvenile corrections, football & weight lifting coach, religious leader (deacon), childcare worker, healthcare worker
Dwight	Org 36	B	Teacher's aide	Some college, AA degree	LBA, B	M, DR	6M	Camp counselor, Boy Scouts, Cub Scouts, teacher's aide
Malik	R-P Joseph 27	B	Training specialist in health department	AA degree	AVG, B	S, NM	–	Basketball & football coach, mentor, camp counselor, juvenile corrections, religious leader, Big Brother
José	R-S3 20	H 1, 4	Student, (finance)	Some college	WO, E	S, NM	–	Camp counselor, religious leader, Big Brother, Junior Achievement
Carlos	R-P Malik 33	H 2	Pastor	AA degree	AVG, C	M	3M 1F	Basketball & football coach, childcare in church setting, camp counselor, Sunday school teacher, religious leader, mentor

(continued)

Participant Profiles

Pseudonym	Recruiting Source	Age	Race	Occupation	Education	Financial Status	Marital Status	Age & Gender of Own & Step Kids	Context of Interaction with Kids
Phillip	Flyer 3	26	W	Graduate student, school psychologist	Post-college degree, PhD student	LBA, A	S, NM	—	Coach, camp counselor, childcare worker, Big Brother, school psychologist
Jackson	Flyer 4	37	B	Intern coordinator, graduate student	Post-college degree	AVG, A	S, NM	—	Big Brother (church program), camp counselor, cuddler program, childcare program, childcare leader, preschool playtime program, guardian ad litem, mentor in elementary school, YMCA coach (boys and girls)
Travis	Flyer 3	24	W	Graduate student	College degree MA studentt	AVG, F[1]	S, NM	—	Camp counselor, tutoring, child-family consultations in obesity clinic, child/adolescent mental health clinic, ES & MS psych. assessments

Name		Age							
Tony	R-S4	35	W	Executive director, juvenile justice alternative program & school	College degree, MA student	LBA, C	S, NM	–	Soccer coach, camp counselor, Sunday school teacher, juvenile corrections, school teacher
Vince	R-S4	42	B	Team leader at alternative school	HS degree	LBA, B	M	24F 21M	Basketball & football coach, volunteer, juvenile corrections, mentor-camp military academy
Ramón	R-F5	41	H 4*	HS math teacher	Post-college degree	AVG, C	M	11M 4F	Soccer coach, camp counselor, school teacher, tutor, engineering club coach
Ricardo	R-F5	44	H 3*	Construction engineer	Post-college degree	AVG, D	S, D	19M 14M[2] 7M	Soccer & swimming coach, Sunday school teacher, Boy Scouts, Cub Scouts, religious leader (young adults), healthcare support in community service program

(continued)

Participant Profiles

Pseudonym	Recruiting Source	Age	Race	Occupation	Education	Financial Status	Marital Status	Age & Gender of Own & Step Kids	Context of Interaction with Kids
Santiago	R-F5	45	H 4*	Landscaping supervisor	HS degree	LBA, C	M	10M 7F	Coach of soccer, baseball, horseback riding, dancing, acting & muppets
Eduardo	R-P Santiago	65	H 1*	Teacher, engineer, junior college math teacher	Post-college degree	WO, E	M	43F 35F	Sunday school teacher, religious leader
Hernando	R-F5	38	H 4*	Staff minister	Some college	LBA, C	M	2F PRG[3]	Soccer coach, camp counselor, Sunday school teacher, clergy, PE teacher, church youth group
Ray	R-P Mark	22	B	Director of HS after-school program, college student	Some college	AVG, C	S, NM	—	Director of HS after-school program, minister of music, Sunday school, track & football coach
Eric	R-S5	22	NAI, W	Preschool teacher	Some college, AA degree	LBA, B	S, LWP	—	Sunday school teacher, preschool teacher, family child-care worker

| Tom | R-P Joseph | 48 | W | Behavior analyst for special needs youth | College degree | AVG, G | M | 24F 14F | Youth minister, school teacher, camp counselor, healthcare worker, baseball, basketball & football coach |
| Jacob | R-S6 | 50 | W | Rabbi | Post-college degree | WO, F | M | 25M 21M | Sunday school teacher, clergy, camp counselor, childcare worker, Boy Scouts, Cub Scouts, Junior Achievement |

[1]This represents data for Travis's parents.
[2]Ricardo sees his 14-year-old son on the weekends.
[3]Hernando's wife was 3 months pregnant at the time of his interview.

Notes

CHAPTER 1. THE MISSION

1. McWhirter et al. 1995; see also Moore's discussion (2006a) regarding the confusing ways the term "at-risk" is used in different settings.

2. Coltrane 1996.

3. de St. Aubin, McAdams, and Kim 2004.

4. Appendix B also offers a relatively detailed profile of the men's personal background characteristics and the types of experiences they have had throughout their lives working and volunteering with kids.

CHAPTER 2. THE LANDSCAPE

1. See Mortimer and Larson (2002) for a comprehensive overview of adolescents' lives and transitional experiences from adolescence to adulthood.

2. Lerner 1995, 1.

3. Land 2007a. High school diploma and bachelor's degree data include persons 18–24 and 25–29, respectively; rate of presidential voting includes persons 18–20 years.

4. U.S. Census Bureau 2006a.

5. Child Trends 2005

6. Land 2007a.

7. National Campaign to Prevent Teen Pregnancy 2006; see National Campaign to Prevent Teen Pregnancy (2008) regarding the slight increase in the teen birth rate for 2006 (41.9).

8. Monitoring the Future Survey.

9. Uniform Crime Reports 2003.

10. U.S. Census Bureau 2006a.

11. Most of the rigorous, nationally representative research has focused on children living in single-parent households resulting from divorce or unmarried childbearing. One notable exception is a study (Biblarz and Gottainer 2000) that used pooled national data from 1972 through 1996 to focus on five family types, including a single-mother family caused by the death of the father.

12. The research literature relevant to children's experiences in single-parent families is extremely diverse; it varies depending on the studies' questions and design—especially

how family structure is measured. Recently, various studies have systematically compared child outcomes across family types, although these studies vary in ways that make it difficult to draw definitive conclusions. Also, researchers have recently looked beyond family composition to examine family processes (e.g., monitoring, interparental decisionmaking and conflict, parental support) by which different family configurations affect children (Cookston 1999; Demo and Acock 1996; Demuth and Brown 2004; Kleist 1999).

13. Cherlin 1999.

14. Wallerstein and Blakeslee 1989; Wallerstein and Lewis 1997.

15. Harris 1998.

16. Cherlin 1999, 422. The classic analyses on this topic were compiled by Sara McLanahan and Gary Sandefur in a 1994 volume, *Growing Up With a Single Parent.* The researchers, using multiple data sets, found that being raised in a single-parent family or stepfamily was associated with a higher probability of dropping out of high school, giving birth as a teenager, and, for young men, being idle, that is, neither in school or employed in the first few years beyond high school. Other recent researchers also conclude that shifts in family structure, whether because of family dissolution or family reconstitution, are related to poor outcomes for children, measured in various ways (Amato 2001; Duncan and Brooks-Gunn 1997; Pryor and Rodgers 2001; Ram and Hou 2003). Numerous scholars have confirmed that living with a single mother is often associated with children's delinquency, alcohol and substance use, lower self-esteem, psychiatric problems, earlier initiation of sexual intercourse, out-of-wedlock fertility, lower educational attainment, and leaving school before graduation (Manning and Lamb 2003; Marsiglio 2006; Painter and Levine 2000). In addition, although a stepfather or a mother's romantic partner can sometimes provide valuable assets to children unrelated to them (Marsiglio 2004), biological fathers are more likely to devote time, energy, and resources to their children (Cooksey and Fondell 1996). Yet, others have concluded that the configuration of the family is of less importance than family processes, or not significant at all for producing negative child outcomes (Demo and Acock 1996; Demuth and Brown 2004), or not significant once the family head's occupational status is taken into account (Biblarz and Raftery 1999).

The debate has been complicated by the mixed findings of the past fifteen years regarding African American single-mother families. Whereas some studies find the same type of negative consequences for African American youth raised in single-mother families (Paschall, Ennett, and Flewelling 1996; Rodney and Mupier 1999; Teachman, Day, Paasch, Carver, and Call 1998), others do not (Dunifon and Kowaleski-Jones 2002; Paschall, Ringwalt, and Flewelling 2003; Salem, Zimmerman, and Notaro 1998).

In a systematic and related review of the 1990s literature on children in general and children of divorce in particular, Paul Amato of Penn State University (2001, 366) provides a measured assessment underscoring the difficulties of drawing firm conclusions about individual cases.

Children with divorced parents, as a group, continue to fare more poorly than children with continuously married parents. In particular, children with divorced parents achieve lower levels of success at school, are more poorly behaved, exhibit more behavioral and emotional problems, have lower self-esteem, and experience more difficulties with interpersonal relationships. . . . [However] the average differences between children with divorced and continuously married parents are not large in absolute terms. . . . The adjustment of children following divorce depends on a variety of factors, including the level of conflict between parents before and after separation, the quality of parenting from both the custodial and noncustodial parent, changes in the child's standard of living, and the number of additional stressors to which children are exposed, such as moving or changing schools. Depending on the specific constellation of factors around the time of divorce, children may exhibit an improvement in functioning, a modest decline in functioning that improves over time, a substantial long-term decline in functioning, or little change. Knowledge of group averages, therefore, cannot predict how a particular child will adjust to family disruption.

17. Manning and Lamb 2003.

18. UNICEF 2005; Land 2007b, 14.

19. Interestingly, national polls reveal that the public tends to overestimate the pervasiveness of children's problems and to have negative perceptions of adolescents (Guzman, Lippman, Moore, and O'Hare 2003; Public Agenda 1999). To assess the statistical reality of children's level of risk, Moore, Vandivere, and Redd (2006) construct a sociodemographic risk index based on five factors (poverty, single-parent family, parents or parent with a low level of education, large family, and family not able to own or buy a home). Using this index, they find that 38 percent of children experience no risk factors and 26 percent experience only one. A total of 29 percent have either two (18%) or three (11%) of the family risk conditions. Finally, 7 percent of kids experience four (5%) or all five (2%) of the conditions. As expected, those children experiencing multiple risk factors are developing less well (Moore 2006b).

20. Abundant Assets Alliance 2005.

21. Marsh 1999.

22. Whiting 1993.

23. Scales and Leffert 1999.

24. P. Y. Martin 2003, 354.

25. Marsh 1999.

26. Hochschild 1989.

27. J. H. Pleck 1997.

28. Pleck and Masciadrelli 2004.

29. Marsiglio, Amato, Day, and Lamb 2000.

30. Kramer and Thompson 2005.

31. U.S. Department of Labor, Bureau of Labor Statistics 2005a.

32. Murray 1996; Sargent 2001.

33. U.S. Department of Labor, Bureau of Labor Statistics 2007a.

34. U.S. Department of Labor, Bureau of Labor Statistics 2005b.

35. U.S. Department of Labor, Bureau of Labor Statistics 2007a.

36. Cazeneuver 1999.

37. Greeley 2004. Though reports are less frequent, the media occasionally remind

the public of the tragedy while reiterating the slow, inadequate response by many of the top decisionmakers of the Catholic Church.

38. Wolak, Mitchell, and Finkelor 2006.

39. National Center for Missing and Exploited Children CyberTipline™.

40. Wolak, Mitchell, and Finkelor 2006.

41. Fisher 2005.

42. Louv 2005.

43. Valentine 2004, 15.

44. Furstenberg 1988; E. Pleck 2004.

45. Coleman 1987.

46. Kimmel 1996.

47. Cited in Kimmel 1996, 168.

48. Kimmel 1996.

49. Cited in Kimmel 1996, 168.

50. Cited in Kimmel 1996, 169.

51. Cited in Kimmel 1996, 70.

52. Mechling (2001) provides a nuanced historical account of the string of court cases culminating in the Supreme Court's 5–4 decision on June 28, 2000, stipulating that the Boy Scouts of America, as a private organization, was free to deny access to persons whose presence would detract from the organization's philosophical message. Part of the Boy Scouts' official response to the Supreme Court decision included the following: "We believe an avowed homosexual is not a role model for the values espoused in the Scout Oath and Law. Boy Scouting makes no effort to discover the sexual orientation of any person. Scouting's message is compromised when prospective leaders present themselves as role models inconsistent with Boy Scouting's understanding of the Scout Oath and Law" (cited in Mechling 2001, 214).

53. Mechling 2001, 227.

54. Iowa State University, University Extension, 4-H Youth Development. 4-H history.

55. Iowa State University, University Extension, 4-H Youth Development. Learn about 4-H.

56. Wessel and Wessel 1982; National 4-H Headquarters 2005.

57. Van Auken and Van Auken 2001.

58. Fine's (1987) ethnographic study of the subculture of Little League baseball during the late 1970s provides an insightful analysis of how men, as coaches, attempt to teach skills and build character in young boys. Although the study focuses primarily on revealing the dimensions of boy culture as expressed in formalized youth sport, Fine also comments on how men participate in defining and managing the "moral order" for boys.

59. T. Martin 2003; MacPherson 2003.

60. National Education Association 2004.

61. Sargent 2001.

62. McCarthy 1998.

63. U.S. Department of Labor, Bureau of Labor Statistics 2006–2007a.

64. Center for the Childcare Workforce 2002.

65. Center for the Childcare Workforce 2002.

66. Puzzanchera, Stahl, Finnegan, Tierney, and Synder 2004.

67. U.S. Department of Labor, Bureau of Labor Statistics 2006–2007b.

68. Strommen, Jones, and Rahn 2001.

69. U.S. Department of Labor Statistics 2007b. See also, Foster-Bey, Dietz, and Grimm 2006.

70. U.S. Census Bureau 2006b.

71. Dote, Cramer, Dietz, and Grimm 2006. See also Corporation for National and Community Service 2006.

72. National 4-H Headquarters 2005.

73. Cary 2004.

74. Pop Warner Little Scholars, Inc. 2007.

75. Boy Scouts of America 2005.

76. Boys & Girls Clubs of America 2008.

77. Personal communication with Pat Wellen, director of research for the National Boy Scouts Office, pwellen@netbsa.org.

CHAPTER 3. SOCIAL PLACES

1. I follow Gieryn's (2000) theorizing by distinguishing between "place" and "space." The former has three distinct features. First, a place has finitude, though its boundaries are elastic and can be negotiated at times. A place could be a van, building, neighborhood, the wilderness, etc. Second, "place is stuff" meaning it has a physicality, that is, there are objects and tangible aspects to a particular location. Some places are present naturally, others are built. It is through these material forms that social life occurs. Third, a place is assigned meaning and value. People imagine, negotiate, feel, understand, and talk about places. Gieryn also asserts that space differs from place because the former is "more properly conceived as abstract geometries (distance, direction, size, shape, volume) detached from material form and cultural interpretation. . . . place is space filled up by people, practices, objects, and representations" (p. 465).

2. Valentine 2004.

3. Marsiglio, Roy, and Fox 2005.

4. Louv 2005.

5. Louv 2005, 97.

6. Marsiglio 2004.

7. Daly 1996, 46.

8. Mechling 2001.

CHAPTER 4. MEN'S MOTIVES

1. Hewlett 2004.

2. Parke 2002.

3. Adams and Coltrane, 2005; Salomone 2003; Thorne 1993.

4. Pleck and Masciadrelli 2004.

5. Adams and Coltrane 2005.

6. Chodorow 1978.

7. Wells-Wilbon and Holland 2001.

8. Gerson 1993, 61.

9. David and Brannon 1976.

10. Pollack 1998; see also Kindlon and Thompson 1999. Geoffrey Canada (1998), the noted child advocate and CEO of Harlem's Children's Zone, Inc., uses an autobiographical storytelling approach to illustrate how aspects of the boy code shaped his life while growing up in poverty in the Bronx.

11. Kimmel 1994.

12. Connell 2000.

13. The Disney Channel often produces comedic series and movies targeting "tweens" (adolescents ages 10–14) that include as one of their main characters an emotionally open, respectful, easygoing boy who resists peer pressure and is not driven by the standard of the boy code. Several examples include the comedies *Phil of the Future* (Summer 2004–Fall 2006) and *That's So Raven* (Winter 2003–Winter 2007) and the made for TV movie series *High School Musical* (2006 and 2007).

14. Kindlon and Thompson 1999.

15. Marsiglio and Hutchinson 2002; Marsiglio 2006.

16. De St. Aubin, McAdams, and Kim 2004.

17. Snarey 1993, 19.

18. Kotre 1984.

19. Although lifespan theorists, including Snarey (1993), tend to define societal generativity as involving adults' care for younger adults, I extend this notion by suggesting that men with generative feelings can strive to establish close ties with children and adolescents who are not their offspring in varied ways and in diverse contexts.

20. Erikson 1975.

CHAPTER 5. RELATING TO KIDS

1. Pleck and Masciadrelli 2004.

2. LaRossa 2005.

3. Morrow and Styles 1995, 89.

4. Kimmel 1994.

5. Messner 1992.

6. Guide to Safe Scouting.

7. Swidler 1986.

8. Collins 1988, 2004.

9. Bly 2004.

10. Coltrane 1996; Connell 1995; Kimmel 1995.

11. Gilmore 1990.

12. Majors 1994; Mills 2000.

13. Majors 1994, 313.

CHAPTER 6. MANAGING KIDS

1. CBS News 2006. The guards were acquitted of manslaughter; the defense argued that the boy's death was due to undiagnosed sickle cell trait.

2. I am grateful to one of my research assistants, Jessica Libbey, who brought this issue to my attention. She noted how grateful she was that she had been able to discuss comfortably with a male coach issues involving her menstruation.

3. Marsiglio, Amato, Day, and Lamb 2000.

4. Barrett, Annis, and Riffey 2004.

CHAPTER 7. MAKING A DIFFERENCE

1. Amato 1998; Furstenberg 1998; Furstenberg and Hughes 1995; Marsiglio and Cohan 2000; Seltzer 1998.

2. Coleman 1987, 1988, 1990.

3. Mortimer and Larson 2002.

4. Coleman 1987, 37.

5. Coleman 1987, 38.

6. An example of such activist groups is MAD DADS Inc. (Men Against Destruction Defending Against Drugs and Social Disorder), founded in 1989 by eighteen men in Omaha, Nebraska, has generated more than sixty chapters in sixteen states. The organization's mission is to "seek out, encourage, motivate, and guide committed men in the struggle to save children, communities, and ourselves from the social ills that presently plague neighborhoods." The organization's neighborhood groups work to curb crime and drug use while keeping children safe. Although it appears that most members are fathers, men without their own children are welcome. Being involved in a group with this type of collective identity increases men's visibility in the community and can potentially influence their personal relations with neighborhood kids, their own as well as others. In the process, group members help shape the kinds of social capital they construct for particular youth. See maddads.com.

7. Marsiglio and Cohan 2000.

CHAPTER 8. MEN AND MENTORING

1. Freedman 1999.

2. Cited in Hamilton 1990, 156.

3. Baruch and Stutman 2003, 38.

4. Freedman 1999; see also Rhodes and DuBois 2006.

5. Freedman 1999.

6. Freedman 1999, 42.

7. Bellah, Madsen, Sullivan, Swidler, and Tipton 1985.

8. Coleman 1987, 36.

9. Halpern 1999.

10. Garbarino, Dubrow, Kostelny, and Pardo 1992.

11. Freedman 1999.

12. Wilson 1987.

13. Hamer 2005.

14. Anderson 1990; Duneier 1992.

15. Anderson 1990, 3.

16. Freedman 1999, 47.

17. Majors and Billson 1990.

18. Du Bois 1899/1967, 317.

19. Duneier 1992, 124.

20. Jencks 1991.

21. Duneier 1992, 127.

22. Luker 1997.

23. Freedman 1999.

24. Dortch 2000.

25. 100 Black Men of America, Inc.

26. In Zimmerman, Bingenheimer, and Notaro's 2002 study of 770 predominately African American eighth graders living in a midwestern city in 1994, with GPAs of 3.0 or lower, 53 percent of the participants reported having a natural mentor. Thirty-six percent of those indicating they had a mentor described the person as an extended-family member (e.g., aunt, uncle, cousin, or grandparent); thus a significant percentage reported mentors outside their extended kin network. About 11 percent of the natural mentors identified were professionals. Other adults develop mentoring relationships with youth through some sort of volunteer effort arranged under the auspices of an organization like the Big Brothers Big Sisters.

27. Rhodes and DuBois 2006; see also Child Trends 2007 for a guide to effective mentoring and tutoring programs for youth, many of which include male youth workers.

28. Roaf, Tierney, and Hunte 1994.

29. Chambliss 2001.

30. DuBois, Holloway, Valentine, and Cooper 2002.

31. DuBois, Holloway, Valentine, and Cooper 2002.

32. DuBois, Holloway, Valentine, and Cooper 2002, 187–188.

33. Tierney and Grossman 2000.

34. Grossman and Rhodes 2002.

35. Levine, Murphy, and Wilson 1993.

36. Ballasy 2004.

37. Blackman 1999; Garringer 2004; Jocovy 2000.

38. Barrett, Annis, and Riffey 2004; Beiswinger 1985.

39. Furano, Roaf, Styles, and Branch 1993; Roaf, Tierney, and Hunte 1994.

40. Furano, Roaf, Styles, and Branch 1993.

41. Roaf, Tierney, and Hunt 1994.

42. Garringer 2004; Blackman 1999.

43. Hopkins 2000.

44. Freedman 1999.

45. Anderson 1990.

46. Freedman 1999.

47. Hopkins 2000.

48. Hamilton 1990.

49. Hamilton 1990, 60–61; see also Hamilton and Hamilton 2004.

50. Blackman 1999.

51. Garringer 2004.

52. Levine, Murphy, and Wilson 1993.

53. Freedman 1999.

54. Blackman 1999.

55. Garrington 2004.

56. Blackman 1999; Garrington 2004.

57. Styles and Morrow's 1992 study included 26 mentor-youth pairs (10 male-male, 14 female-female, 2 female mentor–male child). At about three and a half months into the mentoring relationship, an interviewer separately asked the mentor and youth open-ended questions about their relationship. Second interviews were conducted roughly nine months later. Researchers studied: what types of activities the mentors and youths shared; what they talked about; the positive and negative aspects of how their relationship developed; and indicators of mentors' and youths' level of satisfaction. For both mentors and youths, indicators of satisfaction included feelings of liking, attachment, and commonality, as well as commitment to seeing the relationship continue. In addition, mentors' satisfaction was assessed by whether they felt appreciated. The youths' satisfaction took into account their feelings of whether their mentor was a source of social support for them. Researchers tried to identify the most effective practices in helping relationships develop in a productive way.

58. Styles and Morrow 1992, iii.

59. Styles and Morrow 1992, v.

60. Morrow and Styles 1995.

61. Morrow and Styles 1995.

62. Mecartney, Styles, and Morrow 1994; Styles and Morrow 1992.

63. Sherrod 1987; Walker 1994.

64. De Garis 2000; Dolgin 2001.

65. Styles and Morrow 1992, 44.

66. Canada 1998; Freedman 1999.

67. Baruch and Stutman 2003.

CHAPTER 9. PUBLIC AND PRIVATE LIVES

1. E. Pleck 2004.

2. Diamond 2007; Parke 1996.

3. Griswold 1993.

4. Doucet 2006, 141.

5. LaRossa 1988, 1997.

6. Hewlett 2004.

7. Lupton and Barclay 1997.

8. Marsiglio, Amato, Day, and Lamb 2000; E. Pleck 2004.

9. Lupton and Barclay 1997.

10. Hewlett 2004.

11. Griswold 1993; Lamb 2000; LaRossa 1997; Mintz 1998; E. Pleck 2004; Rotundo 1985; Stearns 1991.

12. Coltrane 1996.

13. Lamb, Pleck, Charnov, and Levine 1985, 1987; Marsiglio, Day, and Lamb 2000; Marsiglio 2004; Palkovitz 1997; Pleck and Masciadrelli 2004; Pleck and Stueve 2001.

14. Strauss and Goldberg 1999.

15. De St. Aubin, McAdams, and Kim 2004.

16. Erikson 1975.

17. My efforts to explore how men's involvement in youth work affects their fathering experience is tangentially connected to research focusing on the links between men's civic engagement (e.g., church, sports groups, cultural activities, and organizations with a fraternal, professional, or service focus) and father involvement (Sikkink and Wilcox 2005). Using national survey data, these researchers argue that the "values, virtues, and social integration associated with civic institutions are conducive to a strong paternal orientation among residential fathers" (p. 13). They also suggest that this pattern is particularly strong for father involvement in youth-related activities and that the benefits of civic engagement are most prominent for lower-income fathers.

CHAPTER 10. PERSONAL GROWTH

1. De St. Aubin, McAdams, and Kim 2004.

2. Although researchers have not studied how doing youth work influences men's fathering or adult development, some have explored how involved fathering affects adult development (Palkovitz 2002).

CHAPTER 11. YOUTH WORK DOMAINS

1. Jensen 1998.

2. Cameron 2001; Mills 2000; Mills, Martino, and Lingard 2004; Owen, Cameron, and Moss 1998; Pringle 1998; Rice and Goessling 2005.

3. Cameron 2001; Cameron and Moss 1998; Finkelhor and Williams, with Burns 1988; Sumsion 2005; see also Mills 2003.

4. Cameron 2001.

5. Allan 1993.

6. Cameron and Moss 1998.

7. Cameron 2001.

8. Finkelhor and Williams, with Burns 1988; Pringle 1992, 1998.

9. Murray 1996.

10. King 1998; Nelson 2002; Rice and Goessling 2005; Sargent 2000.

11. Dee 2006; Kindlon and Thompson 1999; Mead 2006; Mercer 2006; Mills 2000, 2003; Pollack 1998; Sadker and Sadker 1994; Sommers 2000.

12. Chiarella 2006; Tyre 2006; Whitmire 2006, see also Killion 2006; Mercer 2006.

13. Kimmel 1996.

14. See Salomone (2003) for a detailed review of the diverse issues involving possible gendered learning patterns and implications of same-sex schooling.

15. Francis 2000; Mills, Martino, and Lingard 2004; Skelton 2001.

16. S. Mead, 2006, 19.

17. Krieg 2005; Martin and Marsh 2005.

18. A. Martin 2002.

19. Dee 2006.

20. Ladson-Billings 1995.

21. Sargent 2001.

22. King 1998.

23. Kindlon and Thompson 1999, 48.

24. Rice and Goessling 2005.

25. Puzzanchera, Stahl, Finnegan, Tierney, and Synder 2004.

26. See Strommen, Jones, and Rahn 2001 for a practical guide to youth ministry work.

27. Bauldry and Hartmann 2004.

28. According to Goode and Smith (2005, 1) the West African word "Amachi" means, "who knows but what God has brought us through this child?" Although none of the religious leaders specifically referred to the Amachi model, this approach provides faith-based leaders a worthwhile opportunity to reach beyond their borders and coordinate mentoring activities with community organizations. As of July 2005, this program, designed to help the children of prisoners, had partnered with over 1,000 faith organizations located in 100 cities in 38 states. Its motto, "people of faith mentoring children of promise," highlights the prospects of adults contributing to kids so they can make a future for themselves and avoid repeating their parents' mistakes (p. 2). Religious leaders can tap into this model and partner with a correctional facility as well as with the Big Brothers Big Sisters association. A large proportion of prisoners are men, therefore male mentors for prisoners' children are in high demand. These kids may be best motivated by *male* religious figures.

29. Stommen, Jones, and Rahn 2001.

CHAPTER 12. MOVING FORWARD

1. European Union Council Recommendation on Child Care, 1992, Article 6 (cited in Cameron 2001, 437).

2. Cameron 2001; Cushman 2005; Martino and Frank 2006; Mills 2000; Mills, Martino, and Lingard 2004; Odih 2002; Sumsion 2005.

3. Hewlett 2004.

4. Hewlett 1991.

5. Pleck, Lamb, and Levine 1986; Lamb 2004.

6. Commentators have highlighted the increasing prominence of two distinct "faces of fatherhood" in the United States in recent decades: fathers who are more attentive and

nurturing to their children than their own fathers were to them, and the large number of "dead-beat" dads who have little or no contact with their children (Furstenberg 1988).

7. Blankenhorn 1995.

8. Ehrenreich 1983.

9. The participants tend to use phrases like "hip-hop music" or "hip-hop culture" when referring to the broad, powerful cultural force they believe negatively affects kids. Yet, at least some appear to register their harshest indictment for the more narrow type of gangsta rap some social commentators characterize as a particularly destructive and divisive brand of misogynistic masculinity (hooks 2004).

10. Kittilson 2006. In 1997, 42.7 percent of Sweden's representatives to Parliament were women, whereas 13.3 percent of the members of the United States House of Representatives were women.

11. Daune-Richard and Mahon 2001; Hort 1997.

12. Building on his ethnographic study of Boy Scout leaders but drawing conclusions beyond that setting, Mechling (2001, 226) presents a detailed, sober analysis of his provocative questions "Can a homosexual adult male be an appropriate role model for a heterosexual teen?" and "Can a heterosexual male leader be an appropriate role model for a gay teen?" On both accounts he concludes, "yes," if the man models "what it means to be a 'good man.'" I agree.

13. Coltrane 1996.

14. Messner 1992, 2002.

15. Hamilton 1990.

16. Kimmel 1994.

17. Townsend 1998.

18. Finkelhor 1994; Finkelhor and Jones 2004.

19. Neal 2006; Stearns 2003.

20. For example, the National Fatherhood Initiative's relatively recent progam, Double Duty Dad™, encourages experienced fathers to mentor kids who lack active fathers (Mathewes 2006).

21. Such thinking extends what sociologist Patricia Hill-Collins (2000) describes as "othermothering," common in low-income African American communities. Although Hill-Collins focuses primarily on how networks of extended female kin share responsibilities for one another's children in a familial context, one can imagine a much broader, less-well defined constellation of men—those with and without their own children—expressing tacit obligations to help youth. Critical to this perspective is the notion that adults are willing to organize themselves to help kids who are not their own.

22. Letiecq and Koblinsky 2004.

23. Doucet 2000, 2006.

APPENDIX A. REFLECTIONS ON STUDY METHODOLOGY AND FUTURE RESEARCH

1. See Charmaz 2002 and Silverman 1993 for more elaborate discussions about alternative strategies for interpreting qualitative interview data. In describing how researchers can analyze and represent participants' experiences, Charmaz distinguishes between con-

structionist and objectivist forms of grounded theory and Silverman emphasizes competing assumptions associated with positivism and interactionism.

2. Marsiglio, Roy, and Fox 2005.

3. Gergon 1999, 2001.

4. Kimmel, Hearn, and Connell 2005.

5. West and Zimmerman 1987.

6. G. Mead 1934; Stryker 1980.

7. Elder 1998.

8. Erikson 1975.

9. De St. Aubin, McAdams, and Kim 2004; Snarey 1993.

10. Marsiglio and Hutchinson 2002; Marsiglio 2004.

11. Schwable and Wokomir 2002.

12. Schwable and Wokomir 2002.

13. Van den Hoonard 1997.

14. Dey 2003, 86.

15. Strauss and Corbin 1998.

16. Lincoln and Guba 1985.

17. Charmaz 2006.

18. Emerson, Fretz, and Shaw 1995.

19. Doucet 2000, 2006.

References

Abundant Assets Alliance (2005). Developmental assets: Essential building blocks of human development. www.abundantassets.org (accessed May 28, 2005).

Adams, M., and Coltrane, S. (2005). Boys and men in families: The domestic production of gender, power, and privilege. In M. S. Kimmel, J. Hearn, and R. W. Connell, eds., *Handbook of studies on men and masculinities* (pp. 230–248). Thousand Oaks, CA: Sage.

Allan, J. (1993). Male elementary teachers: Experiences and perspectives. In C. L. Williams, ed., *Doing "women's work": Men in nontraditional occupations* (pp. 113–127). Thousand Oaks, CA: Sage.

Amato, P. R. (1998). More than money? Men's contributions to their children's lives. In A. Booth and N. Crouter, eds., *Men in families. When do they get involved? What difference does it make?* (pp. 241–278). Mahwah, NJ: Erlbaum.

——— (2001). Children of divorce in the 1990s: An update of the Amato and Keith (1991) Meta-Analysis. *Journal of Family Psychology* 15: 355–370.

Anderson, E. (1990). *Streetwise: Race, class, and change in an urban community.* Chicago: University of Chicago Press.

Ballasy, L. (2004). *Marketing for the recruitment of mentors: A workbook for finding and attracting volunteers.* Portland, OR: Northwest Regional Educational Laboratory.

Barrett, B., Annis, A., and Riffey, D. (2004). *Little moments, big magic: Inspirational stories of Big Brothers and Big Sisters and the magic they create.* Gilbert, AZ: Magical Moments Publishing.

Baruch, R., and Stutman, S. (2003). The yin and yang of resilience. In E. H. Grotberg, ed., *Resilience for today: Gaining strength from adversity* (pp. 31–52). Westport, CN: Praeger.

Bauldry, S., and Hartmann, T. A. (2004). *The promise and challenge of mentoring high-risk youth: Findings from the National Faith-Based Initiative.* Philadelphia: Public/Private Ventures.

Beiswinger, G. L. (1985). *One to one: The story of the Big Brothers Big Sisters movement in America.* Philadelphia: Big Brothers Big Sisters of America.

Bellah, R., Madsen, R., Sullivan, W. M., Swidler, A., and Tipton, S. M. (1985). *Habits of the heart: Individualism and commitment in American life.* Berkeley: University of California Press.

Biblarz, T. J., and Gottainer, G. (2000). Family structure and children's success: A comparison of widowed and divorced single-mother families. *Journal of Marriage and the Family* 62: 533–548.

Biblarz, T. J., and Raftery, A. E. (1999). Family structure, educational attainment, and socioeconomic success: Rethinking the "pathology of matriarchy." *American Journal of Sociology* 105: 321–365.

Blackman, S. T. (1999). *Recruiting male volunteers: A guide based on exploratory research.* Washington, DC: Corporation for National and Community Service. www.energizeinc .com/download/blackman.pdf (accessed May 16, 2005).

Blankenhorn, D. (1995). *Fatherless America: Confronting our most urgent social problem.* New York: Basic Books.

Bly, R. (2004). *Iron John: A book about men.* Cambridge, MA: Da Capo Press.

Boys & Girls Clubs of America (2008). www. bgca.org/(accessed Dec. 2007).

Boy Scouts of America (2005). Year in review. www.scouting.org/nav/enter.jsp?s=mc (accessed May 24, 2007).

Cameron, C. (2001). Promise or problem? A review of the literature on men working in early childhood services. *Gender, Work and Organization* 8: 430–453.

Cameron, C., and Moss, P. (1998). Men as carers for children: An introduction. In C. Owen, C. Cameron, and P. Moss, eds., *Men as workers in services for young children: Issues of a mixed-gender workforce* (pp. 11–28). London: Thomas Coram Research Unit, Institute of Education, University of London.

Canada, G. (1998). *Reaching up for manhood: Transforming the lives of boys in America.* Boston: Beacon.

Cary, P. (2004). Fixing kids' sports: Rescuing children's games from crazed coaches and parents. *U.S. News and World Report* 1, June.

Cazeneuver, B. (1999). Peter Westbrook is turning inner-city kids into America's top fencers. *Sports Illustrated,* November 16.

CBS News (2006). Autopsy: Beating killed boot camp teen. May 5. www.cbsnews.com/ stories/2006/05/05/national/printable1593568.shtml (accessed May 24, 2007).

Center for the Childcare Workforce (2002). *Estimating the size and components of the U.S. child care workforce and caregiving population: Key findings from the Child Care Workforce estimate (preliminary report).* Washington, DC: Center for the Child Care Workforce.

Chambliss, W. J. (2001). *Power, politics, and crime.* Boulder, CO: Westview.

Charmaz, K. (2002). Qualitative interviewing and grounded theory analysis. In J. F. Gubrium and J. A. Holstein, eds., *Handbook of interview research: Context and method* (pp. 675–694). Thousand Oaks, CA: Sage.

——— (2006). *Constructing grounded theory: A practical guide through qualitative analysis.* Thousand Oaks, CA: Sage.

Cherlin, A. J. (1999). Going to extremes: Family structure, children's well-being, and social science. *Demography* 36: 421–428.

Chiarella, T. (2006). The problem with boys. *Esquire,* July, 94–99, 137–138.

Child Trends (2005). Child Trends Data Bank. www.childtrendsdatabank.org/tables/1 _Table_2.htm (accessed June 15, 2005).

———— (2007). Guide to effective programs for children and youth. www.childtrends
.org/Lifecourse/mentoring_menu.htm.

Chodorow, N. (1978). *The reproduction of mothering: Psychoanalysis and the socialization of gender*. Berkeley: University of California Press.

Coleman, J. S. (1987). Families and schools. *Educational Researcher* 16: 32–38.

———— (1988). Social capital in the creation of human capital. *American Journal of Sociology* 94: S95–S120.

———— (1990). *Foundations of social theory*. Cambridge: Harvard University Press.

Collins, R. (1988). *Theoretical sociology*. New York: Harcourt, Brace & Jovanovich.

———— (2004). *Interaction ritual chains*. Princeton, NJ: Princeton University Press.

Coltrane, S. (1996). *Family man: Fatherhood, housework, and gender equity*. New York: Oxford University Press.

Connell, R. W. (1995). *Masculinities*. Berkeley: University of California Press.

———— (2000). *The men and the boys*. Berkeley: University of California Press.

Cooksey, E. C., and Fondell, M. M. (1996). Spending time with his kids: Effects of family structure on fathers' and children's lives. *Journal of Marriage and the Family* 58: 693–707.

Cookston, J. T. (1999). Parental supervision and family structure: Effects on adolescent problem behaviors. *Journal of Divorce and Remarriage* 32: 107–122.

Corporation for National and Community Service (2006). *Educating for active citizenship: Service-learning, school-based service, and civic engagement*. Brief 2 in Youth Helping America Series. March. Washington, DC: Corporation for National and Community Service.

Cushman, P. (2005). It's just not a real bloke's job: Male teachers in the primary school. *Asia-Pacific Journal of Teacher Education* 33: 321–338.

Daly, K. (1996). *Families and time*. Thousand Oaks, CA: Sage.

Daune-Richard, A., and Mahon, R. (2001). Sweden: Models in crisis. In J. Jenson and M. Sineau, eds., *Who cares? Women's work, childcare, and welfare state redesign* (pp. 146–176). Toronto: University of Toronto Press.

David, D., and Brannon, R. (1976). *The forty-nine percent majority: The male sex role*. Reading, MA: Addison-Wesley.

Dee, T. S. (2006). The why chromosome: How a teacher's gender affects boys and girls. *Education Next*, Fall, 68–55, and at www.education.org (accessed August 29, 2006).

de Garis, L. (2000). Be a buddy to your buddy: Male identity, aggression, and intimacy in a boxing gym. In J. McKay, M. Messner, and D. Sabo, eds., *Masculinities, gender relations, and sport: Research on men and masculinities* (pp. 87–107). Thousand Oaks, CA: Sage.

Demo, D. H., and Acock, A. C. (1996). Family structure, family process, and adolescent well-being. *Journal of Research on Adolescence* 6: 457–488.

Demuth, S., and Brown, S. L. (2004). Family structure, family processes, and adolescent delinquency: The significance of parental absence versus parental gender. *Journal of Research in Crime and Delinquency* 41: 58–81.

de St. Aubin, E., McAdams, D. P., and Kim, T. C. (2004). *The generative society: Caring for future generations*. Washington, DC: American Psychological Association.

Dey, I. (2003). Grounded theory. In C. Seale, G. Gobo, J. Gubrium, and D. Silver, eds., *Qualitative research practice* (pp. 80–93). London: Sage.

Diamond, M. J. (2007). *My father before me: How fathers and sons influence each other throughout their lives.* New York: W. W. Norton.

Dolgin, K. G. (2001). Men's friendships: Mismeasured, demeaned, and misunderstood? In T. F. Cohen, ed., *Men and masculinity: A text reader* (pp. 103–117). Belmont, CA: Wadsworth.

Dortch, T. W., Jr. (2000). *The miracles of mentoring: How to encourage and lead future generations.* New York: Broadway Books.

Dote, L., Cramer, K., Dietz, N., and Grimm, R., Jr. (2006). *College students helping America.* Washington, DC: Corporation for National and Community Service.

Doucet, A. (2000). "There's a huge gulf between me as a male carer and women": Gender, domestic responsibility, and the community as an institutional arena. *Community, Work and Family* 3: 163–184.

——— (2006). *Do men mother? Fathering, care and domestic responsibility.* Toronto: University of Toronto Press.

DuBois, D., Holloway, B., Valentine, J., and Cooper, H. (2002). Effectiveness of mentoring programs: A meta-analytic review. *American Journal of Community Psychology* 30 (2): 157–197.

Du Bois, W. E. B. (1899/1967). *The Philadelphia Negro.* New York: Schocken Books.

Duncan, G. J., and Brooks-Gunn, J. (1997). *Consequences of growing up poor.* New York: Russell Sage Foundation.

Duneier, M. (1992). *Slim's table: Race, respectability, and masculinity.* Chicago: University of Chicago Press.

Dunifon, R., and Kowaleski-Jones, L. (2002). Who's in the house? Race differences in cohabitation, single parenthood, and child development. *Child Development* 73: 1249–1264.

Ehrenreich, B. (1983). *The hearts of men: American dreams and the flight from commitment.* New York: Anchor Books / Doubleday.

Elder, G. H., Jr. (1998). The life course and human development. In R. E. Lerner, ed., Volume 1, *Theories of human development: Contemporary perspectives* in William Damon (editor-in-chief), *The handbook of child psychology,* 5th edition (pp. 939–991). New York: Wiley.

Emerson, R. M., Fretz, R. I., and Shaw, L. L. (1995). *Writing ethnographic fieldnotes.* Chicago: University of Chicago Press.

Erikson, E. (1975). *Life history and the historical moment.* New York: W. W. Norton.

Fine, G. A. (1987). *With the boys: Little league baseball and preadolescent culture.* Chicago: University of Chicago Press.

Finkelor, D. (1994). Current information on the scope and nature of child sexual abuse. *The Future of Children* 4: 31–53.

Finkelor, D., and Jones, J. M. (2004). Explanations for the decline in child sexual abuse cases. Juvenile Justice Bulletin. Washington, DC: Office of Juvenile Justice and Delinquency Prevention, U.S. Department of Justice.

Finkelor, D., and Williams, L., with Burns, N. (1988). *Nursery crimes: Sexual abuse in day care*. Newbury Park, CA: Sage.

Fisher, L. (2005). Are our kids safe? Deaths of two girls bring sex offender issue to forefont. *Gainesville Sun*, June 12, 1A, 6A.

Forbush, W. (1901). *The boy problem: A study in social pedagogy*. Boston: Pilgrim Press.

Foster-Bey, J., Dietz, N., and Grimm, R. (2006). *Volunteers mentoring youth: Implications for closing the mentoring gap*. Youth Helping America Series. Washington, DC: Corporation for National and Community Service.

Francis, B. (2000). *Boys, girls and achievement: Addressing the classroom issues*. London: Routledge.

Freedman, M. (1999). *The kindness of strangers: Adult mentors, urban youth, and the new voluntarism*. Cambridge: Cambridge University Press.

Furano, K., Roaf, P. A., Styles, M. B., and Branch, A. Y. (1993). *Big Brothers/Big Sisters: A study of program practices*. Philadelphia: Public/Private Ventures.

Furstenberg, F. F., Jr. (1988). Good dads—bad dads: Two faces of fatherhood. In A. Cherlin, ed., *The changing American family and public policy* (pp. 193–218). Washington, DC: Urban Institute.

Furstenberg, F. F., Jr. and Hughes, M. E. (1995). Social capital and successful development among at-risk youth. *Journal of Marriage and the Family* 57: 580–592.

Garbarino, J., Dubrow, N., Kostelny, K., and Pardo, C. (1992). *Children in danger: Coping with consequences of community violence*. San Francisco: Jossey-Bass.

Garringer, M. (2004). Putting the "men" back in mentoring. *National Mentoring Center* 2: 1–8.

Gergon, K. J. (1999). *An invitation to social construction*. London: Sage.

——— (2001). *Social construction in context*. London: Sage.

Gerson, K. (1993). *No man's land: Men's changing commitments to family and work*. New York: Basic Books.

Gieryn, T. F. (2000). A space for place in sociology. *Annual Review of Sociology* 25: 463–496.

Gilmore, D. D. (1990). *Manhood in the Making: Cultural concepts of masculinity*. New Haven: Yale University Press.

Goode, W. W., and Smith, T. J. (2005). *Building from the ground up: Creating effective programs to mentor children of prisoners*. Philadelphia: Public/Private Ventures.

Greeley, A. M. (2004). *Priests: A calling in crisis*. Chicago: University of Chicago Press.

Griswold, R. (1993). *Fatherhood in America: A history*. New York: Basic Books.

Grossman, J., and Rhodes, J. (2002). The test of time: Predictors and effects of duration in youth mentoring relationships. *American Journal of Community Psychology* 30 (2): 199–219.

Guide to safe scouting, I: Youth protection and adult leadership, www.scouting.org/pubs/gss/gss01.html (accessed October 14, 2006).

Guzman, L., Lippman, L., Moore, K. A., and O'Hare, W. (2003). *How children are doing: The mismatch between public perception and statistical reality*. Washington, DC: Child Trends.

Halpern, R. (1999). *Fragile families, fragile solutions: A history of supportive services for families in poverty.* New York: Columbia University Press.

Hamer, J. F. (2005). "Gotta protect my own": Men parenting children in an abandoned city. In W. Marsiglio, K. Roy, and G. L. Fox, eds., *Situated fathering: A focus on physical and social spaces* (pp. 255–275). Latham, MD: Rowman & Littlefield.

Hamilton, S. F. (1990). *Apprenticeship for adulthood: Preparing youth for the future.* New York: Free Press.

Hamilton, S. F., and Hamilton, M. A. (2004). *The handbook of youth development: Coming of age in American communities.* Thousand Oaks, CA: Sage.

Harris, J. R. (1998). *The nurture assumption: Why children turn out the way they do.* New York: Free Press.

Hewlett, B. S. (1991). *Intimate fathers.* Ann Arbor: University of Michigan Press.

——— (2004). Fathers in forager, farmer, and pastoral cultures. In M. E. Lamb, ed., *The role of the father in child development,* 4th edition (pp. 182–195). Hoboken, NJ: Wiley.

Hill-Collins, P. (2000). Bloodmothers, othermothers and women-centered networks in African American communities. In *Black feminist thought: Knowledge, consciousness, and the politics of empowerment,* 2nd edition (pp. 178–183). New York: Routledge.

Hochschild, A. (1989). *The second shift: Working parents and the revolution at home.* New York: Viking.

hooks, bell (2004). *We real cool: Black men and masculinity.* New York: Routledge.

Hopkins, J. (2000). Signs of masculinism in an "uneasy" place: Advertising for "Big Brothers." *Gender, Place and Culture* 7: 31–55.

Hort, S. E. O. (1997). Advancing for children in the advanced welfare state: Current problems and prospects in Sweden. In G. A. Cornia and S. Danziger, eds., *Child poverty and deprivation in the industrialized countries, 1945–1995* (pp. 284–306). Oxford: Clarendon Press.

Iowa State University, University Extension, 4-H Youth Development. Learn about 4-H. www.extension.iastate.edu/4H/Hhhh.html#pledge (accessed May 24, 2007).

——— 4-H history. www.extension.iastate.edu/4h/history.html (accessed May 24, 2007).

Jencks, C. (1991). Is the American underclass growing? In C. Jencks and P. E. Peterson, eds., *The urban underclass* (pp. 28–100). Washington, DC: Brookings Institution.

Jensen, J. J. (1998). Men as workers in childcare services: A European perspective. In C. Owen, C. Cameron, and P. Moss, eds., *Men as workers in services for young children: Issues of a mixed-gender workforce* (pp. 118–131). London: Thomas Coram Research Unit, Institute of Education, University of London.

Jocovy, L. (2000). *The ABCs of school-mentoring: Technical assistant packet #1.* Portland, OR: Northwest Regional Educational Laboratory.

Killion, K. (2006). 22 school practices that may harm boys. Illiniosloop.org. Posted March 2006. www.illinoisloop.org/gender.html (accessed July 26, 2006).

Kimmel, M. (1994). Masculinity as homophobia: Fear, shame, and silence in the construction of gender identity. In H. Brod and M. Kaufman, eds., *Theorizing masculinities* (pp. 119–141). Thousand Oaks, CA: Sage.

———— (1995). *The politics of manhood: Profeminist men respond to mythopoetic men's movement (and the mythopoetic leaders answer)*. Philadelphia: Temple University Press.

———— (1996). *Manhood in America: A cultural history.* New York: Free Press.

Kimmel, M., Hearn, J., and Connell, R. W. (2005). *The handbook of studies on men and masculinities.* Thousand Oaks, CA: Sage.

Kindlon, D., and Thompson, M. (1999). *Raising Cain: Protecting the emotional life of boys.* New York: Ballantine Books.

King, J. R. (1998). *Uncommon caring: Learning from men who teach young children.* New York: Columbia University, Teachers College Press.

Kittilson, M. C. (2006). *Challenging parties, changing parliaments: Women and elected office in contemporary Western Europe.* Columbus: Ohio State University Press.

Kleist, D. M. (1999). Single-parent families: A difference that makes a difference? *The Family Journal: Counseling and Therapy for Couples and Families* 7: 373–378.

Kotre, J. (1984). *Outliving the self: Generativity and the interpretation of lives.* Baltimore: Johns Hopkins University Press.

Kramer, B. J., and Thompson, E. H., Jr. (2005). *Men as caregivers.* Amherst, NY: Prometheus Books.

Krieg, J. M. (2005). Student gender and teacher gender: What is the impact on high stakes test scores? *Current Issues in Education* 8. At cie.asu.edu/volume8/number9/index.html (accessed May 25, 2007).

Ladson-Billings, G. (1995). Towards a theory of culturally relevant pedagogy. *American Education Research Journal* 32: 465–491.

Lamb, M. E. (2000). The history of research on father involvement: An overview. *Marriage and Family Review* 29: 23–42.

———— (2004). *The role of the father in child development,* 4th edition. Hoboken, NJ: John Wiley & Sons.

Lamb, M. E., Pleck, J. H., Charnov, E. L., and Levine, L. A. (1985). Paternal behavior in humans. *American Zoologist* 25: 883–894.

———— (1987). A biosocial perspective on paternal behavior and involvement. In J. B. Lancaster, J. Altmann, A. S. Rossi, and L. R. Sherrod, eds., *Parenting across the lifespan: Biosocial dimensions* (pp. 111–142). Hawthorne, NY: Aldine de Gruyter.

Land, K. C. (2007a). *The Foundation for Child Development Child and Youth Well-Being Index (CWI), 1975–2005, with Projections for 2006.* Duke University. www.soc.duke.edu/~cwi/ (accessed September 17, 2007).

Land, K. C. (2007b). 2007 child well-being index (CWI) special focus report on international comparisons. Duke University. www.fcd-us.org/usr_doc/2007CWIIntlReport.pdf.

LaRossa, R. (1988). Fatherhood and social change. *Family Relations* 37: 451–457.

———— (1997). *The modernization of fatherhood: A social and political history.* Chicago: University of Chicago Press.

———— (2005). "Until the ball glows in the twilight": Fatherhood, baseball, and the game of playing catch. In W. Marsiglio, K. Roy, and G. L. Fox, eds., *Situated fathering: A focus on physical and social spaces* (pp. 141–161). Latham, MD: Rowman & Littlefield.

Lerner, R. M. (1995). *America's youth in crisis: Challenges and options for programs and policies*. Thousand Oaks, CA: Sage.

Letiecq, B. L., and Koblinsky, S. A. (2004). Parenting in violent neighborhoods: African American fathers share strategies for keeping children safe. *Journal of Family Issues* 25: 715–734.

Levine, J. A., Murphy, D. T., and Wilson, S. (1993). *Getting men involved: Strategies for early childhood programs*. New York: Families and Work Institute.

Lincoln, Y., and Guba, E. (1985). *Naturalistic inquiry*. Beverly Hills, CA: Sage.

Louv, R. (2005). *Last child in the woods: Saving our children from nature-deficit disorder*. New York: Algonquin Books.

Luker, K. (1997). *Dubious conceptions: The politics of teenage pregnancy*. Cambridge: Harvard University Press.

Lupton, D., and Barclay, L. (1997). *Constructing fatherhood: Discourses and experiences*. Thousand Oaks, CA: Sage.

MacPherson, K. (2003). Study finds few male, minority teachers. August 28. Post-Gazette.com. Pittsburgh, PA. www.post-gazette.com/pg/03240/215857.stm (accessed May 24, 2007).

Mad Dads Against Destruction Defending Against Drugs and Social Disorder. maddads.com/ (accessed June 24, 2006).

Majors, R. G. (1994). Conclusion and recommendations: A reason for hope—an overview of the new black male movement in the United States. In R. G. Majors and J. U. Gordon, eds., *The American black male: His present status and his future*. Chicago: Nelson-Hall.

Majors, R., and Billson, J. M. (1990). *Cool pose: The dilemmas of black manhood in America*. New York: Simon & Schuster.

Manning, W. D., and Lamb, K. A. (2003). Adolescent well-being in cohabiting, married, and single-parent families. *Journal of Marriage and Family* 65: 876–893.

Marsh, P. E. (1999). What does camp do for kids? A meta-analysis of the influence of the organized camping experience on the self-constructs of youth. Master of Science thesis. Recreation and Park Administration, School of Health, Physical Education, and Recreation. Indiana University.

Marsiglio, W. (2004). *Stepdads: Stories of love, hope, and repair*. Latham, MD: Rowman & Littlefield.

—— (2006). Young men and teen pregnancy: A review of sex, contraception, and fertility-related issues. In W. Marsiglio, A. Ries, F. Sonenstein, F. Troccoli, and W. Whitehead. *It's a guy thing: Boys, young men, and teen pregnancy prevention* (pp. 9–100). Washington, DC: National Campaign to Prevent Teen Pregnancy.

Marsiglio, W., Amato, P., Day, R. D., and Lamb, M. E. (2000). Scholarship on fatherhood in the 1990s and beyond. *Journal of Marriage and the Family* 62: 1173–1191.

Marsiglio, W., and Cohan, M. (2000). Contextualizing father involvement and paternal influence: Sociological and qualitative themes. *Marriage and Family Review* 29: 75–95.

Marsiglio, W., Day, R. D., and Lamb, M. E. (2000). Exploring fatherhood diversity: Implications for conceptualizing father involvement. *Marriage and Family Review* 29: 269–293.

Marsiglio, W., and Hutchinson, S. (2002). *Sex, men, and babies: Stories of awareness and responsibility.* New York: New York University Press.

Marsiglio, W., Roy, K., and Fox, G. L. (2005). Situated fathering: A spatially sensitive and social approach. In W. Marsiglio, K. Roy, and G. L. Fox, eds., *Situated fathering: A focus on physical and social spaces* (pp. 3–26). Latham, MD: Rowman & Littlefield.

Martin, A. J. (2002). *Improving the educational outcomes of boys.* Report on ACT Department of Education, Youth and Family Services. Canberra, Australia.

Martin, A., and Marsh, H. (2005). Motivating boys and motivating girls: Does teacher gender really make a difference? *Australian Journal of Education* 49: 320–334.

Martin, P. Y. (2003). "Said and done" versus "saying and doing": Gendering practices, practicing gender at work. *Gender and Society* 17: 342–366.

Martin, T. (2003). Male teachers remain a rarity. Educators: More men needed for healthy balance. *Lansing State Journal,* September 25. ed-web3.educ.msu.edu/news/news-briefs/03/maleteachers.htm (accessed August 12, 2006).

Martino, W., and Frank, Blye. (2006). The tyranny of surveillance: Male teachers and the policing of masculinities in a single-sex school. *Gender and Education* 18: 17–33.

Mathewes, J. (2006). Double Duty Dad™: Dads helping dads, helping kids. *Fatherhood Today* (newsletter of National Fatherhood Initiative) 11: 1, 10.

McCarthy, C. (1998). True heroes. www.aliciapatterson.org/APF1901/McCarthy/McCarthy.html (accessed September 14, 2007).

McLanahan, S., and Sandefur, G. (1994). *Growing up with a single parent: What hurts, what helps.* Cambridge: Harvard University Press.

McWhirter, J. J., McWhirter, B. T., McWhirter, A. M., and McWhirter, H. E. (1995). Youth at risk: Another point of view. *Journal of Counseling and Development* 73: 567–569.

Mead, G. H. (1934). *Mind, self, and society: From the standpoint of a social behaviorist.* Chicago: University of Chicago Press.

Mead, S. (2006). The evidence suggests otherwise: The truth about boys and girls. www.educationsector.org/usr_doc/ESO_BoysAndGirls.pdf#search= Educationsector.org (accessed July 24, 2006).

Mecartney, C. A., Styles, M. B., and Morrow, K. V. (1994). *Mentoring in the juvenile justice system: Findings from two pilot programs.* Philadelphia: Public/Private Ventures.

Mechling, J. (2001). *On my honor: Boy Scouts and the making of American youth.* Chicago: University of Chicago Press.

Mercer, I. (2006). Shafting boys. Worldnetdaily. Posted January 27, 2006. www.wnd.com/news/article.asp?ARTICLE_ID=48527 (accessed July 26, 2006).

Messner, M. A. (1992). *Power at play: Sports and the problem of masculinity.* Boston: Beacon Press.

——— (2002). *Taking the field: Women, men, and sports.* Minneapolis: University of Minnesota Press.

Mills, M. (2000). Issues in implementing boys' programme in schools: Male teachers and empowerment. *Gender and Education* 12: 221–238.

——— (2003). Shaping the boys' agenda: The backlash blockbusters. *International Journal of Inclusive Education* 7: 57–73.

Mills, M., Martino, W., and Lingard, B. (2004). Attracting, recruiting and retaining male teachers: Policy issues in the male teacher debate. *British Journal of Sociology of Education* 25: 355–369.

Mintz, S. (1998). From patriarchy to androgyny and other myths: Placing men's family roles in historical perspective. In A. Booth and A. C. Crouter, eds., *Men in families: Why do they get involved? What difference does it make?* (pp. 3–30). Mahwah, NJ: Erlbaum.

Monitoring the Future Survey. University of Michigan News Service. www .monitoringthefuture.org/pressreleases/04drugpr.pdf (accessed August 12, 2006).

Moore, K. A. (2006a). *Defining the term "at-risk."* Brief: Research-to-Results. October, #2006–12. Washington, DC: Child Trends.

——— (2006b). *Cumulative risks among American children.* Brief: Research-to-Results. October, #2006–13. Washington, DC: Child Trends.

Moore, K. A., Vandivere, S., and Redd, Z. (2006). A sociodemographic risk index. *Social Indicators Research* 75: 45–81.

Morrow, K. V., and Styles, M. B. (1995). *Building relationships with youth in program settings: A study of Big Brothers Big Sisters.* Philadelphia: Public/Private Ventures.

Mortimer, J. T., and Larson, R. W. (2002). *The changing adolescent experience: Societal trends and the transition to adulthood.* Cambridge: Cambridge University Press.

Murray, S. B. (1996). "We all love Charles": Men in child care and the social construction of gender. *Gender and Society* 10: 368–385.

National Campaign to Prevent Teen Pregnancy (2006). Teen birth rates in the United States, 1940–2004. www.teenpregnancy.org/resources/data/pdf/BirthRatesOnePager .pdf (accessed August 12, 2006).

——— (2008). Teen birth rate increase 2006: Some thoughts from the National Campaign to prevent teen and unplanned pregnancy. www.thenationalcampaign.org/ resources/pdf/nchs_statement1.pdf.

National Center for Education Statistics (2006). Digest of Education Statistics, 2006. Chapter 2. Elementary and Secondary Education. nces.ed.gov/pubs2007/ 2007017_2a.pdf (accessed September 17, 2007).

National Center for Missing and Exploited Children CyberTipline. www.missingkids .com/en_US/documents/Presskit_CyberTipline.pdf (accessed May 25, 2007).

National Education Association (2004). Are male teachers on the road to extinction? National teacher day 2004 spotlights disappearing male teacher. www.nea.org/ newsreleases/2004/nr040428.html?mode.

National 4-H Headquarters (2005). 4-H Youth Development ES-237 Statistics. www.national4-hheadquarters.gov/library/2005_ES-237_stats.pdf (accessed May 24, 2007).

Neal, N. (2006). How dangerous is childhood? *Gainesville Sun*, August 13, 1G, 4G.

Nelson, B. G. (2002). *The importance of men teachers: And reasons why there are so few.* National Association for the Education of Youth and Children. Minneapolis: Men Teach and Men in Child Care and Elementary Education Project.

Odih, P. (2002). Mentors and role models: Masculinity and the educational "underachievement" of young Afro-Caribbean males. *Race, Ethnicity and Education* 5: 91–105.

100 Black Men of America, Inc. www.100blackmen.org/index.php?option=com_content &task=view&id=14&Itemid=26 (accessed May 25, 2007).

Owen, C., Cameron, C., and Moss, P. (1998). *Men as workers in services for young children: Issues of a mixed-gender workforce.* London: Thomas Coram Research Unit, Institute of Education, University of London.

Painter, G., and Levine, D. I. (2000). Family structure and youths' outcomes: Which correlations are causal? *Journal of Human Resources* 35: 524–549.

Palkovitz, R. (1997). Reconstructing "involvement": Expanding conceptualizations of men's caring in contemporary families. In A. Hawkins and D. C. Dollahite, eds., *Generative fathering: Beyond deficit perspectives* (pp. 200–216). Thousand Oaks, CA: Sage.

——— (2002). *Involved fathering and men's adult development: Provisional balances.* Mahwah, NJ: Erlbaum.

Parke, R. (1996). *Fatherhood.* Cambridge: Harvard University Press.

——— (2002). Fathers and families. In M. H. Bornstein, ed., *Handbook of parenting*, 2nd edition (vol. 3, pp. 27–73). Mahwah, NJ: Erlbaum.

Paschall, M. J., Ennett, S. T., and Flewelling, R. L. (1996). Relationships among family characteristics and violent behavior by black and white male adolescents. *Journal of Youth and Adolescence* 25: 177–197.

Paschall, M. J., Ringwalt, C. L., and Flewelling, R. L. (2003). Effects of parenting, father absence, and affiliation with delinquent peers on delinquent behavior among African-American male adolescents. *Adolescence* 38: 15–34.

Pleck, E. (2004). Two dimensions of fatherhood: A history of the good dad–bad dad complex. In M. E. Lamb, ed., *The role of the father in child development*, 4th edition (pp. 32–57). Hoboken, NJ: Wiley.

Pleck, J. H. (1997). Paternal involvement: Levels, sources, and consequences. In M. E. Lamb, ed., *The role of the father in child development* (pp. 66–103). New York: Wiley.

Pleck, J. H., Lamb, M. E., and Levine, J. A. (1986). Epilog: Facilitating future change in men's family roles. *Marriage and Family Review* 9: 11–16.

Pleck, J. H., and Masciadrelli, B. P. (2004). Paternal involvement by U.S. residential fathers: Levels, sources, and consequences. In M. E. Lamb, ed., *The role of the father in child development*, 4th edition (pp. 222–271). Hoboken, NJ: Wiley.

Pleck, J. H. and Stueve, J. J. (2001). Time and paternal involvement. In K. Daly, ed., *Minding the time in family experience: Emerging perspectives and issues* (pp. 205–226). Oxford, England: Elsevier Science.

Pollack, W. (1998). *Real boys: Rescuing our sons from the myth of boyhood.* New York: Henry Holt.

Pop Warner Little Scholars, Inc. (2007). Benefits of Participation in Pop Warner. www.popwarner.com/aboutus/benefits.asp?lable=benefits (accessed May 24, 2007).

Pringle, K. (1992). Child sexual abuse perpetuated by welfare personnel and the problem of men. *Critical Social Policy* 12: 4–19.

———— (1998). *Children social welfare in Europe.* Buckingham, England: Open University Press.

Pryor, J., and Rodgers, B. (2001). *Children in changing families: Life after parental separation.* Oxford, England: Blackwell.

Public Agenda (1999). *Kids these days '99: What Americans really think about the next generation.* New York: Public Agenda.

Puzzanchera, C., Stahl, A. L., Finnegan, T. A., Tierney, N., and Synder, H. N. (2004). *Juvenile Court Statistics 2000.* Pittsburgh, PA: National Center for Juvenile Justice.

Ram, B., and Hou, F. (2003). Changes in family structure and child outcomes: Roles of economic and familial resources. *Policy Studies Journal* 31: 309–330.

Rhodes, J. E., and DuBois, D. L. (2006). Understanding and facilitating the youth movement. *Social Policy Report* 20: 3–11, 13, 15–19.

Rice, C., and Goessling, D. P. (2005). Recruiting and retaining male special education teachers. *Remedial and Special Education* 26: 347–356.

Roaf, P. A., Tierney, J. P. , and Hunte, D. E. I. (1994). *Big Brothers / Big Sisters of America: A study of volunteer recruitment and screening.* Philadelphia: Public/Private Ventures.

Rodney, H. E., and Mupier, R. (1999). Behavioral differences between African American male adolescents with biological fathers and those without biological fathers in the home. *Journal of Black Studies* 30: 45–61.

Rotundo, E. A. (1985). American fatherhood: An historical perspective, *American Behavioral Scientist* 29: 7 25.

Sadker, M., and Sadker, D. (1994). *Failing at fairness: How our schools cheat girls.* New York: Touchstone.

Salem, D. A., Zimmerman, M. A., and Notaro, P. C. (1998). Effects of family structure, family process, and father involvement on psychosocial outcomes among African American adolescents. *Family Relations* 47: 331–341.

Salomone, R. C. (2003). *Same, different, equal: Rethinking single-sex schooling.* New Haven: Yale University Press.

Sargent, P. (2000). Real men or real teachers? Contradictions in the lives of men elementary teachers. *Men and Masculinities* 2: 410–433.

———— (2001). *Real men or real teachers? Contradictions in the lives of men elementary school teachers.* Harriman, TN: Men's Studies Press.

Scales, P. C., and Leffert, N. (1999). *Developmental assets: A synthesis of the scientific research on adolescent development.* Minneapolis: Search Institute.

Schwalbe, M., and Wolkomir, M. (2002). Interviewing men. In J. F. Gubrium and J. A. Holstein, eds., *Handbook of interview research: Context and method* (pp. 203–219). Thousand Oaks, CA: Sage.

Seltzer, J. (1998). Men's contributions to children and social policy. In A. Booth and N. Crouter, eds., *Men in families: When do they get involved? What difference does it make?* (pp. 303–314). Mahwah, NJ: Erlbaum.

Sherrod, D. (1987). The bonds of men: Problems and possibilities in close male relationships. In H. Brod, ed., *The making of masculinities: The new men's studies* (pp. 213–239). Boston: Allen & Unwin.

Sikkink, D., and Wilcox, W. B. (2005). Bowling together: Civic engagement, income, and paternal involvement. Unpublished manuscript. Department of Sociology, University of Notre Dame.

Silverman, D. (1993). *Interpreting qualitative data: Methods for analysing talk, text and interaction.* London: Sage.

Skelton, C. (2001). *Schooling the boys: Masculinities and primary education.* Buckingham, England: Open University Press.

Snarey, J. (1993). *How fathers care for the next generation: A four-decade study.* Cambridge: Harvard University Press.

Sommers, C. H. (2000). *The war against boys.* New York: Simon & Schuster.

Stearns, P. N. (1991). Fatherhood in historical perspective: The role of social change. In F. W. Bozett and S. M. H. Hansen, eds., *Fatherhood and families in social context* (pp. 28–52). New York: Springer.

——— (2003). *A history of modern childrearing in America.* New York: New York University Press.

Strauss, A. L., and Corbin, J. (1998). *Basics of qualitative research: Techniques and procedures for developing grounded theory,* 2nd edition. Thousand Oaks, CA: Sage.

Strauss, R., and Goldberg, W. A. (1999). Self and possible selves during the transition to fatherhood. *Journal of Family Psychology* 13: 244–259.

Strommen, M., Jones, K. E., and Rahn, D. (2001). *Youth ministry that transforms: A comprehensive analysis of the hopes, frustrations, and effectiveness of today's youth workers.* Grand Rapids, MI: Zondervan.

Stryker, S. (1980). *Symbolic interactionism: A social structural version.* Menlo Park: CA: Benjamin/Cummings.

Styles, M. B., and Morrow, K. V. (1992). *Understanding how youth and elders form relationships: A study of four linking lifetimes programs.* Philadelphia: Public/Private Ventures.

Sumsion, J. (2005). Male teachers in early childhood education: Issues and case study. *Early Childhood Research Quarterly* 20: 108–123.

Swidler, A. (1986). Culture in action: Symbols and strategies. *American Sociological Review* 51: 273–286.

Teachman, J., Day, R., Paasch, K., Carver, K., and Call, V. (1998). Sibling resemblance in behavioral and cognitive outcomes: The role of father presence. *Journal of Marriage and Family* 60: 835–848.

Thorne, B. (1993). *Gender play: Girls and boys in school.* New Brunswick, NJ: Rutgers University Press.

Tierney, J. P., and Grossman, J. B. (2000). *Making a difference: An impact study of Big Brothers / Big Sisters.* Philadelphia: Public/Private Ventures.

Townsend. J. (1998). *What women want—what men want: Why the sexes still see love and commitment so differently.* New York: Oxford University Press.

Tyre, P. (2006). The trouble with boys. *Newsweek,* January 30, 44–52.

UNICEF (2005). *Child poverty in rich countries, 2005.* Innocenti Report Card No. 6. Florence: UNICEF Innocenti Research Centre, Paris, France.

Uniform Crime Reports (2003). Age-specific arrest rates and race-specific arrest rates for selected offenses, 1993–2001. Uniform Crime Reporting Program, Federal Bureau of Investigation. www.fbi.gov/ucr/adducr/age_race_specific.pdf (accessed June 15, 2005).

U.S. Census Bureau (2006a). Annual demographic survey. CPS 2006 annual social and economic supplement. POVO3: People in families with related children under 18 by family structure, age, and sex, iterated by income-to-poverty ratio and race: 2005 below 100% poverty all races. pubdb3.census.gov/macro/032006/pov/new03_100_01.htm (accessed May 25, 2007).

——— (2006b). Table C2. Household relationship and living arrangements of children under 18 years, by age, sex, race, Hispanic origin: 2006 (black alone). www.census .gov/population/www/socdemo/hh-fam/cps2006.html.

U.S. Department of Labor, Bureau of Labor Statistics (2005a). Table 5. Volunteer activities for main organization for which activities were performed and selected characteristics, September 2005. www.bls.gov/news.release/volun.t05.htm (accessed August 12, 2006).

——— (2005b). May 2003 national occupational employment and wage estimates. www.bls.gov/oes/2003/may/oes_17Ar.htm (accessed August 12, 2006).

——— (2006–2007a). Occupational outlook handbook. Child care workers. www.bls .gov/oco/ocos170.htm (accessed September 17, 2007).

——— (2006–2007b). Occupational outlook handbook. Probation officers and correctional treatment specialists. www.bls.gov/oco/ocos265.htm (accessed July 30, 2006).

——— (2007a). National compensation survey: Occupational wages in the United States, June 2006. www.bls.gov/ncs/ocs/sp/ncbl0910.pdf.

——— (2007b). Volunteering in the United States, 2006. www.bls.gov/news.release/ pdf/volun.pdf (accessed May 24, 2007).

Valentine, G. (2004). *Public space and the culture of childhood*. Burlington, VT: Ashgate.

Van Auken, L., and Van Auken, R. (2001). *Play ball!* University Park: Pennsylvania State University Press.

Van den Hoonard, W. C. (1997). *Working with sensitizing concepts: Analytical field research*. Thousand Oaks, CA: Sage.

Walker, K. (1994). "I'm not friends the way she's friends": Ideological and behavioral constructions of masculinity in men's friendships. *Masculinities* 2: 38–55.

Wallerstein, J. S., and Blakeslee, S. (1989). *Second chances: Men, women, and children a decade after divorce*. New York: Ticknor & Fields.

Wallerstein, J. S. and Lewis, J. (1997). The long-term impact of divorce on children: A first report from a 25-year study. Presented at the Second World Congress of Family Law and the Rights of Children and Youth, June 2–7, San Francisco.

Wells-Wilbon, R., and Holland, S. (2001). Social learning theory and the influence of male role models on African American children in PROJECT 2000. *The Qualitative Report* 6 (4) December. www.nova.edu/ssss/QR/QR6–4/wellswilbon.html (accessed June 24, 2006).

Wessel, T., and Wessel, M. (1982). *4-H: An American idea, 1900–1980: A history of 4-H*. Chevy Chase, MD: National 4-H Council.

West, C., and Zimmerman, D. H. (1987). Doing gender. *Gender and Society* 1: 125–151.

Whiting, B. J. (1993). *Reweaving the tattered web—socializing and enculturating our children.* Kansas City, MO: Ewing Marion Kauffman Foundation.

Whitmire, R. (2006). Boy trouble. *New Republic,* January 23. www.tnr.com/user/nregi .mhtml?i=20060123&s=whitmire012306&pt=l9xVa2UNsTJZ1ydbfQJiaS%3D%3D (accessed July 25, 2006).

Wilson, W. J. (1987). *The truly disadvantaged: The inner city, the underclass, and public policy.* Chicago: University of Chicago Press.

Wolak, J., Mitchell, K., and Finkelor, D. (2006). *Online victimization of youth: Five years later.* National Center for Missing and Exploited Children. www.missingkids.com.

Zimmerman, M., Bingenheimer, J., and Notaro, P. C. (2002). Natural mentors and adolescent resiliency: A study with urban youth. *American Journal of Community Psychology* 30 (2): 221–243.

Index

ABOUT THE AUTHOR

William Marsiglio is a professor of sociology at the University of Florida. He has written extensively on the social psychology of fathering and men's sexuality, fertility, and reproductive health. Among his recent books, *Situated Fathering: A Focus on Physical and Social Spaces*; *Stepdads: Stories of Love, Hope, and Repair*; *Sex, Men, and Babies: Stories of Awareness and Responsibility*; and *Procreative Man* explore how men socially construct and express their identities as persons capable of creating and nurturing human life. His recent research focuses on men's experiences with children and stepchildren, the mothers of their children and stepchildren, and stepchildren's fathers. He has lectured at national and international conferences on fatherhood and consulted on national surveys about male sexuality and fatherhood.